The MacArthur
Quick Reference Guide to the Bible

The MacArthur
Quick Reference Guide to the Bible

By
John MacArthur

W Publishing Group™

A Division of Thomas Nelson, Inc.

THE MACARTHUR QUICK REFERENCE GUIDE TO THE BIBLE

Published by W Publishing Group,
a Division of Thomas Nelson, Inc.,
P.O. Box 141000, Nashville, Tennessee 37214.

Published in association with The Livingstone Corporation,
Carol Stream, Illinois.

ISBN 0-7394-2438-6

Printed in the United States of America

CONTENTS

HOW TO USE THE QUICK REFERENCE GUIDE TO THE BIBLE

This guide has been prepared to help you develop good Bible-reading habits and a better understanding of the depth and breadth of God's Word.

The *MacArthur Quick Reference Guide to the Bible* should be used next to your Bible. It does not replace your Bible; it simply offers you a source of answers for the kinds of questions that might discourage your personal study. By checking the *Guide*, you should be able to get back quickly to the Bible.

If you already own a study Bible, you will note many similarities between the *MacArthur Quick Reference Guide* and your Bible notes. There are, however, some features you will probably not find in your study Bible. In any case, having these materials at your side as you study the Scriptures will help you to stay focused on God's Word itself.

QUICK TUTORIAL

1. Take a look at the Contents. As you read the entries, note which ones seem unfamiliar to you. Turn to those features and make sure you keep a mental record of what you find. Entries like harmonies and chronologies will be of great value to you when you are studying certain parts of Scripture.
2. Open to one of the Bible book entries. Note the features that you will find in each of those quick introductions:
   - Title and Quick Notes
   - Author and Date of the Book
   - Key People in the Book
   - Background and Setting—historical notes about the book
   - Key Doctrines in the Book—central teachings in the book
   - God's Character in the Book—key aspects of God's character illustrated
   - Christ in the Book—how Christ can be found in that book
   - Key Words in the Book—significant words used

- Quick Overview—brief outline of contents
- Meanwhile, in other parts of the world…—historical notes
- Frequently Asked Questions about the book
- Quick Study—basic questions for reflection as you read

1. Using the *MacArthur Quick Reference Guide* may seem a little awkward at first, but with practice, you will find it to be a rich resource of information as you study God's Word.

INTRODUCTION TO THE BIBLE

The Bible is a collection of sixty-six documents inspired by God. These documents are gathered into two testaments, the Old (39) and the New (27). Prophets, priests, kings, and leaders from the nation of Israel wrote the Old Testament books in Hebrew (with two passages in Aramaic). The apostles and their associates wrote the New Testament books in Greek. The Old Testament begins with the creation of the universe and closes about four hundred years before the birth of Jesus Christ.

The History of the Old Testament

- Creation of the universe
- Fall of man
- Flood over the whole earth
- Abraham, Isaac, and Jacob (Israel)—fathers of the chosen nation
- The history of Israel begins
- Exile in Egypt—430 years
- Exodus and wilderness wanderings—40 years
- Conquest of Canaan—7 years
- Era of Judges—350 years
- United Kingdom—Saul, David, Solomon—110 years
- Divided Kingdom—Judah/Israel—350 years
- Exile in Babylon—70 years

The details of Old Testament history are explained in the 39 books, which are divided into 5 categories:

- Return and rebuilding the land—140 years
- The Law—5 books (Genesis–Deuteronomy)
- History—12 books (Joshua–Esther)
- Wisdom—5 books (Job–Song of Solomon)
- Major Prophets—5 books (Isaiah–Daniel)
- Minor Prophets—12 books (Hosea–Malachi)

Prelude and History of the New Testament

After the completion of the Old Testament, there were four hundred years of silence, during which God did not speak or inspire any Scripture.

That silence was broken by the arrival of John the Baptist, who announced that the promised Savior had come. While the thirty-nine Old Testament books focus on the history of Israel and the promise of the coming Savior, the twenty-seven New Testament books focus on the person of Christ and the establishment of the church.

The four gospels give the record of His birth, life, death, resurrection, and ascension. Each of the four writers views the greatest and most important event in history, the life of Jesus Christ, from a different perspective. Matthew looks at Him through His kingdom; Mark through His servanthood; Luke through His humanity; and John through His deity.

The Book of Acts tells the story of the impact of the life, death, and resurrection of Jesus Christ—His ascension, the coming of the Holy Spirit, the birth of the church, and the early years of gospel preaching by the apostles and their associates. The twenty-one epistles (or letters) were written to churches and individuals to teach about the person and work of Jesus Christ and how to live and witness until He returns.

The New Testament closes with Revelation, which begins by addressing the current church age and culminates with the prophecies of Christ's return, when He will establish His earthly kingdom, bring judgment on the ungodly, and bless His believers. Following Christ's millennial reign will be the last judgment, in which all believers of all time will enter the ultimate eternal glory prepared for them, and all the ungodly will be consigned to eternal punishment in hell.

Central Theme

The one, unifying theme unfolding throughout the whole Bible is that for His own glory, God has chosen to create and gather to Himself a group of people, who will live in His eternal kingdom, to praise, honor, and serve Him forever, and through whom He will display His wisdom, power, mercy, grace, and glory. To gather His chosen ones, God must redeem them from sin. The Bible reveals God's plan for this redemption, from its origin in eternity past to its completion in eternity future. All covenants and eras are secondary to the one continuous plan of redemption.

There is one God, who is Creator and Lord. The Bible is one book. It offers one plan of grace, recorded from its initiation in Creation, through its fulfillment in Christ, to its completion in Revelation. The Bible is the story of God's redeeming His chosen people for His glory.

Supporting Themes

As God's redemptive purposes and plan unfold in Scripture, five recurring motifs are constantly emphasized:

- the character of God

- the judgment for sin and disobedience
- the blessing for faith and obedience
- the sacrifice of the Lord Savior for sin
- the glory of the coming kingdom

Everything revealed in both the Old Testament and New Testament falls into these five categories. As one studies Scripture, it is essential to grasp these recurring themes that shape all of the passages and to recognize that what is introduced in the Old Testament is also clarified in the New Testament.

1. The revelation of the character of God

Above all else, Scripture is God's self-revelation. In that self-revelation is established His standard of absolute holiness because of His holy character. From Adam and Eve, the standard of righteousness was established and is sustained through the last page of the New Testament.

2. The revelation of divine judgment for sin and disobedience

Scripture repeatedly deals with the matter of human sin. Of the 1,189 chapters in the Bible, only four do not involve a fallen world: the first two and the last two—before the Fall in Eden and after the creation of the new heaven and new earth. The rest is the chronicle of the tragedy of sin.

In the Old Testament, God showed the disaster of sin—starting with Adam and Eve to Cain and Abel, the relentless record shows the continual devastation produced by sin. In the New Testament, the tragedy of sin becomes clearer as Jesus issues a call to repentance. Disobedience is even more flagrant than in the Old Testament because it involves the rejection of the Lord Jesus Christ in the brighter light of New Testament truth.

3. The revelation of divine blessing for faith and obedience

Scripture repeatedly promises wonderful rewards, in this life and in eternity, to those who trust and seek to obey God. In the Old Testament, God showed the blessings of repentance, faith, and obedience—as seen in the lives of Abel, the patriarchs, the remnant in Israel, and even Gentiles who believed, such as the people of Nineveh. In the New Testament, God showed the blessedness of redemption for those who responded to the preaching of John the Baptist, Jesus, and the apostles. To all those and to all who will believe through all of history, there is blessing promised in this world and the world to come.

4. The revelation of the Savior and His sacrifice for sin

This is the heart of both the Old Testament and the New Testament. The promise of blessing is dependent upon grace and mercy for the sinner. Such forgiveness is dependent upon a payment of sin's penalty to satisfy God's holy justice. That requires a substitute—one to die in the sinner's place. God's chosen substitute—the only one who qualified—is Jesus. Salvation is always by the same gracious means, whether during Old Testament or New Testament times. When any sinner repents, convinced he has no power to save himself from the judgment he deserves, and pleads for mercy, God grants him forgiveness. God then declares him righteous because Christ's sacrifice covers him.

In the Old Testament, God justified sinners that same way, in anticipation of Christ's atoning work. Therefore, there is a continuity of grace and salvation through all of redemptive history. Having fulfilled all righteousness by His perfect life, Christ fulfilled justice by His death. Thus God Himself atoned for our sin, at a very high price. That is what Scripture means when it speaks of salvation by grace.

5. The glory of Christ and His kingdom

As in any book, how the story ends is the most crucial and compelling part—so with the Bible. Redemptive history is controlled by God, so as to culminate in His eternal glory. Scripture notes several very specific features of the end planned by God.

The Old Testament repeatedly mentions a kingdom ruled by the Messiah, accompanied by the salvation of Israel, the salvation of Gentiles, the renewal of the earth from the effects of the curse, and the bodily resurrection of God's people who have died. Finally, the Old Testament predicts the creation of a new heaven and new earth—which will be the eternal state of the godly—and a final hell for the ungodly.

In the New Testament, these features are clarified and expanded. The King will return in glory, bringing judgment, resurrection, and His kingdom for all who believe. The LORD will reign in the renewed earth, exercising power over the whole world and receiving due honor and worship. Following that kingdom will come the dissolution of the renewed but still sin-stained creation, and the subsequent creation of a new heaven and new earth—which will be the eternal dwelling of those who believe.

To understand these five themes reveals the glorious pattern of the Bible. With these in mind, the Bible will unfold, not as sixty-six separate documents, or even two separate testaments—but as one Book, by one divine Author, who wrote it all with one overarching theme.

My prayer is that the magnificent and overwhelming theme of the redemption of sinners for the glory of God will carry every reader with captivating interest from beginning to end of the story. Christian, this is your story. It is from God for you—about you. It tells what He planned for you, why He made you, what you were, what you have become in Christ, and what He has prepared for you in eternal glory.

HOW WE GOT THE BIBLE

Considering the human tendency to doubt God, it is common for a person to be skeptical of the authenticity of the Bible, considering its bold claim to be the only, true Word of God. Many minds have struggled with valid questions, such as these:

- Where did the Bible originate?
- Who wrote the Bible—God or man?
- Has Scripture been protected from human tampering over the centuries?
- How close to the original manuscripts are today's translations?
- How did the Bible get to our time and language?

If the Scriptures were written over a period of fifteen hundred years (about 1405 B.C. to A.D. 95), passed down since then for almost two thousand years, and translated into several thousand languages, what prevented the Bible from being changed by the carelessness or ill motives of men?

A study of the Scriptures alone settles all questions to the extent that someone need never be bothered by them again. Scripture gives this assurance.

Scripture's Self Claims

Take the Bible and let it speak for itself. Does it claim to be God's Word? Yes! Over two thousand times in the Old Testament alone, the Bible asserts that God spoke what is written within its pages. From the beginning (Genesis 1:3) to the end (Malachi 4:3) and continually throughout, this is what Scripture claims.

Passages in Scripture make powerful statements about the Bible, setting it apart from any other religious instruction ever known in the history of mankind. Its content marks it as "sacred" (2 Timothy 3:15) and "holy" (Romans 1:2). The Bible claims ultimate spiritual authority in doctrine, correction, and instruction because it represents the inspired Word of Almighty God. Scripture asserts its spiritual sufficiency, so much so that it claims exclusivity for its teaching (see Isaiah 55:11; 2 Peter 1:3–4).

God's Word declares that it is *inerrant* (Psalms 12:6; 119:140; Proverbs 30:5a; John 10:35) and *infallible* (2 Timothy 3:16–17). In other words, it is true and therefore trustworthy. All of these qualities are dependent on the fact that the Scriptures are God-given (2 Timothy 3:16; 2 Peter 1:20–21), which guarantees its quality at the Source and at its original writing.

THE PUBLISHING PROCESS

Revelation

God took the initiative to reveal Himself to mankind (Hebrews 1:1), sometimes through the created order, visions and dreams, or speaking prophets. However, the most complete and understandable self-disclosures were through the propositions of Scripture (1 Corinthians 2:6–16). The revealed and written Word of God is unique in that it is the only revelation of God that is complete and that so clearly declares man's sinfulness and God's provision of the Savior.

Inspiration

The revelation of God was captured in the writings of Scripture by means of *inspiration.* "All Scripture is given by inspiration of God" (2 Timothy 3:16). Peter explains the process: "Knowing this first, that no prophecy of Scripture is of any private interpretation, for prophecy never came by the will of man, but holy men of God spoke as they were moved by the Holy Spirit" (2 Peter 1:20–21). Through the work of the Holy Spirit, the Word of God was protected from human error.

Canonicity

We must understand that the Bible is actually one book with one Divine Author, though it was written over a period of fifteen hundred years through the pens of almost forty human writers.

The Bible begins with the creation account of Genesis 1–2, written by Moses about 1405 B.C., and extends to the eternity future account of Revelation 21–22, written by the Apostle John about A.D. 95. But this raises a significant question: How was it determined which sacred writings were to be included in the canon of Scripture, and which ones were to be excluded?

Over the centuries, three widely recognized principles were used to validate those writings that were divinely inspired. First, the writing had to have a recognized prophet or apostle as its author (or one associated with them, as in the case of Mark, Luke, Hebrews, James, and Jude). Second, the writing could not disagree with or contradict previous Scripture. Third, the writing had to have general consensus by the church as an inspired book.

Preservation

God anticipated man's and Satan's malice towards the Scripture with divine promises to preserve His Word. The very continued existence of Scripture is guaranteed in Isaiah 40:8: "The grass withers, the flower fades, but the word of our God stands forever" (see 1 Peter 1:25). This even means that no inspired Scripture has been lost in the past and still awaits rediscovery. The battle for the Bible rages, but Scripture has and will continue to outlast its enemies.

"So shall My word be that goes forth from My mouth; it shall not return to Me void, but it shall accomplish what I please, and it shall prosper in the thing for which I sent it" (Isaiah 55:11).

Transmission

Through the centuries, the practitioners of textual criticism, a precise science, have discovered, preserved, catalogued, evaluated, and published an amazing array of biblical manuscripts from both the Old and New Testaments. In fact, the number of existing biblical manuscripts dramatically outdistances the existing fragments of any other ancient literature. By comparing text with text, the textual critic can confidently determine what the original prophetic/apostolic, inspired writing contained.

For example, the discovery of the Dead Sea Scrolls in 1947–1956 (manuscripts that are dated about 200–100 B.C.) proved to be monumentally important. After comparing the earlier Hebrew texts with the later ones, only a few slight variants were discovered, none of which changed the meaning of any passage. Although the Old Testament had been translated and copied for centuries, the latest version was essentially the same as the earlier ones.

The New Testament findings are even more decisive because a much larger amount of material is available for study; there are over five thousand Greek New Testament manuscripts that range from the whole testament to scraps of papyri containing as little as part of one verse. A few existing fragments date back to within fifty years of the original writing.

New Testament textual scholars have generally concluded that 1) 99.99 percent of the original writings have been reclaimed, and 2) of the remaining one-hundredth of one percent, there are no variants substantially affecting any Christian doctrine.

SUMMING IT UP

God intended His Word to abide forever (preservation). Therefore His written self-disclosure (revelation) was protected from error in its original writing (inspiration) and collected in the sixty-six books of the Old and New Testaments (canonicity).

Through the centuries, tens of thousands of copies and thousands of translations have been made (transmission), which did introduce minute errors. Because there is an abundance of existing ancient Old Testament and New Testament manuscripts, however, the exacting science of textual criticism has been able to reclaim the content of the original writings (revelation and inspiration) to the extreme degree of 99.99 percent, with the remaining one-hundredth of one percent having no effect on its content (preservation).

The sacred Book which we read and obey deserves to unreservedly be called The Bible, since its author is God and it bears the qualities of total truth and complete trustworthiness that also characterize its divine source.

IS THERE MORE TO COME?

How do we know that God will not amend our current Bible with a sixty-seventh inspired book? In other words, "Is the canon forever closed?" The most compelling text on the closed canon is the Scripture, to which nothing has been added for nineteen hundred years.

"For I testify to everyone who hears the words of the prophecy of this book: If anyone adds to these things, God will add to him the plagues that are written in this book; and if anyone takes away from the words of the book of this prophecy, God shall take away his part from the Book of Life, from the holy city, and from the things which are written in this book" (Revelation 22:18,19).

THE BIBLE

This Book contains the mind of God, the state of man, the way of salvation, the doom of sinners, and the happiness of believers. Read it to be wise, believe it to be saved, and practice it to be holy. It contains light to direct you, food to support you, and comfort to cheer you. It is the traveler's map, the pilgrim's staff, the pilot's compass, the soldier's sword, and the Christian's charter. It should fill the memory, rule the heart, and guide the feet. Read it slowly, frequently, and prayerfully.

"For this reason we also thank God without ceasing, because when you received the word of God which you heard from us, you welcomed it not as the word of men, but as it is in truth, the word of God, which also effectively works in you who believe" (1 Thessalonians 2:13).

HOW TO STUDY THE BIBLE

Why is God's Word so important? Because it contains God's will for your life (2 Timothy 3:16–17). The Bible is the only source of absolute, divine authority for you as a servant of Jesus Christ. Consider the following descriptive claims from Scripture: "The law of the LORD is perfect, converting the soul; the testimony of the LORD is sure, making wise the simple" (Psalm 19:7). "Every word of God is pure; He is a shield to those who put their trust in Him. Do not add to His words, lest He rebuke you, and you be found a liar" (Proverbs 30:5–6). "For I testify to everyone who hears the words of the prophecy of this book: If anyone adds to these things, God will add to him the plagues that are written in this book; and if anyone takes away from the words of the book of this prophecy, God shall take away his part from the Book of Life, from the holy city, and from the things which are written in this book" (Revelation 22:18–19). "So shall My word be that goes forth from My mouth; it shall not return to Me void, but it shall accomplish what I please, and it shall prosper in the thing for which I sent it" (Isaiah 55:11).

What Are the Basics of Bible Study?
The idea of personal Bible study is simple but requires discipline and long-term goals. I want to share with you five steps for Bible study that will give you a pattern to follow.

STEP 1—Reading.
Develop a plan of how you will approach reading through the Bible. Unlike most books, you will probably not read it straight through from cover to cover. There are quite a number of good Bible reading plans that will help you read the Bible systematically. Read a passage of Scripture repeatedly until you understand its theme, meaning the main truth of the passage.

For example, in the Old Testament I would suggest you read it straight through, spread over time. Since that is a significant reading project, do not feel overwhelmed. Simply try to find the truths that God has revealed for you to learn. In the New Testament, you may want to take a more repetitious approach. You can read one book numerous times in a row so that you will retain what you have read. If you want to try this, begin with a short book, such as 1 John, and read its five chapters carefully through in one sitting. After you have finished, begin again, reading 1 John every day for thirty days. At the end of that time, you will really know what is in the book.

STEP 2—Interpreting.

As you read Scripture, always keep in mind one simple question: What does this mean? Let the Holy Spirit be your teacher (1 John 2:27), for this is the Book that He authored. Pray for wisdom to understand the meaning, and read diligently. As you interpret Scripture, several common errors should be avoided.

1. *Do not draw any conclusions at the price of proper interpretation.* That is, do not make the Bible say what *you* want it to say, but rather let it say what *God* intended.
2. *Avoid superficial interpretation.* You have heard people say, "To me, this passage means," or "I feel it is saying...." Recognize that between your time and the biblical times, you must bridge cultural, geographical, and historical gaps. These gaps do not invalidate biblical truth, but you will understand the message much more clearly if you understand the context in which it was written.
3. *Do not spiritualize the passage.* Interpret and understand the passage in its normal, literal, historical, grammatical sense, just as you would understand any other piece of literature you were reading today.

Four principles should guide us as we interpret the Bible: literal, historical, grammatical, and synthesis.

- *The Literal Principle.* Scripture should be understood in its literal, normal, and natural sense. While the Bible does contain figures of speech and symbols, they were intended to convey literal truth. In general, the Bible speaks in literal terms, and we must allow it to speak for itself.
- *The Historical Principle.* We must ask what the text meant to the people to whom it was first written. In this way we can develop a proper contextual understanding of the original intent of Scripture.
- *The Grammatical Principle.* Ask simple questions about the basic structure. To whom do the pronouns refer? What is the tense of the main verb? Simple details like these make the meaning of the text clearer.
- *The Synthesis Principle.* The Reformers called this *analogia scriptura,* meaning that the Bible does not contradict itself. If an interpretation of one passage contradicts a truth taught elsewhere in the Scriptures, our interpretation cannot be correct. Scripture must be compared with Scripture to discover its full meaning.

STEP 3—Evaluating.
At times you will find it helpful to consult others to ensure that you have interpreted the Bible correctly. Read Bible introductions, commentaries, and background books to enrich your thinking. In your evaluation, be a true seeker. Accept the truth of God's Word even though it may cause you to change what you have always believed or it may require you to alter your life pattern.

STEP 4—Applying.
Studying Scripture without allowing it to penetrate the depths of your soul would be like preparing a banquet without sitting down to eat and enjoy it. Ask the ultimate question: How do the divine truths apply to my attitude and actions? Jesus made this promise to those who would carry their personal Bible study through to this point: "If you know these things, blessed are you if you do them" (John 13:17).

Having read and interpreted the Bible, you should have a basic understanding of what the Bible says and what it means by what it says. But studying the Bible does not stop there. The ultimate goal should be to hear its message and to grow spiritually. That requires personal application.

Bible study is not complete until we ask ourselves, "What does this mean for my life, and how can I practically apply it?" We must take the knowledge we have gained from our reading and draw out the practical principles that apply to our personal lives. If there is a command to be obeyed, we obey it. If there is a promise to be embraced, we claim it. If there is a warning to be followed, we heed it. This is the ultimate step: We submit to Scripture and let it transform our lives. If you skip this step, you will never enjoy your Bible study, and the Bible will never change your life.

STEP 5—Correlating.
Finally, make connections between the doctrine you have learned in a particular passage with divine truths and principles taught elsewhere in the Bible to form the big picture. Always keep in mind that the Bible is a single book in sixty-six parts, and its truths are taught over and over again in a variety of stories and principles. By correlating and cross-referencing, you will begin to build a sound doctrinal foundation.

What Now?
It is not enough just to *study* the Bible. We must *meditate* upon it and *immerse* ourselves in the purifying solution of God's Word. "This Book of the Law shall not depart from your mouth, but you shall meditate in it day and night, that you may observe to do according to all that is written in it. For then you will make your way prosperous, and then you will have good success" (Joshua 1:8).

CHRONOLOGY OF THE BIBLE

OLD TESTAMENT

Book	Approximate Writing Date	Author
1. Job	Unknown	Anonymous
2. Genesis	1445–1405 B.C.	Moses
3. Exodus	1445–1405 B.C.	Moses
4. Leviticus	1445–1405 B.C.	Moses
5. Numbers	1445–1405 B.C.	Moses
6. Deuteronomy	1445–1405 B.C.	Moses
7. Psalms	1410–450 B.C.	Multiple Authors
8. Joshua	1405–1385 B.C.	Joshua
9. Judges	about 1043 B.C.	Samuel
10. Ruth	about 1030–1010 B.C.	Samuel (?)
11. Song of Solomon	971–965 B.C.	Solomon
12. Proverbs	971–686 B.C.	Solomon primarily
13. Ecclesiastes	940–931 B.C.	Solomon
14. 1 Samuel	931–722 B.C.	Anonymous
15. 2 Samuel	931–722 B.C.	Anonymous
16. Obadiah	850–840 B.C.	Obadiah
17. Joel	835–796 B.C.	Joel
18. Jonah	about 775 B.C.	Jonah
19. Amos	about 750 B.C.	Amos
20. Micah	735–710 B.C.	Micah
21. Hosea	750–710 B.C.	Hosea
22. Isaiah	700–681 B.C.	Isaiah
23. Nahum	about 650 B.C.	Nahum
24. Zephaniah	635–625 B.C.	Zephaniah
25. Habakkuk	615–605 B.C.	Habakkuk
26. Ezekiel	590–570 B.C.	Ezekiel
27. Lamentations	586 B.C.	Jeremiah
28. Jeremiah	586–570 B.C.	Jeremiah
29. 1 Kings	561–538 B.C.	Anonymous
30. 2 Kings	561–538 B.C.	Anonymous
31. Daniel	536–530 B.C.	Daniel
32. Haggai	about 520 B.C.	Haggai
33. Zechariah	480–470 B.C.	Zechariah

34. Ezra	457–444 B.C.	Ezra
35. 1 Chronicles	450–430 B.C.	Ezra (?)
36. 2 Chronicles	450–430 B.C.	Ezra (?)
37. Esther	450–331 B.C.	Anonymous
38. Malachi	433–424 B.C.	Malachi
39. Nehemiah	424–400 B.C.	Ezra

NEW TESTAMENT

Book	Approximate Writing Date	Author
1. James	A.D. 44–49	James
2. Galatians	A.D. 49–50	Paul
3. Matthew	A.D. 50–60	Matthew
4. Mark	A.D. 50–60	Mark
5. 1 Thessalonians	A.D. 51	Paul
6. 2 Thessalonians	A.D. 51–52	Paul
7. 1 Corinthians	A.D. 55	Paul
8. 2 Corinthians	A.D. 55–56	Paul
9. Romans	A.D. 56	Paul
10. Luke	A.D. 60–61	Luke
11. Ephesians	A.D. 60–62	Paul
12. Philippians	A.D. 60–62	Paul
13. Colossians	A.D. 60–62	Paul
14. Philemon	A.D. 60–62	Paul
15. Acts	A.D. 62	Luke
16. 1 Timothy	A.D. 62–64	Paul
17. Titus	A.D. 62–64	Paul
18. 1 Peter	A.D. 64–65	Peter
19. 2 Timothy	A.D. 66–67	Paul
20. 2 Peter	A.D. 67–68	Peter
21. Hebrews	A.D. 67–69	Unknown
22. Jude	A.D. 68–70	Jude
23. John	A.D. 80–90	John
24. 1 John	A.D. 90–95	John
25. 2 John	A.D. 90–95	John
26. 3 John	A.D. 90–95	John
27. Revelation	A.D. 94–96	John

GENESIS
The Book of Beginnings

Genesis covers a longer span of history than any other book of the Bible.

God started everything. The Bible doesn't begin with an argument for God's existence; it begins by accepting that our existence depends on God. The ancient Greek translation of the Bible (called the Septuagint, or LXX) titled this first book *Genesis,* meaning "origins." Eventually, English translators borrowed the word directly. The title used in Hebrew texts simply highlights the very first word, which means "in the beginning."

AUTHOR AND DATE

Written by Moses, approximately 1445 to 1405 B.C.

Although Genesis does not name its author, and the events described in the text end almost three centuries before his birth, both the Old Testament and the New Testament designate Moses as the author. In addition, Moses' educational background makes him the likely candidate (Acts 7:22). No compelling reasons have been forthcoming to challenge Mosaic authorship.

KEY PEOPLE IN GENESIS

Adam and Eve—the original human beings (1:26–5:5)
Noah—the faithful builder of the ark (6:5–9:29)
Abraham and Sarah—the parents of a nation called God's chosen people (12:1–25:8)
Isaac and Rebekah—the original members of a new nation (21:1–35:29)
Jacob—the father of the twelve tribes of Israel (25:21–50:14)
Joseph—the preserver of his people and the nation of Egypt (30:22–50:26)

BACKGROUND AND SETTING

The initial setting for Genesis is eternity past. God, by willful act and divine word, spoke all creation into existence, furnished it, and finally breathed life into a lump of dirt that He fashioned in His image to become Adam. God made this human the crowning point of His creation; that is, companions who would enjoy fellowship with Him and bring glory to His name.

Genesis has three distinct and sequential geographical settings: 1) Mesopotamia (chapters 1–11); 2) the Promised Land (chapters 12–36); 3) Egypt (chapters 37–50). The time frames of these three segments are 1) creation to 2090 B.C.; 2) 2090 to 1897 B.C.; 3) 1897 to 1804 B.C.

KEY DOCTRINES IN GENESIS

Most of the central teachings of Christianity have their roots in the Book of Genesis.

God the Father—the authority of God in creation (1:1–31; Psalm 103:19; 145:8–9; 1 Corinthians 8:6; Ephesians 3:9; 4:6)

God the Son—the agent of God in creation (1:1; 3:15; 18:1; John 1:1–3; 10:30; 14:9; Philippians 2:5–8; Colossians 1:15–17; Hebrews 1:2)

God the Holy Spirit—the presence of God in creation (1:2; 6:3; Matthew 1:18; John 3:5–7)

God as one yet three—the Trinity (1:1,26; 3:22; 11:7; Deuteronomy 6:4; Isaiah 45:5–7; Matthew 28:19; 1 Corinthians 8:4; 2 Corinthians 13:14)

Human beings—created in Christ's image yet fallen into sin and needing a Savior (1:26; 2:4–25; 9:6; Isaiah 43:7; Romans 8:29; Colossians 1:16; 3:10; James 3:9; Revelation 4:11)

Sin (the Fall)—the infection of all creation with sin by rebellion toward God (2:16–17; 3:1–19; John 3:36; Romans 3:23; 6:23; 1 Corinthians 2:14; Ephesians 2:1–3; 1 Timothy 2:13–14; 1 John 1:8)

Redemption—the rescue from sin and restoration accomplished by Christ on the cross (3:15; 48:16; John 8:44; 10:15; Romans 3:24–25; 16:20; 1 Peter 2:24)

Covenant—God establishes relationships and makes promises (15:1–20; 17:10–11; Numbers 25:10–13; Deuteronomy 4:25–31; 30:1–9; 2 Samuel 23:5; 1 Chronicles 16:15–18; Jeremiah 30:11; 32:40; 46:27–28; Amos 9:8; Luke 1:67–75; Hebrews 6:13–18)

Promise—God commits Himself into the future (12:1–3; 26:3–4; 28:14; Acts 2:39; Galatians 3:16; Hebrews 8:6)

Satan—the original rebel among God's creatures (3:1–15; Isaiah 14:13–14; Matthew 4:3–10; 2 Corinthians 11:3,14; 2 Peter 2:4; Revelation 12:9; 20:2)

Angels—special beings created to serve God (3:24; 18:1–8; 28:12; Luke 2:9–14; Hebrews 1:6–7,14; 2:6–7; Revelation 5:11–14)

Revelation—*Natural revelation* occurs as God indirectly communicates through what He has made (1:1–2:25; Romans 1:19,20). *Special revelation* occurs when God directly communicates Himself as well as otherwise unknowable truth (2:15–17; 3:8–19; 12:1–3; 18:1–8; 32:24–32; Deuteronomy 18:18; 2 Timothy 3:16; Hebrews 1:1–4; 1 Peter 1:10–12)

Israel—Jacob's God-given name that became the name of the nation he fathered; inheritors of God's covenant with Abraham (32:28; 35:10; Deuteronomy 28:15–68; Isaiah 65:17–25; Jeremiah 31:31–34; Ezekiel 37:21–28; Zechariah 8:1–17; Matthew 21:43; Romans 11:1–29)

Judgment—God's righteous response to sin (3; 6; 7; 11:1–9; 15:14, 18:16–19:29; Deuteronomy 32:39; Isaiah 1:9; Matthew 12:36–37; Romans 1:18–2:16; 2 Peter 2:5–6)

Blessing—a special benefit or a hope-filled statement to someone about their life (1:28; 9:1; 12:1–3; 14:18–20; 27:1–40; 48:1–20; Numbers 6:24–27; Deuteronomy 11:26–27; Psalm 3:8; Malachi 3:10; Matthew 5:3–11; 1 Peter 3:9)

GOD'S CHARACTER IN GENESIS

Many of God's character traits are first revealed in Genesis.
God is the Creator—1:1–31
God is faithful (keeps promises)—12:3,7; 26:3–4; 28:14; 32:9,12
God is just—18:25
God is long-suffering—6:3
God is loving—24:12
God is merciful—19:16,19
God is omnipotent—17:1
God is powerful—18:14
God is provident—8:22; 24:12–14,48,56; 28:20–21; 45:5–7; 48:15; 50:20
God is truthful—3:4–5; 24:27; 32:10
God is wrathful—7:21–23; 11:8; 19:24–25

CHRIST IN GENESIS

Jesus' entrance into humanity was planned from before the beginning of time. God potentially mitigated the curse that resulted from the sin of Adam and Eve by offering a promise that someday a Seed would rise up to crush the serpent (3:15). Even though death came through Adam, Christ's coming brought life to humankind (Romans 5:12–21).

Genesis goes on to trace the first lines in God's divine blueprint for Jesus' birth. From the peoples of the earth, God singled out Abraham to be the father of a chosen nation. This nation continued through Abraham's son Isaac, and then through Isaac's son Jacob, concluding with the account of Jacob's son Joseph. Genesis reveals God's continual protection over the earliest people in Christ's lineage.

KEY WORDS IN GENESIS

God: Hebrew plural *ʾelohim*—1:1,12; 19:29; 24:42; 28:3; 35:11; 45:9; 50:24—the most used Hebrew term for God. The basic meaning is "the Almighty." The Hebrew usage of this term in Genesis is called "the plural of majesty." Unlike a normal plural, the Hebrew uses this plural to mean "the Fullness of Deity" or "God-Very God!" The plural form of this word has traditionally been recognized as indicating the plural nature of God. God is one, but God is also three distinct persons: the Father, the Son, and the Holy Spirit.

Heavens: Hebrew *shamayim*—1:1,8–9; 2:1; 8:2; 11:4; 14:22; 24:3; 28:12. The Hebrew word for heavens may refer to the physical heavens, the sky and the atmosphere of earth (2:1,4,19), or to the dwelling place of God (Psalm 14:2), the spiritual heaven. The expression is related to the term for "to be high, lofty." The physical heavens of creation testify to God's glorious position and also to His creative genius (Psalm 19:1,6).

Land: Hebrew *'erets*—1:1,10; 4:16; 12:1; 13:10; 41:36; 31:3; 35:12. The common Old Testament word *land* possesses several shades of meaning. In essence, all land belongs to God as its Creator (Psalm 24:1). When God promised the Israelites the land of Canaan, it was His to give. The land of Canaan was so representative of God's covenant with the Israelites (12:1) that it became one of their identifying characteristics—the "people of the land" (13:15; 15:7).

Seed: Hebrew *zera'*—1:11,29; 13:15–16; 15:18; 17:19; 28:14; 48:19; 32:12. The Hebrew word for seed can literally mean a plant's seed (1:11–12) or can figuratively mean one's descendants (13:15). In Genesis, it refers specifically to the coming Messiah, in God's promise that the woman's Seed would crush the serpent (3:15; Numbers 24:7; Isaiah 6:13; Galatians 3:16). As such, the term takes on great importance in the Bible: Through Abraham's *seed,* both collectively in Israel and singularly in Christ, God would reach out to save His people (15:3).

QUICK OVERVIEW

I. Primitive History—Four Major Events (1–11)
  A. Creation (1–2)
  B. The Fall into Sin (3–5)
  C. The Flood (6–9)
  D. The Dispersion of Peoples (10–11)
II. Patriarchal History—Four Great Men (12–50)[1]
  A. Abraham (12:1–25:8)
  B. Isaac (21:1–35:29)
  C. Jacob (25:21–50:14)
  D. Joseph (30:22–50:26)

MEANWHILE, IN OTHER PARTS OF THE WORLD . . .
Until after the Flood (chapters 6–9), world events center in the Middle East. Populations expand widely after Babel (chapter 11). By the time of the Patriarchs (about 2150 B. C.), Egypt is the world power. Egyptians are already using papyrus and ink for writing.

FREQUENTLY ASKED QUESTIONS

1. How does the Bible challenge or agree with current scientific theories?

Scientific theories, by their very definition, are subject to change and adjustment. Scripture remains as God's revealed, unchanging declaration of truth. The Bible was not written as a challenge to any particular scientific theory, but scientific theories have often been designed to challenge or undermine biblical statements. They either agree with Scripture or are mistaken.

The description in 1:1 that "God created the heavens and the earth" yields three basic conclusions: 1) creation was a recent event measured in thousands not millions of years ago; 2) creation was *ex nihilo*, meaning that God created out of nothing; 3) creation was special, with light and time being the first of God's creative acts, since the day-count (1:5) began before the creation of sun and moon (1:16).

2. What do Christians mean when they talk about the Fall?

The Fall refers to that moment in time when human beings first disobeyed God. Chapter 3 tells the painful episode. What Eve set into motion, Adam confirmed and completed by joining her. They sinned together. The willful decision of Adam and Eve created a state of rebellion between the creation and her Creator. In the Fall, our first ancestors declared us on Satan's side.

The Bible makes it clear that the Fall brought sin into every subsequent person's life (Romans 5:12). Our capacity for sin is inborn. We are sinners before we have the opportunity to sin. Not only are we sinners because we sin; we first sin because we are sinners. Why? Because we have all inherited the effects of Adam's fall.

3. How significant is the Flood in the overall biblical history?

The Bible treats the Flood as a worldwide event directly brought by God as a judgment on the sin of humanity. The Flood hangs like a warning cloud over all of subsequent history. Fortunately, that cloud also holds a rainbow of God's promised grace.

The Flood illustrates several important aspects of God's character and God's relationship with His creation: 1) God retains ultimate control of world events; 2) God can and will judge sin; 3) God can and does exercise grace even in judgment; 4) an even more universal and final judgment will be carried out on the world based on God's timetable.

4. Why did God cause the multiplication of languages and the dispersion of peoples in Genesis?

After the Flood, human civilization again began to spread across the earth. Later, the people decided to establish a city as a tribute to themselves and as a way to keep from spreading across the earth (11:4). This was a double, prideful rebellion against God. First, their city, with its proposed tower, was to be a monument to their self-reliance. Second, the permanence of their settlement represented an effort to disobey God's direct command to inhabit the whole earth.

Because God purposed to fill the earth with custodians, He responded to the people's prideful rebellion. They had chosen to settle; He forced them to scatter. Their cooperation and self-reliance had been based on their shared language. Instead of using all their resources to obey God, they misused them for disobedience. God chose to complicate communication by multiplying the languages. The location where this confusion took place became known as Babel (related to a Hebrew word meaning "to confuse"). Later it became Babylon, the constant enemy of God's people, and throughout Scripture the capital of human rebellion against God (Revelation 16:19; 17:5).

QUICK STUDY ON GENESIS

1. How important is it to acknowledge God's creative role in the origin of the universe as described in Genesis?
2. What role do Adam and Eve play in the history of the human race?
3. How much would we know about God if we only had the Book of Genesis?
4. What biblical significance is given to such events as the eviction from the Garden of Eden, the Flood, the Tower of Babel?
5. How does God's promise to Abraham (12:1–3) affect the whole world?
6. Who are the heroes of this book? Why?

[1] See also "Chronology of Old Testament Patriarchs and Judges" in the Appendices at the back of this book.

EXODUS
The Great Escape

In Exodus God saves His people and gives them His Ten Commandments.

The descriptive title *Exodus* was given to the second book of Moses by the ancient translators of the Greek Old Testament. The title is simply the Greek expression "a going out," which delightfully understates God's great acts on behalf of His chosen people.

AUTHOR AND DATE

Written by Moses, approximately 1445 to 1405 B.C.

Mosaic authorship of Exodus is unhesitatingly affirmed by Scripture. For example, Moses followed God's instructions when he "wrote all the words of the LORD" (24:4). Similar references to Moses as the writer occur elsewhere in Scripture.

KEY PEOPLE IN EXODUS

Moses—author of the Pentateuch and deliverer of Israel from Egyptian slavery (2–40)

Miriam—prophetess and older sister of Moses (2:7; 15:20–21)

Pharaoh's daughter—the princess who rescued baby Moses from the water and adopted him (2:5–10)

Jethro—Midian shepherd who became Moses' father-in-law (3:1; 4:18; 18:1–12)

Aaron—brother of Moses and first high priest of Israel (4:14–40:31)

Pharaoh—unnamed Egyptian leader at the time of the Exodus (5:1–14:31)

Joshua—assistant to Moses and military leader who led Israel into the Promised Land (17:9–14; 24:13; 32:17; 33:11)

BACKGROUND AND SETTING

Israel's dramatic exit from Egypt occurred during the Eighteenth Dynasty, a setting of great political and economic strength in Egyptian history. Though born a slave, Moses had entered a culture in rapid expansion and growth. Egypt was a world military, economic, and political superpower. God used the educational and governmental systems of Egypt as well as a wilderness exile in Midian to train Moses. Once ready, Moses represented Israel before powerful Pharaoh Amenhotep II and then guided his people on their wilderness journey.

Exodus sketches Moses' early history and records the details of Israel's departure from Egypt. It concludes after the giving of the law and the construction of the Tabernacle at the foot of Mount Sinai. At that point, despite the people's terrible sin of idolatry while Moses was on the mountain, God continued to lead Israel to the Promised Land.

KEY DOCTRINES IN EXODUS

Covenant promises—God's promise to Abraham to preserve his heritage forever (12:1–3,7,31–42; Genesis 17:19; Leviticus 26:45; Judges 2:20; Psalm 105:38; Acts 3:25)

The nature of God—human beings cannot understand God completely but can come to know Him personally (3:7; 8:19; 34:6–7; 2 Samuel 22:31; Job 36:26; Matthew 5:48; Luke 1:49–50)

The Ten Commandments—the basic truths of God (20:1–17; 23:12; Leviticus 19:4,12; Deuteronomy 6:14; 7:8–9; Nehemiah 13:16–19; Isaiah 44:15; Matthew 5:27; 19:18; Mark 10:19; Luke 13:14; Romans 13:9; Ephesians 5:3,5)

GOD'S CHARACTER IN EXODUS

God is accessible—24:2; 34:4–7
God is glorious—15:1,6,11; 33:18–23; 34:5–7
God is good—34:6
God is gracious—34:6
God is holy—15:11
God is long-suffering—34:6
God is merciful—34:6,7
God is all-powerful—6:3; 8:19; 9:3,16; 15:6,11–12
God is provident—15:9–19
God is true—34:6
God is unequaled—9:14
God is wise—3:7
God is wrathful—7:20; 8:6,16,24; 9:3,9,23; 10:13,22; 12:29; 14:24,27; 32:11,35

CHRIST IN EXODUS

As God delivered the nation of Israel out from Egyptian slavery, a new foundation was laid by the presentation of the law. The focus of Exodus remains twofold: 1) a description of the redemption of God's people; 2) the formation of the chosen nation through whom Christ would enter the world. The law prepared Israel to receive Christ, its promised Messiah and King.

KEY WORDS IN EXODUS

Delivered: Hebrew *natsal*—3:8; 5:18; 21:13; 22:7,10,26; 23:31—this verb may mean either "to strip, to plunder" or "to snatch away, to deliver." The word is often used to describe God's work in delivering (3:8), or rescuing (6:6), the Israelites from slavery. Sometimes it signifies deliverance of God's people from sin and guilt (Psalm 51:14). In 18:8–10, however, the word is a statement of God's supremacy over the Egyptian pantheon of deities.

Consecrate: Hebrew *qadash*—28:3,41; 29:9,33,35; 30:30; 32:29—this verb means "to make holy," "to declare distinct," or "to set apart." The word describes dedicating an object or person to God. By delivering the Israelites from slavery in Egypt, God made the nation of Israel distinct. Through His mighty acts of deliverance, God demonstrated that the Israelites were His people, and He was their God (6:7). By having the people wash themselves at Mount Sinai, the Lord made it clear that He was claiming a special relationship with them (19:10).

Washing: Hebrew *rachats*—2:5; 19:10; 29:4,17; 30:18,21; 40:12,30—washing or bathing. The term was used in both religious and cultural settings. The ancient custom of washing a guest's feet was a part of hospitality still practiced in the New Testament period (Genesis 18:4; John 13:5). Ritual washing was an important step in the purification of the priests for service in the Tabernacle (40:12). Washing with water symbolized spiritual cleansing, the preparation necessary for entering God's presence (Psalm 26:6; 73:13). The Old Testament prophets used this imagery of repentance (Isaiah 1:16; Ezekiel 16:4). In the New Testament, Paul describes redemption in Christ as "the washing of regeneration" (Titus 3:5).

QUICK OVERVIEW

I. Israel in Egypt (1:1–12:36)
  A. The Population Explosion (1:1–7)
  B. The Oppression under the Pharaohs (1:8–22)
  C. The Maturation of a Deliverer (2:1–4:31)
  D. The Confrontation with Pharaoh (5:1–11:10)
  E. The Preparation for Departure (12:1–36)

II. Israel on the Road to Sinai (12:37–18:27)
  A. Exiting Egypt and Panicking (12:37–14:14)
  B. Crossing the Red Sea and Rejoicing (14:15–15:21)
  C. Traveling to Sinai and Grumbling (15:22–17:16)
  D. Meeting with Jethro and Learning (18:1–27)

III. Israel Encamped at Sinai (19:1–40:38)
  A. The Law of God Prescribed (19:1–24:18)
  B. The Tabernacle of God Described (25:1–31:18)
  C. The Worship of God Defiled (32:1–35)

D. The Presence of God Confirmed (33:1–34:35)
E. The Tabernacle of God Constructed (35:1–40:38)

MEANWHILE, IN OTHER PARTS OF THE WORLD . . . The Iron Age in Syria and Palestine begins. Also, people in Mediterranean and Scandinavian countries perfect the art of shipbuilding.

FREQUENTLY ASKED QUESTIONS

1. Why don't the Egyptian historical records acknowledge the devastation of the plagues, the defeat of the army, and Israel's escape that occurred during the Exodus?

The absence of references to Israel in the available Egyptian historical records should come as no surprise. Most of these records exist in the form of official inscriptions in the tombs and monuments of ancient leaders. Such public and lasting memorials were rarely used to record humiliating defeats and disasters. Interestingly, one of the subtle proofs of the truth of Scripture is the way in which it records both the triumphs and the tragedies of God's people. The Bible offers as many examples of failure as it does of faith.

2. How are we in the twenty-first century supposed to think about the astonishing miracles that Exodus so matter-of-factly reports, such as the burning bush, the plagues, God's presence in the pillar of fire and cloud, the parting of the Red Sea, and manna, to name a few?

The scientific materialism of many twenty-first-century people makes it difficult for them to consider any so-called miracles. If the laws of nature are considered supreme, the existence of a personal Supreme Being above the laws of nature and able to override them becomes inconceivable. Examples of miracles do little to convince someone who is already convinced that miracles are impossible.

Miracles can demonstrate God's existence; they don't prove it. Human beings display an amazing ability to come up with alternate explanations for God's activity in history. The situation is not that twenty-first-century people can't believe in miracles; rather, it is that twenty-first-century people often won't believe in miracles.

For Christians, the matter is settled by faith. In becoming Christians, we had to believe in the central miracle: God came in the flesh, Jesus Christ, who lived, died, and rose from the dead to reign eternally as Lord and Savior. In the light of that miracle, the miracles of Exodus become less a matter for speculation and more a matter of wonder and worship. They are examples of the lengths to which God went to communicate to people. Even twenty-first-century Christians are humbled and awestruck by God's amazing power!

3. Are the Ten Commandments outmoded expectations or divine demands?

People make a serious error when they speak about "breaking the Ten Commandments." History amply displays the fact that people persist in breaking themselves on the Ten Commandments. The commandments represent God's absolute and unchanging standard despite any arguments over their interpretation and application.

The title Ten Commandments comes from Moses (34:28). The emphasis on God Himself speaking and writing these words makes unacceptable any theories of Israel's borrowing legal patterns or concepts from surrounding nations.

The Ten Commandments may be grouped into two broad categories: the vertical—humanity's relationship to God (20:2–11); and the horizontal—humanity's relationship to the community (20:12–17). By these Ten Commandments, true theology and true worship, the name of God and the Sabbath, family honor, life, marriage, property, truth, and virtue are well protected.

QUICK STUDY ON EXODUS

1. What are the highlights of Moses' early life?
2. In what different ways did God make Himself known throughout Exodus?
3. What were the ten plagues that afflicted the Egyptians?
4. How did the plagues relate to the gods worshiped by the Egyptians?
5. How does the law summarized in the Ten Commandments show us we need God's help?
6. Which of the Ten Commandments direct our relationship with God and which direct our relationships with other people?

LEVITICUS
The Blueprint for Redemption

Leviticus details the laws of approach to and fellowship with God.

Ancient scholars translating this book from Hebrew to Greek gave it a descriptive title—*Leuitikon*—which means "matters of the Levites." Later translators borrowed the word directly.

AUTHOR AND DATE

Written by Moses, approximately 1445 to 1405 B.C.

As if to make the point unmistakable, Leviticus includes fifty-six references in its twenty-seven chapters to the fact that God "called to Moses" or "spoke to Moses" and gave him direct instructions about what to say to the people. The content of Leviticus was given to the people by God through Moses.

KEY PEOPLE IN LEVITICUS

Moses—prophet and leader who acted as God's mouthpiece to explain His law to Israel (1:1; 4:1; 5:14; 6:1–27:34)

Aaron—Moses' brother and first high priest of Israel (1:7; 2:3,10; 3:5,8,13; 6:9–24:9)

Nadab—son of Aaron, in training to become a priest, died because of disobedience to the Lord's commands (8:36; 10:1–2)

Abihu—son of Aaron, in training to become a priest, died because of disobedience to the Lord's commands (8:36; 10:1–2)

Eleazar—son of Aaron who succeeded him as high priest of Israel (10:6–20)

Ithamar—son of Aaron who also became a priest (10:6–20)

BACKGROUND AND SETTING

The Exodus radically changed the way God related to Israel. Until that point in the history of God's people, the following had never occurred: 1) the glory of God had not been visible among the Israelites; 2) a central place of worship, like the Tabernacle, had never existed; 3) the yearly calendar had no feasts or sacrifices that required participation; 4) no formal structure of priests or other religious workers had been appointed.

During Israel's departure from Egypt, however, God made His presence visible to them with a pillar of cloud and fire. At Mount Sinai, Aaron and his family were appointed as priests. The plans for the Tabernacle were also revealed and carried out. These developments set the stage for God's instructions about lifestyle, worship, and the yearly calendar recorded in Leviticus.

Leviticus records no geographical movement. The people of Israel remained at Mount Sinai, the place where God came down to give His law (25:1).

KEY DOCTRINES IN LEVITICUS

Sacrifice—God required sacrifices from the people to atone for sin (1:3,9–13; 16:3; 17:8; 19:5; Exodus 29:34; Deuteronomy 16:5–6; Judges 11:31; Psalm 66:13–15; Matthew 5:23–24; Romans 8:3; 12:1; Hebrews 2:17; 1 John 2:2)

Holiness—the attribute that encapsulates God's perfect character; Israel was called to be holy as God is holy (11:44–45; 19:2; 20:7, 26; 21:6–8; Exodus 6:7; 19:6; Psalm 22:3; 99:5; Isaiah 41:14–16; 1 Thessalonians 4:7; 1 Peter 1:14–16)

Offerings—forms of worship to God, to give expression of the penitent and thankful heart (1:1–17; 2:1–16; 3:1–17; 4:1–5:13; 5:14–6:7; Genesis 4:4–5; Deuteronomy 16:10; 1 Kings 18:33–40; Job 42:8; 2 Corinthians 5:21; 2 Timothy 4:6)

Israel as God's holy nation—the people through whom Christ would enter the world (26:42–46; Genesis 15:12–21; Exodus 19:5–6; 2 Samuel 7:13; 23:5; Hebrews 8:6–13)

GOD'S CHARACTER IN LEVITICUS

God is accessible—16:12–15
God is glorious—9:6,23
God is holy—11:44–45
God is wrathful—10:2

CHRIST IN LEVITICUS

God's explicit instructions about offerings within Leviticus point towards the final substitutionary sacrifice of Christ. Because the sacrifices of the people represented only temporary removal of Israel's sins, they needed to be repeated continually. Jesus lived a perfect life on earth and presented Himself as the final sacrifice for all humankind. In contrast to the Old Testament Passover feast celebrated annually, believers constantly celebrate the "feast" of the new Passover—Jesus Christ, the Passover Lamb (1 Corinthians 5:7).

KEY WORDS IN LEVITICUS

Offering: Hebrew *qorban*—2:3; 4:35; 6:18; 7:14,33; 9:4; 10:14—this Hebrew word is derived from the verb "to bring near" and literally means "that which one brings near to God." The fact that the Israelites could approach to present their gifts to God reveals His mercy. Even though the people were sinful and rebellious, God instituted a sacrificial system in which they could reconcile themselves to Him. The sacrifices foreshadowed Jesus' death on the cross, the ultimate offering, the offering that ended the need for any others. Through Christ's sacrificial death, we have once for all been reconciled to God (Hebrews 10:10–18). An appropriate response to Jesus' death for us is to offer our lives as living sacrifices to God (Romans 12:1).

Memorial Portion: Hebrew *ʾazkarah*—2:2,9,16; 5:12; 6:15; 23:24; 24:7—a memorial portion of a grain offering was a representative portion burnt on the altar in place of the whole amount. The rest was a gift to the priest, to support him in his ministry. The word for *memorial portion* is related to the Hebrew verb *zakar*, which means "to remember." It signifies the worshiper's remembering of God's gracious character and generosity, especially God's remembering and blessing of the worshiper.

Blood: Hebrew *dam*—1:5; 3:17; 4:7; 8:15; 9:9; 16:18; 17:10; 20:11—related to the Hebrew word *ʾadom*, which means "red" (Genesis 25:30) and refers to blood. This may be the blood of animals (Exodus 23:18) or human beings (Genesis 4:10). The word *blood* may also represent a person's guilt, as in the phrase "his blood shall be upon him"; that is, he is responsible for his own guilt (20:9). The Old Testament equates *life* with *blood* (Genesis 9:4; Deuteronomy 12:23), which vividly illustrates the sanctity of human life (Genesis 9:6). According to the New Testament, "without shedding of blood there is no remission" of sin (Hebrews 9:22). Thus the emphasis on blood in the Old Testament sacrifices pointed to the blood that Christ would shed, i.e., the life that He would give on our behalf (Romans 5:9; 1 Corinthians 11:25–26).

Jubilee: Hebrew *yobel*—25:9,12,30,40,54; 27:18,24—literally means "ram" or "ram's horn" (Exodus 19:13; Joshua 6:5). The term is associated with the Year of Jubilee in Leviticus 25:10 and Numbers 36:4. The fiftieth year was a "jubilee" year for the Hebrews, marked by the blowing of a trumpet (25:9). During that year, the Israelites were instructed to practice freedom and liberty: debts were canceled; slaves were freed; the land rested; family property was redeemed (25:10–17). The fact that Jesus quoted Isaiah 48:8,9 seems to indicate that Jesus equated His earthly ministry with the principles of the Year of Jubilee (Luke 4:18–19).

QUICK OVERVIEW

I. Laws Pertaining to Sacrifice (1:1–7:38)
  A. Legislation for the Laity (1:1–6:7)
  B. Legislation for the Priesthood (6:8–7:38)

II. Beginnings of the Priesthood (8:1–10:20)
  A. Ordination of Aaron and His Sons (8:1–36)
  B. First Sacrifices (9:1–24)
  C. Execution of Nadab and Abihu (10:1–20)
III. Prescriptions for Uncleanness (11:1–16:34)
  A. Unclean Animals (11:1–47)
  B. Uncleanness of Childbirth (12:1–8)
  C. Unclean Diseases (13:1–59)
  D. Cleansing of Diseases (14:1–57)
  E. Unclean Discharges (15:1–33)
  F. Purification of the Tabernacle from Uncleanness (16:1–34)
IV. Guidelines for Practical Holiness (17:1–27:34)
  A. Sacrifice and Food (17:1–15)
  B. Proper Sexual Behavior (18:1–30)
  C. Neighborliness (19:1–37)
  D. Capital/Grave Crimes (20:1–27)
  E. Instructions for Priests (21:1–22:33)
  F. Religious Festivals (23:1–44)
  G. The Tabernacle (24:1–9)
  H. An Account of Blasphemy (24:10–23)
  I. Sabbatical and Jubilee Years (25:1–55)
  J. Exhortation to Obey the Law: Blessings and Curses (26:1–46)
  K. Redemption of Votive Gifts (27:1–34)

MEANWHILE, IN OTHER PARTS OF THE WORLD . . .
The Olmec culture in Mexico develops and construction begins on the Mexican Sun Pyramid.

FREQUENTLY ASKED QUESTIONS

1. Why did God have so many specific rules for the Israelites?

God's purpose was to create a separate, holy people (11:44–45). Their lives were to reflect His character and contrast with the behavior of their neighbor nations. They were to obey God's rules even when they didn't necessarily understand the reasons.

Looking back over history, we can often see that God had several reasons behind His rules. One of the interesting discoveries about the Levitical rules for cleanliness is that they measure up to recent standards of hygienic living. They represent just the sort of precautions taken by medical personnel today in order to prevent infections and the spread of diseases. God did not ask His people to behave in ways that were at all harmful to them.

2. What does the phrase *type of Christ* mean when used to describe someone or an event in the Old Testament?

Certain persons and practices recorded in the Old Testament serve as hints, clues, and preillustrations of what Jesus Christ would accomplish by His life, death, and resurrection. In most cases, the similarities or parallels are highlighted in the New Testament. The following events and practices, some introduced in Leviticus, prefigure Christ:

the ark—Genesis 7:16; 1 Peter 3:20–21
atonement sacrifices—16:15–16; Hebrews 9:12, 24
the brazen serpent—Numbers 21:9; John 3:14–15
the mercy seat—Exodus 25:17–22; Romans 3:25; Hebrews 4:16
the Passover lamb—Exodus 12:3–6, 46; John 19:36; 1 Corinthians 5:7
the red heifer—Ephesians 2:14, 16
rock of Horeb—Exodus 17:6; 1 Corinthians 10:4
scapegoat—16:20–22
Tabernacle—Exodus 40:2, 34; Hebrews 9:11; Colossians 2:9
veil of the Tabernacle—Exodus 40:21; Hebrews 10:20.

3. To what degree should believers today submit to the rules and regulations God gave the people of Israel?

Believers' understanding of the Old Testament must be shaped by Jesus and the New Testament. Jesus talked about this when He said, "Do not think I came to destroy the Law or the Prophets. I did not come to destroy but to fulfill" (Matthew 5:17).

In relation to the Old Testament ceremonial law, the Levitical priesthood, and the sanctuary, the New Testament records a number of instances of how this fulfillment by Jesus worked itself out in individual understanding and practice (Matthew 27:51; Acts 10:1–16, Colossians 2:16–17; 1 Peter 2:9; Revelation 1:6; 5:10; 20:6). The very institution of the New Covenant in and by Jesus (Matthew 26:28; 2 Corinthians 3:6–18; Hebrews 7–10) places the Old Testament in a new light.

The most profitable study in Leviticus focuses on the truths contained in the understanding of sin, guilt, substitutionary death, and atonement by noting features that are not explained or illustrated elsewhere in the Old Testament. Later writers of Scripture, especially the New Testament, build on the basic understanding of these matters provided by Leviticus. The sacrificial features of Leviticus point to their ultimate, one-time fulfillment in the substitutionary death of Jesus Christ (Hebrews 9:11–22).

QUICK STUDY ON LEVITICUS

1. How many different kinds of sacrifices and offerings can you identify in Leviticus?
2. What does the term *holy* mean and in what ways is it used in Leviticus?
3. In what ways do the laws in Leviticus contribute to healthy living?
4. What kinds of sacrifices and offerings are part of your relationship with God?

NUMBERS
Travelogue of a Wilderness Journey

Numbers records the thirty-nine years of judgment that Israel spent in the wilderness.

Originally, the Hebrew designation of the fourth book of the Bible was an expression meaning "in the wilderness." The ancient Greek title of this book is *arithmoi,* from which we get the English word *arithmetic*. Later, Latin translators gave the book the title *numeri,* which English has borrowed as its general word *numbers.* The translators were referring to the numberings (censuses) recorded in the book. In another sense, the book numbers the thirty-nine years in which God's people were in the wilderness, counting down the time of their punishment.

AUTHOR AND DATE

Written by Moses, approximately 1445 to 1405 B.C.

Like the other first five books of the Bible, Numbers is identified as Moses' writing by the rest of Scripture. Numbers itself mentions Moses twice (33:2; 36:13) as the recorder of events and commandments.

Numbers was written in the final year of Moses' life. Biblical sequence requires a completion date for Numbers of shortly before the eleventh month of the fortieth year after the Exodus, since that is the specific date given for Deuteronomy (Deuteronomy 1:3).

KEY PEOPLE IN NUMBERS

Moses—great prophet and leader who acted as God's mouthpiece to explain His Law to Israel (1:1,19,48; 5:1,4–5,11—and over two hundred other references)

Aaron—Moses' brother and first high priest of Israel (1:3,17,44; 2:1; 3:1–10; 12:1–5; 20:23–29)

Miriam—sister to Moses and Aaron, also songwriter and prophetess; stricken with leprosy because of jealousy toward Moses (12; 20:1; 26:59)

Joshua—Moses' successor as leader of Israel; one of the only two people to see both the Exodus from Egypt and the Promised Land (11:28; 13; 14; 26:65; 27:15–23; 32:11–12,28; 34:17)

Caleb—one of the men sent to scout Canaan; faithful to God in his desire to conquer the land; one of the only two people to see both the Exodus from Egypt and the Promised Land (13–14; 26:65; 32:12; 34:19)

Eleazar—son of Aaron who succeeded him as high priest of Israel (3:1–4; 4:16; 16:36–40; 20:25–29; 26:1–4,63; 27:2,15–23; 32:2; 34:17)

Korah—Levite who assisted in the Tabernacle; killed because of his rebellion against the Lord (16:1–40; 26:9)

Balaam—prophet and sorcerer who halfheartedly obeyed God; attempted to lead Israel into idol worship (22:1–24:25; 31:7–8,16)

BACKGROUND AND SETTING

Most of the events in Numbers are set in the wilderness. The people were forced to live as nomads for forty years, though their actual moves were infrequent. Chapter 33 lists a complete itinerary of their travels. The Israelites broke camp roughly forty times in forty years.

The greatest portion of the book describes the events leading up to the first failed conquest of the Promised Land as well as the final preparations for the second conquest almost four decades later. In between, the tragedy of thirty-seven wasted years is emphasized by being largely ignored.

KEY DOCTRINES IN NUMBERS

Rebellion against God—resulted from Israel's coupling with heathen nations (14:26–38; Exodus 34:6–7; Joshua 24:19; Psalm 32:1–7; Hosea 10:9–10; 2 Thessalonians 2:3; Jude 1:14–15)

Inheritance of the land—God secured the Promised Land for His people (16:14; 26:52–56; Leviticus 14:34; 1 Chronicles 28:8; Ezra 9:10–12; Psalm 16:5–6; Joel 3:2; Colossians 1:11–12; 1 Peter 1:4)

Divine authority given to Moses—Moses spoke the words of God and led Israel (1:1; 7:89; 12:6–8). God also gave authority to others of His prophets (Jeremiah 5:12–13; 1 Corinthians 1:10) and to Jesus (Matthew 7:29; 9:6; Mark 6:12; Luke 10:22)

Israel's sin and judgment from the Lord—God does not have favorites; Israel's sin demanded punishment (11:1,10,33; 12:9; 14:18; 25:3,4; 32:10,13–14; Leviticus 10:2; Deuteronomy 9:22; 2 Kings 1:12, Psalm 78:21; 106:15; Jonah 4:2; John 3:18–19; Romans 5:9; 1 John 4:17–18; Revelation 20:11–15)

Faithfulness of God to His covenant—when God's people lose faithfulness, God remains faithful (15:2; 26:52–56; 27:12; 33:50–56; 34:1–29; Joshua 11:23; 14:1)

GOD'S CHARACTER IN NUMBERS

God is long-suffering—14:18

God is merciful—14:18

God is provident—26:65

God is true—23:19

God is wrathful—11:1,33; 12:9–10; 14:37,40–45; 16:31,35; 21:6; 25:9; 32:14

CHRIST IN NUMBERS

The New Testament remains a source of insight into the presence of Christ in the Book of Numbers. In chapter 21, verses 4 through 9, the Israelite people who looked upon the serpent lifted up by Moses were healed. John describes this as a picture of the Crucifixion: "And as Moses lifted up the serpent in the wilderness, even so must the Son of Man be lifted up" (John 3:14). The manna that sustained the people also illustrated Christ as the Bread of Life (John 6:31–33). Furthermore, the rock that brought water to the people was also a type of Christ. Paul's letter to the Corinthians refers to this rock as "that spiritual Rock that followed them, and that Rock was Christ" (1 Corinthians 10:4).

KEY WORDS IN NUMBERS

Sacrifice: Hebrew *zebach*—6:17; 7:17,29,47,59,77; 15:3,5,8—from a verb meaning "to slaughter for an offering." In accordance with the law of Moses, a priest would offer sacrifices on behalf of a worshiper by burning them on the altar (Exodus 20:24). Sacrifices could either be grain offerings (the first fruits of the harvest) or animal sacrifices. Animal sacrifices under the law served one primary function—to cover or atone for sin (Leviticus 22:21; Hebrews 9:22). The sin of an individual was symbolically transferred to the sacrificed animal, thereby providing a temporary substitutionary atonement that had to be repeated annually because it only partially dealt with sin (Hebrews 10:4). Ultimately, all sacrifices in the Old Testament point forward to and are types of the final, all-sufficient sacrifice made by Christ (Isaiah 53; 1 Corinthians 5:7; Hebrews 9:10).

Anointed: Hebrew *mashach*—3:3; 6:15; 7:1,10,84,88; 35:25—a verb meaning "to wet or daub a person with olive oil." Kings, priests, and prophets were anointed at the beginning of their service (8:12; 16:32; 2 Samuel 2:4; 5:3; 1 Kings 19:15–16). This ritual identified a person or object as set apart for God's special purposes. During the Exodus, many holy objects were anointed, including the Tabernacle itself. Anointing oil was an exquisite and expensive blend of oil and spices (7:1). This special oil symbolized the consecration of the Tabernacle and its furnishings to God.

Vow: Hebrew *neder*—6:2,21; 15:3; 21:2; 30:2–3,9,13—a vow. A vow to God is a voluntary commitment to do something that pleases Him or to abstain from certain practices to demonstrate devotion to Him. A vivid example of a vow in the Old Testament is the Nazirite vow (6:1–21). Scripture admonishes the believer against making rash vows, since they are made before God, the righteous and holy Judge (Ecclesiastes 5:4). The reason for the warning is that a vow made to Him is binding and must be fulfilled.

Elders: Hebrew *zaqen*—11:16,24–25,30; 16:25; 22:4,7—a word that means "aged" or "old." In the Old Testament, the word *elder* refers to either an aged, feeble person (Genesis 44:20; Job 42:17) or to a mature person who had authority within the Israelite community (Exodus 3:16; Joshua 8:33). Elders could serve as judges (Exodus 18:12), advisers (Ezekiel 7:26), and ruling officials (Deuteronomy 19:12; Ruth 4:2). Their position was one of great honor (Proverbs 31:23; Isaiah 9:15). In addition to age (Hebrew tradition states that an elder had to be a man at least fifty years of age), an elder had to demonstrate his maturity by fearing God, being truthful, and not coveting (Exodus 18:21).

QUICK OVERVIEW

I. The Experience of the First Generation of Israel in the Wilderness (1:1–25:18)
 A. The Obedience of Israel toward the Lord (1:1–10:36)
 B. The Disobedience of Israel toward the Lord (11:1–25:18)

II. The Experience of the Second Generation of Israel in the Plains of Moab: A Renewed Obedience of Israel toward the Lord (26:1–36:13)
 A. The Preparations for the Conquest of the Land (26:1–32:42)
 B. The Review of the Journey in the Wilderness (33:1–49)
 C. The Anticipation of the Conquest of the Land (33:50–36:13)

MEANWHILE, IN OTHER PARTS OF THE WORLD . . .
The Chinese begin to create elaborate sculptures with bronze.

FREQUENTLY ASKED QUESTIONS

1. The size of Israel's population provokes questions about the accuracy of the numbers in Numbers. Did that many people wander in the wilderness? How did they survive? How did they manage themselves?

Twice during the wilderness wanderings a census of the people of Israel was taken (1:46; 26:51). Each time the resulting total count of fighting men exceeded 600,000. These numbers indicate a population for Israel in the wilderness of around 2.5 million people at any time. Viewed naturally, this total appears too high to sustain in wilderness conditions.

Before concluding that Moses inflated the numbers, several factors must be considered. First, the Lord supernaturally took care of Israel for forty years (Deuteronomy 8:1–5). Second, God also spelled out sanitary practices that prevented the kind of health crises that might have occurred under those conditions. Third, while Israel wandered in the wilderness for forty years, they only moved camp about forty times. Spending about a year in each campsite preserved some grazing for the herds while keeping the people's pollution to a manageable amount. Each census was meant to be an accurate accounting of God's people. They ought to be taken at face value.

2. Chapter 21, verses 4 through 9, records an infestation of fiery serpents that attacked the people. Moses was instructed by God to create a bronze serpent and hang it on a pole. When bitten people looked at the serpent on the pole, they were healed. Wasn't this some kind of idol worship?

The circumstances leading up to the casting of the bronze serpent were all too familiar. The people were tired and discouraged. Angry with God, they complained to Moses. They were convinced that things couldn't get any worse, but God showed them otherwise. He sent fiery serpents among the people, and some of the Israelites died. Others suffered excruciating bites.

Realizing their mistake, the people came in repentance to Moses and begged for help. They were not worshiping the bronze serpent but were acting in faith, in obedience to God's and Moses' directions.

3. Why does a pagan and greedy prophet like Balaam receive so much attention in the biblical story?

Balaam, whose story is recorded in 22:2–24:25, does seem to receive special treatment. Even though Balaam claimed to know the Lord (22:18), Scripture consistently refers to him as a false prophet (2 Peter 2:15–16; Jude 11). Apparently, God placed such a priority on the message that the character of the messenger became a secondary consideration. The Lord used Balaam as His mouthpiece to speak the true words He put in his mouth. God had a purpose for Balaam despite the pagan prophet's own plans.

4. What are modern readers to do with Balaam's talking donkey (22:22–35)?

Several observations come to mind when a question like this is asked. First, the question assumes that ancient readers had fewer problems with talking donkeys than modern people do. This incident was not recorded as a commonplace occurrence but as something unusual and noteworthy. Second, one can just as easily wonder why God didn't (or doesn't) use talking animals more often—we would all probably be better off. Third, why not recognize God's sense of humor in this account?

Fourth, God's display of patience and persistence in these events ought to provoke in us a sense of humble worship. Fifth, the incident, unusual as it may be, should be accepted at face value as true.

QUICK STUDY ON NUMBERS

1. What considerations were behind the numbering of the people as they crossed the wilderness?
2. What events led up to God's decision to turn His people back into the wilderness for forty years?
3. In what different ways did the Israelites rebel against God?
4. What benefits could have been accomplished during the forty years in the desert?
5. What principles are illustrated by the plague of fiery serpents in the wilderness (21:4–9)?
6. In what ways does the episode with Balaam illustrate the character of God (22:2–24:25)?

DEUTERONOMY
The Great Review

Deuteronomy records the last words of a great leader—Moses.

The Hebrew title of this fifth biblical book simply uses two words that mean "these are the words." Ancient Greek translators based their title on 17:18, which mentions "a copy of this law." The Greek word actually means "second law." This emphasizes the fact that much of Deuteronomy is a review of God's Law by Moses in his final days.

AUTHOR AND DATE

Written by Moses, approximately 1410 to 1405 B.C.

Moses has generally been accepted as the author of Deuteronomy in large part because the book itself makes that claim. Both the Old Testament and the New Testament support the claim of Mosaic authorship. While 32:48–34:12 was added after Moses' death (probably by Joshua), the rest of the book must have originated with Moses shortly before his death in 1405 B.C.

KEY PEOPLE IN DEUTERONOMY

Moses—leader of Israel; instructed the people on the law of God but was not allowed to enter the Promised Land (chapters 1–5; 27; 29; 31–34)

Joshua—Moses' successor; guided Israel into the Promised Land (1:37–38; 3:21–28; 31:3–23; 32:44; 34:9)

BACKGROUND AND SETTING

Like Leviticus, the events in Deuteronomy take place in one location. The people of Israel were camped in their final staging area before invading the Promised Land. Numbers 36:13 identifies the location as "the plains of Moab."

The first thirty chapters of Deuteronomy record Moses' review and commentary on God's Law. Only two other events are included: 1) Moses' official acts of recording the Law in written form and commissioning Joshua as the new leader (31:1–29); and 2) Moses' death after viewing the Promised Land from the distant peak of Mount Nebo (32:48–52; 34:1–12).

All of the original recipients of Deuteronomy were the generation that had grown up or been born in the wilderness during the forty years since the Exodus from Egypt. Here they stood on the border of the Promised Land, poised to do what their parents had refused to do.

KEY DOCTRINES IN DEUTERONOMY

The Promised Land of Israel (1:8; 6:10; 9:5; 29:13; 30:20; 34:4; Genesis 12:7; 15:5; 22:17; Exodus 33:1; Leviticus 18:24; Numbers 14:23; 34:1–15; Joshua 24:13; Psalm 105:44; Titus 3:5)

The Lord's faithfulness to give Israel victory over its enemies (2:24–3:11; 29:2,7–8; Numbers 21:3,33–34; Joshua 1:7; 10:8–12; Judges 1:1–4; 1 Kings 2:3; Psalm 18:43; Romans 8:37; 1 Corinthians 15:54–57; 1 John 5:4)

Israel's rebellion against the Lord (1:26–46; 9:7–10:11; Exodus 14:11; Numbers 14:1–4; Ezra 4:19; Psalm 106:24; Jeremiah 5:6; Ezekiel 18:31; Daniel 9:24; 2 Thessalonians 2:2; Jude 1:11,15)

The scattering of Israel as judgment from God (4:25–31; 29:22–30:10; 31:26–29; Leviticus 26:33; 1 Kings 14:15; Nehemiah 1:8; Psalm 106:25–27; Ecclesiastes 3:5; Jeremiah 9:15–16; Amos 9:8)

Holiness of God and His people—God declares Israel His chosen people (7:6–11; 8:6,11,18; 10:12,16–17; 11:13; 13:3–4; 14:1–2; Exodus 19:5–6; Proverbs 10:22; Amos 3:2; Micah 6:8; Matthew 22:37; Romans 12:1; 1 Timothy 1:5; 1 Peter 2:9)

GOD'S CHARACTER IN DEUTERONOMY

God is accessible—4:7
God is eternal—33:27
God is faithful—7:9
God is glorious—5:24; 28:58
God is jealous—4:24
God is just—10:17; 32:4
God is loving—7:7–8,13; 10:15,18; 23:5
God is merciful—4:31; 32:43
God is powerful—3:24; 32:39
God is a promise keeper—1:11
God is provident—8:2,15,18
God is righteous—4:8
God is true—32:4
God is unequaled—4:35; 33:26
God is unified—4:32–35,39–40; 6:4–5; 32:39
God is wise—2:7
God is wrathful—29:20,27–28; 32:19–22

CHRIST IN DEUTERONOMY

Deuteronomy speaks directly of the coming of a new Prophet similar to Moses: "The LORD your God will raise up for you a Prophet like me from your midst, from your brethren. Him you shall hear" (18:15). This Prophet is interpreted by both the Old and New Testaments as the Messiah or Christ (34:10; Acts 3:22–23; 7:37).

Moses illustrates a type of Christ in several ways: 1) Both were spared death as babies (Exodus 2; Matthew 2:13–23); 2) Both acted as priest, prophet, and leader over Israel (Exodus 32:31–35; Hebrews 2:17; 34:10–12; Acts 7:52; 33:4–5; Matthew 27:11).

KEY WORDS IN DEUTERONOMY

Statutes: Hebrew *choq*—4:1,14; 5:1; 6:1; 7:11; 10:13; 16:12; 28:15; 30:16—conveys a variety of meanings in the Old Testament, including a verb that means "to decree" or "to inscribe" (Proverbs 8:15; Isaiah 10:1; 49:16). It often refers to commands, civil enactments, legal prescriptions, and ritual laws decreed by someone in authority—whether by humans (Micah 6:16) or by God Himself (6:1). The Law of Moses includes commandments (*miswah*), judgments (*mispat*), and statutes (*choq*) (4:1–2). Israel was charged to obey God's statutes, and they had pledged to do so (26:16–17).

Swore: Hebrew *shabaʿ*—6:13; 7:8; 10:20; 13:17; 19:8; 29:13; 31:7—the verb translated *swore* is related to the word used for the number seven. In effect, the verb means "to bind oneself fully"; that is, "seven times." In ancient times, oaths were considered sacred. People were promising to be faithful to their word no matter what the personal cost. The Old Testament describes God as taking an oath (Genesis 24:7; Exodus 13:5). He was not forced to do this; He did not have to swear in order to ensure His own compliance with His word. Instead, He made an oath so that His people would be assured that His promises were completely trustworthy.

Worship: Hebrew *shachah*—4:19; 8:19; 11:16; 26:10; 30:17—this most common Hebrew word for *worship* literally means "to cause oneself to lie prostrate." In ancient times, a person would fall down before someone who possessed a higher status. People would bow before a king to express complete submission to his rule. Following the example of the ancient people of faith, true Christian worship must express more than love for God; it must also express submission to His will.

Cursed: Hebrew *ʾarar*—7:26; 13:17; 27:15,20,23; 28:16,19—literally means "to bind with a curse." A curse is the opposite of a blessing. It wishes or prays illness or injury on a person or an object. God cursed the serpent and the ground after the sin of Adam and Eve (Genesis 3:14,17). Jeremiah, in despair, cursed the man who brought news of his birth (Jeremiah 20:14–15). The seriousness of God's covenant with His people is illustrated by the threat of a curse on any who violate it (28:60–61). In the New Testament, Paul taught that Jesus Christ became a "curse" for us, so that we might be freed form the curses of the Law (Galatians 3:13).

QUICK OVERVIEW

I. Introduction: The Historical Setting of Moses' Speeches (1:1–4)
II. The First Address by Moses: A Historical Prologue (1:5–4:43)
  A. A Historical Review of God's Gracious Acts from Horeb to Beth Peor (1:5–3:29)
  B. An Exhortation to Obey the Law (4:1–40)
  C. The Setting Apart of Three Cities of Refuge (4:41–43)
III. The Second Address by Moses: The Stipulations of the Sinaitic Covenant (4:44–28:68)
  A. Introduction (4:44–49)
  B. The Basic Elements of Israel's Relationship with the Lord (5:1–11:32)
  C. The Specific Stipulations for Life in the New Land (12:1–26:19)
  D. The Blessings and Curses of the New Covenant (27:1–28:68)
IV. The Third Address by Moses: Another Covenant (29:1–30:20)
V. The Concluding Events (31:1–34:12)
  A. The Change of Leadership (31:1–8)
  B. The Future Reading of the Law (31:9–13)
  C. The Song of Moses (31:14–32:47)
  D. The Final Events of Moses' Life (32:48–34:12)

MEANWHILE, IN OTHER PARTS OF THE WORLD . . . Ethiopia becomes an independent power. The Shang dynasty flourishes in China.

FREQUENTLY ASKED QUESTIONS

1. Is Deuteronomy simply Moses' version of the secular covenants and treaties of his day, or does it represent a unique revelation from God?

The format that Moses used in recording not only the material in Deuteronomy but also the rest of the Pentateuch bears some resemblance to other official documents from a particular time in history. This fact has been used by historians in trying to establish a date for the book. It has also been used by those who question God's unique revelation to support their claim that Moses merely copied the style of other nations of his time.

The people whom God enlisted to record His revelation did not shed their personalities, education, or style as they wrote for God. Moses had the equivalent of advanced degrees in the best training Egypt had to offer young princes (Acts 7:22). If we think of the Pentateuch as Moses' God-guided journaling during the wilderness wanderings, it will not seem unusual that his writing style bears similarities to the official and political writings of his day. What sets Moses' writings, along with the rest of Scripture, apart is not so much the style but their authoritative and God-inspired content.

QUICK STUDY ON DEUTERONOMY

1. What does Moses say about his reasons for taking time to review all that God had done?
2. According to chapter 6, how is the Law to be preserved by each generation?
3. What was the relationship between the Law and the Promised Land?
4. In what ways is God's love revealed throughout this book?
5. Why did Moses die without ever entering the Promised Land?

JOSHUA
God's Bold Warrior

Joshua fought the battle of Jericho
when the walls came tumbling down.

This book heads the list of twelve historical books in the Old Testament. The meaning of Joshua's name matches the significance of his role. Joshua means "Jehovah saves" or "the Lord is salvation" and is an earlier Hebrew form of the New Testament name "Jesus."

AUTHOR AND DATE

Written by Joshua, approximately 1405 to 1385 B.C.

Although the author of this book is not named, the most probable candidate is Joshua, who was the key eyewitness to the events (18:9; 24:26). A trusted assistant may have attached such comments as the description of Joshua's death (24:29–33).

Details like the mention of Rahab still being alive at the time of writing indicate an early date for this book (6:25). Other internal clues, like the ongoing presence of the Jebusites in Jerusalem (15:63), place the completion date before the reign of David (2 Samuel 5:5–9).

KEY PEOPLE IN JOSHUA

Joshua—led Israel to possess the Promised Land (1–24)

Rahab—prostitute from Jericho; saved from death because of her obedience to God; ancestor of David and Jesus (2; 6:17,22–23,25)

Achan—disobeyed God by stealing from the plunder of Jericho; caused Israel to lose the battle against Ai; stoned as punishment (7; 22;20)

Phinehas—priest and son of Eleazar; acted as intermediary among the tribes of Israel to prevent civil war (22:13,31–34; 24:33)

Eleazar—son of Aaron; succeeded him as high priest; helped Joshua lead Israel (14:1; 17:4; 19:51; 21:1–3; 22:13–33; 24:33)

BACKGROUND AND SETTING

When Joshua replaced Moses as leader (Deuteronomy 34), the children of Israel had reached the end of their forty-year wilderness wandering. At that time, Joshua was nearly 90 years old. He eventually died at 110 (24:29) having led Israel in driving out most of the Canaanites and having divided the land among the twelve tribes.

As the Book of Joshua opens, the nation of Israel is camped on the east side of the Jordan River, awaiting God's instructions. Across the river lived nations so devoted to sinfulness that God would cause the land, so to speak, to "vomit out" its inhabitants (Leviticus 18:25). God would give

Israel the land by conquest, primarily to fulfill the covenant He had made with Abraham and his descendants. Through this invasion, God also would pass judgment on the sinful inhabitants (Genesis 15:16). Some of them had possessed part of the land since before Abraham's time (Genesis 10:15–19; 12:6; 13:7). Their persistent moral decline and pagan worship led to God's response. They lost their land.

KEY DOCTRINES IN JOSHUA

God's faithfulness in giving the Promised Land to Abraham's descendants (5:14–6:2; 11:23; 21:45; 22:4; Genesis 12:7; 15:18–21; 17:8; Exodus 33:2; Numbers 34:2–15; Deuteronomy 12:9–10; 25:19; Hebrews 4:8)

GOD'S CHARACTER IN JOSHUA

God is holy—24:19
God is jealous—24:19
God is a promise keeper—22:4; 23:14
God is provident—7:14; 21:45
God is wrathful—10:25; 23:16

CHRIST IN JOSHUA

Although the Book of Joshua lacks explicit messianic prophecy, Joshua represents a type of Christ in name and in deed. The name *Yeshua* represents Joshua's Hebrew name. This name, meaning "Yahweh is Salvation," is also translated as "Jesus." At one point Joshua received a vision of a "Commander of the army of the LORD" (5:13–14). This Commander represents the preincarnate Christ who led Joshua, the commander of Israel's army, to victory over the Canaanites.

KEY WORDS IN JOSHUA

Stone: Hebrew *'eben*—4:3,5,9,20; 7:25; 8:31; 10:11,18. The stones that littered the landscape of the ancient Middle East were used in numerous ways. They were the building material for houses, city walls, and fortifications (1 Kings 5:17; 2 Kings 12:12). Stones were used for religious purposes, to build sacred pillars (Genesis 35:14) and altars (Deuteronomy 27:5). Stones were also piled up as memorials marking the sites of divine revelation (Genesis 28:18,22) or a significant event in the life of an individual (Genesis 31:46) or a nation (4:6). Because a stone was commonly used as a foundation for a structure, God Himself was called the "Stone of Israel" (Genesis 49:24). But Isaiah also described the Lord as a "stone of stumbling" for those Israelites who rejected Him (Isaiah 8:14). These same images were applied to Jesus Christ in the New Testament (Isaiah 28:16; 1 Peter 2:4–8).

Trumpet: Hebrew *shophar*—6:5,8–9,13,16,20—an animal horn (typically from a ram or a goat) used as a trumpet (6:6; Judges 7:8). The word can also refer to a metal trumpet (Numbers 10:2–10; 1 Chronicles 15:28; 2 Chronicles 15:14). The *shophar* was a signaling instrument, used in warfare (Judges 3:27) and for assembling the people together at religious festivals, such as the Day of Atonement (Leviticus 25:8; 2 Samuel 6:5; Joel 2:1). A trumpet blast announced God's descent to Mount Sinai to reveal His law (Exodus 19:20). Both the Old Testament and the New Testament mention a trumpet announcing the Day of the Lord, the day when the Lord will come in judgment (Zephaniah 1:16; Matthew 24:31).

Inheritance: Hebrew *nachalah*—13:14,33; 14:3; 17:4; 19:1,9,49: 21:3; 24:32—meaning "possession" or "property," is linked to the promises of God, particularly those involving the Promised Land (Genesis 13:14–17). When this word is used of the Promised Land, it does not merely refer to what a person wills to his children. Rather God, Creator of the world, granted His people a specific parcel of ground. He fixed its boundaries and promised to deliver it to them. However, the concept of Israel's inheritance transcends a simple association with the land. David and Jeremiah both affirm that God Himself is the real inheritance of His people (Psalm 16:5; Jeremiah 10:16). God's people can find joy and fulfillment in their relationship with God. Nothing this world can offer as an inheritance compares with God Himself (1 Peter 1:4).

Rest: Hebrew *shaqat*—1:13; 3:13; 10:20; 13:27; 17:2; 21:44; 22:4; 23:1—means "to be at peace." Rest implies freedom from anxiety and conflict. God promised the Israelites *rest* in the Promised Land (Exodus 33:14; Deuteronomy 3:1–20; 12:9–10). In the Book of Joshua, the idea of *rest* is related specifically to the conflicts and hostilities Israel had with their neighbors. God promised His people a peaceful place to settle. Obtaining this rest depended on Israel's complete obedience to God's command to drive out the Canaanites (11:23; 14:15). The New Testament writers also speak of the concept of rest. Christians are told that heaven will bring them rest from death, pain, sin, and all other earthly struggles (Hebrews 4:1; Revelation 21:4).

QUICK OVERVIEW

I. Entering the Promised Land (1:1–5:15)
II. Conquering the Promised Land (6:1–12:24)
  A. The Central Campaign (6:1–8:25)
  B. The Southern Campaign (9:1–10:43)
  C. The Northern Campaign (11:1–15)
  D. The Summary of Conquests (11:16–12:24)

III. Distributing Portions of the Promised Land (13:1–22:34)
   A. Summary of Instructions (13:1–33)
   B. West of the Jordan (14:1–19:51)
   C. Cities of Refuge (20:1–9)
   D. Cities of the Levites (21:1–45)
   E. East of the Jordan (22:1–34)
IV. Retaining the Promised Land (23:1–24:28)
   A. The First Speech by Joshua (23:1–16)
   B. The Second Speech by Joshua (24:1–28)
V. Postscript (24:29–33)

MEANWHILE, IN OTHER PARTS OF THE WORLD . . .
In Egypt, the peaceful reign of Amenhotep III improves and expands Egyptian culture and trade (1420–1385 B.C.).

FREQUENTLY ASKED QUESTIONS

1. How can we reconcile the character of God as revealed in the rest of Scripture with the harsh commands of God to utterly destroy cities and peoples in the conquest of the Promised Land?

When Joshua issued orders for the destruction of Jericho, he was echoing God's very clear commands. Passages like Exodus 23:32–33; 34:11–16 and Deuteronomy 7:1–5; 20:16–18 make it impossible to soften or avoid the truth that God ordered the destruction of entire populations. Those were not just soldiers killing soldiers. Many of the victims were women and children. The challenge for serious and humble Bible students is to face these horrors and the hard lessons they teach without trying to explain them away.

If we do not have a growing awe about the holiness of God and His righteous judgment of sin, our understanding of God's grace and mercy will fade away. Without an acknowledgment that God can and does punish, the possibility of mercy and forgiveness carries little weight. If we do not seek to see the entire scope of God's actions and character, we will tend to gravitate to what we like or don't like and miss the connections. The gaps in our understanding can be partly filled by biblical insights.

The people of Israel's role in applying God's judgment had nothing to do with their own righteousness. But for God's grace, they would easily be in the place of the condemned. "Do not think in your heart, after the LORD your God has cast them out before you, saying, 'Because of my righteousness the LORD has brought me in to possess this land'; but it is because of the wickedness of these nations that the LORD is driving them out from before you" (Deuteronomy 9:4).

God could have used sickness, famine, fire, or flood to clear out the land, but He chose to use the people of Israel. In terrible natural disasters, everyone suffers. It isn't easy to accept that little children shared the fate of their parents. But they often do. And they did as Israel carried out God's judgments. Did God unfairly include these children in punishment, or do the parents and leaders bear responsibility for putting the innocent in harm's way by their rejection of God? Some of these issues will have to be settled beyond death, when the final judgment occurs (Hebrews 9:27).

2. Why did God bless Rahab and give her a unique role in history in spite of her lie?

Rahab's life was not spared because of her lie; it was spared because she put her faith in God. Rahab was given a gracious opportunity to side with God by protecting the two Israelite spies, and she acted within her circumstances. She lied daringly and elaborately. Perhaps her initial response was simply a habit of her profession. From the perspective of the king of Jericho, Rahab would have been guilty of treason, not just lying. She had a new allegiance, and she didn't yet know that the God she now wanted to trust had a rule about lying.

The radical change that came into Rahab's life when those spies knocked on her door can be seen in several ways. She risked her life to trust God. The Book of Ruth also reveals that Rahab married and became the great, great-grandmother of King David and one of the ancestors of Jesus. Centuries later, Rahab was one of the women listed in Hebrews 11 because of her faith.

3. How does God's guarantee of success to Joshua carry over to us?

The Book of Joshua begins with God's commissioning of Israel's new leader. God described Joshua's mission—to go in and possess the land (1:2–6). God hinged Joshua's success on three key factors: 1) God's own presence (1:5); 2) Joshua's personal strength and courage (1:7,9); and 3) Joshua's attention to and application of God's Word (1:7–8).

The process of biblical meditation begins with a thoughtful, lingering reading of God's Word. It progresses to familiarity and memorization. In order to "meditate in it day and night" (Joshua 1:8), Joshua needed to spend enough time in the Book of the Law so that the Book would eventually get in Joshua. The purpose of God's Word has been achieved when meditation leads us to application—"observe to do according to all that is written in it" (Joshua 1:8).

"Then," God told Joshua, "you will make your way prosperous, and then you will have good success" (1:8). Joshua found that the ultimate measure of prosperity and success was knowing how God wants His people to live and then living that way. God repeatedly assured Joshua of

His own presence "wherever you go." What greater measure of success could there be than to honor the ever-present God with our obedience?

QUICK STUDY ON JOSHUA

1. What character traits in Joshua made him an excellent leader for Israel?
2. What were Joshua's greatest challenges as a leader?
3. Review Numbers 13–14 and compare the attitudes and actions of the people with the next generation that approached the Promised Land in Joshua 1–2.
4. In what ways did God keep His promises to Israel throughout Joshua?
5. How would you apply Joshua 24:15 in your life?

JUDGES
Chosen Servants for Troubled Times

"In those days there was no king in Israel; everyone did what was right in his own eyes" (21:25).

Israel's failure to evict the peoples of the land as God had commanded led to the results God had predicted (Joshua 1:27–2:4). The Canaanite nations became thorns to Israel, and the land was in constant turmoil. In desperate times, the people of Israel would acknowledge their slide into sinfulness and cry to God for forgiveness and deliverance. At each occasion, God would send unique leaders (judges) to deliver them (2:16–19). In Hebrew, the title of this book can also mean "deliverers," or "saviors." The Book of Judges records the careers of twelve God-chosen leaders.

AUTHOR AND DATE

Probably written by Samuel, approximately 1043 to 1004 B.C.

Though Judges does not indicate an author, ancient Jewish tradition assigns that task to Samuel. Samuel's life spanned the end of the period of the judges and the early years of the monarchy in Israel. Internal evidence in the book indicates the writer was at least a contemporary of Samuel who could summarize the period of history, acknowledge the kings, yet also note that Jerusalem was still under the control of the Jebusites.

A comparison of Judges 1:21 with 2 Samuel 5:6–7 leads to the conclusion that this book was recorded between Saul's rise to the throne in 1043 B.C. and David's capture of Jerusalem in 1004 B.C.

KEY PEOPLE IN JUDGES

Othniel—first judge of Israel; victorious over a powerful Mesopotamian king; brought forty years of peace to Israel (1:13–14; 3:7–11)

Ehud—second judge of Israel; brought Israel eighty years of peace by helping to conquer the Moabites (3:15–31)

Deborah—prophet and Israel's only female judge; succeeded Shamgar as fourth judge of Israel (4:4–16; 5)

Gideon—Israel's fifth judge; destroyed the Midianite army (6–8)

Abimelech—Gideon's evil son who declared himself king over Israel; killed sixty-nine of his half brothers (8:31–9:57)

Jephthah—judge of Israel and warrior who conquered the Ammonites (11:1–12:7)

Samson—dedicated to God as a Nazirite from birth; also a judge of Israel sent to overthrow the Philistines (13:24–16:31)

Delilah—Samson's lover who betrayed him to the Philistines for money (16:4–21)

BACKGROUND AND SETTING

The Book of Judges represents a tragic sequel to Joshua. In the Book of Joshua, most of the people were obedient to God in conquering the land. Judges portrays them as disobedient, idolatrous, and often defeated. After touching on the final days of Joshua and his death (1:1–3:6), the book describes seven distinct cycles in Israel's stormy relationship with God. These cycles reveal five basic reasons that lie behind the downward spiral of Israel's moral and spiritual life:

1. **Disobedience** in failing to drive out the Canaanites from the land (1:19,21,35)
2. **Idolatry** in adopting local gods and religious practices (2:12)
3. **Intermarriage** with wicked Canaanites against God's instructions (3:1–6)
4. **Minimal cooperation** with the judges (2:17)
5. **Turning away from God** after the death of each judge (2:19)

The seven cycles also demonstrate the repeated four-step sequence of God's intervention in Israel's life:

1. **Israel departs from following God's ways.**
2. **God faithfully corrects** by allowing military defeat and foreign domination.
3. **Israel cries out for deliverance.**
4. **God raises up judges** who serve as civil or military champions and lead the people to victories over the oppressors.

KEY DOCTRINES IN JUDGES

God's mercy in delivering Israel (2:16,18–19; Deuteronomy 30:3; Joshua 1:5; Psalm 106:43–45; Luke 1:50; Romans 11:30–32; 2 Corinthians 1:3; Ephesians 2:4)

Israel's apostasy (3:7; 4:1; 6:1; 8:33; 10:6; 13:1; 21:25; Numbers 31:1–3; Deuteronomy 32:18; 1 Samuel 12:9; 1 Kings 11:33; Isaiah 1:4; Ezekiel 6:11–14; John 3:18–21; Romans 7:5–6; Colossians 3:25; Titus 3:3)

GOD'S CHARACTER IN JUDGES

God is righteous—5:11
God is wrathful—9:56

CHRIST IN JUDGES

The Book of Judges traces the people of Israel through seven periods of rebellion and apostasy. During each period, specific judges are brought forth as deliverers and saviors for the fallen people. These judges illustrate Christ as the final Savior and King of His people (Luke 2:11; John 4:42; Mark 15:2).

KEY WORDS IN JUDGES

Judge: Hebrew *shaphat*—2:16,18; 10:2; 11:27; 12:9,11; 15:20; 16:31—this Hebrew word for *judge* means "to deliver" or "to rule." The judges of Israel had a wide range of responsibilities. Like their modern counterparts, Old Testament judges could decide controversies and hand down verdicts (Exodus 18:16). These judges were also involved in the execution of their judgment in both vindicating the righteous (Psalm 26:1) and destroying the wicked (Exodus 7:3). Many judges were God's appointed military leaders who, empowered by God's Spirit (6:34; 15:14), fought Israel's oppressors and thereby delivered the people. Later, Israel's king functioned as the national judge (1 Samuel 8:5). Ultimately, Israel's perfect Judge is God. He alone is capable of flawlessly judging the wicked and delivering the righteous (Isaiah 11:4).

Riddle: Hebrew *chidah*—14:12–19—meaning "an enigmatic saying." In Samson's story, the riddle is used in a contest of wits. Proverbs attributes enigmatic sayings to the wise (Proverbs 1:6). When the Queen of Sheba tested Solomon's wisdom, her questions are described by this same Hebrew word (1 Kings 10:1; 2 Chronicles 9:1). In the Lord's confrontation with Miriam and Aaron, God describes Himself as speaking in "dark sayings" (the same Hebrew word) to the prophets, but to Moses face-to-face (Numbers 12:6–8). Perhaps Paul had this last concept in mind when he admonished the Corinthians that even someone with the ability to understand all mysteries would not amount to anything if that person did not possess the love of God (1 Corinthians 13:2).

QUICK OVERVIEW

I. Introduction and Summary—The Disobedience of Israel (1:1–3:6)
  A. Incomplete Conquest over the Canaanites (1:1–36)
  B. The Decline and Judgment of Israel (2:1–3:6)
II. A Selected History of the Judges—The Deliverance of Israel (3:7–16:31)[1]
  A. First Period: Othniel versus the Mesopotamians (3:7–11)
  B. Second Period: Ehud and Shamgar versus the Moabites (3:12–31)
  C. Third Period: Deborah versus the Canaanites (4:1–5:31)
  D. Fourth Period: Gideon versus the Midianites (6:1–8:32)
  E. Fifth Period: Tola and Jair versus Abimelech's Effects (8:33–10:5)
  F. Sixth Period: Jephthah, Ibzan, Elon, and Abdon versus the Philistines and Ammonites (10:6–12:15)
  G. Seventh Period: Samson versus the Philistines (13:1–16:31)

III. Epilogue—The Dereliction of Israel (17:1–21:25)
   A. The Idolatry of Micah and the Danites (17:1–18:31)
   B. The Crime at Gibeah and War against Benjamin (19:1–21:25)

MEANWHILE, IN OTHER PARTS OF THE WORLD . . .
Prohibition is declared in China, and silk fabrics become widely developed for use in Chinese trade.

FREQUENTLY ASKED QUESTIONS

1. Men like Gideon, Jephthah, and Samson seem to exhibit as many gross failures as they do successes. Why does God make use of leaders with such obvious weaknesses?

One obvious answer to the question is that as long as God chooses to use people at all, He will end up using people with obvious weaknesses. No one escapes that category. The point is that God uses people in His plans in spite of their obvious weaknesses.

Does this mean that the sins of a leader are somehow to be excused? Of course not. In fact, leaders bear a higher level of accountability. Note, for example, the fact that Moses forfeited his opportunity to enter the Promised Land because of an angry outburst (Numbers 20:10; Deuteronomy 3:24–27). Jephthah made a rash vow for which his daughter had to bear the primary consequence (Judges 11:29–40). What probably ought to attract our attention to these servants of God is not so much their weaknesses, or even the great accomplishments that God worked through them, but the fact that they remained faithful to God despite their failures.

2. What can we gain by studying the lives of the judges of Israel?

God's Word includes a rich panorama of human experience. Despite the superficial transformation of much of the world, the people who inhabit it remain the same. When we study the lives of the judges we discover ourselves. The shared victories, defeats, mistakes and right choices form a common link across the centuries and turn our attention to the God who was active in their lives. The invitation from the ancients remains silently compelling: If we were to live as boldly for God, surely we would discover each day that same kind of immediate presence of God that was such a part of their experience.

QUICK STUDY ON JUDGES

1. Who were the twelve judges reviewed in this book, and how well did they carry out their missions of leadership?
2. Which judge do you find most worth imitating?
3. What were the main signs in the lives of the Israelites that indicated their loss of commitment to God and their compromises with the surrounding cultures?
4. Why did God continually rescue the people?
5. How would you illustrate the last verse in Judges to fit the times in which you live: "In those days there was no king in Israel; everyone did what was right in his own eyes" (Judges 21:25)?

---

[1] See also "Chronology of Old Testament Patriarchs and Judges" in the Appendices at the back of this book.

RUTH
God's International Family

The only book in the Old Testament named after an ancestor of Jesus.

Even the title of the Book of Ruth includes several noteworthy facts: 1) this book is the only one in the Old Testament named after a non-Jewish person; 2) this book is one of only two books in the Bible named after a woman (Ruth, like Esther, serves as the central character of the story). The name Ruth was most likely a shared Hebrew/Moabite term meaning "friendship." As her brief biography demonstrates, Ruth certainly lived up to her name.

AUTHOR AND DATE

Probably written by Samuel, approximately 1030 to 1010 B.C.

Ruth itself offers little help in identifying the author. Ancient Jewish traditions name Samuel as the writer. The closing verses mention David, but not Solomon, indicating a date of composition at the end of or shortly after Samuel's life (Ruth 4:17,22). Whoever the author was, the effort yielded an enduring work of exquisite storytelling.

KEY PEOPLE IN RUTH

Ruth—Naomi's daughter-in-law; later married to Boaz; direct ancestor of Jesus (chapters 1–4)

Naomi—widow of Elimelech and mother-in-law of Orpah and Ruth; wisely instructed Ruth (chapters 1–4)

Boaz—prosperous farmer who married Ruth, the Moabite; direct ancestor of Jesus (chapters 2–4)

BACKGROUND AND SETTING

Two geographic locations provide the context of the action in Ruth: the city of Bethlehem, just south of Jerusalem and the country of Moab, to the southeast and beyond the Dead Sea. Moab and Israel shared a distant but shameful ancestral relationship. The Moabites were descendants of Abraham's nephew Lot through incest (Genesis 19:37). Tensions were often high between the two nations. The events in Ruth's life apparently occurred during a time of relative peace between the two peoples.

The famine that had driven Elimelech and Naomi to relocate to Moab illustrates a method God would use, in addition to foreign conflicts, to discipline His unruly people (1:1). According to the book, the events occurred during the time of the judges (1:1). No famines are recorded in Judges, but the brief genealogy of David indicates that Ruth probably lived during the judgeship of Jair (Judges 10:3–5).

KEY DOCTRINES IN RUTH

Redemption for both Jews and Gentiles (2:12; 1 Samuel 24:19; Psalm 58:11; Acts 13:46; Romans 10:11–12; Galatians 3:28; Ephesians 2:14)
Women as coheirs with men of God's salvation grace (2:12; Acts 17:12; Galatians 3:28)
Characteristics of a virtuous woman (3:11; Proverbs 12:4; 31:10–31)
David's right (and thus Christ's right) to the throne of Israel (4:18–22; Genesis 49:8–12; Matthew 1:1–7; Luke 3:32)

GOD'S CHARACTER IN RUTH

God is sovereign—1:6; 4:13
God is provident—2:3

CHRIST IN RUTH

Boaz, as a type of Christ, becomes the kinsman-redeemer of Ruth (see the **Key Word** and **Frequently Asked Questions** below). This account foretells the coming of Jesus as the Redeemer of all believers (1 Peter 1:18–19).

KEY WORDS IN RUTH

Glean: Hebrew *laqat*—2:2,7,15,17–19,23—used here means "to gather together" or "to pick up." In the Old Testament, people are described as gleaning a variety of objects: stones (Genesis 31:46), money (Genesis 47:14), manna (Exodus 16:4–5,26), and even worthless men (Judges 11:3). The prophet Isaiah used this word to describe how the Lord would "gather up" His people from among all the nations and restore them to their own land (Isaiah 27:12). The verb occurs thirty-four times in the Old Testament, with twelve instances here in Ruth 2. In this passage, Ruth makes use of the stipulations the Lord gave to Moses. God had told the Israelites not to completely harvest their fields; instead they were to leave some unharvested grain so that the poor and strangers in the land could gather it up for their survival (Leviticus 19:9–10; 23:22).

Kinsman-Redeemer: Hebrew *ga'al*—2:1,20; 3:9,12–13; 4:1,3,6,14—meaning "kinsman," refers to a "close relative" who acted as a protector or guarantor of the family rights. He could be called upon to perform a number of duties: 1) to buy back property that the family had sold; 2) to provide an heir for a deceased brother by marrying that brother's wife and producing a child with her; 3) to buy back a family member who had been sold into slavery due to poverty; and 4) to avenge a relative who had been murdered by killing the murderer. The Scripture calls God the Redeemer or the "close relative" of Israel (Isaiah 60:16), and Jesus the Redeemer of all believers (1 Peter 1:18–19).

QUICK OVERVIEW

I. Elimelech and Naomi's Ruin in Moab (1:1–5)
II. Naomi and Ruth's Return to Bethlehem (1:6–22)
III. Boaz's Reception of Ruth in His Field (2:1–23)
IV. Ruth's Romance with Boaz (3:1–18)
V. Boaz's Redemption of Ruth (4:1–12)
VI. God's Reward of Boaz and Ruth with a Son (4:13–17)
VII. David's Right to the Throne of Judah (4:18–22)

MEANWHILE, IN OTHER PARTS OF THE WORLD . . .
Civil war breaks out under the reign of Ramses XI during the Twenty-first Dynasty in Egypt (1090 to 945 B.C.).

FREQUENTLY ASKED QUESTIONS

1. What is the "kinsman-redeemer," a prominent part in the story of Ruth?

When Boaz negotiated with another relative about the settlement of Elimelech and Naomi's estate (4:1–12), he referred to a law established by Moses in Deuteronomy 25:5–10. That law set out specific actions to be taken by the surviving family if a married son were to die without a son to inherit or carry on his name. Another (presumably unmarried) man in the family was to marry the widow. The first resulting child would inherit the estate of the man who had died.

Boaz's relative was willing to work out a financial arrangement with Naomi over her estate, but he didn't realize that Ruth was part of the settlement. When Boaz informed the man, he immediately released his right to claim responsibility for the estate. That cleared the way for Boaz and Ruth to marry. The whole exchange conveys a commitment to integrity and honor.

QUICK STUDY ON RUTH

1. In what ways does Naomi's and Ruth's relationship illustrate the best forms of friendship?
2. How does Ruth's story illustrate God's faithfulness?
3. In what ways did Ruth explain and express her faith in God?
4. How did Boaz exhibit wisdom in handling of Naomi's and Ruth's inheritance matters?
5. Describe Naomi's relationship with God throughtout the Book of Ruth.
6. What specific illustrations of God's provision can you think of in your own life?

FIRST AND SECOND SAMUEL

Qualifications for a King and the Establishment of David's Line

The tribes that formed the nation of Israel eventually became a kingdom, and these books tell the story.

First and 2 Samuel continue the history of Israel where Judges left off. Samuel's life spanned significant changes among God's chosen people. He can be called the last and greatest of the judges (Acts 13:20). Samuel's ministry also made him the first of the prophets (Acts 3:24). He anointed the first two kings of Israel (Saul and David). The two books that now bear his name were originally one scroll, divided for convenience by those who hand copied the record.

FIRST SAMUEL

AUTHOR AND DATE

Author(s) unknown, approximately 931 B.C. or later

Although the original human author of 1 and 2 Samuel remains anonymous, ancient traditions of Israel assign the writing to Samuel himself (1 Chronicles 29:29). Other possible writers include Nathan and Gad.

KEY PEOPLE IN 1 SAMUEL

Eli—high priest and Israel's judge for forty years; trained Samuel to be judge (1:3–28; 2:11–4:18)

Hannah—mother of Samuel; dedicated him to the Lord when he was a baby (1:2–2:11,21)

Samuel—priest, prophet, and greatest judge of Israel; anointed Israel's first two kings (1:20; 2:11,18–26; 3:1–21; 7:3–13:15; 15:1–16:13; 19:18–24; 25:1; 28:3–16)

Saul—first king of Israel appointed by God; grew jealous of David and tried to kill him (9:2–11:15; 13:1–19:24; 20:24–33; 21:10–11; 22:6–24:22; 25:44–27:4; 28:3–31:12)

Jonathan—son of Saul; befriended David and protected him against Saul (13:1–14:49; 18:1–23:18; 31:2)

David—greatest king of Israel; also a shepherd, musician, and poet; direct ancestor to Jesus Christ (16:11–30:27)

BACKGROUND AND SETTING

For the first time in Scripture, the events recorded in 1 and 2 Samuel occurred within the borders of the Promised Land. Familiar places like Jerusalem, Bethlehem, Ramah, and Hebron become Jewish cities. Daily life includes continual warfare and strife with the peoples who resisted displacement when Israel conquered the Promised Land. The people demand a king. Saul and particularly David rule the land with power. Samuel lives through the times of upheaval and speaks for God to the people and the leaders.

The action in 1 and 2 Samuel begins in about 1105 B.C. with the birth of Samuel (1 Samuel 1:1–28). The account ends with David's final words in about 971 B.C. (2 Samuel 23:1–7). The books cover about 135 years of history. During those eventful years, Israel was transformed from a loosely knit group of tribes guided by judges into a united nation under a king. Three men stand as giants among their peers of the time: Samuel, who ministered from 1105 to 1030 B.C.; Saul, who reigned as king from 1052 to 1011; and David, who reigned from 1011 to 971.

KEY DOCTRINES IN 1 SAMUEL

Davidic covenant—God's promise to David to extend his throne and kingdom forever (2:10; Genesis 49:8–12; Numbers 24:7–9,17–19; 2 Kings 8:19; 2 Chronicles 13:5; 21:7; Psalm 89:20–37; Isaiah 16:5; Acts 15:16–18; Revelation 22:16)

Work of the Holy Spirit—empowers men for divinely appointed tasks (10:6,10; 16:13; Numbers 11:25,29; Judges 14:6; 27:18; Matthew 4:1; 28:19–20; Mark 13:11; Luke 1:35; John 14:16–17; Acts 1:8; 2:4; Romans 8:5–6; Galatians 5:16–18; James 4:5–6)

Sin—Israel's sin created personal and national consequences (3:10–14; 4:17–18; 6:19; 13:9,13–14; 15:8–9,20–23; Genesis 3; Numbers 4:15; 15:30–31; 1 Kings 11:38; 13:34; 2 Kings 21:12; Psalm 106:43; Isaiah 22:14; Jeremiah 19:3; Ezekiel 7:3; 18:30; John 8:34; Romans 2:5; Hebrews 10:4,26–31)

GOD'S CHARACTER IN 1 SAMUEL

God is holy—2:2
God is powerful—14:6
God is provident—2:7–8; 6:7–10,12; 30:6
God is righteous—12:7
God is sovereign—9:17; 16:12–13; 24:20
God is wise—2:3
God is wrathful—5:6; 6:19; 7:10; 31:6

CHRIST IN 1 SAMUEL

Hannah's prayer (2:10) anticipates a future king anointed by God. This anointed one, also called the Messiah, would fulfill God's promise to establish David's throne forever.

KEY WORDS IN 1 SAMUEL

Hears: Hebrew *shama'*—1:13; 2:23; 4:14; 7:9; 8:18; 17:11; 23:11; 25:24—also means "to listen" or "to obey." This important Old Testament word appears over 1,100 times. It implies that the listener is giving his or her total attention to the one who is speaking. In some cases, the word connotes more than listening and indicates obedience to what has been said. Abraham was blessed not only for hearing, but for obeying God's voice (see Genesis 22:18, where the word is translated "obeyed"). In the third chapter of 1 Samuel, Samuel is listening for God's Word and is determined to obey it. This young man is an example of the kind of person God delights to use—one who is always ready to receive His Word and follow it.

King: Hebrew *melek*—2:10; 8:6; 10:24; 15:11; 18:22; 21:11,16; 24:20—may describe a petty ruler of a small city (Joshua 10:3) or a monarch of a vast empire (Esther 1:1–5). An ancient king's jurisdiction included the military (8:20), the economy (1 Kings 10:26–29), international diplomacy (1 Kings 5:1–11), and the legal system (2 Samuel 8:15). He often served as a spiritual leader (2 Kings 23:1–24), although Israel's kings were prohibited from some priestly functions (13:9–14). The Bible presents David as an example of the righteous king who set his heart on faithfully serving God (Acts 13:22). God's promise to give David an everlasting kingdom (2 Samuel 7:16) has been fulfilled in Jesus Christ, whose human ancestry is through the royal family of David (Luke 2:4).

Utterly Destroyed: Hebrew *charam*—15:3,8–9,15,18,20—refers to the "setting apart" of inappropriate things, usually because of defilement associated with idol worship. In the ancient world, anything sacred or defiled was considered inappropriate for common use and was therefore subject to complete destruction. According to Deuteronomy 13:12–15, Israel was to destroy everyone and everything that was wicked enough to be considered defiled. Violation of this command cost Achan his life (Joshua 7) and Saul his throne (15:9–11). Paul reminds us that we are all wicked, and as a result are defiled and deserve destruction. Yet God in His mercy has chosen to save those who place their trust in Jesus (Romans 3:10–26).

QUICK OVERVIEW OF 1 SAMUEL[1]

I. Samuel: Prophet and Judge to Israel (1:1–7:17)
 A. Samuel the Prophet (1:1–4:1a)
 B. Samuel the Judge (4:1b–7:17)
II. Saul: First King over Israel (8:1–15:35)
 A. The Rise of Saul to the Kingship (8:1–12:25)
 B. The Decline of Saul in the Kingship (13:1–15:35)
III. David and Saul: Transfer of the Kingship in Israel (16:1–31:13)
 A. The Introduction of David (16:1–17:58)
 B. David Driven from the Court of Saul (18:1–20:42)
 C. David's Flight from Saul's Pursuit (21:1–28:2)
 D. The Death of Saul (28:3–31:13)

MEANWHILE, IN OTHER PARTS OF THE WORLD . . .
In areas known today as Nevada and California within the United States, the Pinto people group thrives, leaving behind evidence of huts built with reeds, wood, and loam.

FREQUENTLY ASKED QUESTIONS

See **Frequently Asked Questions** in 2 Samuel.

QUICK STUDY ON 1 SAMUEL

1. In what ways did Samuel's birth and childhood affect his life as a judge and prophet?
2. What remarkable character traits are illustrated in the life of Hannah, Samuel's mother?
3. How did Samuel relate to the first two kings of Israel, and what did that relationship indicate about God's view of kings?
4. To what degree is obedience a central theme of 1 Samuel?
5. How does God's specific call in Samuel's life influence your understanding of God's purposes for your life?

SECOND SAMUEL

AUTHOR AND DATE

See **Author and Date** in 1 Samuel.

KEY PEOPLE IN 2 SAMUEL

David—greatest king of Israel; also a shepherd, musician, and poet; direct ancestor to Jesus Christ (1:1–24:25)

Joab—military commander of David's army (2:13–3:39; 8:16; 10:7–12:27; 14:1–33; 18:2–24:9)

Bathsheba—committed adultery with David; became queen of Israel and mother of Solomon; direct ancestor of Jesus (11:1–26; 12:24)

Nathan—prophet and advisor to David; urged him to repent of his sin (7:2–17; 12:1–25)

Absalom—son of David; attempted to overthrow the throne of Israel (3:3; 13:1–19:10)

BACKGROUND AND SETTING

See **Background and Setting** in 1 Samuel.

KEY DOCTRINES IN 2 SAMUEL

Davidic covenant—God's promise to David to extend his throne and kingdom forever (7:12–16; 22:51; Genesis 49:8–12; Numbers 24:7–9,17–19; 2 Kings 8:19; 2 Chronicles 13:5; 21:7; Psalm 89:20–37; Isaiah 16:5; Acts 15:16–18; Revelation 22:16)

Sin—Israel's sin created personal and national consequences (6:6–7; 12:13–14; Genesis 3; Numbers 4:15; 15:30–31; 1 Kings 11:38; 13:34; 2 Kings 21:12; Psalm 106:43; Isaiah 22:14; Jeremiah 19:3; Ezekiel 7:3; 18:30; John 8:34; Romans 2:5; Hebrews 10:4,26–31)

Messiah—foretold to David by Nathan to be the anointed king who will triumph over all nations opposed to God (7:12–16; 22:51; Matthew 1:16–17; 12:22; Mark 1:1; John 7:42; Acts 2:30–33)

GOD'S CHARACTER IN 2 SAMUEL

God is kind—2:6
God is a promise keeper—7:12–13
God is provident—17:14–15
God is true—2:6
God is unequaled—7:22
God is unified—7:22
God is wise—7:20
God is wrathful—6:7; 21:1; 24:1,15,17

CHRIST IN 2 SAMUEL

The Davidic covenant outlined in 2 Samuel 7:12–16 reveals God's promise to extend the kingdom of David for eternity. Christ fulfills this covenant as the Messiah directly descending from the royal line of David. The life of David recorded in 2 Samuel foreshadows Christ's future kingdom.

KEY WORDS IN 2 SAMUEL

Ark: Hebrew *'aron*—6:2,4,10,12,17; 7:2; 11:11; 15:24—can be translated "chest" (2 Kings 12:9) or "sarcophagus" (Genesis 50:26), but most often appears in the phrase *'aron haberith*, which means "ark of the covenant." The ark was a wooden chest overlaid with gold (Exodus 25:10–22), housing the Ten Commandments (Exodus 40:20), Aaron's staff, and a pot of manna (Hebrews 9:4). It sat in the Most Holy Place as a reminder of Israel's covenant with God and His presence among them. When the Israelites became careless with the ark (1 Samuel 4:1–11), God allowed it to be captured in order to demonstrate that His covenant relationship with them transcended symbols and superstitions. What He required was continual obedience to His covenant and a contrite heart surrendered to Him (Psalm 51:17; Isaiah 57:15).

Jerusalem: Hebrew *yerushalaim*—5:5; 8:7; 11:1, 15:8,29; 16:15; 17:20; 19:19; 24:16—related to the word for "peace." During the reign of King David, Jerusalem was made the political and religious capital of Israel and became central to the unfolding of God's redemptive plan. Jerusalem is described variously in the Old Testament as the city of God (Psalm 87:1–3), the place where God has put His name (2 Kings 21:4), a place of salvation (Isaiah 46:13), the throne of God (Jeremiah 3:17), and a holy city (Isaiah 52:1). The prophets foresaw an approaching time when Jerusalem would be judged because of its iniquity (Micah 4:10–12), but in pronouncing judgment they could also see its glorious restoration (Isaiah 40:2; 44:25–28; Daniel 9:2; Zephaniah 3:16–20). This vision of a restored Jerusalem included the hope of a New Jerusalem in which God would gather all His people (Isaiah 65:17–19; Revelation 21:1–2).

Mighty Men: Hebrew *gibbor*—1:25; 10:7; 16:6; 17:8; 20:7; 23:8,22—emphasizes excellence or unusual quality. In the Old Testament, it is used for the excellence of a lion (Proverbs 30:30), of good or bad men (Genesis 10:9; 1 Chronicles 19:8), of giants (Genesis 6:4), of angels (Psalm 103:20), or even God (Deuteronomy 10:17; Nehemiah 9:32). The Scriptures state that the *mighty man* is not victorious because of his strength (Psalm 33:16) but because of his understanding and knowledge of the Lord (Jeremiah 9:23–24). The phrase *mighty God* is used three times in the Old Testament, including Isaiah's messianic prophecy of the birth of Jesus (Isaiah 9:6; 10:21; Jeremiah 32:18).

QUICK OVERVIEW[1]

I. The Reign of David as King over Israel (1:1–20:26)
   A. David's Accession to Kingship over Judah (1:1–3:5)
   B. David's Accession to Kingship over Israel (3:6–5:16)

  C. David's Triumphal Reign (5:17–8:18)
  D. David's Troubled Reign (9:1–20:26)
II. Epilogue (21:1–24:25)
  A. The Lord's Judgment against Israel (21:1–14)
  B. David's Heroes (21:15–22)
  C. David's Song of Praise (22:1–51)
  D. David's Last Words (23:1–7)
  E. David's Mighty Men (23:8–39)
  F. The Lord's Judgment against David (24:1–25)

MEANWHILE, IN OTHER PARTS OF THE WORLD . . .
The use of wigs becomes popular in Egyptian and Assyrian aristocracy.

FREQUENTLY ASKED QUESTIONS

1. If we accept the scholarly view that the surviving ancient manuscripts of 1 and 2 Samuel were relatively poorly preserved, what should be our attitude toward these books as part of God's Word?

Given the challenges involved in hand copying and preserving scrolls, it is a wonder that we have the ancient documents that we do have. Our attitude ought to lean more towards amazement that we have such few discrepancies rather than concern over the difficulties that may puzzle and challenge us.

Many of the discoveries in the science of analyzing ancient manuscripts involve the typical errors that commonly appear when handwritten documents are copied. For example, when two lines of text end with the same word or words, the eye of the copyist tends to skip the second line, deleting it completely. Careful comparisons between manuscripts and reconstruction of the text often reveal these simple errors.

In the case of 1 and 2 Samuel we have two ancient text families: 1) the Masoretic text, in the Hebrew language, and 2) the LXX (Septuagint) text in Greek, which was translated by Jewish scholars in about 100 B.C. Comparing the two, it is true that they differ more often here than they do in other Old Testament books. There are frequent disagreements between the texts when it comes to numbers. In settling these discrepancies, because of the age and language of the Masoretic text it is generally considered a closer version of the original manuscript unless grammar and context indicate a copying error.

A central fact to remember when thinking about the possibility of textual errors in the Scriptures we have is the following: The central doctrines of the Christian faith are never based on a single verse of Scripture, nor do they rely on a disputed section of Scripture. God's plan of salvation and the main outline of Christian teaching can be found throughout Scripture.

2. How do 1 and 2 Samuel help us understand the role of the Holy Spirit in the time of the Old Testament?

First and 2 Samuel illustrate part of the Holy Spirit's role in the Old Testament. The Spirit's specific actions are noted in the following passages: 1 Samuel 10:6,10; 11:6; 16:13–14; 19:20,23; 2 Samuel 23:2. These references offer several conclusions regarding the Holy Spirit's ministry: 1) it was an occasional "coming upon" a chosen person for a particular task or statement; 2) the Spirit's ministry was not controlled by the person(s); 3) the expectation of the Spirit's help could be given and withdrawn; 4) the Holy Spirit inspired certain people to speak or write God's message.

Jesus promised the indwelling presence of the Holy Spirit, not surprise visits. Certainly at times believers might experience a particular empowering by the Holy Spirit for a task, but the picture of the Holy Spirit's ministry changes from the Old Testament idea of an external visitation by God to the New Testament picture of a resident presence by God in the life of a believer.

3. Was the rule of kings part of God's plan all along, or did the people's demand for a king bring about a monarchy as a form of divine discipline?

When Israel entered the Promised Land, they encountered Canaanite city-states that were ruled by kings (Joshua 12:7–14). Later, during the time of the judges, Israel was enslaved and oppressed by nations led by kings (Judges 3:8,12; 4:2; 8:5; 11:12). The Book of Judges repeatedly mentions the lack of a king (Judges 17:6; 18:1; 19:1; 21:25). The idea of having a king like the surrounding nations became a powerful temptation. According to Deuteronomy 17:14, however, God knew this would be their desire and He foretold His permission. First Samuel 8:4–20 reveals that their motive actually involved a rejection of God.

In spite of Samuel's dire warnings about the drawbacks of monarchy, the people offered what they thought were three compelling reasons why they needed a king (1 Samuel 8:20): 1) to be like the other nations; 2) to have a national judge; 3) to have a war champion. Each of these contradicted God's specific purposes: 1) Israel was to be a holy nation, not like any other; 2) God was their ultimate judge; 3) God had fought their battles for them, whereas a king would send them to battle. Israel's problem was not about having a king but rather, it was about replacing God with a human ruler. They exchanged an awesome and powerful Ruler they could not see for one they could see who was utterly capable of failure.

QUICK STUDY ON 2 SAMUEL

1. What significant character traits of David are illustrated in 2 Samuel?
2. In what ways was he a "man after God's own heart"?
3. What kind of a leader, or king, was David?
4. How does the sequence of events involving David and Bathsheba demonstrate the appeal of sin and its consequences?
5. What prevented the rejection of David by God after his multiple sins?
6. How does David's experience affect your understanding of God's view of you and your sin?

---

[1] See also "Chronology of Old Testament Kings and Prophets" in the Appendices at the back of this book.

FIRST AND SECOND KINGS

Royal Disappointments and Disasters

These books present a powerful case for the failure of human leadership when it turns away from God.

Kings come in many shapes and sizes. Their characters vary widely. Some lead successfully while others fail miserably. Some build, only to be replaced by those who destroy. Some fight, some surrender, and some do practically nothing at all. Some kings leave a legacy of good; others a legacy of evil. At their best or worst, however, monarchs demonstrate one overwhelming truth: Kings simply cannot replace God.

FIRST KINGS

AUTHOR AND DATE

Written by an unknown author, approximately 561 to 538 B.C.

Though Jewish tradition has suggested Jeremiah as the likely author of 1 and 2 Kings, the books themselves raise some objections. For example, 2 Kings 25:27–30 records events that took place in Babylon in 561 B.C. Jeremiah went to Egypt, but not to Babylon (Jeremiah 43:1–7). The central role of God's prophets in these books does indicate, however, that the author was probably a prophet, someone whose name we would recognize, or one of the many nameless prophets who served God among the people.

KEY PEOPLE IN 1 KINGS

David—king of Israel; appointed his son Solomon to be the next king to rule (1–2:10)

Solomon—son of Bathsheba and David; third king to rule Israel and builder of the temple; God made him the wisest man ever born (1:10–11:43)

Rehoboam—son of Solomon; succeeded him as king of Israel; his evil actions led to the division of Israel into two kingdoms; later became king of the southern kingdom of Judah (11:43–12:24; 14:21–31)

Jeroboam—evil king of the northern ten tribes of Israel; erected idols and appointed non-Levitical priests (11:24–14:20)

Elijah—prophet of Israel; accomplished extraordinary acts of faith against the prophets of Baal (17:1–19:21; 21:17–28)

Ahab—eighth and most evil king of Israel; committed more evil than any other Israelite king (16:28–17:1; 18:1–19:1; 20:1–22:40)
Jezebel—married Ahab and became queen of Israel; promoted Baal worship (16:31; 18:4–19; 19:1–2; 21:5–27)

BACKGROUND AND SETTING

Two streams run through 1 and 2 Kings: 1) the accounts of eyewitnesses to events; and 2) the commentary on those events by the final author. The first accurately conveys history; the second accurately interprets history. Using reliable sources, Kings traces the histories of two sets of kings and two nations of disobedient people, Israel and Judah, both of whom grew indifferent to God's law and God's prophets. That indifference led them to humiliation, defeat, and crushing captivity.

The author, exiled in Babylon, produced a book that went beyond a compilation of historical records. He also interpreted the lessons from Israel's history for his fellow exiles. He pointed out clearly that their present condition was a direct consequence of God's judgment over long-established patterns of disobedience (1 Kings 9:3–9).

The book also records God's efforts to confront and warn the people along the way, using the prophets as His spokesmen. The prophets fearlessly foretold the eventual results of national sin, which would culminate in exile. Always, the prophets held out the offer of God's mercy whenever the people would humble themselves.

KEY DOCTRINES IN 1 KINGS

God's judgment of the apostate nations (9:3–9; Deuteronomy 4:26; 28:37; 2 Samuel 14–16; 2 Chronicles 7:19–20; Psalm 44:14; 89:30; Jeremiah 24:9; Hosea 5:11–12; Matthew 23:33–36; John 3:18–19; 12:48; Romans 2:5–6; 2 Peter 3:10; Revelation 18:10)
Fulfilled prophecies of God (13:2–5; 22:15–28; Numbers 27:17; 2 Kings 23:15–20; 2 Chronicles 18:16; Matthew 9:36; Mark 6:34; John 2:18)
God's faithfulness to His covenant with David (11:12–13,34–36; 15:4; 2 Samuel 7:12–16; Luke 1:30–33; Acts 2:22–36)

GOD'S CHARACTER IN 1 KINGS

God fills heaven and earth—8:27
God is glorious—8:11
God is merciful—8:23
God is a promise keeper—8:56
God is provident—21:19; 22:30,34,37–38

CHRIST IN 1 KINGS

The wisdom of Solomon typifies Christ who "became wisdom from God" (1 Corinthians 1:30). Yet, in the book of 1 Kings, Solomon led his kingdom into apostasy by marrying many foreign women (11:1). In contrast, Christ Himself proclaimed that He was "greater than Solomon" (Matthew 12:42). The future kingdom of Christ will not pass away.

KEY WORDS IN 1 KINGS

Baal: Hebrew *ba'al*—16:31; 18:19,21,26,40; 19:18; 22:53—literally means "master," or "husband." Baal refers to pagan gods of fertility and storms throughout the ancient Middle East. Canaanite literature links Baal with the fertility goddess Asherah, who is mentioned numerous times in the Old Testament (2 Kings 21:7). Worship of these pagan deities included self-mutilation, ritual prostitution, and infant sacrifice. God punished the Israelites for adopting the worship of Baal and Asherah (Judges 2:11–15; Jeremiah 19:4–6).

Supplication: Hebrew *techinnah*—8:28,33,45,47,52,54,59; 9:3—refers to the petitioning of God or a specific person for favor or mercy (Jeremiah 37:20; 38:26). Solomon uses this word repeatedly in his dedication prayer over the temple (8:23–9:3; 2 Chronicles 6:14–42). Supplication is often used in relation to impending distress in the midst of one's enemies (Psalms 55:1–3; 119:70; Jeremiah 36:7). The Bible describes the supplications of David (Psalm 6:9), Solomon (9:3), and of wicked King Manasseh, who humbled himself before God (2 Chronicles 33:12–13).

Name: Hebrew *shem*—1:47; 3:2; 5:5; 7:21; 8:17; 9:3; 11:36; 18:24—most likely means "to mark." In biblical history, a person's name often described personal characteristics such as destiny or position (see 1 Samuel 25:25 for the explanation of Nabal's name, which meant "Fool"). Sometimes, God renamed people to reflect a change in their character or status (see Genesis 35:10). The various names of God reveal important aspects of His nature (for example, God Most High, Almighty God, I AM). The name of God should be used with honor and respect (Exodus 20:7). God shared His name with Israel to express His intimate covenantal relationship with them (Exodus 3:13–15).

Gold: Hebrew *zahab*—6:21,28; 7:49; 9:28; 10:14; 12:28; 15:15; 20:3—describes both the substance and the color of gold (1 Kings 10:16; Zechariah 4:12). Gold, usually mentioned with silver, symbolized wealth (Genesis 13:2; 2 Chronicles 1:15; Ezekiel 16:13). Most references to gold in the Old Testament relate to Solomon's temple and palace (Exodus 25:3; 2 Chronicles 2:7; 9:13–27). However precious gold appears, nothing compares to the value of wisdom (Job 28:17), loving favor (Proverbs 22:1), and the commandments of the Lord (Psalms 19:9–10; 119:72,127).

QUICK OVERVIEW OF 1 KINGS[1]

I. The United Kingdom: The Reign of Solomon (1 Kings 1:1–11:43)
   A. The Rise of Solomon (1:1–2:46)
   B. The Beginning of Solomon's Wisdom and Wealth (3:1–4:34)
   C. The Preparations for the Building of the Temple (5:1–18)
   D. The Building of the Temple and Solomon's House (6:1–9:9)
   E. The Further Building Projects of Solomon (9:10–28)
   F. The Culmination of Solomon's Wisdom and Wealth (10:1–29)
   G. The Decline of Solomon (11:1–43)

II. The Divided Kingdom: The Kings of Israel and Judah (12:1–22:53)
   A. The Rise of Idolatry: Jeroboam of Israel/Rehoboam of Judah (12:1–14:31)
   B. Kings of Judah/Israel (15:1–16:22)
   C. The Dynasty of Omri and Its Influence: The Rise and Fall of Baal Worship in Israel and Judah (16:23–22:53)
      1. The introduction of Baal worship (16:23–34)
      2. Elijah and the opposition to Baal worship (17:1–22:53)

MEANWHILE, IN OTHER PARTS OF THE WORLD . . .
The Persian Empire is founded after the overthrow of Lydia, Babylon, and the Medes by King Cyrus the Great (553 to 529 B.C.).

FREQUENTLY ASKED QUESTIONS

See **Frequently Asked Questions** in 2 Kings.

QUICK STUDY ON 1 KINGS

1. What qualities do the successful kings have in common?
2. What character flaws and bad decisions marked the lives of kings who failed?
3. Why did the kingdom of David divide into the kingdom of Israel and the kingdom of Judah?
4. What role did Elijah fulfill throughout 1 Kings?
5. How does the building and dedication of the temple of God teach us about effective and ineffective ways to honor God?
6. What is the single, most concentrated effort you are carrying out in your life for the glory of God?

SECOND KINGS

AUTHOR AND DATE

See **Author and Date** in 1 Kings.

KEY PEOPLE IN 2 KINGS

Elijah—prophet of Israel; escaped death by being carried directly to heaven in a chariot of fire (1:3–2:11; 10:10,17)

Elisha—prophet appointed to be Elijah's successor (2:1–9:3; 13:14–21)

The woman from Shunem—woman who hosted Elisha in her home; Elisha brought her son back to life (4:8–37; 8:1–6)

Naaman—mighty Syrian warrior who suffered from leprosy; healed by Elisha (5:1–27)

Jezebel—evil queen of Israel; attempted to prevent Israel from worshiping God; eventually killed and eaten by dogs (9:7–37)

Jehu—anointed king of Israel; used by God to punish Ahab's family (9:1–10:36; 15:12)

Joash—king of Judah who was saved from death as a child; followed evil advice and was ultimately assassinated by his own officials (11:1–12:21)

Hezekiah—thirteenth king of Judah who remained faithful to God (16:20–20:21)

Sennacherib—king of Assyria who threatened Judah; his army was destroyed by the Lord (18:13–19:36)

Isaiah—prophet who ministered through the reigns of five kings of Judah (19:2–20:19)

Manasseh—son of Hezekiah; became the fourteenth king of Judah; practiced evil and brought judgment upon Jerusalem (20:21–21:18)

Josiah—sixteenth king of Judah; great-grandson of Hezekiah; remained faithful to God (21:24—23:30)

Jehoiakim—eighteenth king of Judah; practiced evil in the eyes of the Lord (23:34–24:6)

Zedekiah—twentieth king of Judah; captured by the Babylonians as God's punishment for practicing evil (24:17–25:7)

Nebuchadnezzar—king of Babylon allowed by God to conquer Jerusalem (24:1–25:22)

BACKGROUND AND SETTING

See **Background and Setting** in 1 Kings.

KEY DOCTRINES IN 2 KINGS

God's judgment of the apostate nations (17:7–23; 21:10–15; Judges 6:10; 1 Samuel 3:11; Jeremiah 6:9; 19:3; Lamentations 2:8; Amos

7:7–8; Matthew 23:33–36; John 3:18–19; 12:48; Romans 2:5–6; 2 Peter 3:10; Revelation 18:10)

Fulfilled prophecies of God (23:16; 24:2; 1 Kings 13:2; Jeremiah 25:9; 32:28; 35:11; Ezekiel 19:8)

God's faithfulness to His covenant with David (8:19; 25:27–30; 2 Samuel 7:12–16; Luke 1:30–33; Acts 2:22–36)

GOD'S CHARACTER IN 2 KINGS

God is compassionate—13:23
God is One—19:15
God is wrathful—19:28,35,37; 22:17

CHRIST IN 2 KINGS

Although great judgment fell on Judah for the nation's disobedience, God still spared the Jewish remnant in Babylonian captivity. This Remnant preserved the royal line of David through which Christ would enter the world. Judah's apostasy demanded judgment from the righteous God, yet God remained faithful to His covenant with David. As David's direct descendant, Jesus the Messiah would ultimately free His people from the captivity that held them in sin.

KEY WORDS IN 2 KINGS

Silver: Hebrew *keseph*—5:5,23; 6:25; 7:8; 12:13; 14:14; 20:13; 23:35—literally referred to as "the pale metal," was the basic unit of money in the Old Testament (1 Kings 21:6; Isaiah 55:1). However, there is no reference to silver coins in the Old Testament because silver was valued by weight in ancient times (Isaiah 46:6; Jeremiah 32:9–10). Silver, along with gold, was one of the valuable materials used to construct the Tabernacle and the Temple (Exodus 25:1–9; 2 Chronicles 2:7). In Ecclesiastes, Solomon voices a warning about silver: "He who loves silver will not be satisfied" (Ecclesiastes 5:10).

Anger: Hebrew *'aph*—13:3; 17:11; 21:6,15; 22:17; 23:26; 24:20—signifies either "nose," "nostril," or "anger" (Genesis 2:7; Proverbs 15:1). This term often occurs with words describing burning. Throughout the Old Testament, figures of speech such as "a burning nose" typically depict anger as the fierce breathing of a person through his nose (Exodus 32:10–12). Most of the Old Testament references using this word describe God's anger (Psalm 103:8; Deuteronomy 4:24–25). The righteous anger of God is reserved for those who break His covenant (Deuteronomy 13:17; 29:25–27; Joshua 23:16; Judges 2:20; Psalm 78:38).

High Places: Hebrew *bamah*—12:3; 14:4; 15:4; 17:9; 23:8,15,20—often refers to a sacred area located on high ground such as a hill or ridge. Before the temple was built, the Israelites worshiped the true God at high places (1 Kings 3:2–4). However, the Israelites began worshiping pagan gods at these sacred sites. Consequently, the term *high places* in the Old Testament became associated with Israel's religious rebellion and apostasy (1 Kings 14:23; Psalm 78:58; Jeremiah 19:5).

QUICK OVERVIEW OF 2 KINGS[1]

I. The Divided Kingdom (continued): The Kings of Israel and Judah (1:1–17:41)
  A. The Dynasty of Omri and Its Influence (continued): The Rise and Fall of Baal Worship in Israel and Judah (1:1–13:25)
    1. Elijah's ongoing clash with Baal worship (1:1–18)
    2. Elisha's ministry and influence for God (2:1–9:13)
    3. The overthrow of Baal worship in Israel (9:14–10:36)
    4. The overthrow of Baal worship in Judah (11:1–12:21)
    5. The death of Elisha (13:1–25)
  B. Kings of Judah/Israel (14:1–15:38)
  C. The Defeat and Exile of Israel by Assyria (16:1–17:41)
II. The Surviving Kingdom: The Kings of Judah (18:1–25:21)
  A. Hezekiah's Righteous Reign (18:1–20:21)
  B. Manasseh's and Amon's Wicked Reigns (21:1–26)
  C. Josiah's Righteous Reign (22:1–23:30)
  D. The Defeat and Exile of Judah by Babylon (23:31–25:21)
III. Epilogue: The People's Continued Rebellion and the Lord's Continued Mercy (25:22–30).

MEANWHILE, IN OTHER PARTS OF THE WORLD . . .
The first use of papyrus by the Greeks is recorded. In the Persian Empire, King Cyrus the Great develops a messenger system using horses.

FREQUENTLY ASKED QUESTIONS

1. How are the six books—1 and 2 Samuel, 1 and 2 Kings, and 1 and 2 Chronicles—related to one another in recording the history of the kingdom of Israel?

First and 2 Samuel and 1 and 2 Kings provide a chronological account of the Kingdom of Israel in its original and divided state. First and 2 Chronicles serve as a special review of the line of David (the kings of Judah).

Those who add up the numbers given for the lengths of reign in these books are sometimes surprised that the math produces inconsistencies. Extra-biblical sources also provide some dating that creates problems when correlated with the text. Two important factors help explain the apparent inconsistencies in these records: 1) a number of cases had co-regencies (fathers and sons sharing the throne) in which each king's years were listed without accounting for the overlap; 2) neither the calendars nor the official reckoning of years was always the same in both kingdoms.

QUICK STUDY ON 2 KINGS

1. In what ways were Elijah and Elisha different, and how did they influence their society?
2. What other prophets are mentioned in 2 Kings?
3. What are God's purposes behind the miracles that occur in 2 Kings?
4. How many kings did Israel and Judah each have and how many were good? How many were evil?
5. What parts of God's character are illustrated and emphasized in 2 Kings?
6. How do you understand and acknowledge God's patience in your own life?

---

[1] See also "Chronology of Old Testament Kings and Prophets" in the Appendices at the back of this book.

FIRST AND SECOND CHRONICLES

Historical Review and Prelude to Disaster

The two-part book of Chronicles provides a summary of history back to the beginning—a review that includes material from Genesis to 2 Kings.

Before video cameras and tape recorders, there were chroniclers. Somewhere in the corner of every throne room sat people whose duty was to record the events of the day. The original Hebrew title for this book meant "the annals of the days." It became two books around 200 B.C. when the Septuagint translators divided the original long scroll.

1 CHRONICLES

AUTHOR AND DATE

Possibly written by Ezra, approximately 450 to 430 B.C.

First and 2 Chronicles contain no specific indications of authorship. Ancient traditions favor Ezra the priest (Ezra 7:6), who lived in the time period and was known as a scribe. The genealogical record in 1 Chronicles 1–9 suggests a date after 450 B.C.

KEY PEOPLE IN 1 CHRONICLES

David—king of Israel and ancestor of Jesus Christ; described by God as "a man after My own heart" (2:8–29:30; see Acts 13:22)

David's mighty men—special group of warriors pledged to fight for King David (11:10–28:1)

Nathan—prophet and advisor to David; relayed God's will for Solomon to build the temple (17:1–15)

Solomon—son of David who became the next king of Israel (3:5–29:28)

BACKGROUND AND SETTING

First and 2 Chronicles provide a large-scale perspective for a people during a time of chaotic change. After seventy years of captivity in Babylon, Jews were returning to Israel. This occurred in three phases: 1) Zerubbabel's group around 538 B.C. (Ezra 1–6); 2) Ezra's group around 458 B.C. (Ezra 7–10); and 3) Nehemiah's group around 445 B.C. (Nehemiah 1–13). The exiles needed to see God's hand in the history of their nation so that they could cope with the setbacks and difficulties of the time in which they lived.

To put it mildly, the exiles' future looked bleak compared to their majestic past, particularly the glory years of David and Solomon. The return to the Promised Land could be described as bittersweet—bitter because their present poverty brought hurtful memories about what was forfeited by God's judgment on their ancestors' sin, and sweet because at least they were back in the land God had given Abraham seventeen centuries earlier (Genesis 12:1–3).

The chronicler's selective genealogy and history of Israel, stretching from Adam (1 Chronicles 1:1) to the return from Babylon (2 Chronicles 26:23), was intended to remind the Jews of God's promises and intentions regarding 1) the land; 2) their identity as a nation; 3) the Davidic royal line; 4) the Levitical priesthood; 5) the temple; and 6) true worship. God made it clear that none of those had been abolished or erased by the Babylonian captivity. By summarizing the Jews' unique spiritual heritage, Chronicles encouraged readers to remain faithful to God in difficult times.

KEY DOCTRINES IN 1 CHRONICLES

Blessing—when the king obeyed and trusted the Lord, God blessed and protected him (11:4–9; 14:8–14; Exodus 23:22; Deuteronomy 11:27; 1 Samuel 15:22; Psalms 5:12; 106:3; Ecclesiastes 12:13; Isaiah 30:18; Matthew 5:6; Luke 11:28)

Judgment—when the king disobeyed God and put his trust in something else, God withdrew His blessing (10:1–7; Deuteronomy 28:41; Job 12:23; Psalm 78:32–33; Isaiah 42:24; Ezekiel 39:23; Hosea 4:17; Amos 3:6; 4:10; Micah 6:9; Malachi 2:2; Matthew 7:22–23; 13:40–42; John 12:48)

The Davidic covenant—God's promise to Israel to restore a king was not abandoned because of the Exile (17:7–15; 2 Samuel 7:1–17; 2 Chronicles 3:1–2; Jeremiah 31:31–34)

GOD'S CHARACTER IN 1 CHRONICLES

God is glorious—16:24
God is holy—16:10
God is merciful—16:34
God is powerful—29:11–12
God is a promise keeper—17:23,26
God is provident—29:12
God is unified—17:20
God is wise—28:9

CHRIST IN 1 CHRONICLES

God's covenant with David promised him an eternal dynasty: "I will set up your seed after you, who will be of our sons; and I will establish his kingdom. He shall build Me a house, and I will establish his throne forever. I will be his Father, and he shall be My son" (17:11–13). As a fulfillment to this promise, Solomon built the temple for the Lord. The final fulfillment of this covenant will come with the establishment of the eternal kingdom of Christ the Messiah, a direct descendant of David.

KEY WORDS IN 1 CHRONICLES

Sons: Hebrew *ben*—1:43; 3:12; 4:25; 5:14; 7:14; 9:4; 11:22; 22:9; 26:28—literally, "to build." The ancient Hebrews considered their children the "builders" of the future generations. *Ben* can refer to a direct son or to one's future descendants (1 Kings 2:1; 1 Chronicles 7:14). Old Testament names such as Benjamin, meaning "Son of my Right Hand," incorporate this Hebrew noun (Genesis 35:18). In the plural, *ben* can be translated as "children" regardless of gender (see Exodus 12:37—"children of Israel"). God Himself uses this term to describe His unique relationship with Israel: "Israel is My son, My firstborn" (Exodus 4:22).

QUICK OVERVIEW OF 1 CHRONICLES

I. Selective Genealogy (1:1–9:34)
  A. Adam to Just before David (1:1–2:55)
  B. David to the Captivity (3:1–24)
  C. The Twelve Tribes (4:1–9:2)
  D. Jerusalem Dwellers (9:3–34)
II. David's Ascent (9:35–12:40)[1]
  A. Saul's Heritage and Death (9:35–10:14)
  B. David's Anointing (11:1–3)
  C. Jerusalem's Conquest (11:4–9)
  D. David's Men (11:10–12:40)
III. David's Reign (13:1–29:30)
  A. The Ark of the Covenant (13:1–16:43)
  B. The Davidic Covenant (17:1–27)
  C. Selected Military History (18:1–21:30)
  D. Temple-Building Preparations (22:1–29:20)
  E. Transition to Solomon (29:21–30)

MEANWHILE, IN OTHER PARTS OF THE WORLD . . .
The Spartans develop the use of chemicals such as sulfur, pitch, and charcoal in warfare.

QUICK STUDY ON 1 CHRONICLES

1. As you read through the historical review of the first nine chapters of 1 Chronicles, what purposes can you discover for this record?
2. What are the highlights and significance of King David's life from the perspective of 1 Chronicles?

3. What happens to the ark of the covenant in 1 Chronicles? What is the background of that event (see 1 Samuel 5–6)?
4. If David was a man after God's own heart, why didn't God allow him to build the great temple in Jerusalem?
5. How is the importance of genuine worship illustrated in 1 Chronicles?
6. In what ways does your own practice of worship match the ideals found in 1 Chronicles?

2 CHRONICLES

KEY PEOPLE IN 2 CHRONICLES

Solomon—king of Israel and builder of the Lord's temple; received great wisdom from God (1:1–9:31)

Queen of Sheba—heard of Solomon's reputation for wisdom; visited Jerusalem to test him with hard questions about his success (9:1–12; see Matthew 12:42)

Rehoboam—evil son of Solomon who became the next king of Israel; soon divided the kingdom and later led the southern kingdom of Judah (9:31–13:7)

Asa—king of Judah; tried to accomplish God's purposes through corrupt means (14:1–16:14)

Jehoshaphat—succeeded his father, Asa, as king of Judah; followed God but made several poor choices (17:1–22:9)

Jehoram—wicked son of Jehoshaphat who succeeded him as king of Judah; promoted idol worship and killed his six brothers (21:1–20)

Uzziah—(also called Azariah) succeeded his father, Amaziah, as king of Judah; mostly followed God yet retained a prideful attitude (26:1–23)

Ahaz—succeeded his father, Jotham, as king of Judah; led the people in Baal worship and other idolatry that included the sacrifice of his own children (27:9–29:19)

Hezekiah—succeeded his father, Ahaz, as king of Judah; obeyed God and restored the temple; started religious reform among the people (28:27–32:33)

Manasseh—succeeded his father, Hezekiah, as king of Judah; did evil in the sight of the Lord but repented toward the end of his reign (32:33–33:20)

Josiah—succeeded his father, Amon, as king of Judah; followed the Lord and discovered the Book of the Law of the Lord while restoring the temple (33:25–35:27)

BACKGROUND AND SETTING

See 1 Chronicles **Background and Setting.**

KEY DOCTRINES IN 2 CHRONICLES

Wisdom—Solomon learned that the attainment of wisdom was more important than riches, honor, or victory (1:7–12; 1 Kings 3:9; Proverbs 3:15; 16:7–8; Matthew 7:7; James 1:5)

Blessing—when the king obeyed and trusted the Lord, God blessed and protected him (7:13,19–20; 9:13–22; Exodus 23:22; Deuteronomy 11:27; 1 Samuel 15:22; 1 Chronicles 11:4–9; 14:8–14; Psalms 5:12; 106:3; Ecclesiastes 12:13; Isaiah 30:18; Matthew 5:6; Luke 11:28)

Judgment—when the king disobeyed God and put his trust in something else, God withdrew His blessing (7:14–15; Deuteronomy 28:41; 1 Chronicles 10:1–7; Job 12:23; Psalm 78:32–33; Isaiah 42:24; Ezekiel 39:23; Hosea 4:17; Amos 3:6; 4:10; Micah 6:9; Malachi 2:2; Matthew 7:22–23; 13:40–42; John 12:48)

The Davidic covenant—God's promise to Israel to restore a king was not abandoned because of the Exile (3:1–2; 2 Samuel 7:1–17; 1 Chronicles 17:7–15; Jeremiah 31:31–34)

GOD'S CHARACTER IN 2 CHRONICLES

God is good—30:18
God is great—2:5
God is just—19:7
God is long-suffering—33:10–13
God is powerful—13:4
God is true—6:17

CHRIST IN 2 CHRONICLES

In 2 Chronicles, the line of David still remains protected by God. Solomon carries on David's preparation to build the temple to the Lord. In the New Testament, Christ likens Himself to the temple: "Destroy this temple, and in three days I will raise it up" (John 2:19). The temple Solomon built was eventually destroyed. Yet, Christ promises believers an eternal temple in Himself. In Revelation 21:22, the New Jerusalem has no temple for "the Lord God Almighty and the Lamb are its temple."

KEY WORDS IN 2 CHRONICLES

Right: Hebrew *yashar*—14:2; 20:32; 24:2; 25:2; 26:4; 27:2; 28:1; 34:2—literally, "to be level" or "to be upright." The Hebrew word *right* refers to being just or righteous. The word is used in many settings to describe the righteousness of God (Deuteronomy 32:4; Psalm 111:7–8), the integrity of one's speech (Job 6:25; Ecclesiastes 12:10), or the lifestyle of a righteous person (Proverbs 11:3,6). Often, this word is used to assess the quality of the kings in 1 and 2 Chronicles. David, as Israel's king, exemplified righteousness in his life (1 Kings 3:6) and became a standard for judging the kings who succeeded him (see 17:3; 34:2).

Passover: Hebrew *pesach*—30:1,15; 35:1,9,11,13,18–19—literally, "to pass" or "to leap over." The Passover celebration commemorated the day God spared the firstborn children of the Israelites from the death plague brought on Egypt. The Lord "passed over" those who sprinkled the blood from the Passover lamb on their doorposts (Exodus 12). Passover, as specified in the Law of Moses, reminds the Israelites of God's great mercy on them (see Leviticus 23:5–8; Numbers 28:16–25; Deuteronomy 16:1–8). In the New Testament, Jesus also celebrated the Passover feast with His disciples (Matthew 26:2,18). Christ became the ultimate Passover Lamb when He sacrificed Himself for our sins (John 1:29; 1 Corinthians 5:7; 1 Peter 1:19).

QUICK OVERVIEW OF 2 CHRONICLES

I. The Reign of Solomon (1:1–9:31)
  A. Coronation and Beginnings (1:1–17)
  B. Temple Building (2:1–7:22)
  C. Wealth/Achievements (8:1–9:28)
  D. Death (9:29–31)
II. The Reign of the Kings of Judah (10:1–36:21)[1]
  A. Rehoboam (10:1–12:16)
  B. Abijah (13:1–22)
  C. Asa (14:1–16:14)
  D. Jehoshaphat (17:1–21:3)
  E. Jehoram (21:4–20)
  F. Ahaziah (22:1–9)
  G. Athaliah (22:10–23:21)
  H. Joash (24:1–27)
  I. Amaziah (25:1–28)
  J. Uzziah (26:1–23)
  K. Jotham (27:1–9)
  L. Ahaz (28:1–27)
  M. Hezekiah (29:1–32:33)
  N. Manasseh (33:1–20)
  O. Amon (33:21–25)
  P. Josiah (34:1–35:27)
  Q. Jehoahaz (36:1–4)
  R. Jehoiakim (36:5–8)
  S. Jehoiachin (36:9–10)
  T. Zedekiah (36:11–21)
III. The Return Proclamation of Cyrus (36:22–23)

MEANWHILE, IN OTHER PARTS OF THE WORLD . . .
Rivals Athens and Sparta strike up a thirty-year truce (445 to 415 B.C.).

FREQUENTLY ASKED QUESTIONS

1. Does the use of outside sources affect the claim of inerrancy for Scripture? Were these other documents also inspired?

First and 2 Chronicles repeatedly quote other sources. Ezra includes many direct quotes from Persian documents. Other Scriptures include extra-biblical references. The answer to this question must reflect not the isolated cases of outside texts, but the numerous places the Bible quotes foreign decrees, pagan leaders, and other secular texts.

The fact that an extra-biblical source is quoted in Scripture does not endorse that entire source as inspired. Biblical content is truth. Sources are not necessarily true because they are in the Bible; facts are in the Bible because they are true. Biblical content remains true even when quoted outside the Bible. Some items of truth that were originally recorded outside Scripture and were available to those whom God inspired to write the Bible were used in Scripture.

These extra-biblical factors have the added effect of reminding us that God's Word was given in real historical situations, lived out and written out by people under God's guidance. These quotes emphasize the Scripture's relationship with reality. God's Word reveals the real God: ultimate reality.

QUICK STUDY ON 2 CHRONICLES

1. Whom would you choose as the two or three best examples of a good king from 2 Chronicles?
2. Which kings most influenced the people towards evil during their reigns?
3. What lessons about prayer can be found in 2 Chronicles?
4. What is the context and significance of 2 Chronicles 7:14?
5. By the end of 2 Chronicles, the nation has collapsed and the temple has been destroyed. How did this disaster come about?
6. In what ways are you benefiting right now from good decisions you made a while ago?

---

[1] See also "A Chronology of Old Testament Kings and Prophets" in the Appendices at the back of this book.

EZRA
The Return of the Exiles

Ancient tradition indicates that Ezra had a key role in the formation of the Old Testament Scriptures as the recognized canon of God's written revelation.

Some people set out to be obedient to God and turn out to be heroes. Ezra was such a man. His name represents the historical significance of the times in which he lived. It means in Hebrew "Jehovah helps" and constantly reminds the reader that God was acting behind the scenes to return His people to the Promised Land.

AUTHOR AND DATE

Possibly written by Ezra, approximately 457 to 444 B.C.

Although Ezra's name does not occur until the seventh chapter of the book that bears his name, he has long been considered the most likely author of both Ezra and Nehemiah. One strong internal clue about authorship has to do with writing perspective. Once his own departure for Jerusalem becomes part of the record (7:28), Ezra switches from writing in the third person to writing in the first. If he wrote 1 and 2 Chronicles, the continued narrative in Ezra makes perfect sense. Ezra begins with the ongoing chronicle of God's people in exile. Babylon had just been defeated by Persia, the new world power. Ezra's own participation in that history allowed him a natural point at which to make the chronicle autobiographical.

Ezra's scribal duties allowed him access to the various administrative documents quoted in Ezra and Nehemiah. He took advantage of special privileges he had in the royal archives of the Persian Empire. These passages are direct quotes from official Persian records: 1:2–4; 4:9–22; 5:7–17; 6:3–12. Other passages reveal Ezra as a devoted student and a strong and godly leader: 7:10; Nehemiah 8:1–9; 12:36.

KEY PEOPLE IN EZRA

Ezra—scribe and teacher of God's Word who began religious reform among the people; led the second group of exiles from Babylon to Jerusalem (Ezra 7:1–10:16)

Cyrus—Persian king who conquered Babylon; assisted the return of the Israelite exiles to their homeland (Ezra 1:1–6:14)

Zerubbabel—led the first group of Israelite exiles from Babylon to Jerusalem; completed the rebuilding of the temple (Ezra 2:2–5:2)

Haggai—post-Exilic (after the Exile) prophet who encouraged Zerubbabel and the Israelite people to continue rebuilding the temple (Ezra 5:1–2; 6:14)

Zechariah—post-Exilic prophet who encouraged Zerubbabel and the Israelite people to continue rebuilding the temple (Ezra 5:1–2; 6:14)

Darius I—Persian king who supported the rebuilding of the temple by the Israelites (Ezra 4:5–6:14)

Artaxerxes—Persian king who allowed Ezra to return to Jerusalem (Ezra 7:1) and reinstitute temple worship and the teaching of the Law

BACKGROUND AND SETTING

Events in the life of the people of Israel must always be seen in the light of God's plan for them. He chose them in their ancestor Abraham. He gave them a land. He brought Israel out of the slave markets of Egypt in the Exodus. Hundreds of years later, still before Ezra, God warned His people that if they chose to break their covenant with Him, He would again allow another nation to take them into slavery (Jeremiah 2:14–25). God's repeated warnings were persistently ignored. Immorality and idolatry were the national pastimes. God was faithful and followed through on His warnings.

In 722 B.C. the Assyrians defeated and deported the ten northern tribes and scattered them all over their empire. Decades later, in 605 to 586 B.C., God allowed the Babylonians to destroy and depopulate Jerusalem. God chastened what was left of His people with seventy years of exile in Babylon. In 539 B.C., Cyrus the Persian overthrew Babylon. A year later, as recorded by Ezra, Cyrus permitted the return of Jews to Jerusalem.

The Jews were originally deported in three waves (605 B.C., 597 B.C., and 586 B.C.). Their return followed the same pattern over nine decades. Zerubbabel led the first group home in 538 B.C. Ezra followed with the second group in 458 B.C. Then Nehemiah led the third group in 445 B.C. Jerusalem and the temple were eventually rebuilt, but, like the nation itself, they were only shadows of their former glory.

KEY DOCTRINES IN EZRA

God's sovereignty—the Lord controlled and guarded the path of the Israelites from their exile to their return to the Promised Land (2:1; Genesis 50:20; Job 42:2; Proverbs 16:1; Matthew 10:29–30; John 6:37; Romans 8:28)

GOD'S CHARACTER IN EZRA

God is good—8:18
God is powerful—8:22
God is righteous—9:15
God is wise—7:25
God is wrathful—8:22

CHRIST IN EZRA

Israel's return to the Land of Promise illustrates the unconditional forgiveness ultimately offered through Christ. God's protection of His people reinforced His covenant with David to preserve his line. Jesus, a direct descendant from the line of David, would later come to bring salvation to the whole world.

KEY WORDS IN EZRA

Jews: Hebrew *yehudi*—4:12,23; 5:1,5; 6:7–8,14—from a root meaning "to praise" or "to give thanks." Jacob used this term during his blessing of his son Judah in Genesis 49:8: "Judah, your brothers will praise you." A Jew may be a person from the tribe of Judah (Numbers 10:14), or an Israelite living in the geographical region known as Judah (see Jeremiah 7:30). During the post-Exilic period, "Jew" referred to the Israelites as a people group. The use of the term "Jew" is also found in the New Testament. Jesus is called "the King of the Jews" (Matthew 27:29). Later, Paul clarified that the true Jew is a person marked by "circumcision of the heart" (Romans 2:28–29).

Remnant: Hebrew *sha'ar*—9:8,15—literally, "to remain" or "to be left over." A *remnant* refers to the few people who survive after a catastrophe, such as the Flood. In the Bible, the word mostly refers to the diminished Israelite population who survived the Exile (9:8). The prophets also use the word to specifically describe the Israelites who remained faithful to God (Amos 5:14–15). The prophet Isaiah described the Messiah as one day gathering the remnant of Israel from all the nations, even attracting some Gentiles to Himself (Isaiah 11:10–11,16). The *remnant* therefore points to God's covenant faithfulness in sparing His people. Through the preservation of Israel, all the world would be blessed by the coming of the Messiah (Genesis 12:3).

QUICK OVERVIEW

I. The First Return under Zerubbabel (1:1–6:22)
- A. Cyrus's Decree of Return (1:1–4)
- B. Treasures to Rebuild the Temple (1:5–11)
- C. Those Who Returned (2:1–70)
- D. Construction of the Second Temple (3:1–6:22)

II. The Second Return under Ezra (7:1–10:44)
- A. Ezra Arrives (7:1–8:36)
- B. Ezra Leads Revival (9:1–10:44)

MEANWHILE, IN OTHER PARTS OF THE WORLD . . .
The Persian Wars finally cease (490 to 449 B.C.) after the Athenian Cimon, son of Miltiades, defeats the Persians at Salamis.

FREQUENTLY ASKED QUESTIONS

1. What parts of the Old Testament and what people were active in the events surrounding the return of the Jews from Exile?

Five historical books (1 and 2 Chronicles, Ezra, Nehemiah, and Esther) come from or cover events after the Exile. Three prophetic books (Haggai, Zechariah, and Malachi) come from the same period. The term *post-Exilic* is often used to describe these books and people.

First and 2 Chronicles provide a summary of history viewed from the final days of the Exile. Ezra and Nehemiah journal the thrilling and trying days of the return to Judah and the rebuilding of the nation. Haggai and Zechariah were prophets active during the time recorded in Ezra 4–6 when the temple was under reconstruction. Malachi wrote and prophesied during Nehemiah's revisit to Persia (Nehemiah 13:6).

Although part of the purpose of these books is to confirm God's continued covenant with the house of David and the unbroken kingly line, the emphasis shifts from royalty to other servants of God. A scribe, a cupbearer, and prophets become God's central agents. Even Esther, although a queen, had to rely on God rather than her position and power to accomplish God's role for her in preserving the Jews in Persia.

All of this sets the stage for the mixed expectations that surrounded the birth of Jesus, the fulfillment of God's covenant with David, God's personal involvement in the history of salvation.

2. How does Ezra's handling of the intermarriage and divorce situation fit into the overall pattern of biblical teaching on these important matters?

Ezra 9 and 10 record a critical time in the reestablishment of the Jewish people in their homeland. In the years before Ezra arrived from Persia, many of the returned Jewish men intermarried with pagan women from the area. This practice reflects no circumstances like those we find in the marriages of Rahab or Ruth, Gentiles who became believers in God. The pagan background of these women was not taken into account by their husbands. Ezra received this news as part of the report when he reached Jerusalem.

For Ezra, this was almost the worst possible news. Intermarriage with pagans had historically been a key in the repeated downfalls of the nation. These marriages were an act of disobedience. Ezra was overwhelmed with shame and distress over the situation (Ezra 9:3–4). His grief was open and convicting. Eventually, the people themselves confessed their error and decided that those who had married pagan women would have to "put away" (divorce) these wives. But God had not changed His mind about divorce. Malachi, who lived in this time period, declared that God hates divorce (Malachi 2:16).

Several important notes can be made about this passage in Ezra. It does not establish a norm about divorce. It is also easy to overlook the fact that while the solution of divorce was a group decision, each of these marriages was examined individually. Presumably, cases in which the women had become believers were treated differently than cases in which the women involved saw questions of faith as a violation of the marriage agreement.

In the humility of the guilty and the care in confronting these issues, a great deal of God's mercy comes through. A strict interpretation of the Law could have led to the stoning death of all involved. The eagerness to set things right opened the doorway for a solution, even though in some of the cases it involved the grief and sadness of divorce.

QUICK STUDY ON EZRA

1. What kind of person was Ezra?
2. Describe the attitudes, emotions, and experiences of the first pilgrims who returned to the Promised Land from captivity.
3. What kinds of opposition to rebuilding Jerusalem and the temple did the people face?
4. What role did God's Word play in the lives of those who returned from captivity?
5. In what ways did the returning exiles demonstrate their faith in God?
6. What ruins from your own past have you trusted God to help you rebuild and enjoy once again?

NEHEMIAH
Rebuilding the Walls

Nehemiah's character provides a powerful case study in leadership, integrity, and faith.

God puts His servants in unlikely places and gets surprising results. Nehemiah was a king's cupbearer in Persia. His name only appears in this book, though Nehemiah certainly fits in the descriptions of various people in the Hall of Faith listed in Hebrews 11. God worked through Nehemiah as a key participant in the reestablishment of the Jewish nation in the Promised Land after the Exile.

AUTHOR AND DATE

Probably written by Ezra, approximately 424 to 400 B.C.

Much of this book was drawn from Nehemiah's personal diaries. But although these reports were written in the first person (1:1–7:5; 12:27–43; 13:4–31), both Jewish and Christian traditions have long identified Ezra as the author. Three clues can be cited to back up Ezra's authorship: 1) the two books Ezra and Nehemiah were originally one book (indicated in the Greek Septuagint and the Latin Vulgate); 2) the recurring phrase *hand of the Lord* in both books points to a single author; 3) the sources used (official Persian documents) probably included Nehemiah's reports and were available to Ezra.

KEY PEOPLE IN NEHEMIAH

Nehemiah—influential cupbearer of the Persian king Artaxerxes; led the third group of exiles to Jerusalem to rebuild the city walls (1:1–13:31)

Ezra—led the second group of exiles to Jerusalem; worked with Nehemiah as Israel's priest and scribe (8:1–12:36)

Sanballat—governor of Samaria who attempted to discourage the people and thwart the rebuilding of Jerusalem's wall (2:10–13:28)

Tobiah—Ammonite official who mocked the rebuilding of the wall and discouraged the people (2:10–13:7)

BACKGROUND AND SETTING

The Book of Nehemiah grows out of a background of pain and glory. The opening scenes occur in Persia. A new chapter in God's dealings with His people begins. Recent history has included the final carrying out of God's promised judgment, with the Promised Land first invaded by the Assyrians, leading to the deportation and loss of the ten northern tribes. Later the Babylonians sacked, destroyed, and nearly depopulated Jerusalem, deporting the best of Judah to Babylon. God chastened His people with seventy years of captivity in Babylon (Jeremiah 25:11).

The ensuing years saw the rise of the Persian Empire. King Cyrus eventually set into motion the events leading to the Jews' return to Jerusalem. Ezra, Esther, Daniel, Nehemiah, and Malachi provide the details for these years in the history of God's faithfulness. The last two books share the distinction of being the final records in the Old Testament.

By the close of Nehemiah, God has allowed His people to reestablish a foothold in the Promised Land. God remains committed to His promises in spite of the fickle nature of His human partners. A four-hundred-year stalemate will follow these events. When God's revelation again takes written form, God will also have taken on flesh and visited the planet.

KEY DOCTRINES IN NEHEMIAH

God's Word—reading the Word of God requires careful attention in order to perform His will (8:1,8,13; 10:29,34,36; 13:1; Ezra 7:10; Psalm 119:16,140; Luke 11:28; John 5:39; James 1:25)

Obedience—God worked through the obedience of Nehemiah (7:5; Exodus 19:5; Deuteronomy 13:4; 1 Samuel 15:22; Jeremiah 7:23; Ecclesiastes 12:13; Hebrews 11:6; 1 Peter 1:2)

Opposition—despite local opposition and heartbreaking corruption, Judah completed the walls of Jerusalem in only fifty-two days (6:15; 8:1,14; Psalm 7:1; 69:26; Zechariah 2:8; Matthew 5:10; Luke 6:22; Romans 8:35; 2 Timothy 3:12)

GOD'S CHARACTER IN NEHEMIAH

God is glorious—9:5
God is good—1:10; 2:8,18; 9:35
God is kind—9:17
God is long-suffering—9:30
God is merciful—9:17, 27
God is powerful—1:10
God is provident—9:6
God is righteous—9:8
God is unified—9:6
God is wise—9:10

CHRIST IN NEHEMIAH

The Book of Nehemiah displays the rebuilding of the city of Jerusalem and the revival of the people. However, Israel still awaited the coming of a king. Christ the Messiah completes this restoration of Israel as the long-awaited King of the Jews (Matthew 27:11).

KEY WORDS IN NEHEMIAH

Confess: Hebrew *yadah*—1:6; 9:2–3—literally, "to throw" or "to cast off." This Hebrew verb conveys the act of "casting off" sin and acknowledging our rebellion against God's commandments (Nehemiah 1:6; 9:2; Psalm 32:3; Proverbs 28:13; Daniel 9:4). Confession also conveys thanksgiving for God's greatness (1 Kings 8:33,35). Confession of sin is thanksgiving because it recognizes the grace and goodness of God's forgiveness (2 Chronicles 30:22; Daniel 9:4).

Awesome: Hebrew *yare'*—1:5,11; 4:14; 6:14,19; 7:2—literally, "to fear." This Hebrew word suggests the virtue that inspires reverence or godly fear. Godly fear is closely related to godly living and respect for God's character (Leviticus 19:14; 25:17; Deuteronomy 17:19; 2 Kings 17:34). Thus while ordinary fear paralyzes a person, godly fear leads to submission and obedience to God. The person who properly fears God follows the will of God (Psalm 128:1) and avoids evil (Job 1:1).

QUICK OVERVIEW

- I. Nehemiah's First Term as Governor (1:1–12:47)
  - A. Nehemiah's Return and Reconstruction (1:1–7:73a)
    1. Nehemiah goes to Jerusalem (1:1–2:20)
    2. Nehemiah and the people rebuild the walls (3:1–7:3)
    3. Nehemiah recalls the first return under Zerubbabel (7:4–73a)
  - B. Ezra's Revival and Renewal (7:73b–10:39)
    1. Ezra expounds the Law (7:73b–8:12)
    2. The people worship and repent (8:13–9:37)
    3. Ezra and the priests renew the covenant (9:38–10:39)
  - C. Nehemiah's Resettlement and Rejoicing (11:1–12:47)
    1. Jerusalem is resettled (11:1–12:26)
    2. The people dedicate the walls (12:27–47)
- II. Nehemiah's Second Term as Governor (13:1–31)

MEANWHILE, IN OTHER PARTS OF THE WORLD . . .
Plato begins to study philosophy under the guidance of Socrates (407 to 399 B.C.).

FREQUENTLY ASKED QUESTIONS

1. What leadership qualities does Nehemiah illustrate by his life?

Like many biblical leaders, Nehemiah demonstrated an understanding of God's call over his life. Whether as cupbearer to a king or as the rebuilder of Jerusalem, Nehemiah pursued his goals with commitment, careful planning, strategic delegation, creative problem solving, focus on the task at hand, and a continual reliance on God, particularly regarding areas beyond his control. Each of the leadership qualities above can be illustrated from Nehemiah's successful completion of the effort to rebuild the walls of Jerusalem.

First, Nehemiah demonstrated his commitment by his interest and his deep concern over the condition of his fellow Jews in Judah. Next, Nehemiah prayed and planned. He claimed God's promise to bring His people back to the Promised Land, but he didn't assume that he would be part of God's action. He declared himself available (1:11; 2:5).

Even when he arrived in Jerusalem, Nehemiah personally inspected the need before he revealed his plans. Then, he enlisted the help of the local leadership. He challenged them to take responsibility for the common good. He placed before them a very specific goal—to rebuild the wall. Workers were assigned to work on the wall where it ran closest to their own homes. That way they could see the benefit in having the protective barrier rebuilt.

As the work sped forward, Nehemiah did not allow himself to be distracted by attacks of various kings or tricks from enemies. He took threats seriously enough to arm the people but not so seriously that the work came to a halt. At every turn, we find Nehemiah conferring in prayer with God, placing every decision before the ultimate Decider. Nehemiah succeeded because he never lost sight of the true reasons for the work and the source of power with which to do the work.

2. How does Nehemiah fit into the time line of world history?

It is unclear how Nehemiah became King Artaxerxes' cupbearer, but the fact that Esther was the king's stepmother may have inclined the king to consider a Jew for such a trusted position. When Nehemiah carried out his mission to rebuild the walls of Jerusalem, the Persian Empire had been dominant for almost a hundred years. King Cyrus's decree of repatriation given back in 539 B.C. had encouraged a group of Jews to return to Israel under Zerubbabel. Their desperate state almost a century later spurred Nehemiah into action.

Ancient Egyptian documents (Elephantine papyri) dated around the fifth century B.C. independently confirm part of Nehemiah's account. Sanballat the governor of Samaria (2:19), Jehohanan (6:18; 12:23), and Nehemiah himself receive mention.

The events recorded in Nehemiah, along with Malachi's prophecies, make up the final inspired writings of the Old Testament. God chose to remain silent for four hundred years after this time. That silence ended with the announcements of John the Baptist's and Jesus' births.

QUICK STUDY ON NEHEMIAH

1. What personal character trait impresses you the most about Nehemiah?
2. What leadership characteristics are illustrated by Nehemiah's life?
3. How did Nehemiah use prayer in his leadership role?
4. How did Nehemiah deal with problems?
5. Nehemiah's great work began with a desire. What was it and how did it guide his actions?
6. What are the desires that provide you with a large perspective about your life?

ESTHER
A Queen Who Served God

One of only two Old Testament books that bear the names of women.

Among Jewish people, Esther, the Jewish girl who became a Persian queen, is remembered by her Hebrew name, *Hadassah* (2:7), which means "myrtle." Her life became a channel through which God continued His protection of His chosen people from the murderous plans of an enemy.

AUTHOR AND DATE

Written by an unknown author, before 331 B.C.

Although Mordecai (Esther's cousin), Ezra, and Nehemiah have all been suggested, the author remains anonymous. The writer may well have been a Persian Jew who had returned to Israel.

Whoever penned Esther reveals a strong sense of Jewish nationalism and a detailed knowledge of Persian customs, etiquette, and history.

KEY PEOPLE IN ESTHER

Esther—replaced Vashti as queen of Persia; saved the Jews against Haman's evil plot (2:7–9:32)

Mordecai—adopted and raised Esther; advisor to Esther as queen; later replaced Haman as second in command under King Xerxes (2:5–10:3)

King Xerxes I—king of Persia; married Esther and made her queen (1:1–10:3)

Haman—second in command under King Xerxes; plotted to kill the Jews (3:1–9:25)

BACKGROUND AND SETTING

During the time of Esther, the Persian Empire ruled the world (539–331 B.C.). Esther's husband, Ahasuerus, reigned from 486 to 465 B.C. The events in this book occurred between 483 and 473 B.C.

Against the backdrop of Jewish history, Esther fits during the time-span between the first return of the Jews to Jerusalem under Zerubbabel around 538 B.C. (Ezra 1–6) and the second return led by Ezra around 458 B.C. (Ezra 7–10). The danger from which Esther rescued her people must have provided an added incentive for many of the Jews to return to Israel.

Like Exodus, Esther chronicles how vigorously foreign powers tried to eliminate the Jewish race as well as how powerfully God preserved His people. God continually honored His covenant promises to Abraham (Genesis 12:1–3; 17:1–8). Esther also documents the origin of a new annual festival among the Jews, called Purim. It is held during the twelfth month (February to March). The festival celebrates God's deliverance through Esther.

KEY DOCTRINES IN ESTHER

Purim as a celebration of God's faithfulness (3:7; 9:21–22,26–28,31; Deuteronomy 16:11,14; Nehemiah 8:10,12)

God's promise to preserve the Jews (4:14; 8:17; Genesis 17:1–8; 2 Samuel 7:8–16; 2 Chronicles 22:10–12; Psalm 121:4; Isaiah 65:8–9; Jeremiah 50:20; Matthew 2:16)

GOD'S CHARACTER IN ESTHER

God is provident—8:5–17

CHRIST IN ESTHER

Although Esther does not mention God specifically, His sovereign protection over His people remains apparent throughout the book. God placed Esther in the key position to impede Haman's plan to destroy the Jews. Esther typifies Christ in her willingness to lay down her life to save her people. Esther also represents the position of Christ as Israel's advocate. In all these events, God declares His love for Israel in His constant watch over the Jews: "Behold, He who keeps Israel shall neither slumber nor sleep" (Psalm 121:4).

KEY WORDS IN ESTHER

Fasting: Hebrew *tsum*—4:3; 4:16—root word simply means "to abstain from food." At times fasting meant abstaining from drinking, bathing, anointing with oil, or sexual intercourse as well. In essence, fasting acknowledges human frailty before God and appeals to His mercy. Fasting was a common practice in the ancient world, associated with mourning for the dead (2 Samuel 12:21–22), intercessory prayer (4:3,16), repentance and contrition for sin (Jeremiah 36:9; Jonah 3:5), and times of distress (Judges 20:26; Nehemiah 1:4). Fasting was required for the Day of Atonement (see the phrase "afflict your souls" in Leviticus 16:31). Fasts varied in length from one day (1 Samuel 14:24; Daniel 6:18) to seven days (1 Samuel 31:13) and could even last up to forty days on extraordinary occasions (Exodus 34:28). But no matter what type of fasting was performed, the prophet Isaiah admonished his people to participate in acts of righteousness and social justice with their fasting (Isaiah 58:3–9).

Pur: Hebrew *pur*—3:7; 9:24,26—in the Book of Esther refers to the Hebrew word for "lot." People cast lots, similar to rolling dice, to make random selections (Nehemiah 11:1). Lots were also used to apprehend the will of certain gods (Jonah 1:7). In Esther, Haman cast lots to determine the right day to destroy the Jews. God, on the other hand, revealed His sovereign power by choosing that particular day to deliver the Jews. Even today, Jews celebrate the festival of Purim in remembrance of their deliverance (9:28).

QUICK OVERVIEW

I. Esther Replaces Vashti (1:1–2:18)
  A. Vashti's Insubordination (1:1–22)
  B. Esther's Coronation (2:1–18)
II. Mordecai Overcomes Haman (2:19–7:10)
  A. Mordecai's Loyalty (2:19–23)
  B. Haman's Promotion and Decree (3:1–15)
  C. Esther's Intervention (4:1–5:14)
  D. Mordecai's Recognition (6:1–13)
  E. Haman's Fall (6:14–7:10)
III. Israel Survives Haman's Genocide Attempt (8:1–10:3)
  A. Esther and Mordecai's Advocacy (8:1–17)
  B. The Jews' Victory (9:1–19)
  C. Purim's Beginning (9:20–23)
  D. Mordecai's Fame (10:1–3)

MEANWHILE, IN OTHER PARTS OF THE WORLD . . .
The Chinese complete the construction of the first wall to prevent the Hun people from entering China (356 B.C.).

FREQUENTLY ASKED QUESTIONS

1. Why isn't God directly mentioned in Esther?

The question naturally arises when reading the book. Even the usual clues about God's presence seem absent. No one refers to the Law of God, sacrifices, worship, or prayer. God does not appear to receive public or private recognition for the preservation of the Jews. When it comes to God, Esther seems strangely silent.

In fact, the silence is so obvious that it becomes an argument. Esther challenges the tendency to demand that God prove His power and presence. Must God be apparent? All too quickly we expect God to demonstrate in unmistakable ways His identity. Yet God has repeatedly resisted human ultimatums. God reveals Himself for His own purposes, not human requirements.

Throughout history, God has more readily operated behind the scenes than in plain sight. The Scriptures are filled with unusual circumstances in which God worked obviously. But Esther comes close to revealing God's standard procedure. God's fingerprints are all over Esther's story. His superficial absence points to a deeper presence. God chose to be subtle, but He was there. The events in Esther give us a model for hope when God works in less than obvious ways in our lives.

2. Why do Esther and Mordecai appear so secular in their lifestyles?

In contrast to their near contemporaries Ezra, Nehemiah, and Daniel, the central people in Esther seem worldly. The lack of references to God is most obvious in Esther and Mordecai's conversations. Are these all subtle indications that Esther and Mordecai were people whose faith had little or no effect on their daily lives?

The Book of Esther does not settle this question. There are several important factors, however, that might hold us back from jumping to conclusions about Esther and Mordecai. Primary among these is the fact that the book has a limited scope. Only a few key events are recorded. Few, if any, details of the inner life of either main character are revealed. Yet the integrity of their actions ought to incline us toward giving them the benefit of the doubt when it comes to faith (4:13–16).

Here are a few other considerations regarding this question: 1) While Mordecai's caution about announcing his and Esther's heritage publicly might be questioned, it must also be pointed out that others were also cautious about this same matter (Nehemiah makes no mention of God in his conversation with Artaxerxes recorded in Nehemiah 2:1–8); 2) Public events such as Passover had fallen out of practice during the captivity, meaning that there were fewer occasions in which faith was practiced in the open (this doesn't mean, however, that the Jews were not a marked people, since they could be identified for the purpose of Haman's law); 3) When it was appropriate, Esther did openly identify her Jewish heritage (7:3–4). These considerations do not remove the charge that Esther and Mordecai seem less devoted to God than, for example, Daniel. But the fact that God did work out His purposes in their lives comes through clearly in the book.

QUICK STUDY ON ESTHER

1. What insights about the evil of racism can you identify in Esther?
2. Although God is not specifically mentioned in Esther, how do you see Him working?
3. What kind of a person was Esther? How do you know?
4. In what different ways did God arrange for the deliverance and safety of His people?
5. Contrast the characters of Haman and Mordecai.
6. In what ways would you say you are actively involved to make a difference in your own time of history?

JOB
The Righteous Can Suffer

The most ancient book in the Bible.

Times change, but people throughout history remain the same. Their deepest questions echo through the centuries. For example, the questions that Job asked thousands of years ago probably crossed your mind in the past week. The Book of Job records the biography of a person who was severely tested. Through Job's experience readers learn a great deal about the character of God.

AUTHOR AND DATE

Written by an unknown author, possibly before 1445 B.C.

Few internal or external clues point to a specific author for this book. Moses and Solomon have been suggested, but with little support. The ancient Jewish tradition of Mosaic authorship is based on the proximity of Moses' lengthy stay in Midian, which was a neighbor of Uz, Job's homeland (1:1). Others simply conclude that the mind-stretching and faith-challenging content of Job certainly fits with Solomon's quest for wisdom. These are only educated guesses, not verifiable conclusions.

KEY PEOPLE IN JOB

Job—patient under suffering; his faith was tested by God but he did not sin by blaming God (1:1–42:16)

Eliphaz the Temanite—a friend of Job; believed Job was suffering because of his sin (2:11; 4:1–5:27; 15:1–35; 22:1–30; 42:7–9)

Bildad the Shuhite—another friend of Job; believed Job had not repented of his sin and therefore suffered (2:11; 8:1–22; 18:1–21; 25:1–6; 42:9)

Zophar the Naamathite—a third friend of Job; believed Job deserved to suffer more for his sins (2:11; 11:1–20; 20:1–29; 42:9)

Elihu the Buzite—stood up against Job's three friends; believed God was using suffering to mold Job's character (32:1–37:24)

BACKGROUND AND SETTING

The divine inspiration of this book becomes clear in the early scene that occurs in heaven (1:6–2:10). The reader learns that Job suffered because God was contesting with Satan. Since neither Job nor his friends were aware of the big picture, their attempts to explain the suffering relied on ignorance and misunderstanding. Job finally rested on nothing but faith in God's goodness and the hope of God's redemption. God's vindication of Job's trust is the central message of the book. The reader must consider the possibility that trust in God sometimes goes beyond rational or theological explanations of pain and suffering.

KEY DOCTRINES IN JOB

Faithfulness in the midst of suffering (2:9; 13:15; Numbers 12:10–12; Luke 22:31–34; John 21:15–19; 2 Corinthians 1:3–7; 12:7–10; Hebrews 12:5–12; 1 Peter 5:10)

GOD'S CHARACTER IN JOB

God is delivering—33:27–28
God is glorious—37:22
God is invisible—23:8–9
God is just—4:17; 8:3; 34:12; 37:23
God is loving—7:17
God is powerful—5:9; 9:4,10; 26:14; 36:22; 40:9
God is provident—1:21; 26:10; 37:9–13
God is righteous—36:3
God is unsearchable—11:7; 37:23
God is wise—9:4; 11:11; 21:22; 23:10; 28:24; 34:21; 36:4–5; 37:16
God is wrathful—9:13; 14:13; 21:17

CHRIST IN JOB

The Book of Job raises many questions over the purpose of suffering. While direct answers are difficult to find in Job, our hope rests in Christ who identifies with our suffering (Hebrews 4:15). Ultimately, Job cries out to Christ, the Mediator between God and man (9:33; 25:4; 33:23).

KEY WORDS IN JOB

Blameless: Hebrew *tam*—1:1,8; 2:3; 8:20; 9:20–22—means "to be complete." This word signifies an individual's integrity: a wholeness and wholesomeness. The word is used as a term of endearment for the Shulamite bride in the Song of Solomon (see "perfect" in 5:2; 6:9). In the Old Testament, blamelessness is frequently associated with the upright (1:1,8; 2:3; Psalm 37:37; Proverbs 29:10) in contrast to the wicked (9:22; Psalm 64:2–4). Job's claim to be blameless agrees with God's assessment of him, but it is not a claim to absolute perfection (1:8; 9:21; 14:16,17). The Psalmist writes that the future of the blameless man is peace, as was the case for Job (42:10–12; Psalm 37:37).

Affliction: Hebrew *'oni*—10:15; 30:16,27; 36:8,15,21—comes from a root meaning "misery" or "poverty." The image evoked by this word is that of a person bowed down under the weight of a heavy burden. Scripture portrays the Lord as seeing the afflictions that bring pain to His people and hearing the anguished cries of those in distress (as in Genesis 16:11; Exodus 2:23–25). The Lord urges us to place our burdens on Him, for He is strong enough to bear them and loves us so much that He will assist us in our time of need (1 Peter 5:7). Moreover, since He controls all events, we can be assured that He is accomplishing good out of the temporary difficulties we are now facing (Romans 8:28). The entire story of Job provides vivid example of this fact (42:10–17; 2 Corinthians 12:7–10).

Behold: Hebrew *ra'ah*—19:27; 22:12; 40:11—common term used in reference to the natural function of the eyes and is thus most often translated as "see" (Genesis 48:10; Deuteronomy 1:8; 2 Kings 3:14; Micah 7:9–10). The word also has a number of metaphorical meanings, such as acceptance (Genesis 7:1; Numbers 23:21) and provision (Genesis 22:8,14; 1 Samuel 16:1). It can even convey the notion of assurance and salvation, as is the case here. In 42:5 the word means "to see" in the sense of "to come to recognize" or "to experience fully" something previously known or understood.

QUICK OVERVIEW

I. The Dilemma (1:1–2:13)
  A. Introduction (1:1–5)
  B. Divine Debates with Satan (1:6–2:10)
  C. Arrival of Friends (2:11–13)
II. The Debates (3:1–37:24)
  A. The First Cycle (3:1–14:22)
  B. The Second Cycle (15:1–21:34)
  C. The Third Cycle (22:1–26:14)
  D. The Final Defense of Job (27:1–31:40)
  E. The Speeches of Elihu (32:1–37:24)
III. The Deliverance (38:1–42:17)
  A. God Interrogates Job (38:1–41:34)
  B. Job Confesses, Worships, and Is Vindicated (42:1–17)

MEANWHILE, IN OTHER PARTS OF THE WORLD . . .
The Egyptians discover the use of papyrus and establish the first libraries in Egypt.

FREQUENTLY ASKED QUESTIONS

1. What kind of relationship did Job have with God?

Job's biography begins with a four-part description of his character: "blameless and upright, and one who feared God and shunned evil" (1:1). He prayed for his children and was concerned about their relationship with God (1:5). He was successful and wealthy, the stereotype of a blessed man. In fact, God adds His own glowing approval of Job, using the same traits that open the book (1:8).

Faced with the sudden, crushing loss of everything—children, servants, herds—Job's initial response was to grieve and recognize God's sovereignty.

"'The Lord gave, and the Lord has taken away; Blessed be the name of the Lord.' In all this Job did not sin nor charge God with wrong" (1:21b–22).

Under the harsh judgments of his friends, Job eventually struggled to understand why God seemed unwilling to settle matters. Once God did speak, at least part of Job's problem becomes clear: He confused a relationship with God with familiarity with God. The Lord did not rebuke Job's faith or sincerity; instead, God questioned Job's insistence on an answer for his difficulties. By allowing Job to hear just a little of the extent of his ignorance, God showed Job that there was a great deal he would never understand. As a creature, Job simply had no right to demand an answer from his Creator. Job's final words are filled with humility and repentance: "I have heard of You by the hearing of the ear, but now my eye sees You. Therefore I abhor myself, and repent in dust and ashes" (42:5–6).

Job spent his last days enjoying the same kind of relationship he had earlier with God. He prayed for his friends and raised another family of godly children. He lived a full life.

2. What kind of relationship does Satan have with God in the Book of Job?

Satan may be God's sworn enemy, but they are not equals. Satan is a creature; God is the Creator. Satan was an angel unwilling to serve in his exalted role, and he rebelled against God.

The continual conflict between Satan and God is illustrated when Satan states that righteous people remain faithful to God only because of what they get. They trust in God only as long as God is nice to them. Satan challenged God's claims of Job's righteousness by calling it untested, if not questionable. Apparently Satan was convinced that he could destroy Job's faith in God by inflicting suffering on him.

Satan suffered another defeat as God demonstrated through Job's life that saving faith can't be destroyed no matter how much trouble the believer suffers or how incomprehensible and undeserved the suffering seems.

After failing to destroy Job, Satan disappears from the story. He remains God's defeated enemy, still raging against God's inevitable triumph.

3. Why do righteous and innocent people suffer?

Of course no human being is truly righteous or innocent. The Bible clearly states that all have sinned (Romans 3:23). And all sinners deserve to be punished, eternally. That's what makes God's grace so amazing!

In understanding that truth, however, it must be admitted that on a relative human scale, righteous and innocent people exist. That is, some people are more moral and virtuous than others and some are more innocent. Consider, for example, a person who strives to live out the Golden

Rule, or another who gives generously to the poor. And certainly most consider small children to have a naive innocence. So this question could be rephrased: "Why do little children and people who live exemplary lives suffer?"

This question reveals the assumption that there is a direct connection between righteousness and innocence on the one hand and pain-free living on the other. There may be a connection, but it is not direct. Indeed, sin eventually does lead to suffering, but suffering is not an infallible indicator of sin. Job's friends could not see beyond this point. For them, a person's suffering was always an effect whose only cause could be that person's sin.

The righteous and the innocent do indeed suffer for a variety of reasons: 1) Sometimes righteous actions in a sinful world involve suffering, as when a righteous person sacrifices his or her life for another; 2) Sometimes the sins of others involve the righteous in suffering, as when a child is deeply hurt as a result of his or her parent's actions; 3) The righteous and innocent are not exempt from the painful situations which arise in an imperfect and sinful world, like toothaches and smashed fingers; 4) People sometimes suffer for no specific reason that can be clarified. Job is a perfect illustration of this last experience.

4. Why doesn't God answer all of Job's (and our) questions?

This question assumes that if God answered all our questions, it would be easier to believe. This is not true. Trust goes beyond answers. Sometimes, questions become a way to avoid trust.

In the end, we must trust God more than our capacity to understand God's ways. The lesson from Job's experience does not forbid us from asking questions. Often these questions will lead us to the reasons for our suffering. But Job's experience also warns us that we may not be able to understand all our suffering all the time, or even any of it some of the time.

God doesn't answer all of our questions because we are simply unable to understand many of His answers.

QUICK STUDY ON JOB

1. What do we learn about the character of Satan from the Book of Job?
2. Summarize the arguments of Job's friends.
3. What does God say to Job's friends?
4. What does God finally say to Job?
5. How does Job change from the righteous man who begins the book to the one who ends the book?
6. How does the Book of Job affect your questions about suffering?

PSALMS
Songbook of a Nation

The Hebrews called the book "Praises."

A person reading through the Bible knows from the first lines of Psalms that he or she has entered into a new and wonderful part of Scripture. It is poetry written for and about God. Psalms explores the full range of human experience and emotion. People meet God in the Psalms, and they discover a lot about themselves as well. As it defined the proper spirit and content of worship throughout Scripture, Psalms continues to influence and guide the worship of the church today.

AUTHOR AND DATE

Written by several authors, approximately 1410 to 450 B.C.

Although the word *inspired* is often used to describe poetry, that word is used in a special way to describe the Psalms and the rest of Scripture. The Bible claims to be "inspired by God" (2 Timothy 3:16). The content, truth, and reliability of Scripture rest on this claim. God employed many writers to compose His Word, but He remained the Author. The uniqueness of the writers can be seen in their style, experiences, and subjects, but God edited the final content.

Among the writers of Psalms, at least seven individuals or groups can be identified: 1) King David wrote at least 75 of the 150 psalms; 2) the sons of Korah are credited with 10; 3) Asaph contributed 12; 4) Solomon, 5) Moses, 6) Heman, and 7) Ethan all wrote at least one psalm each. The writers of 48 psalms are best listed as anonymous.

KEY PERSON IN PSALMS

David—king of Israel; called a man after God's own heart by God Himself (Psalms 2–41; 51–70; 72:20; 78:70–71; 86; 89; 96; 101; 103; 105; 108–110; 122; 124; 131–133; 138–145)

BACKGROUND AND SETTING

The Psalms were first compiled during the early days of Israel's extended worship training in the wilderness. The spontaneous and prepared responses to God that make up many of the Psalms were recorded and reused. Even the intense individual meditations, for example Psalm 23, were incorporated as expressions of universal truths about God.

The Psalms are a product as well as a record of the acts of God in creation and history, particularly the history of Israel. They are the accumulated memories and reflections of a people in relationship with God. The Psalms express and teach proper praise and worship of God.

KEY DOCTRINES IN PSALMS

The sinfulness of man (1:4; 5:4; 32:1–4; 36:1; 51:2; 66:18; 78:17; 106:43; Genesis 6:5; Leviticus 15:14; Deuteronomy 31:18; Job 4:17–19; Psalm 130:3; Jeremiah 17:9; John 1:10–11; Romans 5:15–17; 1 John 1:8)

The law of God (1:1–2; 78:1; 119:97; Exodus 20:1–21; Deuteronomy 5:6-21; Jeremiah 11:4; Romans 7:7–14; James 1:25; 1 John 3:4)

GOD'S CHARACTER IN PSALMS

God is accessible—15:1; 16:11; 23:6; 24:3–4; 65:4; 145:18
God is delivering—106:43–45
God is eternal—90:2; 102:25–27; 106:48
God is glorious—8:1; 19:1; 57:5; 63:2; 79:9; 90:16; 93:1; 96:3; 102:16; 104:1,31; 111:3; 113:4; 138:5; 145:5,11–12
God is good—23:6; 25:8; 31:19; 33:5; 34:8; 52:1; 65:4; 68:10; 86:5; 104:24; 107:8; 119:68; 145:9
God is gracious—116:5
God is great—86:10
God is holy—22:3; 30:4; 47:8; 48:1; 60:6; 89:35; 93:5; 99:3,5,9; 145:17
God is immutable—102:26–27
God is just—9:4; 51:4; 89:14; 98:9; 99:3–4
God is kind—17:7; 24:12; 25:6; 26:3; 31:21; 36:7,10; 40:10–11; 42:7–8; 48:9; 63:3; 89:33,49; 92:2; 103:4; 107:43; 117:2; 119:76,88,149; 138:2; 143:8
God is long-suffering—78:38; 86:15
God is merciful—6:2,4; 25:6; 31:7; 32:5; 36:5; 51:1; 52:8; 62:12; 86:5,15; 89:28; 103:4,8,11,17; 106:1; 107:1; 115:1; 118:1–4; 119:64; 130:7; 145:9; 147:11
God is the Most High—83:18
God is omnipresent—139:7
God is omniscient—139:1–6
God is powerful—8:3; 21:13; 29:5; 37:17; 62:11; 63:1–2; 65:6; 66:7; 68:33,35; 79:11; 89:8,13; 106:8; 136:12
God is a promise keeper—89:3–4,35–36; 105:42
God is provident—16:8; 31:15; 33:10; 36:6; 37:28; 39:5; 73:16; 75:6–7; 77:19; 91:3–4,11; 104:5–9,27–28; 119:15; 121:4; 127:1–2; 136:25; 139:1–5,10; 140:7; 145:9,17; 147:9
God is righteous—5:8; 7:9,17; 11:7; 19:9; 22:31; 31:1; 35:24,28; 36:6,10; 40:10; 48:10; 50:6; 51:14; 69:27; 71:2,15–16,19,24; 73:12–17; 85:10; 96:13; 97:2,6; 98:2,9; 103:17; 111:3; 116:5; 119:7,40, 62, 123,137–138,142,144,172; 143:1,11; 145:7,17
God is sovereign—2:4–5; 3:3; 72:5
God is true—9:14; 11:7; 19:9; 25:10; 31:5; 33:4; 57:3,10; 71:22; 85:10; 86:15; 89:14,49; 96:13; 98:3; 100:5; 119:160; 139:2; 146:6

God is unified—83:18; 86:10
God is unsearchable—145:3
God is upright—25:8; 92:15
God is wise—1:6; 44:21; 73:11; 103:14; 104:24; 136:5; 139:2–4,12; 142:3; 147:5
God is wrathful—2:2–5,12; 6:1; 7:11–12; 21:8–9; 30:5; 38:1; 39:10; 58:10–11; 74:1–2; 76:6–8; 78:21–22,49–51,58–59; 79:5; 80:4; 89:30–32; 90:7–9,11; 99:8; 102:9–10

CHRIST IN PSALMS

Many of the psalms directly anticipate the coming of the Messiah and King through the line of David (2; 18; 20; 21; 24; 47; 110; 132). Since Christ directly descended from the royal life of David, messianic psalms often refer to Christ as a Son of David, or use David as a type of Christ. Some specific messianic prophecies and their fulfillments include 2:7 (and Matthew 3:17; 16:10; Mark 16:6–7); 22:16 (and John 20:25,27; 40:7–8; Hebrews 10:7); 68:18 (and Mark 16:19; 69:21; Matthew 27:34); 118:22 (and Matthew 21:42).

KEY WORDS IN PSALMS

Selah: Hebrew *selah*—3:2; 24:10; 39:11; 47:4; 60:4; 76:3; 88:10; 140:3—derived from the verb *salal,* "to lift up." It occurs in thirty-nine psalms and in the "Psalm of Habakkuk" (Habakkuk 3). No one is certain of the exact meaning of this word, that is, what is to be lifted up. Some think that *Selah* is an emphatic word, marking a point in the psalm for "lifting up" one's thoughts to God. But most scholars think it is simply some form of musical notation, such as a marker of a musical interlude, a pause, or a change of key.

Hope: Hebrew *yachal*—31:24; 42:11; 71:14; 119:49,116; 130:5; 131:3—signifies "to wait with expectation." Almost half of its occurrences are in the Psalms, and it is especially frequent in 119. Sometimes the idea of hope is expressed with confidence (Job 13:15; Isaiah 51:5), and sometimes hope is clearly in vain (Ezekiel 13:6). The Bible describes Noah as waiting for seven days to send out the dove (Genesis 8:12) and men as waiting to hear the counsel of Job (Job 29:21). But by far the main object of "expectant waiting" or "hope" is God—His word, His judgment, and His mercy (33:18; 119:43; Micah 7:7). That hope is not misplaced, for the One in whom we hope is completely faithful to His promises.

Psalm: Hebrew *mizmor*—the titles of chapters 3; 9; 32; 54; 72; 84; 100; 101—derived from the verb *zamar,* "to make music." The word occurs only in the Psalms, and there it appears in fifty-seven of the psalm headings. It may designate a praise song or possibly a song accompanied by a certain type of instrumental music. In thirty-four psalm titles, *mizmor* follows the phrase "To the Chief Musician," perhaps indicating that the psalms were typically songs accompanied by instruments. Frequently the author of the psalm is also identified, such as the sons of Korah (48; 84), Asaph (50; 82), and especially David (23; 29; 51).

Law: Hebrew *torah*—1:2, 19:7; 37:31; 89:30; 119:1,55,174—usually translated "law," the noun *torah* is derived from the verb *yarah*, meaning "to teach," and should be understood as carrying the idea of "instruction." The term can refer to any set of regulations, such as the instructions of parents (Proverbs 1:8) or of a psalmist (78:1). But usually the word refers to God's Law. The writer of Psalm 119 expressed great love for God's Law because it led him to wisdom and righteousness (119:97–176). In the New Testament, Paul also praised God's Law because it pointed out his sin and made him realize his desperate need for a Savior (Romans 7:7).

Truth: Hebrew *'emet*—15:2; 25:10; 30:9; 43:3; 71:22; 108:4; 146:6—signifies truth that conforms to a standard, either to created reality or to God's standards. Truth is often associated with mercy, especially God's mercy (57:3; 117:2; Genesis 24:49). This word is also frequently used in the context of legal language. In secular contexts it is used in speaking of witnesses and judgments (Proverbs 14:25; Zechariah 8:16), while in the religious contexts it is used in reference to the Law and commandments of God (119:142,151). Truth is precious, and its absence was lamented by the prophets (Isaiah 59:14; Jeremiah 9:5; Hosea 4:1). God desires truth in the inward parts of His people (15:2; 51:6); thus it is the basis of a lifestyle that pleases Him (25:5,10; 26:3).

QUICK OVERVIEW

This outline simply follows the ancient Hebrew way of organizing the Psalms.

I. Book 1 (1—41)
II. Book 2 (42—72)
III. Book 3 (73—89)
IV. Book 4 (90—106)
V. Book 5 (107—150)

MEANWHILE, IN OTHER PARTS OF THE WORLD . . .
The Chinese compile their first dictionary containing 40,000 characters. The Hebrew alphabet develops beyond earlier Semitic forms.

FREQUENTLY ASKED QUESTIONS

1. Why are so many uncomfortable expressions in the Psalms, sometimes right in the middle of favorite chapters—for example, Psalms 23 and 139?

Because the Psalms genuinely reflect real life, we should expect that they will be uncomfortable in the same places that life is uncomfortable. According to the best-known Psalm 23, life isn't just about green pastures and still waters; it also includes death and enemies. The psalmists were convinced they knew the only true God. When someone was picking on them or their people, they would at times cry out for very specific judgment to be applied by God on their enemies. An amazing fact about Psalms is their unblushing record of these cries to God that, if we're honest, echo some of our deepest hidden complaints before God.

In David's case, the role that he filled as the king and representative of God's people often blurs with his individual self-awareness. At times it is difficult to tell whether he is speaking for himself alone or for the people as a whole. This explains some of the vehemence behind the curse-pronouncing psalms. They unabashedly invoke God's righteous wrath and judgment against his enemies.

2. What are the different kinds of psalms?

The Psalms cover the full breadth of human experience. Some speak in general terms, while others express in very specific terms the shifting events of life. There's a psalm for almost any kind of day.

One way to categorize the Psalms groups them by five general types:

Wisdom Psalms: instructions for wise living (1; 37; 119)
Lamentation Psalms: meditations on the pangs of life (3; 17; 120)
Penitential Psalms: meditations on the pangs of sin (51)
Kingship Psalms: meditations on God's sovereign rule (2; 21; 144)
Thanksgiving Psalms: praise and worship offered to God (19; 32; 111)

QUICK STUDY ON PSALMS

1. Which psalms are you most familiar with, and what impact do they have on your life?
2. What aspects of a healthy relationship with God can you find in Psalm 23?
3. How could you use Psalm 51 to help explain genuine repentance?
4. Read the first and the last psalms (1 and 150) and consider why each of those was chosen for the spot it holds.
5. What is the central theme of Psalm 119, and how does the length of the psalm add to its impact?
6. Which psalm or portion of a psalm do you find most useful for prayer?

PROVERBS
The Way of the Wise

Solomon composed over three thousand proverbs.

The Proverbs of Solomon contains a collection of 513 of the king's sayings. These are joined by selections from other wise people. Proverbs are simple, moral statements or illustrations that highlight and teach fundamental truths and tendencies in life. They originated as insights drawn from common objects and daily events. The Hebrew word for *proverb* means "to be like." Many of the sayings are, in fact, comparisons between a vivid image and a vivid desire or consequence. For example, "Like one who takes away a garment in cold weather, And like vinegar on soda, Is one who sings songs to a heavy heart" (25:20).

AUTHOR AND DATE

Created and compiled by Solomon and several other authors, approximately 971 to 686 B.C.

Proverbs provides a sample of the kind of wisdom that made Solomon famous. He set the standard for wisdom among his people. Perhaps that is why this collection has traditionally been named after Solomon even though he was not the source of the entire book. In fact, the final compilation of these sayings did not occur until the time of Hezekiah, long after Solomon's reign. Two other sages Agur and Lemuel are also specifically mentioned as contributors to Proverbs.

BACKGROUND AND SETTING

The contents of Proverbs reflect a threefold self-identity: 1) general wisdom literature; 2) insights from the royal court; 3) instructions offered in the mentoring relationship of a father and mother with their children. In each case, the purpose of the proverbs is to focus attention on godly living.

Wisdom Literature describes the part of the Old Testament that supplements the Law (Genesis to Deuteronomy), the History (Joshua to Esther), and the Prophets (Isaiah to Malachi). This category includes Job, Psalms, Proverbs, Ecclesiastes, and Song of Solomon. In Proverbs, Solomon the sage gives insight into the knotty issues of life (1:6). Though it is practical, Proverbs is not superficial or external because it contains moral and ethical elements stressing upright living that flows out of a right relationship with God. Proverbs contains the principles and applications of Scripture that the godly characters of the Bible illustrate throughout their lives.

KEY DOCTRINES IN PROVERBS

Practical righteousness (1:3; John 14:21)

The benefits of wisdom (2:20–22; 3:13–18; 9:11; 12:21; Job 28:17; Psalms 37:3; 91:10; 1 Peter 3:13)
Man's relationship to God (1:7; 3:34; 6:23; 10:22; 12:28; 15:11; 22:19; Genesis 24:35; 26:12; Deuteronomy 8:18; Job 28:28; Psalms 19:8; 111:10; Ecclesiastes 12:13; Acts 1:24; James 4:6; 1 Peter 5:5; 2 Peter 1:19)
Man's relationship to himself (1:5; 3:3; 6:9–11; 11:4; 13:4; 20:11; 29:11; Exodus 13:9; Deuteronomy 6:8; Jeremiah 17:1; Ezekiel 7:19; Zephaniah 1:18; Matthew 7:16; 2 Corinthians 3:3)
Man's relationship to others (3:1–3; 4:1–4; 8:17; 17:17; 19:27; 20:19; 23:23; Deuteronomy 8:1; Ruth 1:16; 1 Samuel 2:30; Psalm 34:11; Romans 16:18)

GOD'S CHARACTER IN PROVERBS

God is merciful—28:13
God is omniscient—5:21
God is provident—3:6; 16:3,9,33; 19:21; 20:24; 21:30–31
God is wise—3:19; 15:11

CHRIST IN PROVERBS

The writers of Proverbs desired that believers not only listen to the truth but apply this wisdom to their own lives. Proverbs calls for wisdom to become incarnate (chapter 8), and indeed it did when "all the treasures of wisdom and knowledge" became flesh in Christ (Colossians 2:3). While the Old Testament readers of Proverbs were guided by wisdom through the written word, the New Testament believers came to know the Word of God in human form. Therefore, Christ not only encompasses Proverbs but actually "became for us wisdom from God" (1 Corinthians 1:30).

KEY WORDS IN PROVERBS

Wisdom: Hebrew *chokmah*—1:2; 4:5; 9:10; 14:6; 16:16; 18:4; 23:23; 31:26—can also mean "skill" but is most commonly used to describe daily application of practical wisdom. Proverbs teaches that true wisdom reaches beyond mere knowledge of truth to living a life of moral integrity (8:7–9). Whereas the sinful life leads ultimately to self-destruction; abundant life is found within the wisdom of God (2:6; Job 11:6).

Foolish: Hebrew *ʾivvelet*—14:1; 12:23; 14:24; 15:2, 14; 19:3; 22:15; 24:9; 27:22—signifies an absence of wisdom. Except for two occurrences in the Psalms, this term occurs only in Proverbs, where the foolishness of fools is frequently contrasted with the wisdom of the wise and prudent (13:16; 14:8,18,24). Foolishness characterizes the speech of fools and the reactions of the impulsive person (12:23; 14:17,29; 15:2,14; 18:13). Foolishness affects the lifestyle of a person, causing his or her heart to fret against God (15:21; 19:3). Indeed, foolishness is often identified with iniquity and sin (5:22,23; 24:9; Psalm 38:4,5). Although Proverbs does not hold out much hope for separating an adult fool from his foolishness, the rod of correction is identified as a remedy for children (22:15; 26:11; 27:22).

QUICK OVERVIEW

I. Prologue (1:1–7)
  A. Title (1:1)
  B. Purpose (1:2–6)
  C. Theme (1:7)
II. Praise and Wisdom to the Young (1:8–9:18)
III. Proverbs for Everyone (10:1–29:27)
  A. From Solomon (10:1–22:16)
  B. From Wise Men (22:17–24:34)
  C. From Solomon Collected by Hezekiah (25:1–29:27)
IV. Personal Notes (30:1–31:31)
  A. From Agur (30:1–33)
  B. From Lemuel (31:1–31)

MEANWHILE, IN OTHER PARTS OF THE WORLD . . .
Peking becomes an established city in China, later to be renamed Beijing, the present-day capital city of China.

FREQUENTLY ASKED QUESTIONS

1. Some of the proverbs seem unclear or even contradictory. How can we study and apply them if we don't understand them?

More often than not, those proverbs that at first seem unclear or contradictory turn out, instead, to be elusive and deep. Proverbs sometimes do state obvious truths. Their meaning is crystal clear: "A foolish son is a grief to his father, and bitterness to her who bore him" (17:25). But many proverbs require thoughtful meditation: "The lot is cast into the lap, but its every decision is from the Lord" (16:33) or "There is a way that seems right to a man, but its end is the way of death" (16:25). The fact that we may have to search the rest of Scripture or work at thinking ought to make Proverbs dearer to us. If God has chosen this unusual approach to help us grow, why would we hesitate to give our full attention to Proverbs?

Given the context that surrounds Proverbs—the rest of God's Word—a student's failure to grasp a proverb ought not to lead to the conclusion that there's something wrong with the proverb. A better conclusion would be that the student doesn't know enough yet or hasn't paid enough attention. A wise person puts an elusive proverb on hold for further understanding rather than rejecting it as useless. God's further lessons in that person's life may well cast a new light on parts of the Bible that have been difficult to interpret.

2. What are some general, time-tested principles that will help rightly interpret Proverbs?

One of the most common characteristics of Proverbs is the use of parallelism; that is, placing truths side-by-side so that the second statement expands, completes, defines, and emphasizes the first. Sometimes a logical conclusion is reached; at other times, a logical contrast is demonstrated.

The following directions will assist a student in gaining greater confidence as he or she interprets these Proverbs:

1. Determine what facts, principles, or circumstances make up the parallel ideas in that proverb—what two central concepts or persons are being compared or contrasted.
2. Identify the figures of speech and rephrase the thought without those figures, for example, restate the idea behind "put a knife to your throat" (23:1–3).
3. Summarize the lesson or principle of the proverb in a few words.
4. Describe the behavior that is being taught or encouraged.
5. Think of examples from elsewhere in Scripture that illustrate the truth of that proverb.

3. Many of the proverbs appear to impose absolutes on life situations that prove to be unclear. How do the proverbs apply to specific life decisions and experiences?

Proverbs are divine guidelines and wise observations that teach underlying principles of life (24:3–4). They are not inflexible laws or absolute promises. This is because they are applied in life situations that are rarely clearcut or uncomplicated by other conditions. The consequences of a fool's behavior as described in Proverbs apply to the complete fool. Most people are only occasionally foolish and therefore experience the occasional consequences of foolish behavior. It becomes apparent that the proverbs usually do have exceptions due to the uncertainty of life and the unpredictable behavior of fallen people.

The marvelous challenge and principle expressed in 3:5–6 puts a heavy emphasis on trusting the Lord with "all your heart" and acknowledging Him "in all your ways." Even partly practicing the conditions of those phrases represents a major challenge. Because of God's grace, we don't have to perfectly carry out these conditions in order to experience the truth that "He shall direct your paths."

God does not guarantee uniform outcome or application for each proverb. By studying them and applying them, a believer is allowed to contemplate God's mind, character, attributes, works, and blessings. In Jesus Christ are hidden all the treasures of wisdom and knowledge partly expressed in Proverbs (Colossians 2:3).

QUICK STUDY ON PROVERBS

1. Using the language of Proverbs, how would you define wisdom?
2. What guidelines does Proverbs offer regarding relationships between people?
3. What recurring themes do you find in Proverbs regarding work?
4. How does God fit in with the teaching of Proverbs?
5. What warnings and guidance does Proverbs offer about speech, or the tongue?
6. Comment on Proverbs 3:5–6 as it relates to your own life.

ECCLESIASTES
Life without God

Words about life's meaning from history's wisest man.

What makes life meaningful? Will enough friends, success, achievement, money, or recognition lead to happiness? King Solomon had the chance to test all the theories of what brings meaning to life. He took full advantage of his opportunity! In the end he declared them all "vanity." The Book of Ecclesiastes serves as Solomon's journal of his failed experiment with life in the fast lane. He discovered that everything that offers to make life full turns out to make life empty. His final conclusion points to the only source of true meaning: "Fear God and keep His commandments, for this is man's all" (Ecclesiastes 12:13).

AUTHOR AND DATE

Written by Solomon, no later than 931 B.C.

Solomon, an experienced elder and king, wrote the Book of Ecclesiastes to young people. The dispassionate wisdom that makes up Proverbs is illustrated in Ecclesiastes by an intimate, painful, firsthand wisdom learned in the hard school of life. Solomon warned his readers to avoid walking through life on the path of human wisdom. He pointed, instead, to the revealed wisdom of God (12:9–14) as the true answer to life's meaning.

KEY PEOPLE IN ECCLESIASTES

Solomon—king of Israel; God granted Solomon's desire for wisdom, and he became the wisest person ever born (Ecclesiastes 1:1–12:14)

BACKGROUND AND SETTING

Ecclesiastes presents itself as an eyewitness account of a misdirected quest: "I set my heart to seek and search out by wisdom concerning all that is done under heaven" (1:13). Solomon decided to test intuitive wisdom by direct experiments. The risks of disillusionment, despair, and death that Solomon faithfully reported make his experiment a warning to those who would insist on copying Solomon's behavior rather than learning from his mistakes.

David recognized his son's wisdom (1 Kings 2:6, 9) even before God deepened Solomon's capacity. After Solomon received a "wise and understanding heart" from the Lord (1 Kings 3:7–12), he became known for rendering insightful decisions (1 Kings 3:16–28). His reputation for wisdom attracted "all the kings of the earth" to his courts (1 Kings 4:34). Solomon's impressive outpouring of songs, proverbs, and opinions set the stage for his personal engagement in the events of Ecclesiastes. Solomon found himself in a position to try anything and everything. He decided to do just that.

KEY DOCTRINES IN ECCLESIASTES

Vanity of life—the futile attempt to be satisfied apart from God (1:2; 12:8; Genesis 3:17–19; Psalms 39:5–6; 62:9; 144:4; Romans 8:19–21; James 4:14)

The meaning of life (1:3; 2:24; 3:9; 12:13–14; Isaiah 56:12–57:2; Luke 12:19–21; John 10:10; 1 Corinthians 15:32; 1 Timothy 6:17)

Balance in life—there is a time and a season for everything (3:1–8,17; Exodus 15:20; Psalm 126:2; Amos 5:13; Romans 12:15–16; Hebrews 9:27)

The fear of the Lord (12:13–14; Deuteronomy 6:2; 10:12; Micah 6:8; Matthew 12:36; Acts 17:30–31; Romans 2:16; 1 Corinthians 4:5; 2 Corinthians 5:10)

GOD'S CHARACTER IN ECCLESIASTES

God is long-suffering—8:11
God is powerful—3:11

CHRIST IN ECCLESIASTES

Solomon wrote Ecclesiastes as a warning to those who attempt to find joy without God. In fact, living without God is impossible for He has "placed eternity in the hearts [of men]" (3:11). Solomon's pursuit of happiness through experiences and philosophy remained unattainable without God. Christ did not come into the world to make life bearable for humans. He came to provide life "more abundantly" (John 10:9–10). Christ remains the "one Shepherd" who is the source of all wisdom (12:11). Therefore, every pursuit without Christ is futile.

KEY WORDS IN ECCLESIASTES

Vanity: Hebrew *hebel*—1:2; 2:1; 4:4; 6:2,11; 7:15; 8:14; 9:9—basically means "vapor" or "breath," such as the rapidly vanishing vapor of one's warm breath in cool, crisp air. With this word, the preacher described worldly pursuits, such as wealth, honor, fame, and various other pleasures, as similar to desperately grasping at air (2:17). It is absurd and useless. Jeremiah used the same word to denounce idolatry as "worthless" (Jeremiah 18:15), and Job used it to bemoan the brevity of human life (Job 7:16). But the preacher of Ecclesiastes used the word more than any other Old Testament author. According to him, all of life is vanity unless one recognizes that everything is from the hand of God (2:24–26).

Labor: Hebrew *'amal*—1:3; 2:10,21; 3:13; 4:8; 5:19; 6:7; 10:15—generally means "toil," or work for material gain (Psalm 127:1; Proverbs 16:26), but it can also mean "trouble" or "sorrow" (see Job 3:10). The effort required for work and human achievement produces "sorrow" and "troubles" in the sense that it can never satisfy the deeper needs of the human soul (6:7). However, when believers recognize that their work is a gift from God, work can become a joy (5:18–20). Our work is part of God's plan to establish His eternal kingdom. In this sense, we can be assured that our faithful commitment to our work will have eternal consequences and reap eternal rewards (see 1 Corinthians 3:8,14; 15:58).

QUICK OVERVIEW

I. Introduction (1:1–11)
   A. Title (1:1)
   B. Poem—A Life of Activity That Appears Wearisome (1:2–11)
II. Solomon's Investigation (1:12–6:9)
   A. Introduction (1:12–18)
   B. Investigation of Pleasure Seeking (2:1–11)
   C. Investigation of Wisdom and Folly (2:12–17)
   D. Investigation of Labor and Rewards (2:18–6:9)
III. Solomon's Conclusions (6:10–12:8)
   A. Introduction—The Problem of Not Knowing (6:10–12)
   B. A Person Cannot Always Find Out Which Route Is the Best to Take Because Wisdom Is Limited (7:1–8:17)
   C. One Does Not Know What Will Come Afterwards (9:1–11:6)
   D. One Should Enjoy Life, But Not Sin, Because Judgment Will Come to All (11:7–12:8)
IV. Solomon's Final Advice (12:9–14)

MEANWHILE, IN OTHER PARTS OF THE WORLD . . .
Chinese culture advances as written script, brush and ink paintings, and mathematical theories such as multiplication and geometry develop.

FREQUENTLY ASKED QUESTIONS

1. How does the author's declaration that "all is vanity" relate to the message of the Book of Ecclesiastes?

By stating one of his conclusions in the opening lines, the author of Ecclesiastes challenges readers to pay attention. The word translated "vanity" is used in at least three ways throughout the book. In each case, the term refers to the nature and value of human activity "under the sun."

1. Vanity refers to the "fleeting" nature of human accomplishments that James later described as vaporlike (James 4:14).

2. Vanity can mean "futile" or "meaningless," which points to the cursed condition of the universe and the debilitating effects it has on human earthly experience.
3. Vanity can represent "incomprehensible" or "enigmatic," which gives consideration to life's unanswerable questions. Solomon found that the word applied to his entire experiment.

While the context in each of the thirty-seven appearances of "vanity" helps determine the particular meaning Solomon had in mind, his most frequent usage conveyed the idea of "incomprehensible" or "unknowable." He was expressing the human limits when faced with the mysteries of God's purposes. Solomon's final conclusion to "fear God and keep His commandments" (12:13–14) represents more than the book's summary; it states the only hope of the good life and the only reasonable response of faith and obedience to the sovereign God. God precisely superintends all activities under the sun, each in its time according to His perfect plan, while He discloses only as much as His perfect wisdom dictates. All people remain accountable. Those who refuse to take God and His Word seriously are doomed to lives of the severest vanity.

2. When the writer of Ecclesiastes encourages his readers to "enjoy life," does he have any conditions or cautions in mind?

Solomon balanced his enjoyment theme with repeated reminders of divine judgment. Even the best moments in life ought not to cut a person off from awareness of God as Provider to whom all will give an account. Solomon declared that the possibility of enjoyment was based on faith (Ecclesiastes 2:24–26).

Part of Ecclesiastes reports the king's experiment in trying to enjoy life without regard for God's judgment. Solomon discovered that such an effort was in vain. In the end, he came to grasp the importance of obedience.

The tragic results of Solomon's personal experience, coupled with the insight of extraordinary wisdom, make Ecclesiastes a book from which all believers can receive warnings and lessons in their faith (2:1–26). This book demonstrates that a person who sees each day of existence, labor, and basic provision as a gift from God, and accepts whatever God gives, will actually live an abundant life. However, anyone who seeks to be satisfied apart from God will live with futility regardless of personal successes.

QUICK STUDY ON ECCLESIASTES

1. How many different major pursuits did Solomon experiment with in Ecclesiastes?
2. What was Solomon seeking?
3. What conclusions did Solomon reach regarding life's meaning?
4. What insights about time and its uses do you get from chapter 3:1–8?

5. What does the phrase "eternity in their hearts" (3:11) mean in Ecclesiastes?
6. In what specific ways do Solomon's discoveries challenge your life?

SONG OF SOLOMON

God Honors Pure Marital Love

The Song of Solomon expands on the ancient marriage instructions of Genesis 2:24 by providing shameless and spiritual music for a lifetime of marital harmony.

The oldest songs are love songs. Among the most intimate ever written are these lyrics authored by Solomon and named after him. The ancient Hebrew versions of this book entitle it "Song of Songs." Based on the biblical record that Solomon composed 1,005 songs (1 Kings 4:32), the title indicates that this was his best.

AUTHOR AND DATE

Written by Solomon, shortly after 971 B.C.

Solomon included his own name seven times in the book (1:1, 5; 3:7, 9, 11; 8:11–12). His unequaled reputation as a thinker, writer, and composer point favorably toward the king as the original author. The style of this book also indicates a single, highly creative mind, composing an example of Wisdom Literature as complex and delightful as the relationship about which it was written.

KEY PEOPLE IN SONG OF SOLOMON

King Solomon—the bridegroom; called "beloved" by his wife (1:7–8:12)
The Shulamite woman—the new bride of King Solomon (1:1–8:13)
The daughters of Jerusalem—unidentified virgins who encouraged the Shulamite woman (1:4; 2:14; 3:5,10,11; 5:1,8; 6:1,12; 8:4)

BACKGROUND AND SETTING

Two people dominate this true-to-life, dramatic love song. Solomon the king takes on the role of "the beloved." The identity of the Shulamite maiden (6:13) remains obscure. Her name may indicate her hometown was Shunem in Galilee. Although some suggest she was the daughter of Pharaoh mentioned in 1 Kings 3:1, the Song itself provides no confirmation. Others have suggested the woman in this song is Abishag, the Shunammite maiden who cared for the aging King David (1 Kings 1:1–4, 15), but there is little evidence of this. We are left with an unknown maiden from Shunem who was Solomon's first wife (9:9). The relationship immortalized in the Song knows nothing of the sin into which Solomon fell when he added 699 other wives and 300 concubines to his household (1 Kings 11:3).

Various small groups fill the supporting roles in this love story. "The daughters of Jerusalem" (1:5), Solomon's friends (3:6–11), and the Shulamite's brothers (8:8, 9) each supply an outside perspective for the couple.

The setting includes rural and urban scenes. Part of the story takes place in the hill country north of Jerusalem, where the Shulamite lived (6:13). They may have met while Solomon carried out duties as a vine grower and shepherd (2:4–7). The events of the wedding and the early married life of the couple occur in Jerusalem (Song of Solomon 3:6–7:13).

KEY DOCTRINES IN SONG OF SOLOMON

The love of God reflected in human love (6:2,3; Genesis 29:20; Leviticus 19:18; 2 Chronicles 36:15; Matthew 14:14; Luke 15:20–24; Philippians 1:8)

God's grace given through marriage (Ruth 1:9; Ezekiel 16:6–8; Matthew 1:20; Hebrews 13:4; 1 Peter 3:7)

GOD'S CHARACTER IN SONG OF SOLOMON

God is faithful—8:5
God is loving—8:6
God is pure—3:5; 4:1–16

CHRIST IN SONG OF SOLOMON

The words of Solomon intimately paint a picture of marriage. Yet, Song of Solomon illustrates the spiritual relationship between God and Israel, His chosen nation, and even the relationship God desires with individuals. Solomon attempts to express the love of the beloved for his bride. This mystery can only be fully revealed in the intimate relationship between Christ and the church (Ephesians 5:32).

KEY WORDS IN SONG OF SOLOMON

Beloved: Hebrew *dod*—1:14; 2:8; 4:16; 5:1,6,10; 6:1; 8:14—in Hebrew love poetry, *dod* is a term of endearment used for a male loved one, usually translated "beloved" (Isaiah 5:1). The writer of the Song of Solomon uses this word thirty-two times. The name David is derived from *dod* and carries the same sense, meaning "beloved one." When *dod* is used in narrative, it means "uncle" or another close male relative (1 Samuel 14:50).

Myrrh: Hebrew *mor*—1:13; 3:6; 4:6,14; 5:1,5,13—describes a taste that is bitter. The word is derived from the verb *marar,* which means "to be bitter." Myrrh is made from the gum or sap of an Arabian balsa tree. The resin was pressed and mixed with oil to make perfume (1:13; 5:1), incense (3:6), and lotion (Esther 2:12). Naomi took the name Mara as a symbol of the bitterness she had experienced in her life (Ruth 1:20), and the Christ-child was presented with a gift of myrrh by the wise men (see Matthew 2:11). Myrrh was also an embalming spice in New Testament times and was used on Jesus' body (John 19:39).

QUICK OVERVIEW

I. The Courtship: Leaving (1:2–3:5)
  A. The Lovers' Remembrances (1:2–2:7)
  B. The Lovers' Expression of Reciprocal Love (2:8–3:5)
II. The Wedding: Cleaving (3:6–5:1)
  A. The Kingly Bridegroom (3:6–11)
  B. The Wedding and First Night Together (4:1–5:1a)
  C. God's Approval (5:1b)
III. The Marriage: Weaving (5:2–8:14)
  A. The First Major Disagreement (5:2–6:3)
  B. The Restoration (6:4–8:4)
  C. Growing in Grace (8:5–14)

MEANWHILE, IN OTHER PARTS OF THE WORLD . . .
Greek worship of gods and goddesses becomes fully developed. Major deities include Zeus, Hera, Poseidon, Apollo, Ares, Demeter, Athena, Hermes, and Artemis.

FREQUENTLY ASKED QUESTIONS

1. Should Song of Solomon be interpreted as person-to-person love or as an allegory of God's love for Israel or Christ's love for the church?

Allegorical interpretations of this book tend to be strained. Denying the human and historical setting of this Song creates more discomfort with the subject matter than insight into the nature of Scripture. The idealistic and allegorical language that lovers use might lead one to assume the freedom to allegorize the entire experience, but the lovers themselves would strongly object. The practice of allegorizing the book comes from outside theological and philosophical frameworks, not the content of the book itself.

One form of interpretation similar to allegorizing takes a "typological" approach. It begins by admitting the historical validity of the story. But it also insists that the idealized language of the lovers can ultimately only accurately describe the kind of love that Christ has demonstrated toward His church.

A more satisfying way to approach Solomon's Song takes the story at face value, interprets it in a normal historical sense, and understands the idealized use of poetic language to depict reality. This interpretation affirms Solomon's account of three phases in his relationship with the Shulamite: his early days of courtship, the early days of his marriage, and the maturing of the royal couple through the good and bad days of married life.

The book serves as God's demonstration of His intentions for the romance and loveliness of marriage, the most precious of human relations and "the grace of life" (1 Peter 3:7).

QUICK STUDY ON SONG OF SOLOMON

1. In what ways does the Song of Songs capture the intensity and shamelessness of romantic love?
2. How does the Song of Songs express and encourage commitment?
3. What factors make the Song of Songs' descriptions of sexuality healthy and good in comparison with much that is available in the rest of culture?
4. What insights about expressing enjoyment over the beauty of one's mate can you find in Song of Songs?
5. How would you describe Song of Song's role within the rest of Scripture?

ISAIAH
Announcing the Suffering King

Isaiah is the Old Testament prophet most often quoted in the New Testament.

Isaiah's thoughts are echoed sixty-five times and his name is mentioned on at least twenty occasions in the New Testament. "Isaiah," which means "the Lord is salvation," shares roots with the names Joshua, Elisha, and Jesus.

AUTHOR AND DATE

Written by Isaiah, approximately 700 to 681 B.C.

Isaiah, the son of Amoz, prophesied in and around Jerusalem during the reigns of four kings of Judah: Uzziah, Jotham, Ahaz, and Hezekiah. The prophet probably grew up in a prominent family, which explains his easy access to the higher levels of Jewish society, including the kings (7:3). Isaiah was a contemporary of fellow prophets Hosea and Micah. His writing style has no rival in its versatility of expression, brilliance of imagery, and richness of vocabulary.

KEY PEOPLE IN ISAIAH

Isaiah—prophet who ministered throughout the reigns of four kings of Judah; gave both a message of judgment and hope (1–66)

Shear-Jashub—Isaiah's son; name means "a remnant shall return," denoting God's promised faithfulness to His people (7:3; 8:18; 10:21)

Maher-Shalal-Hash-Baz—Isaiah's son; name means "hasting to the spoil, hurrying to the prey" denoting God's coming punishment (8:1,3,18)

BACKGROUND AND SETTING

Isaiah grew up in the closing years of King Uzziah's fifty-two-year reign. During those years Judah developed into a strong commercial and military state. Her distant commercial port on the Red Sea and the extensive construction of walls, towers, and fortifications all served as examples of prosperous times (2 Chronicles 26:3–15). Yet the period also witnessed a decline in Judah's spiritual health. Uzziah eventually overstepped his royal bounds by assuming the role of a priest (2 Chronicles 26:16–19). That act sealed his downfall. He was judged with leprosy, from which he never recovered (2 Chronicles 26:20–21).

The spiritual decline begun under Uzziah continued during the reigns of his son Jotham and his grandson Ahaz. Second Kings 15:34 describes Jotham's passive preservation of the spiritual legacy that had been part of Uzziah's reign. Ahaz, however, actively rejected God's ways

(2 Kings 16:2–4). The depth of his idolatry included child sacrifice. Meanwhile, the nation was becoming increasingly weak and under the influence of other nations.

By the time Hezekiah came to the throne, the Assyrian empire was a threat held at bay only through the payment of crushing tribute. Hezekiah realized that a spiritual reformation was a priority (2 Kings 18:4, 22). Isaiah served as a valuable counselor to Hezekiah. When Assyria did invade Judah, Isaiah's influence caused Hezekiah to trust in God's protection. The nation gained a divine reprieve.

KEY DOCTRINES IN ISAIAH

Christ as the Suffering Servant (49:1–57:21; Psalms 68:18; 110:1; Matthew 26:39; John 10:18; Acts 3:13–15; Philippians 2:8,9; Hebrews 2:9)

The first coming of the Messiah (7:14; 8:14; 9:2,6–7; 11:1–2; Ezekiel 11:16; Matthew 1:23; Luke 1:31; 2:34; John 1:45; 3:16; Romans 9:33; 1 Peter 2:8; Revelation 12:5)

The second coming of the Messiah (4:2; 11:2–6,10; 32:1–8; 49:7; 52:13,15; 59:20–21; 60:1–3; 61:2–3; Jeremiah 23:5; Zechariah 3:8; Matthew 25:6; 26:64; Romans 13:11–12; Philippians 4:5; Revelation 3:11)

Salvation through Christ (9:6–7; 52:13–15; 53:1–12; Isaiah 12:2; Psalm 103:11–12; Luke 19:9; John 3:16; Acts 16:31; Romans 3:21–24; 1 Timothy 1:15)

GOD'S CHARACTER IN ISAIAH

God is accessible—55:3,6
God is eternal—9:6
God is faithful—49:7
God is glorious—2:10; 6:3; 42:8; 48:11; 59:19
God is holy—5:16; 6:3; 57:15
God is just—45:21
God is kind—54:8,10; 63:7
God is Light—60:19
God is long-suffering—30:18; 48:9
God is loving—38:17; 43:3–4; 49:15–16; 63:9
God is merciful—49:13; 54:7–8, 55:3,7
God is powerful—26:4; 33:13; 41:10; 43:13; 48:13; 52:10; 63:12
God is a promise keeper—1:18; 43:2
God is provident—10:5–17; 27:3; 31:5; 44:7; 50:2; 63:14
God is righteous—41:10
God is true—25:1; 38:19; 65:16
God is unequaled—43:10; 44:6; 46:5,9

God is unified—44:6,8,24; 45:5–8,18,21–22; 46:9–11
God is unsearchable—40:28
God is wise—28:29; 40:14,28; 42:9; 44:7; 46:10; 47:10; 66:18
God is wrathful—1:4; 3:8; 9:13–14,19; 13:9; 26:20; 42:24–25; 47:6; 48:9; 54:8; 57:15–16; 64:9

CHRIST IN ISAIAH

The Book of Isaiah presents one of the most startling examples of messianic prophecy in the Old Testament. With vivid imagery, Isaiah depicts the future Christ as the Suffering Servant who was "led as a lamb to the slaughter" (53:7) and "shall justify many, for He shall bear their iniquities" (53:11).

Other messianic prophecies found in Isaiah with New Testament fulfillments include 7:14 (Matthew 1:22–23); 9:1–2 (Matthew 4:12–16); 9:6 (Luke 2:11; Ephesians 2:14–18); 11:1 (Luke 3:23,32; Acts 13:22–23); 11:2 (Luke 3:22); 28:16 (1 Peter 2:4–6); 40:3–5 (Matthew 3:1–3); 42:1–4 (Matthew 12:15–21); 42:6 (Luke 2:29–32); 50:6 (Matthew 26:67; 27:26,30); 52:14 (Philippians 2:7–11); 53:3 (Luke 23:18; John 1:11; 7:5); 53:4–5 (Romans 5:6,8); 53:7 (Matthew 27:12–14; John 1:29; 1 Peter 1:18–19); 53:9 (Matthew 27:57–60); 53:12 (Mark 15:28); 61:1 (Luke 4:17–19,21).

KEY WORDS IN ISAIAH

Light: Hebrew *'or*—2:5; 5:30; 10:17; 13:10; 30:26; 45:7; 58:10; 60:20—refers to literal or symbolic light. This Hebrew word often denotes daylight or daybreak (Judges 16:2; Nehemiah 8:3), but it can also be symbolic of life and deliverance (Job 33:28,30; Psalm 27:1; 36:9; 49:19; Micah 7:8,9). In the Bible, light is frequently associated with true knowledge and understanding (42:6; 49:6; 51:4; Job 12:25), and even gladness, good fortune, and goodness (Job 30:26; Psalm 97:11). The Bible describes light as the clothing of God: a vivid picture of His honor, majesty, splendor, and glory (Psalm 104:2; Habakkuk 3:3–4). A proper lifestyle is characterized by walking in God's light (2:5; Psalm 119:105; Proverbs 4:18; 6:20–23).

Blessing: Hebrew *berakah*—19:24,25; 44:3; 51:2; 61:9; 65:8,16; 66:3—comes from a verb expressing several significant ideas, namely "to fill with potency," "to make fruitful," or "to secure victory." The word alludes to God's promise to benefit all nations through Abraham's descendants (Genesis 12:3). When people offer a blessing, they are wishing someone well or offering a prayer on behalf of themselves or someone else (Genesis 49; Deuteronomy 33:1). Old Testament patriarchs are often remembered for the blessings they gave to their children. When God gives a blessing,

He gives it to those who faithfully follow Him (Deuteronomy 11:27), providing them with salvation (Psalm 3:8), life (Psalm 133:3), and success (2 Samuel 7:29).

Servant: Hebrew *'ebed*—20:3; 24:2; 37:35; 42:1; 44:21; 49:5; 53:11—derives from a verb meaning "to serve," "to work," or "to enslave." While *'ebed* can mean "slave" (Genesis 43:18), slavery in Israel was different than in most places in the ancient Middle East. Slavery was regulated by the law of Moses, which prohibited indefinite slavery and required that slaves be freed on the Sabbath (seventh) year (Exodus 21:2) and the Year of Jubilee, the fiftieth year (Leviticus 25:25–28). Sometimes the Hebrew word can refer to the subjects of a king (2 Samuel 10:19). But usually the word is best translated "servant." God referred to His prophets as "My servants" (Jeremiah 7:25) and spoke of the coming Messiah as His Servant, the One who would perfectly obey His will (see 42:1–4; 49:1–6; 50:4–9; 52:13–53:12).

Salvation: Hebrew *yeshu'ah*—12:2; 25:9; 33:6; 49:6; 51:8; 59:11; 62:1—describes deliverance from distress and the resultant victory and well-being. The term occurs most often in Psalms and Isaiah, where it is frequently used along with the word *righteousness*, indicating a connection between God's righteousness and His saving acts (45:8; 51:6,8; 56:1; 62:1; Psalm 98:2). This word can be used for a military victory (1 Samuel 14:45), but it is normally used of God's deliverance (Exodus 15:2; Psalm 13:5,6). The expressions *the salvation of the Lord* and *the salvation of our God* speak of God's work on behalf of His people. The expression *the God of my salvation* is more private in nature, referring to the deliverance of an individual (12:2; 52:10; Exodus 14:13; 2 Chronicles 20:17; Psalms 88:1; 98:3).

QUICK OVERVIEW

I. Judgment (1:1–35:10)
  A. Prophecies Concerning Judah and Jerusalem (1:1–12:6)
  B. Oracles of Judgment and Salvation (13:1–23:18)
  C. Redemption of Israel through World Judgment (24:1–27:13)
  D. Warnings against Alliance with Egypt (28:1–35:10)
II. Historical Interlude (36:1–39:8)
  A. Sennacherib's Attempt to Capture Jerusalem (36:1–37:38)
  B. Hezekiah's Sickness and Recovery (38:1–22)
  C. Babylonian Emissaries to Jerusalem (39:1–8)
III. Salvation (40:1–66:24)
  A. Deliverance from Captivity (40:1–48:22)

B. Sufferings of the Servant of the Lord (49:1–57:21)
C. Future Glory of God's People (58:1–66:24)

MEANWHILE, IN OTHER PARTS OF THE WORLD . . .
Romulus, legendary founder of Rome, institutes a new calendar in which the year is divided into ten months. In Italy, dentistry advances with the creation of false teeth.

FREQUENTLY ASKED QUESTIONS

1. Does Isaiah indicate God's permanent abandonment of the chosen people, or does God reveal through Isaiah an ongoing plan for them?

The long view that Isaiah's prophecies provide supports the future role of Israel in God's plan. God, according to Isaiah, may arrange for harsh punishment of His people, but He has not replaced ethnic Israel with an alleged "new Israel." Isaiah has too much to say about God's faithfulness to Israel. He would not utterly reject the people whom He has created and chosen (43:1). The nation is on the palms of His hands, and Jerusalem's walls are ever before His eyes (49:16). God is bound by His own Word to fulfill the promises He has made to bring them back to Him and bless them in that future day (55:10–12).

The imagery in the New Testament confirms Isaiah's views. Passages like Romans 11 certainly picture Gentiles being grafted into the tree of God's salvation plan, but the message does not imply complete replacement. God does not forget those who belong to Him.

2. In what ways are Isaiah's prophecies still open to fulfillment, and how?

The literal fulfillment of many of Isaiah's prophecies makes up part of the ancient historical record. Manuscripts like the complete copy of Isaiah found among the Dead Sea scrolls were already well worn when the events of Jesus' life were taking place. The trustworthiness of Isaiah's prophetic statements about the intervening events strongly suggests that his prophecies for the future will also be accurate. To argue that those yet unfulfilled can only be fulfilled nonliterally is biblically and historically shortsighted. God's Word remains steadfast. The case for proposing that the church receives some of the promises made originally to Israel rests on shaky ground. The kingdom promised to David still belongs to Israel, not the church. The future exaltation of Jerusalem will be on earth, not in heaven. Christ will reign personally on this earth as we know it, as well as in the new heavens and the new earth (Revelation 22:1,3).

QUICK STUDY ON ISAIAH

1. Isaiah's call in 6:1–8 represents a memorable event in Scripture.
2. What does it indicate about God's holiness?
3. In the great chapter on salvation (53), how is God's plan described?
4. What components of Isaiah's character can be found throughout this book?
5. In what ways do Isaiah's prophecies balance hope/salvation with judgment/punishment?
6. What prophecies about the Messiah/Savior stand out for you in Isaiah?
7. How do you understand God's call in your own life (see 6:1–8 again)?

JEREMIAH
The Testimony of Tears

Jeremiah's life was so filled with sorrow and conflict that he has long been known as the "weeping prophet."

Anyone serious about knowing what life was like for a prophet must read Jeremiah's writing. His books are autobiographical in more intimate ways than in any other prophet. He not only includes the details of his ministry and the responses he received, but he also recounts the difficulties he faced and the rejection and anger he felt. Jeremiah's name means "Jehovah throws," a term used to refer to laying a foundation. It can also mean "Jehovah establishes, appoints, or sends."

AUTHOR AND DATE

Written by Jeremiah during his ministry, approximately 627 to 570 B.C.

Jeremiah served in two vocations during his lifetime: priest and prophet. His hometown was the small village of Anathoth (1:1). He never married. God instructed him to use his celibacy as an object lesson about the hopelessness of days to come for Judah (16:1–4).

KEY PEOPLE IN JEREMIAH

King Josiah—sixteenth king of the southern kingdom of Judah; attempted to follow God (1:1–3; 22:11,18)

King Jehoahaz—evil son of Josiah and seventeenth king of the southern kingdom of Judah (22:9–11)

King Jehoiakim—evil son of Josiah and eighteenth king of the southern kingdom of Judah (22:18–23; 25:1–38; 26:1–24; 27:1–11; 35:1–19; 36:1–32)

King Jehoiachin (Coniah)—evil son of Jehoiakim and nineteenth king of the southern kingdom of Judah (13:18–27; 22:24–30)

King Zedekiah—evil uncle of Jehoiachin and twentieth king of the southern kingdom of Judah (21:1–14; 24:8–10; 27:12–22; 32:1–5; 34:1–22; 37:1–21; 38:1–28; 51:59–64)

Baruch—served as Jeremiah's scribe (32:12–16; 36:4–32; 43:3–45:4)

Ebed-Melech—Ethiopian palace official who feared God and helped Jeremiah (38:7–39:16)

King Nebuchadnezzar—greatest king of Babylon; led the people of Judah into captivity (21–52)

The Rechabites—obedient descendants of Jonadab; contrasted to the disobedient people of Israel (35:1–19)

BACKGROUND AND SETTING

Second Kings 22–25 and 2 Chronicles 34–36 describe the background details of Jeremiah's times. His messages paint word pictures of 1) his people's sin; 2) the invader God would send; 3) the rigors of siege; 4) the horrors of destruction. For forty years Jeremiah faithfully preached an unwelcome message of impending judgment. During that time, five different kings reigned in Judah: Josiah (640–609 B.C.), Jehoahaz (609 B.C.), Jehoiakim (609–598 B.C.), Jehoiachin (598–597 B.C.), and Zedekiah (597–586 B.C.).

Flagrant idol worship was the primary symptom of the desperate spiritual condition of Judah in Jeremiah's day. Even the horrific practice of child sacrifice, introduced by King Ahaz almost a hundred years earlier and temporarily halted under King Hezekiah, was again part of the religious life of Judah. King Josiah's reforms reached their apex in 622 B.C. with the abolishment of the worst of these practices, but the deadly cancer of sin simply hid in a temporary remission and flourished again after the shallow revival. Jeremiah's messages aimed at many of the ongoing symptoms of moral and spiritual disease: religious insincerity, dishonesty, adultery, injustice, tyranny against the helpless, and slander. Jeremiah's writing did little more than document the headlong rush of his people toward judgment.

Momentous events on the world stage occurred in Jeremiah's day. Assyria saw its power wane. By 612 B.C., Assyria's seemingly invincible capital, Nineveh, was destroyed. The rising Babylonian empire under Nabopolassar (625–605 B.C.) established its military dominance with victories over Assyria (612 B.C.), Egypt (609–605 B.C.), and Israel (605 B.C.—Daniel 1; 597 B.C.—2 Kings 24:10–16; and 586 B.C.—Jeremiah 39; 40; 52).

Jeremiah was rarely a lone voice of prophecy. His ministry followed the ringing warnings of Joel and Micah. Jeremiah's early contemporaries were Habakkuk and Zephaniah. In Jeremiah's later years, Ezekiel and Daniel also ministered for God to His scattered people.

KEY DOCTRINES IN JEREMIAH

Sin—Israel's sin demanded punishment from God (2:1–13, 23–37; 5:1–6; 7:16–34; 11:1–17; 17:1–4; 18:1–17; 23:9–40; Exodus 23:33; Deuteronomy 9:16; 1 Kings 11:39; Ezra 6:17; Job 1:22; Psalm 5:4; Micah 3:8; Matthew 5:30; Luke 17:1; Romans 1:29)

Judgment/Punishment (4:3–18; 9:3–26; 12:14–17; 15:1–9; 16:5–13; 19:1–15; 24:8–10; 25:1–38; 39:1–10; 44:1–30; 46:1–51:14; Exodus 12:12; Psalm 1:5; Hosea 5:1; Amos 4:12; John 12:31–32; Romans 14:10; 2 Thessalonians 1:7–10)

Restoration of Israel (23:3–8; chapters 30–33; Deuteronomy 30:1–5; Psalm 71:20–21; Isaiah 49:6; Nahum 2:2; Acts 1:6–8; 15:16; 1 Peter 5:10)

GOD'S CHARACTER IN JEREMIAH

God fills heaven and earth—23:24

God is good—31:12,14; 33:9,11

God is holy—23:9
God is just—9:24; 32:19; 50:7
God is kind—31:3
God is long-suffering—15:15; 44:22
God is loving—31:3
God is merciful—3:12; 33:11
God is omnipresent—23:23
God is powerful—5:22; 10:12; 20:11; 37:27
God is a promise keeper—31:33; 33:14
God is righteous—9:24; 12:1
God is sovereign—5:22, 24; 7:1–15; 10:12–16; 14:22; 17:5–10; 18:5–10, 25:15–38; 27:5–8; 31:1–3; 42:1–22; 51:15–19
God is true—10:10
God is unequaled—10:6
God is wise—10:7,12; 32:19
God is wrathful—3:12–13; 4:8; 7:19–20; 10:10; 18:7–8; 30:11; 31:18–20; 44:3

CHRIST IN JEREMIAH

The picture of Christ remains interwoven throughout the prophecies of Jeremiah. Christ as the "fountain of living waters" (2:13; John 4:14) stands in stark contrast to the judgment poured over the unrepentant nation of Judah. Jeremiah also portrays Christ as the "balm in Gilead" (8:22), the good Shepherd (23:4), "a righteous Branch" (23:5), "the Lord our righteousness" (23:6), and David the King (30:9).

KEY WORDS IN JEREMIAH

Heal: Hebrew *raphaʾ*—3:22; 6:14; 8:11; 15:18; 17:14; 30:17; 51:8—applies literally to the work of a physician. Occasionally it refers to inanimate objects and can best be translated *repair* (1 Kings 18:30). More commonly, this word connotes the idea of restoring to normal, as in 2 Chronicles 7:14, where God promises to restore the land if His people pray. In the Psalms, God is praised for His role in healing disease (Psalm 103:3), healing the brokenhearted (Psalm 147:3), and healing the soul by providing salvation (Psalms 30:2; 107:20). Isaiah declared that the healing of God's people results from the sacrificial wounds of His Son (Isaiah 53:5–12).

Shepherd: Hebrew *roʿah*—6:3; 23:4; 31:10; 43:12; 49:19; 50:44; 51:23—refers to someone who feeds and tends domestic animals. David spoke of God as his Shepherd because God provided, sustained, and guided him (Psalm 23). Kings and other leaders were also seen as shepherds of their people, and the title "shepherd" was frequently applied to kings in the ancient Middle East. David was a true shepherd-king, responsibly leading and protecting his people (2 Samuel 5:1,2). Jeremiah rebuked the leaders of Israel who were false shepherds and failed in their responsibility of caring for the spiritual well-being of God's people (23:1–4).

Prophet: Hebrew *nabi'*—1:5; 6:13; 8:10; 18:18; 23:37; 28:9; 37:3; 51:59—probably comes from the root word meaning "to announce" or "to proclaim" (19:14; Ezekiel 27:4). Another possible derivation is from a Hebrew word meaning "to bubble up" or "to pour forth." Prophecy can be compared to the "bubbling up" of the Holy Spirit in a person who delivers a divine message (compare Amos 3:8; Micah 3:8). In Old Testament times, prophets were heralds or spokesmen who delivered a message for someone else (see 1:5; 2:8; 2 Kings 17:13; Ezekiel 37:7). In the case of the Hebrew prophets, they spoke for God Himself. This is the reason the prophets introduced their messages with "thus says the LORD of hosts" on countless occasions (see 9:7,17).

Word: Hebrew *dabar*—1:2; 5:14; 13:8; 21:11; 24:4; 32:8; 40:1; 50:1—is derived from the verb "to speak," and signifies the word or thing spoken. The phrase *word of the Lord* is used by the prophets at the beginning of a divine message (see 1:13). In the case of prophetic literature, *word* can be a technical term for a prophecy. In the Bible, the word of revelation is associated with prophets (26:5), just as wisdom is associated with wise men and the law with priests (18:18). Jeremiah used *dabar* more than any other prophet in order to clarify the authority given to him by God.

QUICK OVERVIEW

I. Preparation of Jeremiah (1:1–19)
   A. The Context of Jeremiah (1:1–3)
   B. The Choice of Jeremiah (1:4–10)
   C. The Charge to Jeremiah (1:11–19)
II. Proclamations to Judah (2:1–45:5)
   A. Condemnation of Judah (2:1–29:32)
   B. Consolation to Judah—New Covenant (30:1–33:26)
   C. Calamity on Judah (34:1–45:5)
III. Proclamation of Judgment on the Nations (46:1–51:64)
   A. Introduction (46:1; see 25:15–26)
   B. Against Egypt (46:2–28)
   C. Against Philistia (47:1–7)
   D. Against Moab (48:1–47)
   E. Against Ammon (49:1–6)
   F. Against Edom (49:7–22)
   G. Against Damascus (49:23–27)
   H. Against Kedar and Hazor—Arabia (49:28–33)

I. Against Elam (49:34–39)
J. Against Babylon (50:1–51:64)
IV. The Fall of Jerusalem (52:1–34)
A. The Destruction of Jerusalem (52:1–23)
B. The Deportation of Jews (52:24–30)
C. The Deliverance of Jehoiachin (52:31–34)

MEANWHILE, IN OTHER PARTS OF THE WORLD . . .
Water systems develop that enable water to be brought into certain cities: Jerusalem by means of subterranean water tunnels, Nineveh by means of bucket wells, which were improved under Sennacherib through the construction of aqueducts.

FREQUENTLY ASKED QUESTIONS

1. How can one explain God's forbidding prayer for the Jews (7:16) and His saying that even Moses and Samuel's intervention would not prevent judgment (15:1)?

General questions about God's willingness or unwillingness to hear someone's prayer must be answered with reference to specific passages. God's direction to Jeremiah not to pray for the people flows from the people's determined attitude of rejection towards God. Jeremiah 7:16 begins with "therefore" and indicates that what follows expresses God's conclusion. The people have no interest in the prayers of Jeremiah, so they are as useless as if God did not hear them.

Later, in Jeremiah 15:1, God describes the desperate sinful condition of His people by stating that even prayers by Moses and Samuel would not stop the consequences that were on the horizon. The spiritual error that God exposes in this passage has to do with the temptation to offer the "right prayer" as a substitute for genuine repentance. The idea that an empty religious ceremony can satisfy the righteous indignation of a holy God was not just an ancient error. Now, as then, God allows people to experience the full results of their behavior as a final opportunity for correction and repentance.

2. Part of Jeremiah's prophecy includes God's promise of a New Covenant with His people. What is this New Covenant, and how does it relate to Israel, the New Testament, and the church?

In Jeremiah 31:31–34 God announced the coming establishment of a New Covenant with His people, saying "I will put My law in their minds, and write it on their hearts; and I will be their God, and they shall be My people" (31:33). This covenant will be different than the one that, God says, "I made with their fathers in the day that I took them by the hand to lead them out of the land of Egypt, My covenant which they broke" (verse 32). The fulfillment of this New Covenant would be to individuals as well as to Israel as a nation (verse 36; Romans 11:16–27). Among the final external indicators of this covenant are 1) a reestablishment of the people in their land (verses 38–40 and chapters 30–33); and 2) a time of ultimate difficulty (30:7).

In principle, this Covenant, also announced by Jesus (Luke 22:20), began to be exercised on behalf of both Jewish and Gentile believers in the church era (1 Corinthians 11:25; Hebrews 8:7–13; 9:15; 10:14–17; 12:24; 13:20). The idea of a Jewish remnant that appears so often in the Old Testament prophecies, the New Testament identifies as the "remnant according to the election of grace" (Romans 11:5). The New Covenant will be finalized for the people of Israel in the last days, including the regathering to their ancient land, Palestine (chapters 30–33). The streams of the Abrahamic, Davidic, and New Covenants will eventually flow as one in the millennial kingdom ruled by the Messiah.

QUICK STUDY ON JEREMIAH

1. What does the first chapter of Jeremiah indicate about God's plans for individual persons?
2. Jeremiah served as God's prophet for more than forty years. In what ways was he a failure? In what ways was he successful?
3. What does Jeremiah mean when he writes about the New Covenant (chapter 31)?
4. What was Jeremiah's relationship to the kings of his time?
5. How do Jeremiah's prophecies in chapters 46–52 emphasize God's sovereignty in the face of seemingly powerful nations?
6. What does Jeremiah teach you about faithfulness?

LAMENTATIONS
Hope in the Devastation

Here is the surprising source of the phrase "Great is Thy faithfulness!" (3:23)

Sometimes life just makes you want to scream. It can be a shout of victory, a cry of defeat, or a moan of agony, but it expresses the deepest emotions of your soul. Jeremiah lived life with passion. He was seldom passive and often angry. No other book in the Old Testament contains the kind of raw grief that gives this book its name—Lamentations. By allowing us into his pain and sorrow, Jeremiah teaches believers how to deal with suffering.

AUTHOR AND DATE

Written by Jeremiah, approximately 586 B.C.

The author of Lamentations is not named within the book, but internal and external indicators, such as vocabulary and style, point to Jeremiah. References to Jeremiah himself (Jeremiah 7:29; 2 Chronicles 35:25) highlight his tendency to lament over events around him. Jeremiah wrote Lamentations as an anguished eyewitness account of the shameful destruction of Jerusalem. It is likely that Jeremiah saw the destruction of the walls, towers, homes, palace, and temple. He wrote with these painful scenes fresh on his mind.

KEY PEOPLE IN LAMENTATIONS

Jeremiah—prophet of Judah; mourned the destruction of Jerusalem (1:1–5:22)

People of Jerusalem—people judged by God because of their great sins (1:1–5:22)

BACKGROUND AND SETTING

Eight hundred years before the Fall of Jerusalem, Joshua predicted the tragedy (Joshua 23:15, 16). Jeremiah had invested forty years in warning his people of coming judgment. Both he and his message had been rejected. Still, when the predicted calamities fell on the disbelieving people, Jeremiah responded with sorrow and compassion. He took no pleasure in the exact confirmation of his prophecies.

Jeremiah recorded his predictions about the Fall of Jerusalem in the first twenty-nine chapters of the book that bears his name. In Lamentations, Jeremiah provided the details of the bitter suffering and heartbreak that he and others felt over Jerusalem's devastation. The defeat and destruction of Jerusalem represented a critical moment in the story of God's dealings with Israel and the world. The facts of the tragedy are recorded in four separate Old Testament passages: 2 Kings 25; Jeremiah 39:1–11; 52; and 2 Chronicles 36:11–21.

KEY DOCTRINES IN LAMENTATIONS

God's judgment of Judah's sin (1:5,8,18,20; 3:42; 4:6,13,22; 5:16; Deuteronomy 28:43; Nehemiah 9:26; Psalm 137:7; Jeremiah 14:20; 30:14; 52:28; Ezekiel 16:37; Daniel 9:5,7,16; Hosea 2:10; Zephaniah 3:4; Matthew 23:31)

Hope found in God's compassion (3:22–24,31–33; Psalm 30:3–5; Isaiah 35:1–10; Jeremiah 30:1–31:40; Ezekiel 37:1–28; Hosea 3:5; 14:1–9; Joel 3:18–21; Amos 9:11–15; Micah 7:14–20; Zephaniah 3:14–20; Zechariah 14:1–11; Malachi 4:1–6)

GOD'S CHARACTER IN LAMENTATIONS

God is faithful—3:22–25; 5:19–22
God is good—3:25
God is merciful—3:22–23,32
God is wrathful—1:5,12,15,18; 2:1,17,20–22; 3:37–39

CHRIST IN LAMENTATIONS

The tears of Jeremiah flowed from the deep love he had for the people of Israel (3:48–49). In this same way, Christ Himself wept over the city of Jerusalem, crying, "O Jerusalem, Jerusalem, the one who kills the prophets and stones those who are sent to her! How often I wanted to gather your children together, as a hen gathers her chicks under her wings, but you were not willing" (Matthew 23:37–39; Luke 19:41–44)! While Christ must judge those who rebel against Him, He also feels great sorrow over the loss of His beloved people.

KEY WORDS IN LAMENTATIONS

Weeps: Hebrew *bakah*—1:2,16—describes the act of wailing, which expresses emotions ranging from grief to happiness. While the word is often associated with lamentation, the "bitter wailing" of ancient people who were mourning their dead (2 Samuel 1:12), it is also used with expressions of joy (Genesis 29:11). The ancients wept when saying farewell (Ruth 1:9), over impending doom (Jeremiah 9:1), to express their joy over the rebuilt temple (Ezra 3:12), and at the burial of an individual (Genesis 50:1). In Lamentations, Jeremiah weeps over the sins of the people, the sins that would eventually result in the destruction of Jerusalem (1:1,16).

Renew: Hebrew *chadash*—5:21—can mean "to renew" (Psalm 51:10) or "to repair" (Isaiah 61:4). As an adjective, the word identifies something new in contrast to something old (such as the "old harvest" versus the "new harvest;" see Leviticus 26:10), or something different when compared to the status quo (such as "a new spirit;" see Ezekiel 11:19; 18:31). The Bible teaches that God alone is the One who makes things new, whether a new song in the heart of the faithful (Psalm 40:3), a new phase in His plan of redemption (Isaiah 42:9; 43:19), a new name (Isaiah 62:2), or a new heaven and earth (Isaiah 65:17).

QUICK OVERVIEW

I. The First Lament: Jerusalem's Devastation (1:1–22)
  A. Jeremiah's Sorrow (1:1–11)
  B. Jerusalem's Sorrow (1:12–22)
II. The Second Lament: The Lord's Anger Explained (2:1–22)
  A. The Lord's Perspective (2:1–10)
  B. A Human Perspective (2:11–19)
  C. Jeremiah's Prayer (2:20–22)
III. The Third Lament: Jeremiah's Grief Expressed (3:1–66)
  A. His Distress (3:1–20)
  B. His Hope (3:21–38)
  C. His Counsel/Prayer (3:39–66)
IV. The Fourth Lament: God's Wrath Detailed (4:1–22)
  A. For Jerusalem (4:1–20)
  B. For Edom (4:21–22)
V. The Fifth Lament: The Remnant's Prayers (5:1–22)
  A. To Be Remembered by the Lord (5:1–18)
  B. To Be Restored by the Lord (5:19–22)

MEANWHILE, IN OTHER PARTS OF THE WORLD . . .

Pythagoras, the famous mathematician and creator of the Pythagorean Theorem, is born in 581 B.C.

FREQUENTLY ASKED QUESTIONS

1. How does the promise of Christ appear in a book like Lamentations?

Jeremiah serves as one of the strong foreshadowing personalities of Jesus in the Old Testament. Jeremiah's tears over Jerusalem (3:48–49) compare closely with Jesus' weeping over the same city (Matthew 23:37–39; Luke 19:41–44). Jeremiah's grief prepares believers to think about God as the righteous Judge who can execute punishment while at the same time experiencing grief over the suffering of His people. Isaiah described the principle with this statement: "In all their affliction, He [God] was afflicted" (Isaiah 63:9).

Jeremiah's tears also serve as a reminder of the utter hopelessness of a person without God. Tears point to God's promise to one day remove every cause for tears, and then the tears themselves (Isaiah 25:8; Revelation 7:17; 21:4) when sin shall be no more.

2. What appears to be God's purpose in including a book like Lamentations in the Bible?

The Book of Lamentations presents an implied warning to every reader. Through Jeremiah's words, we see consequences from within. The sorrow and sadness that flow from judgment offer a deterrent. If God did not hesitate to judge His beloved people (Deuteronomy 32:10), what will He do to the nations and peoples of the world who reject His Word?

3. What lessons can we find in Jeremiah's bold call for judgment on the enemies of Judah (1:21–22; 3:64–66) and his report that God has shut out his prayers (3:8)?

The prayers of the prophets and psalmists often sound harsh to us. The boldness of their expressions remind us that it is often a good thing that God has not promised to answer our prayers as we have prayed them. We may express our real desires and real emotions in prayer, but we would be foolish to think that God would limit Himself to our perceptions. Jeremiah's call for retribution was partially answered in the fall of Babylon (Isaiah 46–47; Jeremiah 50–51; Daniel 5). God will exercise justice in His time. All accounts will be settled ultimately at the Great White Throne (Revelation 20:11–15).

Jeremiah's description of his prayer life offers a vivid picture of how he felt rather than what God was actually doing. God's negative response to Jeremiah's prayers was not because Jeremiah was guilty of personal sin; rather, it was due to Israel's perpetual sin without repentance. Jeremiah knew that, yet he prayed, wept, and longed to see repentance from his people.

QUICK STUDY ON LAMENTATIONS

1. How does Lamentations compare and contrast with Jeremiah?
2. How does Lamentations 3:22–32 fit with the rest of the book?
3. What powerful feelings does Jeremiah express in Lamentations?
4. What unique role does Lamentations fill within Scripture?
5. In what ways could Lamentations help you during times of grief?

EZEKIEL
Reflections of God's Glory

Neither the author nor his book are mentioned anywhere else in Scripture.

Ezekiel stands like a lonely pillar in the center of the Bible. His name means "strengthened by God." The location and the loneliness that surrounded his ministry required the truth of his name. Ezekiel used vivid and memorable visions, prophecies, parables, signs, and symbols to proclaim and dramatize the message of God to His exiled people. Those who listened to Ezekiel were also strengthened by God.

AUTHOR AND DATE

Written by Ezekiel during his ministry, approximately 593 to 570 B.C.

Like his contemporary Daniel, Ezekiel was born in Judah but died in Babylon. He was exiled from Judah in 597 B.C. There he waited with his fellow exiles during the final years of Jerusalem. Five years after his captivity, Ezekiel received God's call to be a prophet to the exiles. His ministry lasted twenty-two years. This book that bears his name was probably written throughout his years as a prophet. The last prophecy with a date (29:17) was delivered in 572 or 571 B.C., so the book was completed sometime after that date.

KEY PEOPLE IN EZEKIEL

Ezekiel—prophet to the people of Israel in Babylonian captivity (1:1–48:35)

Israel's leaders—led the people of Israel into idolatry (7:26–8:12; 9:5–6; 11; 14:1–3; 20:1–3; 22:23–29)

Ezekiel's wife—unnamed woman whose death symbolized the future destruction of Israel's beloved temple (24:15–27)

Nebuchadnezzar—king of Babylon used by God to conquer Tyre, Egypt, and Judah (26:7–14; 29:17–30:10)

BACKGROUND AND SETTING

The Babylonian Empire ruled the world during Ezekiel's lifetime. After defeating the other world powers (Assyria, 612–605 B.C., and Egypt, 605 B.C.), Nebuchadnezzar turned his attention toward lesser kingdoms. The defeat of Judah and the destruction of Jerusalem came in three stages. The first occurred in 605 B.C. when the Babylonians besieged Jerusalem and deported a large group of captives, including Daniel, to Babylon. In 598 B.C. Nebuchadnezzar again besieged Jerusalem. The defeat of the city led to a deportation of ten thousand more captives, including Ezekiel, in

597 B.C. A decade later, the Babylonians again invaded Judah and completely destroyed Jerusalem. The last group of survivors was shipped to Babylon in 586 B.C.

The background of Ezekiel's ministry includes religious, domestic, and prophetic factors. Born during King Josiah's reign, Ezekiel experienced the real but short-lived effects of the spiritual revival that swept the land. Josiah's death in 609 B.C. set the stage for Judah to plunge headlong into a final abyss of sin. The last years (609–586 B.C.) saw four kings rise and fall in Judah (Jehoahaz, Jehoiakim, Jehoiachin, and Zedekiah). Ezekiel witnessed the tragedy of superficial religion.

Once in Babylon, life went on for Ezekiel and the other captives more as immigrants than as prisoners of war. They were allowed to farm tracts of land, and they experienced other favorable conditions. Ezekiel owned his own home (3:24; 20:1). There were strong domestic temptations to minimize the tragedy of the loss of the Promised Land.

On the prophetic front, Ezekiel witnessed the work of false prophets who assured the people that God would never allow Jerusalem to fall completely and that they would soon be returned to Judah. They said this despite abundant prophetic evidence to the contrary. Ezekiel's first prophecies confronted the people's false hopes. Jerusalem would be destroyed, and their exile would be long. Ezekiel received word in 586 B.C. that Jerusalem had indeed fallen. His message then changed to offer hope beyond the Exile, when Israel would be restored to her homeland, and the final blessings of the messianic kingdom would follow.

KEY DOCTRINES IN EZEKIEL

The work of angels—who carry out God's program behind the scenes in many ways by demonstrating God's glory (1:5–25; 10:1–22), destroying evil (Genesis 19:12–13), and worshiping God (Deuteronomy 32:43; Isaiah 6:2–4; Revelation 4:6–8)

The sinfulness of Israel (2:3–7; 5:6; 8:9,10; 9:9; 1 Samuel 8:7,8; 2 Kings 21:16; Psalms 10:11; 94:7; Isaiah 6:9; 29:15; Jeremiah 3:25; Micah 3:1–3; 7:3; John 3:20,21; Acts 13:24; Revelation 2:14)

GOD'S CHARACTER IN EZEKIEL

God is glorious—1:28; 3:12,23; 9:3; 10:4,18–19; 11:23; 43:4,5; 44:4
God is holy—1:26–28; 8–11; 43:1–7
God is just—18:25,29; 33:17,20
God is long-suffering—20:17
God is provident—28:2–10
God is wrathful—7:19

CHRIST IN EZEKIEL

Ezekiel contains several passages illustrating Israel's triumph through the work of the Messiah. Christ is pictured as "one of the highest branches of the high cedar" (17:22–24). This messianic prophecy demonstrates Christ's royal lineage connected to David. The branch, used consistently in Scripture to depict the Messiah, shows Christ as a "young twig, a tender one" who will be planted on the mountain of Israel (34:23,24; 37:24,25; Isaiah 4:2; Jeremiah 23:5; 33:15; Zechariah 3:8; 6:12). On this height, Ezekiel pictures Christ as growing into a "majestic cedar" able to protect Israel in its shadow.

Christ also appears as the Shepherd over His sheep (34:11–31). However, Ezekiel also describes the Shepherd's judgment on those who abuse the people of Israel (34:17–24; see Matthew 25:31–46).

KEY WORDS IN EZEKIEL

Son of Man: Hebrew *ben 'adam*—2:1; 3:17; 12:18; 20:46; 29:18; 39:17; 44:5; 47:6—used over one hundred times referring to Ezekiel. It serves both to emphasize the difference between God the Creator and His creatures, and to mark the prophet Ezekiel as a representative member of the human race. Ezekiel's life was a living parable or object lesson to the Hebrew captives in Babylon (compare 1:3; 3:4–7). In word and deed, Ezekiel was a "sign" to the house of Israel (12:6). Jesus adopted the title Son of Man because He, too, is a representative person—the "last Adam" who became a life-giving spirit (see Matthew 8:20; 1 Corinthians 15:45). The title Son of Man also alludes to Daniel's vision of the heavenly being who is "like the Son of Man" (Daniel 7:13). Thus the title highlights the mystery of the Incarnation, the fact that Christ is both divine and human. As the God-man, Jesus became a glorious sign for all of sinful humanity (Luke 2:34).

Idols: Hebrew *gillulim*—6:4; 8:10; 14:6; 20:24; 23:30; 36:18; 44:10—related to a verb which means "to roll" (Genesis 29:3; Joshua 10:18). The word refers to "shapeless things" like stones or tree logs of which idols were made (6:9; 20:39; 22:3; 1 Kings 21:26). The prophet Ezekiel uses this Hebrew term for *idols* nearly forty times, always contemptuously, as these false gods had led Israel away from the true God (14:5). The word *gillulim* may be related to a similar Hebrew expression meaning "dung pellets." Later Jewish commentators mocked the *gillulim* as the "dung idols," idols worthless as dung.

Glory: Hebrew *kabod*—1:28; 3:23; 9:3; 10:18; 31:18; 43:2; 44:4—derived from a Hebrew verb which is used to describe the weight or worthiness of something. It can refer to something negative. For example, in reference to Sodom, it depicts the severe degree of sin that had reached the point of making that city worthy of complete destruction (Genesis 18:20). But usually the word is used to depict greatness and splendor (Genesis 31:1). The noun form is translated *honor* in some instances (1 Kings 3:13). God's glory is described in the Old Testament as taking the form of a cloud (Exodus 24:15–18) and filling the temple (1 Kings 8:11). The appropriate response to God's glory is to reverence Him by bowing before Him, as Ezekiel did (3:23; 43:3).

QUICK OVERVIEW

I. Prophecies of Jerusalem's Ruin (1:1–24:27)
  A. Preparation and Commission of Ezekiel (1:1–3:27)
  B. Proclamation of Jerusalem's Condemnation (4:1–24:27)
II. Prophecies of Retribution to the Nations (25:1–32:32)
  A. Ammon (25:1–7)
  B. Moab (25:8–11)
  C. Edom (25:12–14)
  D. Philistia (25:15–17)
  E. Tyre (26:1–28:19)
  F. Sidon (28:20–24)
    Excursus: The Restoration of Israel (28:25–26)
  G. Egypt (29:1–32:32)
III. Provision for Israel's Repentance (33:1–33)
IV. Prophecies of Israel's Restoration (34:1–48:35)
  A. Regathering of Israel to the Land (34:1–37:28)
  B. Removal of Israel's Enemies from the Land (38:1–39:29)
  C. Reinstatement of True Worship in Israel (40:1–46:24)
  D. Redistribution of the Land in Israel (47:1–48:35)

MEANWHILE, IN OTHER PARTS OF THE WORLD . . .
Aesop, a former Phrygian slave, writes his famous fables. Greek settlers bring the olive tree to Italy.

FREQUENTLY ASKED QUESTIONS

1. When reading Ezekiel, it is sometimes difficult to decide whether the language he uses is descriptive of a literal event or symbolic of an idea or principle. Can we use some examples in Ezekiel to demonstrate the difference?

Ezekiel's life offered his audience a sequence of experiences and actions that became teachable moments. Some of these were scenes in visions that held special significance. For example, the first three chapters of the book report extended visions in which the prophet saw a whirlwind, heavenly creatures, and an edible scroll; he also received his call to the prophetic ministry.

In addition, Ezekiel carried out certain unusual or highly symbolic actions that were intended to picture a message or convey a warning. In 4:1–3, the prophet was directed to carve on a clay tablet and then use an iron plate as a sign about the danger facing Jerusalem. Other acted-out sermons followed: symbolic sleeping postures (4:4–8), siege bread making and baking (4:9–17), and haircutting and burning (5:1–4). God instructed Ezekiel to respond even to the tragedies in his life in such a way that a message was communicated to the people. The prophet learned of his wife's impending death but was told by God that his loss would provide an important lesson the people needed to hear. Just as Ezekiel was not allowed to mourn, the people would not be allowed to mourn when they finally faced the "death" of Jerusalem. "Thus Ezekiel is a sign to you; according to all that he has done you shall do; and when this comes, you shall know that I am the Lord GOD" (24:24).

The unique nature of Ezekiel's approach creates a striking contrast between the clarity of his message and the willful rejection of that message by the people. His ministry removed every excuse.

2. Is there a contradiction between 18:1–20, in which individual responsibility for sin is emphasized, and 21:1–7, in which God applies judgment to both the "righteous and wicked" (verse 4)?

The specific subject of these two passages is quite different. The first deals with the personal consequences and responsibilities that are part of each person's life. No amount of blaming others or offering excuses can remove a person's accountability before God. The second passage deals with the corporate consequences of living in a fallen world. When God chose to use Babylon as a weapon of punishment, He did so fully aware that some people who honored Him would suffer and die as a result. A person's connection with a society means that the good and evil that fall on that society may fall on members who have not directly contributed to the cause.

The principles in 18:1–20 prevail in the end because they describe the way in which God will eventually settle moral accounts. Each person will be held responsible for his or her own life. Only those "in Christ" can face that event with hope.

QUICK STUDY ON EZEKIEL

1. What memorable visions were given to Ezekiel as part of his prophetic role?
2. How does Ezekiel illustrate and describe God's holiness?
3. What differences are there between the false hopes being offered to

the people by Ezekiel's contemporaries and the promises of restoration he preached?

4. What scathing words of judgment did Ezekiel have for leaders?
5. How does Ezekiel emphasize the importance of true worship throughout his book?

DANIEL
Portrait of a Godly Man

What Revelation is to the New Testament prophetically and apocalyptically, Daniel is to the Old Testament.

Long before he faced down a den of lions, Daniel demonstrated courage, wisdom, and integrity. He faced the loss of family and homeland with youthful dignity. He never used outside pressure or the humiliation of slavery to excuse a loss of personal standards. He served God and king without getting the two confused. When he emerged unscathed from the lions' den, the king knew Daniel had received God's protection. The king understood Daniel's ultimate loyalty. Therefore, Daniel left a mark on history because he was a man of God.

AUTHOR AND DATE

Written by Daniel during his ministry, before 530 B.C.

Several internal and external references indicate that Daniel wrote this book (8:15,27; 9:2; 10:2,7; 12:4–5; Ezekiel 14:14,20; 28:3; Matthew 24:15). The name Daniel means "God is my Judge."

Daniel, a teenager from a noble Jewish family, was captured and taken from Israel to Babylon. Daniel made the most of his exile, successfully exalting God by his integrity and service. He quickly rose to the role of statesman by official royal appointment and served as an advisor to kings and a prophet of God in two world empires (Babylonian, 2:48; and Medo-Persian, 6:1–2).

KEY PEOPLE IN DANIEL

Daniel—also called Belteshazzar; Israelite captive who became a royal advisor (1:1–12:13)

Nebuchadnezzar—great king of Babylon; went temporarily insane for not acknowledging God's sovereign position (1:1–4:37)

Shadrach—also called Hananiah; exiled Jew placed in charge of the province of Babylon; saved by God from the "fiery furnace" (1:7; 2:49; 3:8–30)

Meshach—also called Mishael; exiled Jew placed in charge of the province of Babylon; saved by God from the "fiery furnace" (1:7; 2:49; 3:8–30)

Abed-Nego—also called Azariah; exiled Jew placed in charge of the province of Babylon; saved by God from the "fiery furnace" (1:7; 2:49; 3:8–30)

Belshazzar—successor of Nebuchadnezzar as king of Babylon; also used Daniel as an interpreter (5:1–30)

Darius—Persian successor of Belshazzar as ruler of Babylon; his advisors tricked him into sending Daniel to the lions' den (5:31–6:28)

BACKGROUND AND SETTING

The Book of Daniel opens in the heat and humiliation of Nebuchadnezzar's siege of Jerusalem in 605 B.C. With Israel's defeat, treasures from the temple and children from the best families were deported to Babylon. Among them were Daniel and three friends. Daniel's book continues to record the eventual demise of Babylon and the rise of the Medo-Persian Empire.

With the exception of the opening verses, the events recorded by Daniel occurred in Babylon. The captivity of the people of Judah had been prophesied by generations of God's servants. The group that included Daniel was the first of three major deportations from Judah to Babylon. The other two occurred in 597 B.C. and 586 B.C. The defeat came in stages. Eventually, Jerusalem and the beloved temple were destroyed. Daniel provides part of the description of life during the exile years.

Daniel was probably born during the reign of the last righteous king of Judah, Josiah (about 641–609 B.C.). He was captured following King Jehoiakim's defeat. He was old enough to remember his homeland. Writing seventy years later, Daniel's passion for Judah, particularly the temple in Jerusalem, still flowed from his pen.

KEY DOCTRINES IN DANIEL

God's sovereign control (2:20-22,44; 1 Kings 3:9,10; 4:29; Psalm 31:15; Esther 1:13; Job 12:18,22; Hebrews 4:13; James 1:5)

Miracles of God (6:16–23; Exodus 4:3–4; 14:21,22; Joshua 6:6–20; 1 Kings 18:36,38; Matthew 9:5–13; Luke 17:14; John 2:6–10; 3:2; Acts 14:13; 19:11)

The promised Messiah (2:35,45; 7:13,14,27; 9:26; Isaiah 28:16; Ezekiel 1:26; Matthew 16:16–20; 24:30; Luke 20:18; John 3:35,36; 1 Corinthians 15:27; Ephesians 1:22; Philippians 2:9–11)

GOD'S CHARACTER IN DANIEL

God is merciful—9:9
God is powerful—3:17; 4:35
God is provident—4:29–31,37
God is righteous—9:7,16
God is true—4:37
God is wise—2:20–22
God is wrathful—9:16

CHRIST IN DANIEL

In Daniel, Christ is portrayed as a Stone that "became a great mountain and filled the whole earth" (2:35). Daniel's prophecies describe Christ's kingdom as standing forever and "consuming all [other] kingdoms" (2:44). Christ is called the coming Messiah who shall be cut off (9:25–26). Daniel identifies the date of His coming, which corresponds to the date of the triumphal entry of Jesus into Jerusalem.

Daniel also describes Christ as "One like the Son of Man" (7:13). This title was used by Christ Himself (Matthew 16:26; 19:28; 26:64) and demonstrates the humanity of Jesus. However, Daniel describes the Son of Man as one who approaches Almighty God and is given universal authority.

KEY WORDS IN DANIEL

Interpretation: Aramaic *peshar*—2:6,30; 4:7,18; 5:7,15,17; 7:16—literally means "to untie" or "to loose." In other words, Daniel could unravel the mysteries of dreams and visions: He could explain or solve them. Yet he was always quick to give God the credit for his ability (2:28).

Vision: Hebrew *chazon*—8:1,13,15,26; 9:21,24; 11:14—dream or a vision, derived from a common Hebrew verb meaning "to see." Dreams and visions were often recognized by the ancients as revelations from the gods, or from God Himself in the case of the Hebrews (Isaiah 1:1). Daniel received a visionary message from God that spoke about the future of the kingdoms of Persia and Greece. His dream was encoded in symbols which required the interpretive assistance of the angel Gabriel (8:15–27). The author of Proverbs insists that revelation from God is essential to the well-being of a society. Without God's law revealed in Scripture, the foundation of a society crumbles (see Proverbs 29:18).

QUICK OVERVIEW

I. The Personal Background of Daniel (1:1–21)
  A. Conquest of Jerusalem (1:1–2)
  B. Conscription of Jews for Training (1:3–7)
  C. Courage of Four Men during Trials (1:8–16)
  D. Choice of Four Men for Royal Positions (1:17–21)
II. The Prophetic Course of Gentile Dominion (2:1–7:28)
  A. Dilemmas of Nebuchadnezzar (2:1–4:37)
  B. Debauchery and Demise of Belshazzar (5:1–31)
  C. Deliverance of Daniel (6:1–28)
  D. Dream of Daniel (7:1–28)

III. The Prophetic Course of Israel's Destiny (8:1–12:13)
  A. Prophecy of the Ram and Male Goat (8:1–27)
  B. Prophecy of the Seventy Weeks (9:1–27)
  C. Prophecy of Israel's Humiliation and Restoration (10:1–12:13)

MEANWHILE, IN OTHER PARTS OF THE WORLD . . .
Confucius, the Chinese philosopher, is born and later spreads his philosophies around Asia.

FREQUENTLY ASKED QUESTIONS

1. How can those who believe in the miraculous nature of Daniel's prophecies and other miracles answer those skeptics who actually doubt Daniel's authorship and early date because the predictions are so astonishingly accurate?

Confidence in the divine origin of Scripture does not rely on blind faith. There are reasonable explanations and acceptable corroborating evidence that point to the trustworthiness of the Bible. Daniel's use of what is now called Imperial Aramaic in writing the book points to an early date. The Dead Sea scrolls offer evidence that also pushes back the date for Daniel.

When accurate prophecy and possible miracles are discounted by definition as unacceptable, proving Daniel's value becomes challenging. But the problem has little to do with lack of evidence and much to do with willful unbelief. Skeptical interpreters, unwilling to acknowledge supernatural prophecies in Daniel that came to pass (over a hundred in chapter 11 alone that were fulfilled) attempt to replace miraculous foresight with simple observation. They assume that the writer of Daniel was actually living in the time of Antiochus and reported current events in prophetic form. That is, the writer wrote as though he was predicting certain events, when, in reality, he was writing after the events had occurred. For scholars like these, no amount of fulfilled prophecy will be enough to convince. They actually become a reminder to believers that people are not argued into the kingdom of God. The most compelling evidence needs the assistance of God's Spirit in bringing resistant people to genuine faith.

2. Who was the fourth person in the fiery furnace of 3:19–25?

The delivery of Shadrach, Meshach, and Abed-Nego from the flames was an astonishing, miraculous event. The furnace was real, and the flames were hot. The guards who carried the young men close enough to cast them into the furnace were killed. Why complicate this miracle with a fourth person in the furnace? Because the king himself noticed the discrepancy between the number he had thrown into the flames and the number he saw strolling about. The truth usually includes unexpected complications.

The king concluded the fourth person was a heavenly being. He identified the visitor in two different ways: "like the Son of God" (3:25) and "angel" (3:28). When he commanded the three friends to exit the furnace, the king did not extend an invitation to God's special servant.

Viewed from the context of all of Scripture, the fourth person could possibly have been the second person of the Godhead (Jesus Christ) in a preincarnate appearance. For other, similar, Old Testament instances, see Exodus 3:2, Joshua 5:13–15, and Judges 6:11 and following. While the term *angel* is used in these reports, the person had a special connection with the Lord. He wasn't an angel, but the Angel of the Lord. His presence may be startling, but He does not have the stunning and awe-inspiring appearance of an angel. The king saw four men in the furnace. The One who appeared miraculously he identified as the Son of God. It may well have been an inspired exclamation.

3. Why is the Book of Daniel often called the Old Testament equivalent of the New Testament Book of Revelation?

The books of Daniel and Revelation complement one another in many ways. Written about six hundred years apart, they both deal with God's plan in history. Though much of Daniel's prophetic vision had already come true by the time John wrote Revelation, there are two specific ways in which John's work complements Daniel's:

1. Both books deal in part with final events and offer parallel prophetic views of the closing days of the original universe and God's design of the new heaven, earth, and kingdom.
2. Revelation confirms the understanding of prophecy that suggests fulfillment can often happen in stages or waves. For instance, many of the prophecies given to Daniel were fulfilled to some degree in the historic events preceding the life of Christ, but will be ultimately and completely fulfilled in the final events of history.

QUICK STUDY ON DANIEL

1. Develop a biographical sketch of Daniel. What kind of person was he?
2. How would you hold Daniel up as an example for young people?
3. How did Daniel balance responsibility as a government official and his relationship with God?
4. What do Daniel's friends teach us about faith?
5. What prophetic visions in Daniel most pique your curiosity to learn more?
6. What does Daniel teach us about God?

HOSEA
Unconditional Love and Compassion

God loves us so much that He gives us tough assignments, and then He helps us accomplish them.

Can you think of anything God asks you to do that seems hard or unfair? If you can't, you haven't been paying careful enough attention to God's Word. Start with some of Jesus' words: "Love your enemies, bless those who curse you, do good to those who hate you" (Matthew 5:44). Hosea's life offers us a heart-wrenching example of just how hard God's instructions can be and just how great His love remains.

AUTHOR AND DATE

Written by Hosea during his ministry, approximately 755 to 710 B.C.

Our information about Hosea and his family comes entirely from this book. Hosea and Jonah share the distinction of being the only two writing prophets from the northern kingdom of Israel. Hosea had a lengthy ministry of forty-five years, spanning the reigns of seven kings in Israel and four kings in Judah. Both Isaiah and Micah were contemporaries of Hosea, though they only prophesied in Judah.

KEY PEOPLE IN HOSEA

Hosea—prophet to the northern kingdom of Israel; his marriage reflected God's relationship with Israel (1:1–14:9)

Gomer—prostitute who became Hosea's wife (1:3–9)

Their children—Jezreel, Lo-Ruhamah, Lo-Ammi; the name of each child illustrated God's relationship with Israel (1:3–2:1)

BACKGROUND AND SETTING

God called Hosea to be a prophet during the closing days of Jeroboam II. Although Israel was enjoying a time of political peace and material prosperity, the nation was also rife with moral corruption and spiritual bankruptcy. Jeroboam II's death ushered in anarchy and the nation rapidly declined. During the next twenty years leading up to the complete overthrow by Assyria, Israel experienced six short reigns, four of which were ended by assassination.

Hosea spoke for God during those chaotic times. His messages were filled with warnings against Israel's moral waywardness and her violation of the covenant relationship that she had with the Lord. His life illustrated the truth of his messages. Hosea announced the coming judgment.

KEY DOCTRINES IN HOSEA

God's unconditional love for His covenant people (6:1–3; 11:1–12; Deuteronomy 7:7; Job 7:17; Isaiah 49:15,16; John 3:16; Titus 3:4)

GOD'S CHARACTER IN HOSEA

God is accessible—14:2
God is good—3:5
God is kind—2:19
God is loving—11:4
God is merciful—2:23; 14:3–4
God is provident—2:8–9

CHRIST IN HOSEA

Hosea pictures the relationship between a faithful husband (Hosea, God) and an unfaithful bride (Gomer, Israel). The presence of Christ permeates the Book of Hosea as the Lover and redeemer of His people, just as Hosea acted as the redeemer of his wife, Gomer. Hosea also depicts Christ's position as Savior of His people: "And you shall know no God but Me; for there is no savior besides Me" (13:4).

KEY WORDS IN HOSEA

Stumble: Hebrew *kashal*—4:5; 5:5—literally means "to totter," "to trip and fall," or "to stumble." The prophets frequently used this word to describe the spiritual life of the Hebrews. For example, Hosea likens both false prophets and their followers to those who stumble in the dark: They are stumbling over the sin of idolatry and falling to their ruin (4:5; 5:5; Isaiah 3:8). Isaiah warns that those who rely on their own strength will stumble and fall (Isaiah 40:30), but those who are led by the Lord will not stumble (Isaiah 63:13). In fact, the Lord will provide strength to those who have stumbled in the past and now call upon Him (1 Samuel 2:4).

Commit Harlotry: Hebrew *zanah*—2:5; 3:3; 4:15—refers to having illicit sexual relations, especially involving prostitution. Two forms of prostitution were practiced in the ancient world: common prostitution and ritual, or "religious," prostitution, which involved pagan fertility rites. Both forms were strictly forbidden in God's Law (Leviticus 19:29; Deuteronomy 23:17). The Old Testament frequently uses prostitution as an image of the sin of idolatry. Israel was pledged to serve one God (Exodus 20:3), so idolatry was like marital unfaithfulness against the Lord. Hosea actually married a prostitute as a living symbol of God's patience with Israel's infidelities (see chapter 1).

QUICK OVERVIEW

I. Adulterous Wife and Faithful Husband (1:1–3:5)
   A. Hosea and Gomer (1:1–11)
   B. God and Israel (2:1–23)
   C. Both Parties Reconciled (3:1–5)
II. Adulterous Israel and Faithful Lord (4:1–14:9)
   A. Adulterous Israel Found Guilty (4:1–6:3)
   B. Adulterous Israel Put Away (6:4–10:15)
   C. Adulterous Israel Restored to the Lord (11:1–14:9)

MEANWHILE, IN OTHER PARTS OF THE WORLD . . .
The city of Rome is founded (753 B.C.).

FREQUENTLY ASKED QUESTIONS

1. Did God instruct Hosea to actually marry a prostitute?

Some interpreters try to ease the question by suggesting that the marital scenes in the first three chapters of Hosea are merely an allegory of God's relationship to His people. Nothing in the account encourages such an interpretation. Much of the impact of the lesson would have been lost if it had not been literal. Those who object usually do so on the grounds that too many negative moral implications arise if God did ask Hosea to marry such a woman.

The language of God's command in the original provides some support for the chastity of Gomer at the time of her marriage to Hosea. The words "take yourself a wife of harlotry" (1:2) can be understood prophetically (looking to the future). Thus, Gomer would have taken up immoral behavior after marriage. This explanation fits better with God's description of Israel coming out of Egypt as a young woman (2:15; 9:10), who then wandered away from God (11:1). The moral power behind Hosea's action in taking back Gomer after her adultery (chapter 3) depends on the purity of their original union, which she violated. Had Hosea married an acknowledged prostitute, he would have had no grounds for offense over her adultery.

QUICK STUDY ON HOSEA

1. As you read through Hosea, how many different word pictures for God can you find?
2. In how many different ways does Hosea depict God's love for His people?
3. What is the significance of the name of each of Hosea and Gomer's children?
4. On a scale of increasing difficulty, how would you rate God's command to Hosea to marry a prostitute?

5. How would you describe the most difficult action God has asked you to take?

JOEL
The Day of the Lord

Joel provided the scripture for Peter's first sermon (Joel 2:28–32; Acts 2:16–21).

The locusts struck like a firestorm. In their wake they left a devastated nation and a prophet speaking out the "word of the LORD" (1:1). Joel survived the plague of devouring insects and delivered a ringing message of explanation, a bold call to action, and a gift of hope. His timeless words still call those who believe in God to trust even when the waves of devastation and evil seem overwhelming. His message continues to inspire hope, "For the day of the LORD is coming" (2:1).

AUTHOR AND DATE

Written by Joel approximately 835 to 796 B.C.

The author identified himself only as "Joel, the son of Pethuel" (1:1). His father's name is not mentioned in the rest of the Old Testament. Even the internal evidence in the book provides little help in identifying Joel's background. Though tradition claims Joel was from the tribe of Reuben, his language and tone seem to indicate that he was from near Jerusalem.

KEY PEOPLE IN JOEL

Joel—prophet to the people of Judah during the reign of Joash (1:1–3:21)

The people of Judah—the southern kingdom punished for their sins by a locust plague (1:2; 2:1; 3:1–2,19–21)

BACKGROUND AND SETTING

Israel discovered that enemies come in many shapes and sizes. They were almost used to the frequent raids by bandits from Tyre, Sidon, and Philistia (3:2). Suddenly, however, destruction came in a new form—swarms of locusts overran the land like an insatiable army. Judah, suffering the ravages of a long drought, now faced economic devastation (1:7–20).

The national disasters gave Joel a vivid illustration of God's judgment. Although the locusts were a severe judgment on sin, God's future judgments will be far worse. On the Day of the Lord, God will judge His enemies and bless the faithful. Joel did not mention specific sins, but he called the people to genuine repentance. He urged them to "rend your heart, and not your garments" (2:13).

KEY DOCTRINES IN JOEL

The Day of the Lord—a general period of wrath and judgment from the Lord; the day in which God unveils His character (1:15; 2:1-11, 31; 3:16; Isaiah 2:12; 13:6; Ezekiel 13:5; Zephaniah 1:14; Malachi 4:5,6; Acts 2:20; 1 Corinthians 5:5; 2 Corinthians 1:14; 2 Peter 3:10).

GOD'S CHARACTER IN JOEL

God is accessible— 2:12
God is longsuffering—2:13
God is merciful—2:13
God is wrathful—2:12–14

CHRIST IN JOEL

Joel's prophecy described God pouring out His Spirit on the people so that one day, "Your sons and your daughters shall prophesy, your old men shall dream dreams, your young men shall see visions" (2:28–32). Peter quotes from this passage in Joel as the prophecy previewed and sampled at the Day of Pentecost (Acts 2:16–21). The final fulfillment of Joel's prophecy will come in the millennial kingdom of Christ when God's Spirit is poured out on all creation.

KEY WORDS IN JOEL

Spirit: Hebrew *ruach*—2:28—related to a verb meaning "to breathe" or "to blow." It can signify breath (Job 9:18; 19:17), wind (Genesis 8:1; Exodus 10:13), air (Ecclesiastes 1:14; Isaiah 26:18), the breath of life (whether animal or human, see Genesis 6:17; 7:15), disposition or mood (Genesis 41:8; Ezekiel 21:7), an evil or distressing spirit (1 Samuel 16:14–16), or the Spirit of God (Genesis 1:2; Psalm 51:11). The spirit of life is the gift of God to all creatures (Job 12:10; 33:4; Ecclesiastes 12:7). The endowment of God's Holy Spirit is a special gift to believers, which brings spiritual life (Psalms 51:10,11; 143:10), power (Judges 6:34), wisdom and understanding (Isaiah 11:2), and divine revelation that leads to a better understanding of God's Word and His perfect ways (2:28; Isaiah 61:1,2).

QUICK OVERVIEW

I. Day of the Lord Experienced: Historical (1:1–20)
   A. Source of the Message (1:1)
   B. Command to Contemplate the Devastation (1:2–4)
   C. Completeness of the Devastation (1:5–12)
   D. Call to Repent in Light of the Devastation (1:13–20)
II. Day of the Lord Illustrated: Transitional (2:1–17)
   A. Alarm Sounds (2:1)
   B. Army Invades (2:2–11)

C. Admonition to Repent (2:12–17)
III. Day of the Lord Described: Eschatological (2:18—3:21)
A. Introduction (2:18–20)
B. Material Restoration (2:21–27)
C. Spiritual Restoration (2:28–32)
D. National Restoration (3:1–21)

MEANWHILE, IN OTHER PARTS OF THE WORLD . . .
The caste system develops in India, creating centuries of racial segregation.

FREQUENTLY ASKED QUESTIONS

1. Does Joel's account mean the land of Israel was actually overrun with locusts?

Insect plagues such as the one reported by Joel are well known in many parts of the world. Joel described at length the different stages of life, or the different types of locusts (1:4). The vivid details included by Joel increase the usefulness of the event as a teaching tool, but they also emphasize the fact that the prophet saw before his eyes the devastated remains of his nation.

Joel's prophetic vision of the Day of the Lord elevated the tragedy of the locusts to become an illustration of the final devastation. In the prophet's similes, the locusts are "like the appearance of horses" (2:4) and "like mighty men" (2:7), but the underlying message announces the coming Day when real horses and men will arrive on the scene bringing God's judgment.

2. When Peter quoted Joel 2:28–32 at the beginning of his sermon in Acts 2:16–21, how did his interpretation relate to the ultimate fulfillment of that prophecy?

Some have viewed the events of Acts 2 and the destruction of Jerusalem in A.D. 70 as the fulfillment of the Joel passage. Others have reserved its ultimate fulfillment for the final Day of the Lord. It appears likely that the initial pouring out of the Holy Spirit at Pentecost was not a fulfillment but a preview and sample of the Spirit's power and work. The full outpouring of the Holy Spirit will come in the Messiah's kingdom after the Day of the Lord. That was the ultimate vision in Joel's prophecy.

QUICK STUDY ON JOEL

1. What are the details of Joel's description of the plague of locusts?
2. How does Joel use the phrase *day of the Lord*?
3. How do the locusts illustrate the ways God judges nations?
4. What principles of grace and mercy does Joel include in his messages?
5. What does Peter's use of Joel's prophecy teach you about the ministry of the Holy Spirit (Joel 2; Acts 2)?

AMOS
The Necessity of True Justice and Worship

Amos was the only prophet to report his occupation before receiving his divine commission.

God finds people almost anywhere to serve Him. Most of the people we meet in the Bible had minimal formal religious training. God showed little interest in their occupations, positions, or successes in life. He looked for men and women with the right kind of heart. God simply met them wherever they were and gave them directions. We have God's Word because these men and women were faithful. Among the unusual people God called to be His prophets was a lowly shepherd named Amos.

AUTHOR AND DATE

Written by Amos approximately 760 to 750 B.C.

Among the prophets, Amos was a contemporary of Jonah, Hosea, and Isaiah. In his book, Amos gave his readers two significant clues about himself: his hometown (Tekoa) and his occupation (sheepbreeder). At one point he expressed some amazement that God called him to deliver a message. After all, he wrote, "I was no prophet, nor was I a son of a prophet, but I was a sheepbreeder and a tender of sycamore fruit" (7:14).

KEY PEOPLE IN AMOS

Amos—Judean prophet who warned Israel of God's judgment (1:1–9:15)
Amaziah—king of southern kingdom of Judah; son of Joash (7:10–17)
Jeroboam II—wicked king of Israel after his father, Jehoash (7:7–13)

BACKGROUND AND SETTING

Although Amos identified himself as a Judean prophet, God directed him to deliver a message intended for the northern tribes of Israel (7:15). Amos confronted Israel during a time of extended prosperity and security. King Jeroboam II had followed his father Jehoash's example and "restored the territory of Israel" (2 Kings 14:25). The widespread peace throughout the region was due in part to the subdued threat of Assyria following Nineveh's repentance under the preaching of Jonah. On the home front, Amos was called to confront the rampant corruption and moral decay that permeated his society.

KEY DOCTRINES IN AMOS

Genuine worship of God (4:4,5; 5:4–6; Numbers 28:3; Deuteronomy 4:29; 14:28; Leviticus 7:13; 2 Chronicles 15:2; Jeremiah 29:13; Isaiah 55:3,6,7; John 4:20–24; Romans 1:25; Revelation 4:10–11)

Justice—God gave Israel a standard of fairness with their neighbors (5:10–13; 6:12; Deuteronomy 16:20; 1 Kings 22:8; Proverbs 31:9; Isaiah 29:21; 56:1; 59:15; 66:5; Jeremiah 17:16–18; Colossians 4:1; 1 Thessalonians 2:10)

Future restoration of the faithful remnant of Israel (9:7–15; Isaiah 27; 42–44; 65; 66; Jeremiah 30–33; Ezekiel 36; 37; 40–48; Daniel 9:20–27; 12:1–3; Hosea 2:14–23; 14:4–7; Joel 3:19–21; Obadiah 17,21; Micah 7:14–20; Zephaniah 3:14–20; Haggai 2:20–23; Zechariah 13; 14; Malachi 4:1–3)

GOD'S CHARACTER IN AMOS

God is holy—4:2
God is provident—3:6

CHRIST IN AMOS

The references to Christ in the Book of Amos point to the permanent restoration of Israel. The Lord speaks through Amos, declaring, "I will plant them in their land, and no longer shall they be pulled up from the land I have given them" (9:15). Israel's complete restoration and recovery of the land will only be fulfilled during the second advent of Christ the Messiah.

KEY WORDS IN AMOS

Seek: Hebrew *darash*—5:4–6,14—describes the act of seeking, inquiring, or asking. The people of Israel began to worship the false gods of Bethel and Gilgal (5:4). Yet, Amos encourages the people to seek the one, true God. Throughout history, none of those who have sought God in need of safety or forgiveness have been disappointed by Him (Psalms 34:4; 77:2; 1 Chronicles 16:11; 2 Chronicles 30:19).

QUICK OVERVIEW

I. Judgment against the nations (1:1–2:16)
  A. Introduction (1:1–2)
  B. Against Israel's Enemies (1:3–2:3)
  C. Against Judah (2:4–5)
  D. Against Israel (2:6–16)
II. Condemnations against Israel (3:1–6:14)
  A. Sin of Irresponsibility (3:1–15)
  B. Sin of Idolatry (4:1–13)
  C. Sin of Moral/Ethical Decay (5:1–6:14)
III. Visions of Judgment and Restoration (7:1–9:15)
  A. The Lord Will Spare (7:1–6)
  B. The Lord Will No Longer Spare (7:7–9:10)
  C. The Lord Will Restore (9:11–15)

MEANWHILE, IN OTHER PARTS OF THE WORLD . . . **The Greeks begin to settle the area known today as Spain. Greek art also develops, influenced heavily by the Chinese.**

FREQUENTLY ASKED QUESTIONS

1. Since Amos 9:11 was quoted as prophecy in the New Testament, to what degree has it been fulfilled?

This verse promises that the Lord "will raise up the tabernacle of David, which has fallen down." James quoted the same promise in Acts 15:15–16 during the first Jerusalem Council discussion. At stake was whether Gentiles should be allowed into the church without being circumcised. Peter had just reported that God had "visited the Gentiles to take out of them a people for His name" (Acts 15:14). James apparently thought of this passage because it makes the point that part of God's plan all along was to include the Gentiles.

Some, however, have concluded that James's usage indicates the complete fulfillment of Amos's prophecy. They assign the phrase above to Jesus as the greater Son of David, through whom the dynasty of David was reestablished.

It seems better, however, to see James's use as an illustration of Amos's words rather than a fulfillment. The original prophecy contains the key phrase *in that day* (9:11), indicating along with the details of the passage that the prophet was speaking of the Messiah's return at the second advent to sit upon the throne of David. The establishment of the church by the apostles and the inclusion of the Gentiles set the stage for that eventual fulfillment.

QUICK STUDY ON AMOS

1. How does a passage like Amos 5:21–24 get applied or overlooked by Christians in today's world?
2. How does Amos make the point that every person must give an account to God for his or her life?
3. What does Amos have to say to Christians who live in prosperous times?
4. How does Amos's message attack those who would live superficial spiritual lives?
5. To what degree do you seek to live your life by God's standard of justice?

OBADIAH

God's Judgment of Israel's Enemies

Edom ranks as God's least favored nation in the Old Testament.

Eight different books devote space to words of God's condemnation and wrath on the nation of Edom. Among the most serious charges against it were those leveled by Obadiah, in this brief book that bears his name.

AUTHOR AND DATE

Written by Obadiah during King Jehoram's reign in Judah, approximately 848 to 841 B.C.

Obadiah's brief writing contains few clues to indicate much about him. The name Obadiah appears frequently in the Old Testament, but none of those instances refer to the prophet. Geographic allusions seem to indicate that he was from the southern kingdom. Obadiah was probably a contemporary of Elijah and Elisha.

KEY PEOPLE IN OBADIAH

The Edomites—the nation originating from Esau, despised and judged by God (1–16)

BACKGROUND AND SETTING

The Edomites traced their origin to Esau, the firstborn (twin) son of Isaac and Rebekah (Genesis 25:24–26). In the womb, Esau struggled with his brother, Jacob (Genesis 25:22), and they struggled thereafter. Genesis 25:30 explains the origin of the nickname Edom. The term means "red" and refers to the "red stew" Esau chose in exchange for his birthright as the oldest son.

The tensions between Esau and Jacob became part of the heritage of the nations they fathered. Edom resented Israel and repeatedly tried to prevent God's chosen people from entering and keeping the Promised Land. God instructed Israel to be kind to Edom (Deuteronomy 23:7–8). Later, Obadiah was sent to confront Edom with its sins and to convey God's judgment on the nation for its treatment of Israel.

Edom had an ongoing role in biblical history even past the close of the Old Testament. Herod the Great, one of Esau's descendants, tried to kill Jesus shortly after He was born. The Edomites were eventually wiped out during the conquest and destruction of Jerusalem that occurred in A.D. 70. Their extinction fulfilled Obadiah's longstanding prophecies that they would be "cut off forever" (verse 10) and that "no survivor shall remain of the house of Esau" (verse 18).

KEY DOCTRINES IN OBADIAH

The judgment of God on Edom and the nations (verses 1–16; Psalms 83:5–18; 137:7; Isaiah 11:14; 21:11–12; 34:5; 63:1–6; Jeremiah 49:7–22; Lamentations 4:21–22; Ezekiel 25:12–14; 35:1–15; Joel 3:19; Amos 1:11–12; 9:11–12; Malachi 1:2–5)

God's covenant mercy on Israel (verses 17–21; Psalm 22:28; Isaiah 14:1–2; Daniel 2:44; Joel 2:32; Amos 9:8; James 5:20; Revelation 11:15)

GOD'S CHARACTER IN OBADIAH

God is judging—verses 1–16
God is restoring—verses 17–21

CHRIST IN OBADIAH

In Obadiah, Christ both acts as Judge over Israel's enemies (verses 15,16), and Savior of His chosen nation (verses 17–20). Israel's final triumph comes only through Christ Himself.

KEY WORDS IN OBADIAH

Pride: Hebrew *zadon*—verse 3—literally means "to act proudly or presumptuously" (Deuteronomy 18:22; 1 Samuel 17:28). The Old Testament writers used this noun to characterize the prideful nation of Edom (verse 3; Jeremiah 49:16). Pride comes when humans think they can live without God. However, this godlessness only leads to shame and ultimate destruction (Proverbs 11:2; 13:10; Jeremiah 49:16; Ezekiel 7:10–12).

QUICK OVERVIEW

I. God's Judgment on Edom (1–14)
  A. Edom's Punishment (1–9)
  B. Edom's Crimes (10–14)
II. God's Judgment on the Nations (15–16)
III. God's Restoration of Israel (17–21)

MEANWHILE, IN OTHER PARTS OF THE WORLD . . .
Homer writes the classic Greek epics the *Iliad* and the *Odyssey*.

FREQUENTLY ASKED QUESTIONS

1. The striking similarity between Obadiah verses 1–9 and Jeremiah 49:7–22 brings up the question: Who borrowed from whom?

Assuming there was not a third common source, it appears that Jeremiah borrowed, where appropriate, from Obadiah. This conclusion rests on the observation that the verses in question form a single unit in Obadiah, while in Jeremiah, they are scattered among other verses.

2. Why did God include such a short book in Scripture?

First, Obadiah is not the shortest book in Scripture. Two others, in fact, are shorter: 2 John (13 verses) and 3 John (14 verses). These short books should not be overlooked because of their length. God manages to communicate a great deal in a small amount of space.

Second, Obadiah and other short books offer highly concentrated views of single issues. The prophet may have had years of ministry and dozens of messages, but he had one vision. God gave him a powerful warning to deliver, and even the echoes of its truth can offer hope today. In Obadiah's closing words, "And the kingdom shall be the LORD'S" (21b).

QUICK STUDY ON OBADIAH

1. What are God's specific charges against the Edomites?
2. How does God describe His own attitude toward Israel in Obadiah?
3. What illustrations of pride does Obadiah include?
4. How do the warnings in Obadiah about pride apply at the personal level in your life?

JONAH
The Reluctant Missionary

One of the clearest Old Testament examples of God's love for the world

God often works through people in spite of themselves. Jonah was a reluctant prophet. He tried to run from his mission. He tried to hide from God. He even offered himself as a noble sacrifice. But he discovered that even attempted suicide couldn't get him out of God's plans. God offered him an opportunity to learn to love the people of Nineveh by having him preach a message that transformed the city. Jonah chose to hold on to his hatred. He resented the mercy God poured out on Nineveh because he didn't fully appreciate the mercy God poured out on him. Jonah's account ends with a haunting rhetorical question from God, "Should I not pity Nineveh?"

AUTHOR AND DATE

Written or told by Jonah during his ministry, approximately 793 to 758 B.C.

Although Jonah never speaks in the first person in this book, there are good reasons to think he was the author. First, the Old Testament offers other examples of authors writing in the third person (Moses—Exodus 11:3; Samuel—1 Samuel 12:11). Second, certain intimate autobiographical material in this book could only have come from Jonah himself. The fish held no other witnesses. Even the introductory verse that establishes the third person account is characteristic of most of the prophets' writings.

A reference to Jonah in 2 Kings 14:25 establishes his hometown as Gath Hepher, near Nazareth. His ministry years coincide with the reign of Jeroboam II (about 793–758 B.C.). Jonah preceded Amos as a prophet to the northern tribes of Israel.

KEY PEOPLE IN JONAH

Jonah—reluctant missionary to the Ninevites; needed to be swallowed by a whale in order to comply with God's command (1:1–9:9)

The captain and crew of Jonah's getaway ship—tried to avoid killing Jonah; threw Jonah overboard to stop the storm (1:5–16)

BACKGROUND AND SETTING

Jonah represented God to the ten northern tribes during a time of relative peace and prosperity. He and Amos shared very similar political and cultural conditions. Both Syria and Assyria were weak, allowing King Jeroboam II to enlarge the northern borders of Israel.

Spiritually, however, the nation was in poverty. Genuine faith in God had been forgotten and replaced by religious rituals. Idolatry had rapidly increased. Justice had become perverted and meaningless. Peace and wealth were being misused to bring about spiritual, moral, and ethical bankruptcy.

God's judgment was devastating. He eventually allowed the Assyrians to bring destruction and captivity to the northern kingdom in 722 B.C., years after Jonah's ministry.

Jonah's mission to Nineveh probably occurred close to the end of his active years. It appears that God arranged for a couple of plagues (765 and 759 B.C.) and a solar eclipse (763 B.C.) that may have contributed to the softening of Nineveh for Jonah's message.

KEY DOCTRINES IN JONAH

The mercy of God towards all nations (4:2,10,11; Exodus 34:6; Numbers 14:18; Psalm 86:5,15; Joel 2:13; 1 Timothy 2:4; 2 Peter 3:9)

God's sovereign rule (1:4,9,17; 2:10; 4:6,7; Job 42:2; Psalms 107:25; 146:6; Nehemiah 9:6; Matthew 10:29–30; Acts 17:24; Romans 8:28)

GOD'S CHARACTER IN JONAH

God is merciful—4:2,10–11
God is provident—1:4,15
God is wrathful—4:2

CHRIST IN JONAH

Jonah attains notoriety as the only prophet whom Jesus Christ identified with Himself (Matthew 12:39–41). Just as Jonah remained three days and three nights in the belly of the whale, Christ uses this experience as an example of the three days and three nights He would be "in the heart of the earth" after His crucifixion.

KEY WORDS IN JONAH

Prepared: Hebrew *manah*—1:17; 4:6–8—describes God's sovereign power to bring about His will. Literally, *manah* signifies the power to appoint or ordain. God's great power in the Book of Jonah in the *preparing* of the fish, the plant, and the worm, illustrated His sovereignty over all His creation. God used these created animals to reveal to Jonah His mercy and love for all people. Through all Jonah's plans, Jonah's path was carefully guided by God (see 4:6–8).

Slow to Anger: Hebrew *ʾerek ʾappayim*—4:2—idiom meaning "the nose burns" or "the nose becomes hot" characterizing the heavy breathing of an angry person (Genesis 30:2; Exodus 4:14). In the Old Testament, the word for anger was directly related to the nose. Thus, when the Old Testament writers describe God as "slow to anger," they literally say "long of nose" (Psalms 86:15; 103:8). The Hebrew idiom for slow to anger reveals God's great mercy and patience (Psalm 145:8; Joel 2:13).

QUICK OVERVIEW

I. Running from God's Will (1:1–17)
   A. The Commission of Jonah (1:1–2)
   B. The Flight of Jonah (1:3)
   C. The Pursuit of Jonah (1:4–16)
   D. The Preservation of Jonah (1:17)
II. Submitting to God's Will (2:1–10)
   A. The Helplessness of Jonah (2:1–3)
   B. The Prayer of Jonah (2:4–7)
   C. The Repentance of Jonah (2:8–9)
   D. The Deliverance of Jonah (2:10)
III. Fulfilling God's Will (3:1–10)
   A. The Commission Renewed (3:1–2)
   B. The Prophet Obeys (3:3–4)
   C. The City Repents (3:5–9)
   D. The Lord Relents (3:10)
IV. Questioning God's Will (4:1–11)
   A. The Prophet Displeased (4:1–5)
   B. The Prophet Rebuked (4:6–11)

MEANWHILE, IN OTHER PARTS OF THE WORLD . . .
The first authenticated solar eclipse in Chinese history was documented on September 6, 775 B.C.

FREQUENTLY ASKED QUESTIONS

1. Were Jonah's adventures some kind of mythical story, or did the prophet actually experience those amazing miracles?

Those who have a problem with the idea of miracles have a great problem with Jonah. The miracles in this book happen on a grand scale: an implacable storm; survival inside a large fish; repentance by the leader of a recognized world power. These are not for the timid in faith. Some skeptics and critics simply deny Jonah's historical validity. Others attempt to offer substitute spiritual lessons by making parts of Jonah allegorical or interpreting the whole book as a parable.

Two factors speak strongly in favor of taking Jonah at face value: 1) The role of the miracles in Jonah offended the central character. Those miracles made him look cowardly, mean, and bitter. Given the constant tension between the prophet and the mission God had given to him, the greatest miracle of all is probably that Jonah eventually recorded these God-glorifying and prophet-humiliating historical events. 2) Jesus referred to Jonah several times as a historical person, not a parable (see Matthew 12:38–44; 16:4; Luke 11:29–32).

2. Why did God care about what happened to Nineveh?

That was precisely Jonah's question. He certainly did not care about Nineveh. He hoped and prayed that God would carry out His intention to overthrow the city. But Jonah also knew that God usually gives warnings as opportunities. Jonah did not want Nineveh to have another chance.

Jonah hated Nineveh and its reputation. He resented the suffering that had befallen his own people through the rulers of Nineveh. He failed to identify with the people of Nineveh, seeing them simply as a faceless enemy. God offered Jonah a priceless lesson in compassion. He stirred up Jonah's sense of outrage through a plant and then explained to the prophet that He had the divine right to exercise compassion on the many thousands in Nineveh who were ignorant of their own condition (4:1–11).

QUICK STUDY ON JONAH

1. Why didn't Jonah want to go to Nineveh?
2. Describe the ups and downs of Jonah's attitude throughout this book.
3. Why does God rescue Jonah in spite of the prophet's blatant disobedience?
4. What insights does the Book of Jonah give about God's love?
5. In what specific ways can you identify with Jonah? What would you like to avoid about his experiences?

MICAH
Who Is like God?

The book that told the wise men where to find Jesus.

"Order in the court!" The words have a powerful effect on a room full of people. The words demand attention. The judge is about to render judgment.

The Book of Micah reads like a court document. Micah's prophecies record God's judgment on three groups of plaintiffs: 1) Samaria and Jerusalem; 2) the leaders of Israel and Judah; 3) the people in Israel and Judah. God holds nations, leaders, and individuals responsible for their failure to acknowledge or obey Him. Micah's words ring with an urgency and truth that still apply today.

AUTHOR AND DATE

Written by Micah, approximately 735 to 710 B.C.

The first verse names Micah as the author. Little else is known about this prophet of God, but his name (which means "Who is like the Lord?") suggests a godly heritage. Micah noted his hometown as Moresheth (1:1), a village about twenty-five miles southwest of Jerusalem. This scant information implies that Micah, like Amos, grew up in a rural area, removed from the powerful and influential. He, like Amos, had been chosen by God (3:8) to deliver a message of judgment to the princes and citizens of Jerusalem and Samaria.

KEY PEOPLE IN MICAH

The people of Israel—the northern kingdom which was about to fall into Assyrian captivity (1:2–7:20)

BACKGROUND AND SETTING

The fact that Micah only mentions the names of the kings of Judah probably indicates the reality of Samaria's defeat in 722 B.C. The prophet did include the northern kingdom in some of his messages (1:5–7), but his attention was primarily directed toward the southern kingdom of Judah. Although Judah's days were also numbered, the nation outlasted her northern neighbor by several decades.

During Micah's lifetime, much of the economic prosperity and political influence that had marked the reign of Jeroboam II soon faded. Conditions between the northern and southern kingdoms rapidly deteriorated. Although Micah's ministry was directed at both houses of God's people, the divisions between them created constant hostility. At one point Israel and Syria invaded Judah and took wicked King Ahaz hostage for a while

(2 Chronicles 28:5–16; Isaiah 7:1–2). After the fall of the northern kingdom, God used Hezekiah, the good king of Judah, to lead Judah back to true worship.

Micah witnessed and influenced all of this. His message from God may not have turned the people away from coming judgment, but some listened. God's hopeful notes in Micah's words about the future (5:2) kept alive the hope of God's promise. Centuries later, when wise men visited Jerusalem looking for a child born to be the king of the Jews, the priests knew where to look for the prophecy of the birthplace of God's Messiah (5:2).

KEY DOCTRINES IN MICAH

God's judgment of sin (1:2–2:5; 1 Chronicles 16:33; Psalm 96:13; Ecclesiastes 3:17; Matthew 7:22–23; John 12:48; Romans 2:12; 2 Timothy 4:1; Revelation 20:12)

God's covenant with Israel's forefathers (7:20; Genesis 15:7–18; 17:2–14,19,21; 26:3–4; 28:13,14; Exodus 6:4; 2 Samuel 23:5; 1 Chronicles 16:16–17; Psalm 89:3–4; Luke 1:72–75; Acts 3:25; Galatians 3:16)

GOD'S CHARACTER IN MICAH

God is long-suffering—7:1
God is merciful—7:18,20
God is provident—5:2
God is righteous—6:4–5; 7:9
God is true—7:20
God is unified—7:18
God is wrathful—7:9,11

CHRIST IN MICAH

Micah provides one of the most significant prophecies in the Bible referring to Christ's birthplace and eternality: "But you, Bethlehem Ephrathah, though you are little among the thousands of Judah, yet out of you shall come forth to Me the One to be Ruler in Israel, whose goings forth are from the old, from everlasting" (5:2). This passage was used by the scribes and chief priest to answer Herod's query about the birthplace of Jesus (Matthew 2:6). Micah 7:6 was also used by Jesus to explain the nature of His coming (Matthew 10:35,36).

KEY WORDS IN MICAH

Complaint: Hebrew *rib*—6:2—can mean "dispute" or "quarrel" in the sense of a feud (Judges 12:2), "controversy" or "strife" (Proverbs 17:14; 18:6) prompted by a rebellious spirit (Numbers 20:13; Proverbs 17:14; 18:6), or even a "legal case" or "lawsuit" (Job 31:13,35; Jeremiah 11:20). The prophets frequently used this word as a technical, legal term in contexts pertaining to the Lord's covenant relationship with Israel (Jeremiah 25:31; Joshua 4:1; 12:2). In this chapter, Micah was informing Judah that God had registered a formal, legal complaint against His people. He was ordering them to stand trial for violating covenant stipulations forbidding idolatry and requiring social justice (6:2–16).

Compassion: Hebrew *raham*—7:19—translated here as *compassion,* means "to love from the womb" and is also frequently translated *mercy* (Isaiah 14:1). The noun form of this verb means "womb," and consequently this verb depicts the tender love of a mother for her own helpless child (1 Kings 3:26). "From the womb" speaks of the depth of emotion associated with this expression of love. God loves His people with a deep compassion and love that is almost beyond description. God used a form of this Hebrew word to reveal His character and name to Moses: "And the Lord passed before him and proclaimed: 'The LORD, the LORD God, merciful and gracious, longsuffering, and abounding in goodness and truth'" (Exodus 34:6).

QUICK OVERVIEW

I. Superscription (1:1)

II. God Gathers to Judge and Deliver (1:2–2:13)
- A. Samaria and Judah Punished (1:2–16)
- B. Oppressors Judged (2:1–5)
- C. False Prophets Renounced (2:6–11)
- D. Promise of Deliverance (2:12–13)

III. God Judges Rulers and Comes to Deliver (3:1–5:15)
- A. The Contemporary Leaders Are Guilty (3:1–12)
- B. The Coming Leader Will Deliver and Restore (4:1–5:15)

IV. God Brings Indictments and Ultimate Deliverance (6:1–7:20)
- A. Messages of Reproof and Lament (6:1–7:6)
- B. Messages of Confidence and Victory (7:7–20)

MEANWHILE, IN OTHER PARTS OF THE WORLD . . .
The Celtic people begin to move southward from the country known today as Scotland to settle the rest of Great Britain.

FREQUENTLY ASKED QUESTIONS

1. How is a book like Micah used in the New Testament?

Twice in the Book of Matthew, passages from Micah play a significant part in events. In Matthew 2:6, the chief priests and scribes quote 5:2 in response to Herod's query about the birthplace of the Messiah. Later, in Matthew 10:35–36, Jesus quotes 7:6 while commissioning His disciples. The people in the New Testament were intimately familiar with the Old Testament prophets. Their writing and thinking were permeated with the phrases as well as the predictions that God had given to those messengers of old.

QUICK STUDY ON MICAH

1. If the religious scholars of Jesus' day knew the prophecy about the Messiah and Bethlehem, why didn't they believe Jesus was the Savior?
2. Does Micah 6:6–8 teach that we can please God and gain eternal favor by being good?
3. What is the purpose of living to please God?
4. How did Micah confront the national and personal oppression that was rampant in his day?
5. How did Micah confront false faith in his own society? What would he say about today?

NAHUM
Postponed Judgment Applied

Jonah's prophecy did come true!

God gave the ancient city of Nineveh an extra one hundred years of life. Jonah's reluctant missionary visit resulted in a genuine repentance by the city. She avoided destruction but, unfortunately, the change wasn't lasting. The city and the empire she represented soon continued on their evil ways. A century later, God announced her final judgment through the prophet Nahum.

AUTHOR AND DATE

Written by Nahum, approximately 650 B.C.

As is true of most of the prophets, we know little about Nahum's life. This fact highlights the importance of their message. Their primary purpose was to speak for God, not about themselves. In Nahum's case, even the location of his hometown remains a mystery. He called himself an Elkoshite (1:1), but no location fitting that name has been clearly identified. Nahum could have been a survivor living in Judah or an exile living in Assyria.

KEY PEOPLE IN NAHUM

The people of Nineveh—Assyrians who returned to evil and were destined for destruction (2:1–3:19)

BACKGROUND AND SETTING

A century after Nineveh repented at the preaching of Jonah, the Assyrian capital returned to idolatry, violence, and arrogance (3:1–4). Assyria was at the height of her power, quickly forgetting the humiliation of Sennacherib's defeat (701 B.C.) at Jerusalem (Isaiah 37:36–38). Assyria's borders extended all the way to Egypt. Conquered peoples were moved from the homelands to other places, making them easier to control. Samaria and Galilee were resettled by exiles in 670 B.C.

Assyria seemed like an unstoppable force, yet God announced to the world through Nahum and other prophets that the nation's days were numbered. Nineveh's destruction happened just as God had prophesied.

KEY DOCTRINES IN NAHUM

God's judgment—the sovereign God would bring vengeance upon those who violated His law (1:8,14; 3:5–7; Exodus 20:5; Deuteronomy 28:41; Job 12:23; Ezekiel 39:23; Joel 3:19; Amos 3:6; Acts 17:31; Romans 2:16; Revelation 6:17)

God's loving-kindness toward the faithful (1:7,12,13,15; 2:2; Numbers 6:22–27; Psalm 46:1; Isaiah 33:2–4; 37:3–7,29–38; Matthew 11:28–29; 19:13–14; 2 Timothy 2:24; Titus 3:4; 1 John 4:11)

GOD'S CHARACTER IN NAHUM

God is good—1:7
God is jealous—1:2
God is powerful—1:3
God is provident—1:4
God is sovereign—1:2–5
God is wrathful—1:2–3,6

CHRIST IN NAHUM

Nahum's portrayal of God's attributes also describes the person of Christ in His future coming. Christ first came to earth as the promised Messiah drawing the faithful unto Himself. Nahum depicts God's protection of the faithful revealing, "The LORD is good, a stronghold in the day of trouble" (1:7). However, the second coming of Christ will bring judgment as Christ takes "vengeance on His adversaries" (1:2).

KEY WORDS IN NAHUM

Jealous: Hebrew *qanno'*—1:2—related to a root word that can mean "to be eager, zealous for" (1 Kings 19:10,14), or even "to be furious" (Zechariah 8:2). One of God's names is Jealous (Exodus 34:14). When the expression "the LORD your God is a jealous God" is used in the Old Testament, it is usually associated with an injunction against idol worship (Exodus 20:5; Deuteronomy 4:24; 5:9; 6:15). God's jealousy for His people is a claim for exclusive allegiance rooted in His holiness (Joshua 24:19) and His role as their Creator and Redeemer (Psalms 95:6–7; 96:2–5). We tend to associate jealousy with a self-serving emotion that usually results from feelings of inadequacy. God's jealousy, in contrast, proceeds from His holiness. Because He alone is the Holy One (see Isaiah 6:3; 40:25), He will tolerate no rival (Exodus 20:5).

QUICK OVERVIEW

I. Superscription (1:1)
II. Destruction of Nineveh Declared (1:2–15)
  A. God's Power Illustrated (1:2–8)
  B. God's Punishment Stated (1:9–15)
III. Destruction of Nineveh Detailed (2:1–13)
  A. The City Is Assaulted (2:1–10)
  B. The City Is Discredited (2:11–13)

IV. Destruction of Nineveh Demanded (3:1–19)
   A. The First Charge (3:1–3)
   B. The Second Charge (3:4–7)
   C. The Third Charge (3:8–19)

MEANWHILE, IN OTHER PARTS OF THE WORLD . . .
Japan becomes a recognized nation (660 B.C.).

QUICK STUDY ON NAHUM

1. How is the entire Book of Nahum an example of God's patience?
2. What are God's charges against the city of Nineveh?
3. Why does God call Himself a jealous God?
4. What examples of God's sovereignty are included in Nahum?
5. What is your own perspective on the possibility of God's judgment on your life?

HABAKKUK
The Just Shall Live by Faith

Its writer holds a place of dubious honor
as the last prophet sent to Judah before the Exile.

"It's just not fair!" Arguments between friends, within families, and between nations often boil down to an issue of fairness. One of the unwritten basic assumptions about life is that it ought to be fair. This assumption leads us into dangerous territory when it comes between us and God. The prophet Habakkuk asked God two very familiar questions about fairness:

- Why aren't things fair, God?
- Why don't you do something when things aren't fair, God?

God's answers and Habakkuk's conclusions make his book a valuable spiritual resource.

AUTHOR AND DATE

Written by Habakkuk, approximately 615 to 605 B.C.

As with most of the minor prophets, little is known about Habakkuk except minimal internal information in his book. His simple introduction as "the prophet Habakkuk" may imply that he was a well-known prophet of his day. Habakkuk was a contemporary of Jeremiah, Ezekiel, Daniel, and Zephaniah.

KEY PEOPLE IN HABAKKUK

Habakkuk—the last prophet sent to Judah before its fall into Babylonian captivity (1:1–3:19)

The Chaldeans—Babylonians raised up by God to punish Judah (1:6–11; 2:2–20)

BACKGROUND AND SETTING

Habakkuk prophesied during the final days of the Assyrian Empire and the beginning of the Babylonian domination of the world. The most recognizable world figure of his time was Nebuchadnezzar, prince and then king of Babylon. The Babylonians began their ascent to power in 626 B.C. and by 605 B.C. had defeated their primary enemies.

Judah got involved in this chapter of world events when King Josiah challenged Assyria's ally Egypt in the battle of Megiddo in 609 B.C. Josiah was killed during the fighting. Although Josiah had instituted significant spiritual reforms in Judah (2 Kings 22–23), his successors did not follow his godly direction. The nation quickly reverted to evil ways (Jeremiah 22:13–19), causing Habakkuk to question God's silence and apparent lack of punitive action to purge His covenant people.

KEY DOCTRINES IN HABAKKUK

The nature of God's judgment—God used the Babylonians to judge the people of Judah (1:5–11; 2:2–20; Deuteronomy 28:49,50; 2 Kings 24:2; 2 Chronicles 36:17; Jeremiah 4:11–13; Ezekiel 7:24; 21:31; Micah 4:10; Acts 17:31; Romans 2:16; Revelation 6:17)

Proper worship of God—God is not to be worshiped merely because of temporal blessings but for His own sake (3:17–19; Deuteronomy 28:1–14; Psalm 97:12; Isaiah 12:2; 41:16; 61:10; Luke 1:47; Philippians 4:4; Revelation 4:10–11)

Justification by faith—Humans are saved through faith in God alone and not through works (2:4; Genesis 15:6; Leviticus 18:5; Isaiah 45:25; 50:8,9; Zechariah 3:4–5; John 3:36; Romans 1:17; 5:1; Galatians 3:11; Colossians 1:22,23; Hebrews 3:12–14; 10:38)

GOD'S CHARACTER IN HABAKKUK

God is glorious—2:14
God is wrathful—3:2

CHRIST IN HABAKKUK

Although Habakkuk never mentions Christ's name, he rejoices in the saving ministry of Jesus as the "God of my salvation" (3:18). Habakkuk also foreshadows Christ's coming salvation: "You went forth for the salvation of Your people; For salvation with Your Anointed" (3:13). The Old and New Testaments clearly point to Christ as the Anointed One (Psalm 28:8; Daniel 9:25,26; Acts 4:27; 10:38; Hebrews 1:9).

KEY WORDS IN HABAKKUK

Image: Hebrew *pesel*—2:18—related to a verbal root meaning "to hew out stone" or "to cut or carve wood" (see Exodus 34:4). A *pesel* is an image or idol in the likeness of a human being or animal made from stone, wood, or metal. God prohibited the Hebrews from making such idols at Mount Sinai (Exodus 20:4). God intended the lack of images among the Hebrews to be one distinguishing feature of their true religion. Tragically, Israel followed the example of their pagan neighbors and worshiped carved images (Judges 18:30; 2 Chronicles 33:7). The psalmist describes such images as worthless and those who worship them as shameful (Psalm 97:7). Both Isaiah (Isaiah 40:19,20; 44:9–20) and Habakkuk (2:18,19) mock those who would put their trust in images made with mere human hands. They have no capacity to see, hear, speak, or do anything for their devotees.

QUICK OVERVIEW

I. Superscription (1:1)
II. The Prophet's Perplexities (1:2–2:20)
  A. Habakkuk's First Complaint (1:2–4)
  B. God's First Response (1:5–11)
  C. Habakkuk's Second Complaint (1:12–2:1)
  D. God's Second Response (2:2–20)
III. The Prophet's Prayer (3:1–19)
  A. Petition for God's Mercy (3:1–2)
  B. Praise of God's Power (3:3–15)
  C. Promise of God's Sufficiency (3:16–19)

MEANWHILE, IN OTHER PARTS OF THE WORLD . . .
The Temple of Artemis, one of the seven wonders of the world, is built in Ephesus.

FREQUENTLY ASKED QUESTIONS

1. In what ways do God's answers to Habakkuk's deep questions offer help to modern people reading his book?

Habakkuk certainly expressed some of the most fundamental questions in all of life. God's answers provide crucial foundation stones on which to build a proper understanding of God's character and sovereign actions in history. Ultimately, Habakkuk demonstrates that life's meaning does not rest in finely argued intellectual answers, but in trusting God. The prophet echoes the theme of genuine holy living: "The just shall live by his faith" (2:4). Those who read the prophet today will find a fellow traveler who may well lead them to trusting the God he came to trust.

2. What impact does Habakkuk have on the New Testament?

The writers of the New Testament quoted Habakkuk in a way that gave him importance. The writer of Hebrews quoted 2:4 to amplify the believer's need to remain strong and faithful in the midst of affliction and trials (Hebrews 10:38). The apostle Paul, on the other hand, employed that same verse twice (Romans 1:17; Galatians 3:11) to accentuate the doctrine of justification by faith. Though these different uses might indicate an interpretive conflict, such is not the case. All of these references point beyond a single act of faith to include the continuity of faith. Faith in the Scriptures is not a one-time act but a way of life. The true believer, declared righteous by God, will persevere in faith throughout his or her life (Colossians 1:22–23; Hebrews 3:12–14). The believer will trust the sovereign God who only does what is right.

QUICK STUDY ON HABAKKUK

1. How does God answer Habakkuk's first question: Why aren't things fair, God?
2. How does God answer the prophet's second question: Why don't you do something when things aren't fair, God?
3. When you experience struggles and doubt, how do you resolve them?
4. In what ways is Habakkuk a tribute to the sovereignty of God?
5. For Habakkuk, what is the ultimate source of hope in this world?

ZEPHANIAH
Shelter in the Midst of Judgment

Zephaniah was the only prophet descended from royal blood.

Standing on a busy corner, the prophet lifts a rough sign inscribed with the short message: "Repent, for the end is near!" People rush by. They don't notice, or don't want to notice the message. God has become someone they can ignore.

Zephaniah's moment in history was an ancient version of that scene. He repeatedly warned the people: "The Day of the Lord is at hand!" He used this expression more than did any other prophet. His work set the stage for a last-minute revival under Josiah that proved short-lived. Within a few years, Judah was defeated and sent into exile. People who ignored God discovered they could not ignore the Day of the Lord.

AUTHOR AND DATE

Written by Zephaniah approximately 635 to 625 B.C.

Among the few facts about Zephaniah included in Scripture, one stands out: The prophet claimed a place in the royal lineage. He appears to have been the only prophet descended from royal blood. Zephaniah was a contemporary of the prophet Jeremiah.

KEY PEOPLE IN ZEPHANIAH

Zephaniah—prophet who warned Judah of coming judgment and also future hope (1:1–3:20)

The people of Judah—led by King Josiah to repent but eventually fell into Babylonian captivity (1:2–2:3; 3:1–20)

BACKGROUND AND SETTING

Zephaniah prophesied during a time of almost universal upheaval. The rise of the Babylonians and the fall of the Assyrians left much of the world between conquerors. Judah experienced relative freedom for the first time in fifty years. King Josiah was able to initiate certain reforms that eventually led to a brief spiritual revival in Judah.

The warnings of impending judgment voiced by Zephaniah probably found little response from the people. The effects of half a century of evil leadership left a nation steeped in sin, and King Josiah's reforms resulted in little more than surface changes. Even the discovery of the Law of God in the temple rubble that occurred after Zephaniah, while it energized Josiah's efforts, had little long-term effect on the attitudes of the people.

KEY DOCTRINES IN ZEPHANIAH

The Day of the Lord (1:7,14–16,18; 3:8; Isaiah 2:12; 13:6,9; Ezekiel 13:5; 20:3; Joel 1:15; 2:1,11,31; 3:14; Amos 5:18–20; Obadiah 1–21; Zechariah 14:1; Malachi 4:5)

God's grace in the midst of judgment (2:3; 3:14–20; Psalm 45:2; Isaiah 26:20; Joel 2:14; Amos 5:14–15; Zechariah 12:10; Romans 5:21; 2 Corinthians 12:9; Hebrews 4:16)

Salvation for the believing remnant (2:7; 3:9–20; Isaiah 35:4; 45:17; Jeremiah 29:14; Micah 5:7–8; Zechariah 9:16; John 3:16; Luke 1:68; Acts 5:31; Romans 11:26)

GOD'S CHARACTER IN ZEPHANIAH

God is judging—1:2–3; 2:2; 3:6–7
God is just—3:5
God is loving—3:17
God is wrathful—1:14–18

CHRIST IN ZEPHANIAH

Even though Zephaniah explicitly portrays the judgment of God, Christ is present as the "Mighty One" who will bring salvation to the earth (3:17). Christ Himself made allusions to Zephaniah (1:3, see Matthew 13:41; and 1:15, see Matthew 24:29), further connecting the prophecies of Zephaniah and the second coming of Christ.

KEY WORDS IN ZEPHANIAH

Meek: Hebrew *'anav*—2:3—may be translated *humble* (Psalm 34:2) or *meek* (Psalm 37:11; see also Matthew 5:5) and is derived from a verb meaning "to be afflicted" or "to be bowed down" (Psalm 116:10). Forms of this word occur twice in 2:3: first translated as *meek* and then as *humility*. The word frequently refers to the poor or oppressed (see Proverbs 14:21; Amos 2:7). But it also signifies strength of character in enduring suffering without resentment. Such character is rooted in a strong faith in God and His goodness and a steadfast submission to the will of God.

QUICK OVERVIEW

I. Superscription (1:1)
II. The Lord's Judgment (1:2–3:8)
  A. On the Whole Earth (1:2–3)
  B. On Judah (1:4–2:3)
  C. On the Surrounding Nations (2:4–15)
  D. On Jerusalem (3:1–7)
  E. On All Nations (3:8)

III. The Lord's Blessing (3:9–20)
  A. For the Nations (3:9–10)
  B. For Judah (3:11–20)

MEANWHILE, IN OTHER PARTS OF THE WORLD . . .
In India, Brahminic religion develops with the completion of the Vedas, sacred writings of religion, education, and philosophy.

FREQUENTLY ASKED QUESTIONS

1. How much validity can be given to the interpretation that takes Zephaniah's phrase "I will restore to the peoples a pure language" (3:9) as a prophetic anticipation of God's restoration of a universal language?

Although some have taken this phrase to refer to an undoing of God's decision to confuse the languages at the Tower of Babel (Genesis 11:1–9), the context of the phrase does not lend much support to that interpretation. True, the word *language* in Zephaniah is identical to the one used in Genesis. The overall context, however, indicates that Zephaniah had in mind a purification of heart and life (Zephaniah 3:13). Throughout the Old Testament, the word *language* is most often translated "lip." When combined with "pure," the reference to speech refers to an inward cleansing from sin (Isaiah 6:5) that is demonstrated in speech (Matthew 12:34). This kind of speech is purified by the removal of the names of false gods from their lips (Hosea 2:17). It is unlikely that Zephaniah had in mind a single world language.

QUICK STUDY ON ZEPHANIAH

1. Why does God indicate such a strong reaction towards idol worship?
2. What aspects does Zephaniah reveal about what he calls the "day of joy"?
3. In the Book of Zephaniah, what does mercy have to do with judgment?
4. In what ways were the lives of the people being offensive to God?
5. As you read God's indictment of the people, think about ways in which people today practice the same attitudes toward God.

HAGGAI
God Will Have His Temple

Haggai helped motivate the exiles to rebuild the temple.

Solomon said it well, "A time for every purpose under heaven" (Ecclesiastes 3:1). This rule applies particularly when the purpose at hand comes from God. His plans take precedence. Haggai prophesied to a people with an agenda of their own. They were procrastinating over God's instructions. The prophet's task was to convince the people of Israel that the time had come to carry out God's purposes.

AUTHOR AND DATE

Written by Haggai approximately 520 B.C.

This is the second shortest book in the Old Testament. Haggai's biography is even shorter, and neither his name nor his writing offer clues about his background and personality. Although Ezra mentions Haggai twice (Ezra 5:1; 6:14), he adds no details other than to identify Haggai as a prophet. Apparently Haggai and his companion Zechariah succeeded in their ministry, for Ezra reported that the people responded to their leadership and rebuilt the temple.

KEY PEOPLE IN HAGGAI

Haggai—prophet of Judah after return from the Babylonian exile; urged the people to rebuild the temple (1:3–2:23)

Zerubbabel—led the Jews out of Babylonian exile; stood as the official representative of the Davidic dynasty; called the signet ring (1:1–2:23)

Jeshua—high priest of Judah; coleader with Zerubbabel (1:1–2:4)

The people of Judah—encouraged by Haggai to complete the rebuilding of the temple (1:2,12; 2:2)

BACKGROUND AND SETTING

Eighteen years before Haggai prophesied, Cyrus the Persian had allowed the exiled Jews to return from Babylon to their homeland (538 B.C.; Ezra 1:1–4). About fifty thousand Jews had returned under the civil leadership of Zerubbabel. External resistance from neighbor nations and internal indifference from the Jews themselves had brought the reconstruction work to a standstill (Ezra 3:1–4:24). Sixteen years later, Haggai and Zechariah were called by God to stir up the people to 1) rebuild the temple and 2) reorder their spiritual priorities (Ezra 5:1–6:22). The temple was completed four years later (about 516 B.C.). Haggai wrote his book in order to motivate the people to work.

KEY DOCTRINES IN HAGGAI

God's presence in the temple (1:7–8; 2:7–9; 1 Kings 8:10–11; 2 Chronicles 5:13–14; Ezekiel 43:5; 1 Corinthians 6:19–20; 2 Corinthians 6:16–18; Revelation 21:22; 22:1–21)

Obedience by the people who feared God (1:12–15; Deuteronomy 11:8; 1 Chronicles 24:19; 2 Chronicles 19:9; Ezra 5:2; Proverbs 15:33; Colossians 2:6–7; 3:22)

GOD'S CHARACTER IN HAGGAI

God is glorious—2:1–9

CHRIST IN HAGGAI

The Book of Haggai reveals Zerubbabel's significant place in the messianic line of David. His position, illustrated by a signet ring (2:23; see **Key Words**), continued the royal line of David through which Christ would come. Zerubbabel's name is found in both the ancestries of Mary (Luke 3:27) and Joseph (Matthew 1:12), demonstrating his importance in grafting both branches of Christ's lineage together.

KEY WORDS IN HAGGAI

Signet Ring: Hebrew *chotham*—2:23—derived from a verbal root meaning "to affix a seal," "to seal up," or "to fasten by sealing." The signet in Old Testament times was an engraved stone set in a gold or silver finger ring, bracelet, or armband (see Song of Solomon 8:6). When pressed upon wax or soft clay, the ring left the impression of the personal insignia of the bearer (see Exodus 28:11,21,36; 39:6,14,30). The signet ring was like an identification card or badge in the ancient world (Genesis 38:18). It symbolized status or position and the binding nature of the authority attached to items sealed by the ring (1 Kings 21:8; Job 38:14). Haggai's comparison of Zerubbabel to a signet ring (2:23) has messianic implications, since Zerubbabel would overturn the curse of Jeremiah on King Jehoiachin's dynasty and restore royal authority to the line of King David (Jeremiah 22:24–30).

QUICK OVERVIEW

I. Rebuke for Disobedience (1:1–11)
II. Remnant Responds and Rebuilds (1:12–15)
III. Return of God's Glory (2:1–9)
IV. Religious Questions (2:10–19)
V. Reign of the Lord (2:20–23)

MEANWHILE, IN OTHER PARTS OF THE WORLD . . .
Forsaking worldly comforts, Buddha leaves his home to begin his study of philosophy. In 521 B.C., he preaches his first sermon in the holy city of Barnares.

FREQUENTLY ASKED QUESTIONS

1. What exactly did Haggai mean when he used the phrase *the Desire of All Nations* (2:7)?

A number of translations of the original phrase have been offered, but only two interpretations seem possible. Pointing to "The silver is Mine, and the gold is Mine" (2:8), as well as to references such as Isaiah 60:5 and Zechariah 14:14, some argue that Haggai had Jerusalem in mind, to which the wealth of the nations will be brought during the millennium. The preferable interpretation, however, seems to be to see here a reference to the Messiah Himself, the Deliverer for whom all the nations ultimately long. Not only is this interpretation supported by the ancient rabbis and the early church, the mention of "glory" in the latter part of the verse suggests a personal reference to the Messiah (Isaiah 40:5; 60:1; Luke 2:32).

QUICK STUDY ON HAGGAI

1. What approaches and arguments did Haggai use to get the people to rebuild the temple?
2. Illustrate from Haggai the concept of priorities.
3. What did God do to provide a warning and incentive for the people to work?
4. What special message did God have Haggai deliver to Zerubbabel the leader of the Israelites?
5. What long-term tasks have you undertaken in your life to accomplish for God?

ZECHARIAH
Preparations for the Coming Messiah

A prophet who gave his life in God's service.

When a team is losing, the coach's halftime talk holds special significance. The game isn't over, but the team may be discouraged, and they need an effective motivation to pursue victory.

Zechariah and his prophet-partner Haggai offered the people of Jerusalem some necessary halftime encouragement. They were losing the contest of wills to the opposition and had stopped rebuilding the temple. God's spokesmen described the benefits that would come if the people worked hard for God, who would ultimately gain the victory.

AUTHOR AND DATE

Written by Zechariah during his ministry, from approximately 520 to 518 B.C., with another section written near 480 to 470 B.C.

Like Jeremiah and Ezekiel, Zechariah was also a priest (Nehemiah 12:12–16). Born in Babylon, he had joined his grandfather, Iddo, in the first group of exiles to return to Jerusalem under the leadership of Zerubbabel and Joshua, the high priest (Nehemiah 12:4). Because Zechariah is sometimes called the son of Iddo (Ezra 5:1; 6:14; Nehemiah 12:16), scholars have concluded that Zechariah may have lost his father, Berechiah, at an early age and therefore had inherited the priesthood directly from his grandfather.

Ancient Jewish tradition also holds that Zechariah was a member of the Great Synagogue, a council of 120 members that was originated by Nehemiah and presided over by Ezra. This council later developed into the ruling elders of the nation, referred to as the Sanhedrin in the New Testament.

Matthew 23:35 reports that the prophet Zechariah was murdered between the temple and the altar. Jesus said that the consequences for Zechariah's death would make up part of God's judgment on his own generation.

KEY PEOPLE IN ZECHARIAH

Zechariah—prophet of Judah after the Exile; encouraged Judah to finish building the temple (1:1–14:20)

Zerubbabel—leader of the Judean exiles; carried out the work on the temple (4:6–10)

Joshua—Israel's high priest after the remnant returned to Israel (3:1–10; 6:11–13)

The Jews rebuilding the temple—who returned to Jerusalem after the Exile to obey God (1:16; 4:9; 6:15; 8:13)

BACKGROUND AND SETTING

Zechariah and Haggai share the same historical background and setting. God had called both prophets into action sixteen years after the arrival of the original fifty thousand Jewish exiles returning from Babylon in 538 B.C. At first the exiles had worked hard to rebuild the temple and repair the city, but opposition had eventually intimidated and discouraged them. All the work had stopped. In 520 B.C., however, Zechariah and Haggai served to spur the people back to action. Ezra 6:15 records that the temple was completed in four years (516 B.C.).

KEY DOCTRINES IN ZECHARIAH

Repentance—true repentance involves more than mere words; actions must also change (1:1–6; 7:8–14; Isaiah 31:6; 44:22; Jeremiah 3:12; 18:11; Ezekiel 18:30; Micah 7:19; Malachi 3:7–10; Luke 15:20; James 4:8; 1 Corinthians 10:11; 2 Corinthians 6:6; Revelation 21:3)

Divine care—the coming glory of Jesus Christ will be a comfort to Israel (1:13,17; Psalm 23:4; Isaiah 30:26; 40:1–2; 51:3; Jeremiah 29:10; 50:4; Hosea 6:1; 14:4; 2 Corinthians 1:3–7; Philippians 2:1–2; 2 Thessalonians 2:16–17)

Messiah's rejection at the first coming (9:1–11:17; 13:7–9; Psalm 22:1–18; Isaiah 52:13–15; 53:1–12; Acts 2:23; 1 Peter 1:18–20)

Messiah's acceptance at the second coming (12:1–14:21; Jeremiah 33:15–16; Daniel 7:13–14; Romans 14:11; Philippians 2:10; Revelation 16:15)

Holy living (7:1–7; Leviticus 20:7; Isaiah 1:10–15; 58:3–9; Ecclesiastes 3:12; Ephesians 5:1; Philippians 1:21; Colossians 3:12; 2 Timothy 3:16–17)

GOD'S CHARACTER IN ZECHARIAH

God is good—9:17

CHRIST IN ZECHARIAH

The Book of Zechariah abounds with passages prophesying the coming Messiah. Christ is portrayed as "My Servant the Branch" (3:8), "a priest on His throne" (6:13), and as "[Him] whom they pierced" (12:10). Zechariah accurately depicts Christ as both humble and triumphant. Christ is the King who provides salvation but comes "lowly and riding on a donkey" (9:9).

KEY WORDS IN ZECHARIAH

Angel: Hebrew *mal'ak*—1:9,13; 2:3; 3:1,5; 4:1; 5:5; 6:5; 12:8—may refer to angelic beings (4:1,5; Genesis 19:1; Psalm 91:11), human messengers (Genesis 32:3; Deuteronomy 2:26), or ambassadors (Isaiah 30:4; Ezekiel 17:15). A special use is the manifestation of the Godhead known as the Angel of God or the Angel of the Lord in the Old Testament (2:6; see Genesis 16:7–13; 21:17; 22:15; Exodus 14:19). In the Old Testament, prophets (Haggai 1:13) and priests (Malachi 2:7) function as messengers from God. In Zechariah, angels bring revelations from God about the future and interpret the meaning of dreams and visions (1:14; 6:4,5). Jesus identified the messenger who prepared the way for the Day of the Lord, forecast in Malachi 3:1, as John the Baptist (Matthew 11:10,11).

Branch: Hebrew *tsemach*—3:8; 6:12—means "shoot" or "twig." This is one title for the coming Messiah, the "Branch" who would "shoot" up from the royal stock of David, a dynasty that had been interrupted with the Babylonian exile (Isaiah 11:1). Many of the prophets promised that a king from David's line would reign in righteousness (Jeremiah 23:5,6) and as a priest would reestablish true worship of the Lord (6:12,13). In His ministry, Jesus Christ fulfilled these predictions by taking on both a royal (see John 12:13–15; 1 Timothy 6:13–16) and a priestly role (see Hebrews 4:14).

QUICK OVERVIEW

I. Call to Repentance (1:1–6)
II. Eight Night Visions of Zechariah (1:7–6:15)
  A. Man among the Myrtle Trees (1:7–17)
  B. Four Horns and Four Craftsmen (1:18–21)
  C. Man with Measuring Line (2:1–13)
  D. Cleansing of High Priest (3:1–10)
  E. Gold Lampstand and Two Olive Trees (4:1–14)
  F. Flying Scroll (5:1–4)
  G. Woman in Basket (5:5–11)
  H. Four Chariots (6:1–8)
  I. Appendix: Coronation of Joshua the High Priest (6:9–15)
III. Four Messages of Zechariah (7:1–8:23)
  A. Question about Fasting (7:1–3)
  B. Four Responses (7:4–8:23)
IV. Two Burdens of Zechariah (9:1–14:21)
  A. Messiah's Rejection at First Advent (9:1–11:17)
  B. Messiah's Acceptance at Second Advent (12:1–14:21)

MEANWHILE, IN OTHER PARTS OF THE WORLD . . .
Two philosophers of worldwide significance were born within one year of each other (550 and 551 B.C.) and died within one year of each other (480 and 479 B.C.): Buddha, the originator of Buddhism, and Confucius, the renowned Chinese philosopher.

FREQUENTLY ASKED QUESTIONS

1. Why is Zechariah sometimes called the "apocalypse of the Old Testament"?

Zechariah's message functions in much the same way as Revelation (the Apocalypse of the New Testament). His prophecies related both to Zechariah's immediate audience as well as to future generations. This conclusion is borne out in the structure of the prophecy itself. In each of the three major sections (chapters 1–6; 7–8; 9–14), the prophet begins historically and then moves forward to the time of the second advent, when Messiah returns to His temple to set up His earthly kingdom.

The prophet reminded the people that Messiah had both an immediate and a long-term commitment to His people. Thus Zechariah's words were "good and comforting" (1:13), both to the exiles of his own day as well as to the remnant of God's chosen people in that future day. It is this dual function of speaking to the present and to the future that has caused some to give Zechariah this title of "apocalypse of the Old Testament."

QUICK STUDY ON ZECHARIAH

1. How do you apply the well-known verse Zechariah 4:6 in your life?
2. To what historical event does Zechariah 12:10 refer?
3. In what ways does Zechariah speak about God's jealousy?
4. How did Zechariah add his voice to Haggai's to encourage the people to rebuild the temple?
5. What does Zechariah have to say about future events beyond the time of Christ?

MALACHI
Final Prophetic Words

God's final words in the Old Testament include a promise: "I will send you Elijah the prophet" (Malachi 4:5).

After Malachi, the next prophet to speak was born more than four hundred years later. John the Baptist picked up the prophetic mantle and prepared the way for Jesus Christ. God's prophetic silence for four centuries certainly makes His final words worth careful attention. God sent that message through the prophet Malachi.

AUTHOR AND DATE

Written by Malachi during his ministry, approximately 433 to 424 B.C.

Because the name Malachi means "my messenger" or "the LORD's messenger," some have suggested that the book may have been written anonymously. Only here is this phrase used as a personal name in the Old Testament. Since all other prophetic books consistently identify their authors in the introductory heading, however, there is good reason to identify the author of this last book as the prophet Malachi.

Ancient Jewish tradition numbers Malachi among the members of the Great Synagogue who collected and preserved the Scriptures. Similar to Revelation 2 and 3, in which Christ writes about what He thinks of the conditions of the churches, here God writes through Malachi to impress upon Israel His thoughts about the nation.

KEY PEOPLE IN MALACHI

Malachi—prophet to Judah; last of the Old Testament prophets until John the Baptist (1:1–4:6)

The priests—revealed their unfaithfulness by marrying foreign wives and giving false interpretation of the Law (1:7–8; 2:1–9)

The people of Judah—married foreign wives and fell into idolatry (2:11–17)

BACKGROUND AND SETTING

During the first return, fifty thousand exiles went back to Judah from Babylon (538–536 B.C.). By 516 B.C., the temple was rebuilt and back in use. Ezra returned to Jerusalem in 458 B.C., followed by Nehemiah in 445 B.C. The people's desire to return to their homeland had not translated into a desire to walk with God. As time passed, religious practices became meaningless routines, with little attention given to God's Law. Into this chaos stepped the last of the Old Testament prophets. Malachi rebuked and condemned these abuses, forcefully indicting the people and calling them to repentance. Later, Nehemiah would return from almost a decade back in Persia and add his stinging confrontation of the temple abuses, Sabbath violations, and the Jewish men's unlawful divorce of their Jewish wives in order to marry foreign women. God's people sank into anonymity among the lost and aimless nations of the world.

As over two millennia of Old Testament history since Abraham concluded, none of the glorious promises of the Abrahamic, Davidic, or New Covenants had been fulfilled in the ultimate sense. Despite a few high points in Israel's history, such as Joshua, David, and Josiah, the Jews seemed determined to turn away from God's favor. Less than a century after returning from crushing captivity, they were again deeply mired in sin. The long-anticipated Messiah had not arrived and did not seem to be in sight.

Malachi wrote the capstone prophecy of the Old Testament in which he delivered 1) God's message of judgment on Israel for their continuing sin and 2) God's promise that one day in the future, when the Jews would repent, Messiah would be revealed and God's covenant promises would be fulfilled.

KEY DOCTRINES IN MALACHI

The Lord's covenant with Israel (2:4–5,8,10,14; 3:1; Numbers 3:44–48; 18:8–24; 25:12; Deuteronomy 33:8–11; Ezekiel 34:25)

Israel's unfaithfulness (1:2–5; Joshua 7:1; 1 Chronicles 5:25; Ezra 9:4; Psalm 78:8; Isaiah 1:21; Ezekiel 44:10; Hosea 1:2; Matthew 25:29; Luke 12:46; Romans 3:3; 2 Timothy 2:13)

The coming of the Lord (3:1–3; Isaiah 40:3; 63:9; Jeremiah 10:10; Joel 2:11; Nahum 1:6; Habakkuk 2:7; Matthew 11:10; Mark 1:2; Luke 1:76; 7:27; John 1:23; 2:14–15)

GOD'S CHARACTER IN MALACHI

God is loving—1:2–3

CHRIST IN MALACHI

The last prophetic words from the Old Testament still reveal hope in the coming of Christ the Messiah. Malachi speaks of two messengers: the messenger that will precede Christ, whom the New Testament identifies as John the Baptist (see Matthew 3:3; 11:10,14; 17:12; Mark 1:2; Luke 1:17; 7:26,27; John 1:23), and Christ, "the Messenger of the covenant" (3:1). The Book of Malachi closes the Old Testament and marks the beginning of four hundred years of prophetic silence. However, Malachi leaves readers with the striking proclamation, "Behold, He is coming" (3:1).

KEY WORDS IN MALACHI

Day: Hebrew *yom*—3:2,17; 4:1,3,5—has a variety of uses in the Old Testament. It can refer to the daylight hours in contrast to the night (Amos 5:8) or to a twenty-four-hour day, such as a certain day of the month (Genesis 7:11). It may also refer to a time period, such as the "time" or harvest (Proverbs 25:13), or even to a year (2 Samuel 13:23). The word is used in the significant phrase "the Day of the LORD" (see Isaiah 2:12; Ezekiel 13:5; Joel 1:15; Zephaniah 1:14). For the prophets, the Day of the Lord would be the future day when God would decisively triumph over all His foes. That day would be a day of great rejoicing and blessing for God's faithful servants (Isaiah 2), whereas for God's enemies it will be a day of "darkness" (Amos 5:18).

Try: Hebrew *bachan*—3:10—means "to try" or "to put to the test" (Job 23:10; Psalm 139:23; Zechariah 13:9). The word can mean "to test" in the sense of separating or discriminating one thing from another (Job 34:3). When this word is used to depict God's "testing" of people, it means the proving of individuals in such a way that their faith becomes more established (see Psalm 66:10–12; Jeremiah 17:10; 20:12). Malachi's challenge to the Israelites to *try* God is a rare instance in which people are encouraged to test the faithfulness of the Lord (3:10). This word for *try* can be contrasted with another Hebrew verb for testing, *nasah*. That word is frequently used in a negative sense, to describe the way Israel was testing God with their unbelief (Exodus 17:7; Psalm 78:18; 95:9). The law of Moses warned the Israelites not to tempt God (Deuteronomy 6:16; Psalms 95:9); it was a mark of spiritual adultery (Matthew 12:38–39). According to James, God tests people in order to grant them the crown of life, but He tempts no one (James 1:12–14).

QUICK OVERVIEW

I. The Denunciation of Israel's Sins (1:1–2:16)
  A. Reminder of God's Love for Israel (1:1–5)
  B. Rebuke of the Priests (1:6–2:9)
  C. Contempt for God's Altar (1:6–14)
  D. Contempt for God's Glory (2:1–3)
  E. Contempt for God's Law (2:4–9)
  F. Rebuke of the People (2:10–16)
II. The Declaration of Israel's Judgment and Blessing (2:17–4:6)
  A. Coming of a Messenger (2:17–3:5)
  B. Challenge to Repent (3:6–12)
  C. Criticism by Israel against the Lord (3:13–15)
  D. Consolation to the Faithful Remnant (3:16–4:6)

MEANWHILE, IN OTHER PARTS OF THE WORLD . . .
The Greeks begin building the temple of Zeus at Olympia and a marble temple in honor of Apollo at Delphi.

FREQUENTLY ASKED QUESTIONS

1. In what ways does John the Baptist fulfill Malachi's final prophecy in which God promises to send Elijah "before the coming of the great and dreadful day of the LORD" (4:5)?

The identity and meaning of Malachi's "Elijah" has been debated. Was this prophecy fulfilled in John the Baptist, or is it yet to be fulfilled? Could God have been announcing the reincarnation of Elijah? Evidence seems to weigh in favor of seeing Malachi's prophecy fulfilled by John the Baptist. Not only did the angel announce that John the Baptist would "go before Him in the spirit and power of Elijah" (Luke 1:17), but John himself stated that he was not Elijah (John 1:21). We conclude that John was like Elijah: 1) internally in "spirit and power"; 2) externally in rugged independence and nonconformity. To the Jews who received the Messiah, John would be the Elijah spoken of (Matthew 11:14; 17:9–13). But, since the Jews as a whole refused the King, then another Elijah-like prophet would be sent in the future, perhaps as one of the two witnesses (Revelation 11:1–19).

QUICK STUDY ON MALACHI

1. What makes Malachi significant as the last Old Testament prophet?
2. When God speaks in Malachi 3:6, what conclusions does God want people to reach?
3. What different aspects of the subject of sin did Malachi address in his prophecies?
4. What do we learn about God's love in Malachi?
5. In what ways has God's love left an indelible mark on your life?

MATTHEW
Jesus Is the Promised Messiah

Matthew focused on teaching his fellow Jews that their hopes had been answered in Jesus.

Although all the gospel writers had the same biography to write, each one approached the subject in a different way. For Matthew, Jesus was the promised King. Matthew backed up this claim by repeatedly pointing out the way that Jesus fulfilled the Old Testament prophecies concerning the Messiah.

AUTHOR AND DATE

Written by Matthew, between A.D. 50 and 70

One day near Capernaum, Jesus passed Matthew at his tax collector's table and called him to follow. Matthew, also known as Levi, immediately left everything to join Jesus. But he took with him certain personal characteristics that affected the gospel he would write. This disciple put his tax-collecting experience to unique use in compiling one of the biographies of Jesus. When writing he approached his task with an accountant's mind. His version of Christ's life placed a higher priority on categories than on chronology. Consequently, parables, miracles, and sayings tend to be grouped by shared characteristics and not by when the events occurred.

Matthew also took pains to account for the claims of Christ. He frequently noted the ways that Jesus' words and actions fulfilled prophecy. Matthew's use of Greek is consistent with that of a Palestinian Jew writing to Hellenistic Jews elsewhere. He wrote as an eyewitness of many of the events he described, giving firsthand testimony to the words and works of Jesus of Nazareth.

KEY PEOPLE IN MATTHEW

Jesus—the promised Messiah and King of the Jews (1:1–28:20)

Mary—the mother of Jesus the Messiah (1:1–2:23; 13:55)

Joseph—husband of Mary and descendant of David; carried the royal line to Jesus (1:16–2:23)

John the Baptist—prophet and forerunner who announced the coming of Christ (3:1–15; 4:12; 9:14; 11:2–19; 14:1–12)

The twelve disciples—Simon Peter, Andrew, James, John, Philip, Bartholomew, Thomas, Matthew, James (son of Alphaeus), Thaddaeus, Simon, Judas Iscariot; twelve men chosen by Jesus to aid His ministry on earth (4:18–22; 5:1; 8:18–27; 9:9–28:20)

Religious leaders—comprised of Pharisees and Sadducees; two religious groups who joined together in their hatred of Jesus (3:7–10; 5:20; 9:11–34; 12:10–45; 15:1–20; 16:1–12; 19:1–9; 21:23–28:15)

Caiaphas—high priest and leader of the Sadducees; held an illegal trial that led to Jesus' death (26:3–4,57–68)

Pilate—Roman governor who ordered the crucifixion of Jesus in place of Barabbas (27:1–65)

Mary Magdalene—devoted follower of Jesus; first person to see Jesus after His resurrection (27:56–28:11)

BACKGROUND AND SETTING

The Jewish flavor of Matthew's gospel is remarkable. Even the opening genealogies only trace Jesus' lineage as far back as Abraham. In contrast, Luke, who aimed to show Christ as the Redeemer of humanity, follows Jesus' family tree all the way back to Adam. Matthew's purpose was somewhat narrower: to demonstrate that Christ is the King and Messiah of Israel. This gospel quotes more than sixty times from Old Testament prophetic passages, emphasizing how Christ fulfilled all those promises.

The conclusion that Matthew's audience was predominantly Jewish also comes from several other facts:

1. Matthew usually mentions Jewish customs without explaining them, in contrast to the other gospels (see Mark 7:3; John 19:40).
2. Matthew consistently refers to Christ as "the Son of David" (1:1; 9:27; 12:23; 15:22; 20:30; 21:9,15; 22:42,45).
3. Matthew even respects Jewish sensibilities regarding the name of God by using the phrase "the kingdom of heaven" where the other evangelists write "the kingdom of God."
4. All the gospel's major themes are rooted in the Old Testament and interpreted in light of Israel's messianic expectations.

Matthew's purpose is clear: to demonstrate that Jesus is the Jewish nation's long-awaited Messiah. His frequent quoting of the Old Testament emphasizes the tie between the Messiah of promise and the Christ of history. This purpose is never out of focus for Matthew. He even points to incidental details from Old Testament prophecies as proofs of Jesus' messianic claims (2:17–18; 4:13–15; 13:35; 21:4–5; 27:9–10).

KEY DOCTRINE IN MATTHEW

Jesus is the Messiah—also called the Christ; prophesied in the Old Testament as the awaited One who would die for the sins of the world (2:17–18; 4:13–15; 13:35; 21:4–5; 27:9–10; Genesis 49:10; Deuteronomy 18:15–18; 2 Samuel 7:12–14; Isaiah 52:13–53:12; Daniel 9:26; Micah 5:2–5; Mark 1:1; Luke 23:2–3; John 4:26; Acts 18:28)

GOD'S CHARACTER IN MATTHEW

God is accessible—6:6; 27:51
God is good—5:45; 19:17

God is holy—13:41
God is long-suffering—23:37; 24:48–51
God is perfect—5:48
God is powerful—6:13; 10:28; 19:26; 22:29
God is provident—6:26,33–34; 10:9,29–30
God is unequaled—19:17
God is unified—4:10; 19:17
God is wise—6:8,18; 10:29–30; 24:36
God is wrathful—10:28; 25:41

CHRIST IN MATTHEW

Matthew writes primarily to the Jews defending Jesus as the King and Messiah of Israel. He supports the fulfillment of Christ as the Messiah by quoting Old Testament prophetic passages more than sixty times in his gospel. Matthew demonstrates the royalty of Jesus by constantly referring to him as "the Son of David" (1:1; 9:27; 12:23; 15:22; 20:30; 21:9,15; 22:42,45).

KEY WORDS IN MATTHEW

Jesus: Greek *Iēsous*—1:1; 4:23; 8:22; 11:4; 19:1; 24:1; 26:52; 27:37—equivalent to the Hebrew name *Yeshua* (Joshua), literally, "The LORD shall save." In the Old Testament times, the name Jesus was a common Jewish name (Luke 3:29; Colossians 4:11). However, the meaning of this name expresses the redemptive work of Jesus on earth. The messenger angel sent to Joseph affirmed the importance of Jesus' name: "for He will save His people from their sins" (1:21). After Jesus sacrificed Himself for the sins of His people and rose from the dead, the early apostles proclaimed Jesus as the one and only Savior (Acts 5:31; 13:23).

Christ: Greek *Christos*—1:1,18; 2:4; 11:2; 16:20; 23:8; 26:68; 27:22—literally, "the Anointed One." Many speak of Jesus Christ without realizing that the title *Christ* is actually a confession of faith. *Messiah*, the Hebrew equivalent for Christ, was used in the Old Testament to refer to prophets (1 Kings 19:16), priests (Leviticus 4:5,16), and kings (1 Samuel 24:6,10), in the sense that all of them were anointed with oil. This anointing symbolized a consecration for ministry by God. Jesus Christ, as the Anointed One, would be the ultimate Prophet, Priest, and King (Isaiah 61:1; John 3:34). With his dramatic confession, "You are the Christ, the Son of the living God" (16:16), Peter declared his faith in Jesus as the promised Messiah.

Blessed: Greek *makarios*—5:3–5,11; 16:17; 24:46—literally, "fortunate" or "happy." This term appears in classical Greek literature, in the

Septuagint (the Greek translation of the Old Testament), and in the New Testament to describe the kind of happiness that comes only from God. In the New Testament, *makarios* is usually written passively: God is the One who is blessing or favoring the person.

The Kingdom of Heaven: Greek *hē basileia tōn ouranōn*—3:2; 4:17; 5:3,10; 10:7; 25:1—literally, "the kingdom of God." To show respect and honor, the Jews avoided saying the name of God out loud. Instead, they often used the word *heaven* as an alternate way to refer to God. The word *heaven* also points to the kingdom of Jesus. Jesus proclaimed His kingdom as residing in the hearts of His people. This spiritual kingdom required internal repentance, not just external submission. It provided deliverance from sin rather than the political deliverance many Jews desired.

QUICK OVERVIEW

I. (Prologue) The King's Advent (1:1–4:25)
   A. His Birth (1:1–2:23)
   B. His Entry into Public Ministry (3:1–4:25)[1]
II. The King's Authority (5:1–9:38)
   A. Discourse 1: The Sermon on the Mount (5:1–7:29)
   B. Narrative 1: The Authenticating Miracles (8:1–9:38)
III. The King's Agenda (10:1–12:50)
   A. Discourse 2: The Commissioning of the Twelve (10:1–42)
   B. Narrative 2: The Mission of the King (11:1–12:50)
IV. The King's Adversaries (13:1–17:27)
   A. Discourse 3: The Kingdom Parables (13:1–52)
   B. Narrative 3: The Kingdom Conflict (13:53–17:27)
V. The King's Administration (18:1–23:39)
   A. Discourse 4: The Childlikeness of the Believer (18:1–35)
   B. Narrative 4: The Jerusalem Ministry (19:1–23:39)
VI. The King's Atonement (24:1–28:15)
   A. Discourse 5: The Olivet Discourse (24:1–25:46)
   B. Narrative 5: The Crucifixion and Resurrection (26:1–28:15)
VII. (Epilogue) The King's Assignment (28:16–20)

MEANWHILE, IN OTHER PARTS OF THE WORLD . . .
The first recorded wrestling match in history takes place in Japan.

FREQUENTLY ASKED QUESTIONS

1. The first three gospels share many similarities in wording. Who copied from whom?

It is true that even a cursory reading of Matthew, Mark, and Luke reveals many striking similarities. Compare, for example, Matthew 9:2–8; Mark 2:3–12; and Luke 5:18–26. But there are also significant differences in the way each writer views the life, ministry, and teaching of Jesus. The question about how to explain these similarities and differences is known as the "synoptic problem" (*syn* means "together" and *optic* means "seeing").

The modern solution—even among evangelicals—has been to assume that some form of literary dependence exists between the synoptic Gospels. This means that there was some copying among the gospel writers. The most commonly accepted theory to explain such an alleged literary dependence is known as the "two-source" theory. According to that theory, Mark was the first gospel written, and Matthew and Luke then used Mark as a source in writing their gospels. Proponents of this view suggest there was a second source, labeled Q (from the German word *Quelle*, meaning "source"), and argue that this no-longer-available source must have supplied the material in Matthew and Luke that does not appear in Mark. They offer the following evidence to support their theory:

- First, most of Mark is paralleled in Matthew and Luke. Since it is much shorter than Matthew and Luke, the latter must be expansions of Mark.
- Second, the first three gospels follow the same general chronological outline, but when either Matthew or Luke departs from Mark's chronology, the other agrees with Mark. Put another way, Matthew and Luke do not both depart from Mark's chronology in the same places. That pattern, it is argued, shows that Matthew and Luke used Mark for their historical framework.
- Third, in passages common to all three gospels, Matthew's and Luke's wording doesn't often agree when it differs from Mark's. Proponents of the two-source theory see this as confirmation that Matthew and Luke used Mark's gospel as a source.

There is a viable alternative to this two-source theory: the synoptic answer. The arguments above do not prove that Matthew and Luke used Mark's gospel as a source. In fact, the weight of all the evidence strongly resists such a theory:

- The nearly unanimous testimony of the church until the nineteenth century was that Matthew was the first gospel written. Such a consistent and impressive chorus cannot be ignored.

- Why would Matthew, an apostle and eyewitness to the events of Christ's life, depend on Mark (who was not an eyewitness) even for the account of Matthew's own conversion?
- A careful statistical analysis of the synoptic Gospels has revealed that the parallels between them are far less extensive and the differences more significant than is commonly acknowledged. The differences, in particular, argue against literary dependence among the gospel writers.
- Since the gospels record actual historical events, it would be surprising if they did not follow the same general chronological sequence. For example, the fact that three books on American history all discussed the Revolutionary War, the Civil War, World War 1, World War 2, the Vietnam War, and the Gulf War in the same order would not prove that the authors had read each others' books. General agreement in content does not prove literary dependency.
- The passages in which Matthew and Luke agree against Mark (see the third argument in favor of the two-source theory above) amount to about one-sixth of Matthew and one-sixth of Luke. If they used Mark's gospel as a source, there is not satisfactory explanation for why Matthew and Luke would so often both change Mark's wording in the same way.
- The two-source theory cannot account for the important section in Mark's gospel (6:45–8:26) that Luke omits. That omission suggests Luke had not seen Mark's gospel when he wrote.
- There is no historical or manuscript evidence that the Q document ever existed. It is purely a fabrication of modern skepticism and a way to possibly deny the verbal inspiration of the gospels.
- The theories of literary dependence between the gospel writers are notorious for downplaying the significance of their personal contacts with each other. Mark and Luke were both companions of Paul (Philemon 24). The early church (including Matthew) met for a time in the home of Mark's mother (Acts 12:12). Luke may well have met Matthew during Paul's two-year imprisonment at Caesarea. Such contacts make theories of mutual literary dependence unnecessary.

The simplest solution to the synoptic problem is that no such problem exists! Because critics cannot prove literary dependency between the gospel writers, there is no need to explain it. The traditional view that the gospel writers were inspired by God and wrote independently of each other—except that all three were moved by the same Holy Spirit (2 Peter 1:20)—remains the only plausible view.

2. Why are some events in Matthew in a different order from the order in Mark and Luke?

In general, Matthew presents a topical or thematic approach to the life of Christ. He groups Jesus' teaching into five major discourses:

- The Sermon on the Mount (chapters 5–7)
- The commissioning of the apostles (chapter 10)
- The parables of the kingdom (chapter 13)
- The childlikeness of the believer (chapter 18)
- The discourse on His second coming (chapters 24–25).

Matthew makes no attempt to follow a strict chronology. A comparison of the synoptic Gospels reveals that he freely placed things out of order. He was dealing with themes and broad concepts, not laying out a timeline. Mark's and Luke's gospels follow a chronological order more closely.

3. Why are three similar gospels necessary?

Readers who examine the gospels carefully, noting the viewpoints of the authors and the details they include make two important discoveries: 1) The differences between the gospels highlight their independence and their value as part of a complete picture; 2) The similarities affirm their common subject and message. The accounts are never contradictory, but complementary. When seen together, they present a fuller understanding of Christ.

4. How should Jesus' prophetic statements, many of which are found in Matthew 24 and 25, be interpreted?

The prophetic passages present a particular challenge for those seeking to understand and correctly interpret Jesus' words. The Olivet discourse (Matthew 24,25), for example, contains some details that evoke images of the violent destruction of Jerusalem in A.D. 70. Jesus' words in 24:34 have led some to conclude that all these things were fulfilled—albeit not literally—in the Roman conquest of that era. This view is known as "preterism." But it is a serious error. The preterist interpreter has to read into these passages allegorical meanings that don't fit normal exegetical study methods. The approach that honors the language and history behind the biblical texts (called the grammatical-historical hermeneutical approach) makes better sense and yields a consistent, futuristic interpretation of crucial prophecies.

5. Why is Jesus' genealogy in Matthew different from the one in Luke?

The genealogies of Jesus recorded by Matthew and Luke have two significant differences: 1) Matthew's genealogy traces the line of descent through Joseph, while Luke's traces Jesus' ancestry through Mary; and 2) Matthew begins his genealogy with Abraham, since his concern has to do with the Jewish connection with Christ and God's plan of salvation; and Luke's genealogy begins with Adam and sees Christ's role in the salvation of mankind.

6. Does Matthew include any material not found in the other gospels?

Matthew includes nine events in Jesus' life that are unique to his gospel:

1. Joseph's dream (1:20–24)
2. Visit of the wise men (2:1–12)
3. Flight into Egypt (2:13–15)
4. Herod kills the children (2:16–18)
5. Judas repents (27:3–10; but see Acts 1:18–19)
6. The dream of Pilate's wife (27:19)
7. Other resurrections (27:52)
8. The bribery of the soldiers (28:11–15)
9. The Great Commission (28:19–20)

QUICK STUDY ON MATTHEW

1. In what special ways does Matthew choose to introduce Jesus' biography?
2. Choose one or two of the kingdom parables from Matthew 13. What central idea was Jesus teaching with those parables?
3. In the section called the Sermon on the Mount (Matthew 5–7), how many different subjects did Jesus speak about?
4. How does Matthew reveal Jesus as the King in his gospel?
5. What reasons can you come up with for why Matthew referred so often to the Old Testament in his gospel?
6. How does the Gospel of Matthew inform your relationship with Jesus Christ?

[1] See also "The Ministries of Jesus Christ" in the Appendices at the back of this book.

MARK
Jesus Is the Suffering Servant

The Gospel for the Romans.

As the chilly shadows of evening lengthen into night, the travelers draw closer to the fire. Among them stands a storyteller, spotlighted by the flames. His story is vivid, colorful, and full of action. His voice conveys a sense of conviction. Some in his audience find themselves deeply moved by the storyteller's account. It sounds to them like good news. If the story is true, then it is the best story ever shared, for it tells about God's personal visit to earth. That rapid, condensed, but fascinating storyteller's approach to the life of Jesus was used by Mark to record his gospel.

AUTHOR AND DATE

Written by Mark, between A.D. 50 and 70

Unlike the Epistles, the Gospels do not name their authors. The early church fathers, however, unanimously affirm that Mark wrote the Second Gospel. Among these witnesses are Papias, bishop of Hierapolis (about A.D. 140), Justin Martyr (about A.D. 150), and Irenaeus (about A.D. 185). Justin Martyr referred to the Gospel of Mark as "the memoirs of Peter." Irenaeus called Mark "the disciple and interpreter of Peter." Papias also strongly supported the authorship of Mark.

KEY PEOPLE IN MARK

Jesus—the Servant who offered Himself as a sacrifice for the sins of the world (1:1–16:19)

The twelve disciples—Simon Peter, Andrew, James, John, Philip, Bartholomew, Thomas, Matthew, James (son of Alphaeus), Thaddaeus, Simon, Judas Iscariot; twelve men chosen by Jesus to aid His ministry on earth (1:16–16:20)

Pilate—Roman governor who ordered the crucifixion of Jesus in place of Barabbas (15:1–45)

The Jewish religious leaders—comprised of Pharisees and Sadducees; two religious groups who joined together in their hatred of Jesus (3:22; 11:27–15:32)

BACKGROUND AND SETTING

In contrast to Matthew's Jewish audience, Mark seems to have targeted Roman believers, particularly Gentiles. When he employed Aramaic terms, Mark translated them for his readers (3:17; 5:4; 7:11,34; 10:46; 14:36; 15:22,34). Further, in some places he used Latin (Roman) expressions instead of their Greek equivalents (5:9; 6:27; 12:15,42; 15:16,39).

Mark also used the Roman system when referring to time (6:48; 13:35), and he took care to explain Jewish customs (7:3–4; 14:12; 15:42).

Some of Mark's omissions (primarily the genealogies) make sense if his audience had little interest in such material. This gospel also includes fewer references to the Old Testament and fewer instances that would be of particular interest to Jewish readers—such as details of the conflict between Jesus and the Pharisees and Sadducees. When mentioning Simon of Cyrene (15:21), however, Mark identifies him as the father of Rufus, a prominent member of the church at Rome (Romans 16:13). These details support the traditional view that Mark was written for a Gentile audience initially at Rome.

KEY DOCTRINES IN MARK

The humanity of Christ—Jesus humbled Himself and became a man in order to reconcile humanity to God (1:41; 3:5; 4:38; 6:34; 8:12; 9:36; 11:12; 13:32; Isaiah 50:6; 53:7; Micah 5:2; Luke 2:4–7; John 1:14; Romans 1:3–4; 8:3; Philippians 2:6–11; Colossians 2:9; Hebrews 4:15; 5:7)

Servanthood—Jesus was the perfect example of true servanthood, even unto death (8:34–37; 9:35; 10:43–45; Zechariah 9:9; Matthew 20:28; 21:5; Luke 22:27; John 13:5; 2 Corinthians 8:9; Philippians 2:7)

GOD'S CHARACTER IN MARK

God is accessible—15:38
God is unified—2:7; 12:29

CHRIST IN MARK

Omitting all accounts of Jesus' ancestry and birth, Mark emphasizes Jesus' role as the Suffering Servant of the Lord (10:45). More than any other gospel, Mark focuses on the humble deeds of Jesus over His teachings.

KEY WORDS IN MARK

Faith: Greek *pistis*—2:5; 4:40; 5:34,36; 10:52; 11:22—"trust" or "belief." To have faith is to relinquish trust in oneself and transfer that trust to someone or something else. The woman who had a hemorrhage for years had first put her trust in physicians. Then as she reached for Jesus' robe, she believed and trusted Jesus to cure her. After she was healed, Jesus declared her faith had made her well (see Matthew 8:10; 9:22,29; 15:28; Luke 7:50; 8:48). Within the Epistles, the word *pistis* sometimes refers to the content of one's faith and beliefs—God's revelation in the Scripture (see Galatians 1:23).

Gospel: Greek *euangelion*—1:1,14–15; 13:10; 14:9; 16:15—literally, "good news" or "good message." Messengers bringing news of victory in battle originally used this Greek term. In the New Testament it points to the Good News of salvation: Jesus Christ came to earth to abolish the power of sin in the lives of His people by offering Himself as a perfect sacrifice on the cross. Christ commands believers to share this Good News with the rest of the world. This Good News is Christ's life-giving message to a dying world (16:15).

Scribes; Chief Priests: Greek *grammateus*—2:6; 3:22; 8:31; 9:14; 11:18; 12:38; 15:31—literally, "writer." Originally, scribes functioned as transcribers of the Law and readers of the Scripture. Later they acted as lawyers and religious scholars by interpreting both civil and religious law. The Greek word for *chief priests* translates as "the leading priests." This group included the high priest and other priests who were experts in the Scriptures. Ironically, these priests did not realize that by mocking Jesus they were fulfilling Isaiah's prophecy regarding the Messiah: "He was despised and rejected by men, a Man of sorrows and acquainted with grief" (Isaiah 53:3).

QUICK OVERVIEW

I. Prologue: In the Wilderness (1:1–13)
  A. John's Message (1:1–8)
  B. Jesus' Baptism (1:9–11)
  C. Jesus' Temptation (1:12–13)
II. Beginning His Ministry: In Galilee and the Surrounding Regions (1:14–7:23)[1]
  A. He Announces His Message (1:14–15)
  B. He Calls His Disciples (1:16–20)
  C. He Ministers in Capernaum (1:21–34)
  D. He Reaches Out to Galilee (1:35–45)
  E. He Defends His Ministry (2:1–3:6)
  F. He Ministers to Multitudes (3:7–12)
  G. He Commissions the Twelve (3:13–19)
  H. He Rebukes the Scribes and Pharisees (3:20–30)
  I. He Identifies His Spiritual Family (3:31–35)
  J. He Preaches in Parables (4:1–34)
  K. He Demonstrates His Power (4:35–5:43)
  L. He Returns to His Hometown (6:1–6)
  M. He Sends Out His Disciples (6:7–13)
  N. He Gains a Powerful Enemy (6:14–29)
  O. He Regroups with the Disciples (6:30–32)

P. He Feeds the Five Thousand (6:33–44)
Q. He Walks on Water (6:45–52)
R. He Heals Many People (6:53–56)
S. He Answers the Pharisees (7:1–23)

III. Broadening His Ministry: In Various Gentile Regions (7:24–10:52)
A. Tyre and Sidon: He Delivers a Gentile Woman's Daughter (7:24–30)
B. Decapolis: He Heals a Deaf-Mute (7:31–37)
C. The Eastern Shore of Galilee: He Feeds the Four Thousand (8:1–9)
D. Dalmanutha: He Has Disputes with the Pharisees (8:10–12)
E. The Other Side of the Lake: He Rebukes the Disciples (8:13–21)
F. Bethsaida: He Heals a Blind Man (8:22–26)
G. Caesarea Philippi and Capernaum: He Instructs the Disciples (8:27–9:50)
H. Concluding His Ministry: He Takes the Road to Jerusalem (10:1–52)

IV. Consummating His Ministry: Jerusalem (11:1–16:20)
A. Triumphal Entry (11:1–11)
B. Purification (11:12–19)
C. Teaching in Public and in Private (11:20–13:37)
D. Arrangements for Betrayal (14:1–2,10–11)
E. Anointing, the Last Supper, Betrayal, Arrest, Trial (Jewish Phase) (14:3–9; 12–72)
F. Trial (Roman Phase), Crucifixion (15:1–41)
G. Burial in Joseph of Arimathea's Tomb (15:42–47)
H. Resurrection (16:1–8)
I. Postscript (16:9–20)

MEANWHILE, IN OTHER PARTS OF THE WORLD . . .
The Han dynasty begins in China, creating the country's largest ethnic group.

FREQUENTLY ASKED QUESTIONS

1. How did Mark come to write one of the Gospels if he wasn't one of the original disciples?

Although Mark was not one of the original apostles of Jesus, he was involved in many of the events recorded in the New Testament. He traveled as a close companion of the Apostle Peter and appears repeatedly throughout the Book of Acts, where he is known as "John whose surname was Mark" (Acts 12:12,25; 15:37,39). When he was miraculously freed from prison, Peter's first action was to go to John Mark's mother's home in Jerusalem (Acts 12:12).

John Mark was also a cousin of Barnabas (Colossians 4:10), and he joined Paul and Barnabas on their first missionary journey (Acts 12:25; 13:5). But Mark deserted the mission team while in Perga and returned to Jerusalem (Acts 13:13). Later, when Barnabas wanted to give Mark another opportunity to travel with Paul's second missionary team, Paul refused. The friction that resulted between Paul and Barnabas led to their separation (Acts 15:38–40).

Eventually, Mark's youthful vacillation gave way to great strength and maturity. In time he proved himself even to the Apostle Paul. When Paul wrote to the Colossians, he instructed them that if John Mark came, they were to welcome him (Colossians 4:10). Paul even listed Mark as a fellow worker (Philemon 24). Later, Paul told Timothy to "get Mark and bring him with you, for he is useful to me for ministry" (2 Timothy 4:11).

John Mark's restoration to useful ministry and preparation for writing his gospel was due, in part, to his extended close relationship with Peter (1 Peter 5:13). The older apostle was no stranger to failure and his influence on the younger man was no doubt instrumental in helping him out of the instability of his youth and into the strength and maturity he would need for the work to which God had called him. As is explained in the introduction, Mark's gospel represents primarily Peter's version of the life of Jesus.

2. Were the last twelve verses of chapter 16 originally part of Mark's gospel?

The external evidence strongly suggests that Mark 16:9–20 were not originally part of Mark's gospel. While the majority of Greek manuscripts contain these verses, the earliest and most reliable ones do not. A shorter ending also existed, but it is not included in this text. Further, some manuscripts that include the passage note that it was missing from older Greek copies, while others have scribal marks indicating the passage was considered doubtful. The fourth-century church fathers Eusebius and Jerome noted that almost all Greek manuscripts available to them lacked verses 9–20.

The internal evidence from this brief passage also weighs heavily against Mark's authorship. The grammatical transition between verses 8 and 9 is abrupt and awkward. The vocabulary in these verses does not match with the rest of Mark. Even the events and people mentioned in these verses appear in awkward fashion. For example, Mary Magdalene is introduced as if she was a new person on the scene rather than someone Mark has mentioned three times (verse 1; 15:40,47). Clearly, Mark 16:9–20 represents an early attempt to complete Mark's gospel.

While for the most part summarizing truths taught elsewhere in Scripture, these verses should always be compared with the rest of

Scripture, and no doctrines should be formulated based solely on them. Further, in spite of all these considerations of the likely unreliability of this section, it is possible to be wrong on the issue. Therefore, it is good to consider the meaning of this passage and leave it in the text, just as is done with the other text with a similar history, John 7:53–8:11.

3. Does Mark include any material not found in the other gospels?

There are three passages found in Mark that are only recorded in his gospel:

- The parable of the growing seed (4:26–29)
- A deaf and mute man is healed (7:31–37)
- A blind man is healed (8:22–26)

QUICK STUDY ON MARK

1. In what different ways does Mark illustrate Jesus' attitude of servanthood in his gospel?
2. What answer did Jesus expect when He asked His disciples, "Who do you say that I am?" (Mark 8:29)?
3. How does Jesus reveal His identity as the Son of God in the Gospel of Mark?
4. What role do miracles play in demonstrating Jesus' special identity in Mark?
5. How does Mark make it clear in his gospel that those who believe in Jesus have a responsibility to pass on the Good News to others?

[1] See also "The Ministries of Jesus Christ" in the Appendices at the back of this book.

LUKE
Jesus Is the Son of Man

A historian's view of the Lord Jesus

People write biographies for different reasons. Usually, they are convinced the subject of their writing ought to be introduced to as many people as possible. An effective biographer uses good sources and interviews people who can give firsthand accounts of events, words, and habits from the subject's life. A good biographer presents an honest and full record of the subject's impact on others.

The gospel writer Luke approached his task with each of these objectives. His opening verses describe in detail how he gathered his materials and why he decided to compose his biography of Jesus Christ.

AUTHOR AND DATE

Written by Luke, approximately A.D. 60

The Gospel of Luke and the Book of Acts were clearly written by the same individual (Luke 1:1–4; Acts 1:1). Although never identifying himself by name, the writer's use of "we" in many sections of Acts indicates that the author was a close companion of Paul (Acts 16:10–17; 20:5–15; 21:1–18; 27:1–28:16). Only Luke, among the colleagues whom Paul mentions in his own epistles (Colossians 4:14; 2 Timothy 4:11; Philemon 24), fits the profile of the author of these books. That agrees perfectly with the earliest tradition of the church, which unanimously attributed this gospel to Luke.

KEY PEOPLE IN LUKE

Jesus—the Son of Man who lived a perfect life to reconcile sinful men and women to God (1:26–24:53)

Elizabeth—godly wife of Zechariah and mother of John the Baptist (1:5–60)

Zechariah—Jewish priest and father of John the Baptist (1:4–79)

John the Baptist—prophet and forerunner who announced the coming of Christ (1:13–80; 3:2–9:9)

Mary—the virgin mother of Jesus (1:26–2:51)

The twelve disciples—Simon Peter, Andrew, James, John, Philip, Bartholomew, Thomas, Matthew, James (son of Alphaeus), Thaddaeus, Simon, Judas Iscariot; twelve men chosen by Jesus to aid His ministry on earth (1:2; 5:30–12:55; 16:1–24:53)

Herod the tetrarch—son of Herod the Great; had John the Baptist executed and participated in the trials of Jesus (3:1–20; 9:7–9; 23:6–16)

Pilate—Roman governor who ordered the crucifixion of Jesus in place of Barabbas (3:1; 13:1; 23:1–52)

Mary Magdalene—devoted follower of Jesus; first person to see Jesus after His resurrection (8:2; 24:10)

BACKGROUND AND SETTING

Luke expressly stated that his knowledge of the events recorded in his gospel came from the reports of those who were eyewitnesses (1:1–2), strongly implying that he personally was not an eyewitness. The prologue makes it clear that Luke's aim was to give an ordered account of the event of Jesus' life, but this does not mean that he always followed a strict chronological order in all instances.

Luke's acknowledgment that he compiled his account from various extant sources does not invalidate the claim of divine inspiration for his work. The process of inspiration never bypasses or overrides the personalities, vocabularies, and styles of the human authors of Scripture. The unique traits of the human authors are always indelibly stamped on the book of Scripture. Luke's research creates no exception to this rule. The research itself was orchestrated by divine Providence. Most importantly, when Luke wrote, he was moved by the Spirit of God (2 Peter 1:21). Therefore, his account is infallibly true.

The Apostle Paul referred to Luke as a physician (Colossians 4:14). This is helpful background for Luke's obvious interest in medical phenomena. He gave special emphasis to Jesus' healing ministry throughout his gospel (4:38–40; 5:15–25; 6:17–19; 7:11–15; 8:43–47, 49–56; 9:2,6,11; 13:11–13; 14:2–4; 17:12–14; 22:50–51). Luke also displays a physician's sensitivity in including Jesus' compassion for Gentiles, Samaritans, women, children, tax collectors, sinners, and others often regarded as outcasts in Israel.

KEY DOCTRINES IN LUKE

Human fear in the presence of God—this response is normal and appropriate when confronted with the mighty work of God (1:30,65; 2:9,10; 5:10,26; 7:16; 8:25,37,50; 9:34,45; 12:5; 23:40; Leviticus 19:14,32; 25:17,36,43; Deuteronomy 25:18; Judges 6:22; 2 Samuel 23:3; 2 Chronicles 20:29; 26:5; Proverbs 1:7; Nehemiah 5:15; 13:22; Mark 16:5; Acts 9:31; 1 Timothy 5:20)

The mysteries of divine truth—wonderment surrounds the mysteries of Christ's words and works (1:21,63; 2:18–19,33,47–48; 5:9; 8:25; 9:43–45; 11:14; 20:26; 24:12,41; Job 11:7; Daniel 2:47; Matthew 13:35; Mark 4:10–20; Romans 11:25; 1 Corinthians 2:7; 4:1; Ephesians 5:32; Colossians 1:25–27; 4:3; 1 Timothy 3:16; Revelation 10:7)

Forgiveness—its place in human life (3:3; 5:20–25; 6:37; 7:41–50; 11:4; 12:10; 17:3–4; 23:34; 24:47; Genesis 50:20–21; Psalm 7:4; Proverbs 19:11; Matthew 6:14–15; 18:22; Mark 11:25; 2 Corinthians 2:5–11; James 2:13; 1 Peter 4:8)

The role of the Holy Spirit—the Spirit in our lives (1:15,35,41,67; 2:25–27; 3:16,22; 4:1,14,18; 10:21; 11:13; 12:10,12; Genesis 1:2; Job 26:13; Psalm 104:30; Ezekiel 37:11–14; Zechariah 4:6–7; Matthew 12:28; John 14:16; 15:26; Acts 1:8; 8:29; Romans 8:11; 15:19; 1 Corinthians 2:4,13; 1 Thessalonians 1:5; 1 Peter 3:18)

Christ's death on the cross—the very purpose for which Christ came to earth (9:22–23; 17:25; 18:31–33; 24:25–26,46; Isaiah 53:7–9; Acts 13:29; 1 Corinthians 1:18; 5:7; Galatians 5:11; 6:14; Ephesians 5:2; Philippians 2:8; Colossians 2:14; Hebrews 10:1,11–12)

GOD'S CHARACTER IN LUKE

God is accessible—23:45
God is holy—1:49
God is long-suffering—13:6–9
God is merciful—1:50, 78
God is powerful—11:20; 12:5
God is a promise keeper—1:38,45,54–55,69–73
God is provident—2:1–4; 21:18,32–33; 22:35
God is wise—16:15

CHRIST IN LUKE

Luke, a physician himself, presents Jesus as the Great Physician (5:31,32; 15:4–7,31,32; 19:10). Luke examines Jesus' interaction with tax collectors, women, children, Gentiles, and Samaritans, demonstrating His unique ministry to the outcasts of society. Luke also describes Jesus as the Son of Man, emphasizing His offer of salvation to the world.

KEY WORDS IN LUKE

Baptize: Greek *baptizō*—3:7,16,12,21; 7:29,30; 12:50—literally, "to dip" or "to immerse." People came to John to be immersed by him in the Jordan River. The baptism of Gentile proselytes to Judaism was common to the Jews, but this kind of baptism for Jews was new and strange to them. John called them to be baptized as a public renunciation of their old way of life. Their baptism also symbolized the preparation of their hearts for the coming of the Messiah. Paul connected baptism with the believers' identification with Christ. Just as a cloth soaked in dye absorbs the color of the dye, so a person immersed in Christ should take on the nature of Christ.

Mammon: Greek *mamōnas*—16:9,11,13—literally, "wealth," "money," or "property." In Luke 16, this word is used for "riches." *Mammon* is also considered an idol or god of the human heart that is in conflict with the true God. The Bible proclaims it is impossible to serve this god of the world and the true God at the same time.

Paradise: Greek *paradeisos*—23:43—literally, "garden" or "park." The Septuagint uses this word literally in Ecclesiastes 2:5 and Song of Solomon 4:13, although the term also refers to the Garden of Eden (see Genesis 2:8). Later, Paradise was described as the place of the righteous dead in Sheol (Luke 16:19–31). When Jesus spoke to the thief on the cross, He assured him that he would that day reside with Him in Paradise (23:42). This seems to indicate that this word refers to a pleasant place for the righteous among the dead. Revelation 2:7 speaks of Paradise as the restitution of an Edenic paradise, an everlasting home for believers (compare Genesis 2 and Revelation 22).

QUICK OVERVIEW

I. The Prelude to Christ's Ministry (1:1–4:13)
  A. Preamble (1:1–4)
  B. The Birth of Jesus (1:5–2:38)
  C. The Boyhood of Jesus (2:39–52)
  D. The Baptism of Jesus (3:1–4:13)
II. The Ministry in Galilee (4:14–9:50)[1]
  A. The Commencement of His Ministry (4:14–44)
  B. The Calling of His Disciples (5:1–6:16)
  C. The Continuation of His Work (6:17–9:50)
III. The Journey to Jerusalem (9:51–19:27)
  A. Samaria (9:51–10:37)
  B. Bethany and Judea (10:38–13:35)
  C. Perea (14:1–19:27)
IV. The Passion Week (19:28–23:56)
  A. Sunday (19:28–44)
  B. Monday (19:45–48)
  C. Tuesday (20:1–21:38)
  D. Wednesday (22:1–6)
  E. Thursday (22:7–53)
  F. Friday (22:54–23:55)
  G. The Sabbath (23:56)
V. The Consummation of Christ's Ministry (24:1–53)
  A. The Resurrection (24:1–12)
  B. The Road to Emmaus (24:13–45)
  C. The Ascension (24:46–53)

MEANWHILE, IN OTHER PARTS OF THE WORLD . . .
Mark Antony and Cleopatra are defeated by Octavian in the Battle of Actium in 30 B.C. and commit suicide. As a result, Egypt becomes a Roman province.

FREQUENTLY ASKED QUESTIONS

1. What do we know about Luke himself?

Very little is actually known about Luke. According to tradition and limited internal evidence, Luke was a Gentile. The Apostle Paul seems to confirm this, distinguishing Luke from those who were "of the circumcision" (Colossians 4:11,14). That would make Luke the only Gentile to pen any books of Scripture.

Luke almost never included personal details about himself. Nothing definite is known about his background or his conversion. Both Eusebius and Jerome identified him as a native of Antioch, which may explain why so much of the Book of Acts centers on Antioch (Acts 11:19–27; 13:1–3; 14:26; 15:22–23,30–35; 18:22–23).

Luke was a frequent companion of the Apostle Paul. They were apparently inseparable from the time of Paul's Macedonian vision (Acts 16:9,10) right up to the time of Paul's martyrdom (2 Timothy 4:11). Paul referred to Luke as a physician (Colossians 4:14). This explains Luke's interest in medical phenomena and the high profile he gave to Jesus' healing ministry (for more on Luke, see **Background and Setting**).

2. What passages in Luke are unique to his gospel?

Luke included twelve events or major passages not found in the other gospels:

- Events preceding the birth of John the Baptist and Jesus (1:5–80)
- Scenes from Jesus' childhood (2:1–52)
- Herod imprisons John the Baptist (3:19–20)
- The people of Nazareth reject Jesus (4:16–30)
- The first disciples are called (5:1–11)
- A widow's son is raised (7:11–17)
- A woman anoints Jesus' feet (7:36–50)
- Certain women minister to Christ (8:1–3)
- Events, teaching, and miracles during the months leading up to Christ's death (10:1–18:14)
- Christ abides with Zacchaeus (19:1–27)
- Herod tries Christ (23:6–12)
- Some of Jesus' final words before His ascension (24:44–49)

3. For whom did Luke write?

Luke shares some similarities with Mark that indicate he intended his gospel for a Gentile readership. He took pains to identify locations that would have been familiar to all Jews (4:31; 23:51; 24:13), suggesting that he had in mind readers who did not have a knowledge of Palestinian geography. He usually preferred Greek terms over Hebrew ones—for example, "Calvary" instead of "Golgotha" (23:33). Luke avoided the use of Semitic terms such as "Abba" (Mark 14:36), "rabbi" (Matthew 23:7–8; John 1:38,49), and "hosanna" (Matthew 21:9; Mark 11:9–10; John 12:13).

The third gospel writer quoted the Old Testament more sparingly than Matthew. When citing Old Testament passages, Luke nearly always employed the Septuagint (LXX), a Greek translation of the Hebrew Scriptures. Furthermore, most of Luke's Old Testament references are actually allusions rather than direct quotations. They appear in Jesus' words rather than in Luke's narrative sections (2:23–24; 3:4–6; 4:4,8,10–12,18–19; 7:27; 10:27; 18:20; 19:46; 20:17–18,37,42–43; 22:37).

4. What about those who claim to see a wide gap between Luke's theology and Paul's theology?

Although Luke, more than any of the other gospel writers, highlighted the universal scope of the gospel invitation, some have questioned why a companion of Paul's would use so little of Paul's language in explaining the process of salvation. But a difference in vocabulary does not necessarily imply a difference in thought or underlying theology.

Luke certainly wrote with his own style. He was an astute observer and careful thinker. In writing the gospel, he was careful not to insert Pauline language back into the gospel account. The theology of Luke's record parallels Paul's exactly. Luke repeatedly related accounts of Gentiles, Samaritans, and other outcasts who found grace in Jesus' eyes. This emphasis not only records Jesus' appeal but also proves to be precisely what we would expect from the close companion of the "apostle to the Gentiles" (Romans 11:13).

A compelling illustration of this parallel involves Luke's treatment of the centerpiece of Paul's doctrine—justification by faith. Luke highlighted and illustrated justification by faith in many of the incidents and parables he related in his gospel. For example, the account of the Pharisee and the publican (18:9–14), the familiar story of the Prodigal Son (15:11–32), the incident at Simon's house (7:36–50), and the salvation of Zacchaeus (19:1–10) all serve to demonstrate that Jesus taught justification by faith long before Paul wrote about it.

QUICK STUDY ON LUKE

1. What evidence would you point to in the Gospel of Luke that would indicate he was a physician?
2. How can you tell the writer of Luke's gospel was a historian?
3. What details about Jesus' birth and early life do you find particularly significant? Why?
4. How does Jesus particularly demonstrate compassion in the Gospel of Luke?

5. In what ways does Luke note and acknowledge the presence of the Holy Spirit throughout his gospel?
6. What aspects of Luke's resurrection account make it clear that he recognized the historical importance of the events he was recording?

---

[1] See also "The Ministries of Jesus Christ" in the Appendices at the back of this book.

JOHN
Jesus Is the Son of God

The gospel by the disciple Jesus loved.

When an exciting event happens, some people can't wait to talk about it. Others like to think about the reasons and details for a while before they offer their comments. One of the four biographies of Jesus fits this second category. John must have spoken many times about his experiences with Jesus, but he did not write down his gospel until long after the other three writers had published theirs. The passage of time did not change the central character in John's account, but it allowed him to express some conclusions about Jesus that could best be made after lifelong reflection on the significance of God's visit to earth.

AUTHOR AND DATE

Written by the Apostle John, approximately A.D. 80 to 90

Although the author's name does not appear in the gospel, early church tradition strongly and consistently identifies him as the Apostle John. Ireneaus (about A.D. 130–200), who was a disciple of Polycarp (about A.D. 70–160), a disciple of the Apostle John, testified on Polycarp's authority that John wrote this gospel (*Against Heresies* 2.22.5; 3.1.1). Subsequent to Ireneaus, all the church fathers assumed John to be the gospel's author. One of them, Clement of Alexandria (about A.D. 150–215), wrote that John, aware of the facts set forth in the other gospels, and being moved by the Holy Spirit, composed a "spiritual gospel" (see Eusebius's *Ecclesiastical History* 6.14.7).

Reinforcing early church tradition are significant internal characteristics of the gospel. While the synoptic Gospels (Matthew, Mark, and Luke) frequently identify the Apostle John by name, he is not directly mentioned by name at all in the Gospel of John. Instead, the author prefers to identify himself as the disciple "whom Jesus loved" (13:23; 19:26; 20:2; 21:7, 20). The absence of John's name is remarkable when one considers the important part played by other named disciples in this gospel. Yet, the recurring designation of himself as the disciple "whom Jesus loved," a deliberate avoidance by John of his personal name, reflects his humility and celebrates his relation to his Lord Jesus. John's authorship is established by conspicuous absence.

KEY PEOPLE IN JOHN

Jesus—the Word of God who came into the world; both fully God and fully human (1:1–21:25)

John the Baptist—prophet and forerunner who announced the coming of Christ (1:6–42; 3:23–27; 4:1; 5:33; 10:40–41)

The disciples—Simon Peter, Andrew, James, John, Philip, Bartholomew, Thomas, Matthew, James (son of Alphaeus), Thaddaeus, Simon, Judas Iscariot; twelve men chosen by Jesus to aid His ministry on earth (1:53–21:14)

Mary—sister of Lazarus; believed and anointed Jesus before His death (11:1–12:11)

Martha—sister of Lazarus; known for her hospitality; grew in faith when Jesus raised her brother from the dead (11:17–45)

Lazarus—raised from the dead by Jesus, his friend (11:1–12:17)

Mary, Jesus' mother—demonstrated her servanthood to Jesus; entrusted to the care of John at Jesus' death (2:1–12; 19:25–27)

Pilate—Roman governor who ordered the crucifixion of Jesus in place of Barabbas (18:29–19:38)

Mary Magdalene—devoted follower of Jesus; first person to see Jesus after His resurrection (19:25–20:18)

BACKGROUND AND SETTING

John's gospel is the only one of the four that contains a precise statement regarding the author's purpose (20:30–31). He declares, "These are written that you may believe that Jesus is the Christ, the Son of God, and that believing you may have life in His name" (20:31). The motivating purposes for writing this book, therefore, are twofold: evangelistic and apologetic.

John emphasized his evangelistic purpose by using the word "believe" approximately a hundred times in the gospel—twice as often as the synoptics use the term. He composed his gospel to provide reasons for saving faith in his readers and, as a result, to assure them that they would receive the divine gift of eternal life (1:12).

John's apologetic purpose often overlapped his evangelistic purpose. He wrote to convince his readers of Jesus' true identity as the incarnate God-man whose divine and human natures were perfectly united into one person who was the prophesied Christ ("Messiah") and Savior of the world (1:41; 3:16; 4:25–26; 8:58). John organized his gospel around eight "signs" or proofs (apart from the central sign of the Resurrection itself) that reinforce Jesus' true identity leading to faith. Seven of the miraculous signs lead up to the Resurrection and one follows it:

- Turning water into wine (2:1–11)
- Healing the royal official's son (4:46–54)
- Healing the lame man (5:1–18)
- Feeding multitudes (6:1–15)
- Walking on water (6:16–21)
- Healing the blind man (9:1–41)
- Raising Lazarus (11:1–57)
- Catching fish miraculously (21:6–11)

KEY DOCTRINES IN JOHN

The divinity of Jesus Christ—who Jesus really is (6:35; 8:12; 10:7,9; 10:11,14; 11:25; 14:6; 15:1,5; 20:28–31; Isaiah 9:6; 40:9; Jeremiah 23:5–6; Zechariah 13:7; Matthew 1:23; Mark 2:7–10; Romans 9:5; 1 Corinthians 1:30; Philippians 2:6; Colossians 2:9; Titus 2:13; 1 John 5:20; Revelation 22:13)

Salvation through Jesus Christ—how people should respond to Jesus (1:1–18; 6:35,48; 8:12; 10:7,9; 10:11–14; 11:25; 14:6; 17:3; Genesis 3:15; Psalms 3:8; 37:39; Isaiah 45:21–22; 49:6; 59:16; 63:9; Luke 1:69; Acts 4:12; 16:31; Romans 5:8; 10:9; Ephesians 2:8; 5:23; 2 Timothy 1:10; Hebrews 2:10; 5:9; 1 Peter 1:5; 1 John 1:1–4)

GOD'S CHARACTER IN JOHN

God is accessible—1:51; 10:7,9; 14:6
God is glorious—1:14
God is invisible—1:18; 5:37
God is loving—3:16; 15:9–10; 16:27; 17:23,26
God is righteous—17:25
God is spirit—4:24
God is true—17:3,17
God is unified—10:30; 14:9–11; 17:3
God is wrathful—3:14–18,36

CHRIST IN JOHN

Unquestionably, the Gospel of John stands as a proclamation of the divinity of Jesus Christ. John reveals the nature of Jesus in his first sentence: "In the beginning was the Word, and the Word was with God, and the Word was God" (1:1). Whereas the Gospel of Mark focuses on Jesus as the Son of Man, the message of John is that "Jesus is the Christ, the Son of God" (20:31). Notably, Jesus asserts Himself as God in seven explicit statements designating Himself as "I AM" (6:35; 8:12; 10:7,9; 10:11,14; 11:25; 14:6; 15:1,5).

KEY WORDS IN JOHN

The Word: Greek *ho logos*—1:1,14; 2:22; 5:24; 8:43; 15:3; 17:14,17—used to speak of the Creator of the universe, even the creative energy that generated the universe. In the Old Testament, the term *logos* may also be connected with wisdom as a personification or attribute of God (see Proverbs 8). In both Jewish and Greek usage, the Logos was associated with the idea of beginnings—the world began with the Word (Genesis 1:3). John specifically used this word to identify the Son of God as divine. Jesus is the image of the invisible God (Colossians 1:15), and the very substance of God (Hebrews 1:3). In the Godhead, the Son functions as the revelation of God and is God in reality.

Born Again: Greek *gennaō anōthen*—3:3,7—literally, "again" or "from above." Jesus spoke of a birth that was either a new birth, or a heavenly birth, or both. Most likely Jesus was speaking of a heavenly birth because He described this birth using an analogy of the wind, coming from some unknown, heavenly source. Nicodemus clearly understood Jesus to be speaking of a second natural birth—being born again. Jesus explained this birth in 3:6–8 by contrasting being born of the flesh and being born of the Spirit.

I AM: Greek *egō eimi*—6:36; 8:58; 10:7,14; 15:1; 18:5—literally, "self-identity in self-sufficiency." In one breath, Jesus proclaimed His eternal preexistence and His absolute deity. Jesus Christ, the Son of God, unlike any human, never had a beginning. He is the eternal God. Jesus clearly states His deity by using the words "I AM" to refer to Himself. In Exodus 3:14, God reveals His identity as "I AM WHO I AM." Thus, Jesus claimed before His judges to be the ever-existing, self-existent God.

Believe: Greek *pisteuō*—1:7; 5:44; 6:64; 7:5; 10:26; 11:48; 13:19; 20:31—literally, "to place one's trust in another." True belief in Jesus requires one to completely trust Him for salvation (3:15–16). When Jesus walked the earth, many people believed in His miraculous powers, but they would not put their faith in Jesus Himself (6:23–26). Others wanted to believe in Jesus only as a political defender of Israel (Mark 15:32). However, we must be careful to believe and trust in the Jesus presented in the Scriptures—the Son of God who humbly sacrificed Himself to deliver us from the bondage of sin (Galatians 1:3–4; Philippians 2:5–8).

QUICK OVERVIEW

I. The Incarnation of the Son of God (1:1–18)
   - A. His Eternality (1:1–2)
   - B. His Preincarnate Work (1:3–5)
   - C. His Forerunner (1:6–8)
   - D. His Rejection (1:9–11)
   - E. His Reception (1:12–13)
   - F. His Deity (1:14–18)

II. The Presentation of the Son of God (1:19–4:54)
   - A. Presentation by John the Baptist (1:19–34)
   - B. Presentation to John's Disciples (1:35–51)
   - C. Presentation in Galilee (2:1–12)
   - D. Presentation in Judea (2:13–3:36)

E. Presentation in Samaria (4:1–42)
F. Presentation in Galilee (4:43–54)
III. The Opposition to the Son of God (5:1–12:50)
A. Opposition at the Feast in Jerusalem (5:1–47)
B. Opposition during Passover (6:1–71)
C. Opposition at the Feast of Tabernacles (7:1–10:21)
D. Opposition at the Feast of Dedication (10:22–42)
E. Opposition at Bethany (11:1–12:11)
F. Opposition in Jerusalem (12:12–50)
IV. The Preparation of the Disciples by the Son of God (13:1–17:26)
A. In the Upper Room (13:1–14:31)
B. On the Way to the Garden (15:1–17:26)
V. The Execution of the Son of God (18:1–19:37)
A. The Rejection of Christ (18:1–19:16)
B. The Crucifixion of Christ (19:17–37)
VI. The Resurrection of the Son of God (19:38–21:23)
A. The Burial of Christ (19:38–42)
B. The Resurrection of Christ (20:1–10)
C. The Appearances of Christ (20:11–21:23)
VII. Conclusion (21:24–25)[1]

MEANWHILE, IN OTHER PARTS OF THE WORLD . . .
Music develops in Asia as the Chinese octave is subdivided into sixty different musical notes.

FREQUENTLY ASKED QUESTIONS

1. How do scholars conclude that the expression "whom Jesus loved" was John's way of referring to himself in the Gospel of John?

Three obvious clues about John's gospel help identify the unnamed disciple who called himself the disciple "whom Jesus loved" (13:23; 19:26; 20:2; 21:7,20).

- Early church fathers invariably identify the Apostle John as the author of this gospel.
- John is frequently mentioned by the other gospel writers as an active participant among the disciples of Jesus.
- John's name is absent from the fourth gospel.

If four people take a trip together and each carries a camera, the group shots each person takes will naturally not include them. In fact, someone else could probably guess who took which pictures by which member of the group was absent. The Gospel of John functions this way. John's absence by name shouts his presence.

As for his signature phrase, the words "whom Jesus loved" convey both a sense of the apostle's humility and the depth of his relationship to Jesus. The phrase doesn't mean that John thought of himself as the only disciple Jesus loved. It simply expresses with disarming honesty the wonder of this disciple over the fact that the Lord loved him!

2. What makes the Gospel of John so different from the other three gospels?

Clement of Alexandria (about A.D. 150–215), one of the early church fathers, may have been the first to describe John's biography of Jesus as a "spiritual gospel." Apparently, John wrote his gospel in order to make a unique contribution to the records of the Lord's life and to be supplementary as well as complementary to Matthew, Mark, and Luke.

Because John wrote in such a clear and simple style, one might tend to underestimate the depth of his gospel. True to its description as a "spiritual gospel," however, the truths John conveys are profound. A reader must prayerfully and meticulously explore the book in order to discover the vast richness of the spiritual treasure that the apostle, under the guidance of the Holy Spirit, has lovingly deposited in his gospel (14:26; 16:13).

3. The timing of events in parts of the Gospel of John seems to differ from the other gospels. How can we explain those apparent differences?

The chronological reckoning between John's gospel and the synoptics does present a challenge in the accounts of the Last Supper (13:2). While the synoptics portray the disciples and the Lord at the Last Supper as eating the Passover meal on Thursday evening (Nisan 14) and Jesus being crucified on Friday, John's gospel states that the Jews did not enter into the Praetorium "lest they should be defiled, but that they might eat the Passover" (18:28). So, the disciples had eaten the Passover on Thursday evening, but the Jews had not. In fact, John (19:14) states that Jesus' trial and crucifixion were on the day of preparation for the Passover and not after the eating of the Passover. This means that since the trail and crucifixion occurred on Friday, Christ was actually sacrificed at the same time the Passover lambs were being slain (19:14). The question then becomes, "Why did the disciples eat the Passover meal on Thursday?"

The answer lies in the fact that there were two distinct ways the Jews in Jesus' day reckoned the beginning and ending of days. Jews in northern Palestine calculated days from sunrise to sunrise. At least one nonregional group, the Pharisees, used that system of timekeeping. But the Jews in southern Israel, which centered in Jerusalem, calculated day from sunset to sunset. In contrast to the Pharisees, the priests and Sadducees, who for the most part lived around Jerusalem, followed the southern scheme.

In spite of the confusion these two calendars must have created at times, they were kept for practical reasons. During the Passover season, for instance, it allowed for the feast to be celebrated legitimately on two adjoining days. This also permitted the temple sacrifices to be made over a total of four hours rather than two. The size of the population made this a complicated project. By lengthening the time for sacrifices, the double calendar had the effect of reducing both regional and religious clashes between the different groups.

The double calendar easily explains the apparent contradictions in the gospel accounts. Being Galileans (northerners), Jesus and the disciples considered Passover day to have started at sunrise on Thursday and end at sunrise on Friday. The Jewish leaders who arrested and tried Jesus, being mostly priests and Sadducees, considered Passover day to begin at sunset on Thursday and end at sunset on Friday. This explains how Jesus could thereby legitimately celebrate the last Passover meal with His disciples and yet still be sacrificed on Passover day.

In these meticulous details one can see how God sovereignly and marvelously provided for the precise fulfillment of His redemptive plan. Jesus was anything but a victim of men's wicked schemes, much less of blind circumstance. Every word He spoke and every action He took were divinely directed and secured. Even the words and actions by others against Him were divinely controlled (11:49–52; 19:11).

QUICK STUDY ON JOHN

1. How would you describe the difference in style and approach between John and the other three gospels?
2. What are John's purposes in the first eighteen verses of his gospel?
3. Compare the use of the word *believe* in John 3:16 with the same word in other verses in John. What kind of belief does God require?
4. Summarize Jesus' teaching on the Holy Spirit in John 14:15–31 and 16:5–16?
5. How have you responded to Jesus' question in John 11:25–26?
6. As in each of the Gospels, the Resurrection of Jesus is the climax of John's gospel. Why is that event so crucial in Christianity?

---

[1] See also "The Ministries of Jesus Christ" in the Appendices at the back of this book.

ACTS
Christ Builds His Church

The second half of Luke's masterpiece, Acts, records the story of the early church.

Everyone underestimated the possibility and the power of the resurrection of Jesus Christ. Even those who had advance warning were taken by surprise. The truth of His victory over death transformed the lives of His followers. They became living witnesses to Jesus' resurrection. That good news spread like wildfire.

Those first disciples were filled with more than a message, however; they were also filled with a Motivator—the Holy Spirit. Their travels, trials, and triumphs changed the course of history. Led by the Holy Spirit, the apostles carried the gospel throughout the world. In fact, this book that describes the early years of the Christian church could most properly be called "The Acts of the Holy Spirit through the Apostles." The Holy Spirit's directing, controlling, and empowering ministry strengthened the church and caused it to grow in numbers, spiritual power, and influence.

AUTHOR AND DATE

Written by Luke, approximately A.D. 60–62

The opening verses of Luke and Acts strongly suggest that both books had the same writer because both are addressed to Theophilus. The writer of Acts specifically claims to have written an earlier book to this mystery person named Theophilus (1:1) about the life and teaching of Jesus. Early church fathers such as Irenaeus, Clement of Alexandria, Tertullian, Origen, Eusebius, and Jerome all affirm Luke's authorship in their writings. So does the Muratorian Canon (about A.D. 170). Because Luke is a relatively obscure figure, mentioned only three times in the New Testament (Colossians 4:14; 2 Timothy 4:11; Philemon 24), it is unlikely that anyone would have forged a work to make it appear to be his. A forger surely would have attributed his work to a more prominent person, such as one of the original twelve disciples or Paul.

KEY PEOPLE IN ACTS

Peter—one of the twelve disciples of Jesus; called "the Rock" (1:13–12:18; 15:7–14)

John—one of the twelve disciples of Jesus; called "the disciple whom Jesus loved" (1:13; 3:1–4:31; 8:14–25; see John 21:20)

James—one of the twelve disciples; first disciple to die for his faith in Christ (1:13; 12:1–2)

Stephen—appointed as a manager of food distribution in the early church; martyred for his faith in Christ (6:3–8:2; 22:20)

Philip—appointed as a manager of food distribution in the early church; one of the first missionaries to Samaria (1:13; 6:5; 8:1–40; 21:8)

Paul—New Testament writer and missionary; originally named Saul; early persecutor of Christians before his conversion (7:58–8:3; 9:1–30; 11:25–30; 12:25–28:30)

Barnabas—name means "Son of Encouragement"; traveled as a missionary with Paul and then with John Mark (4:36; 9:27; 11:22–15:39)

Cornelius—Roman officer; one of the first Gentile Christians (10:1–48)

Timothy—Paul's assistant; later became a pastor in Ephesus (16:1–20:4)

Lydia—believer and hostess to Paul and Silas; seller of purple cloth (16:13–40)

Silas—served as a missionary; involved in the ministries of Paul and Timothy and Peter (15:22–18:5)

Apollos—Alexandrian preacher who ministered in Achaia; instructed by Aquila and Priscilla (18:24–19:1)

Felix—Roman governor of Judea; kept Paul in prison for two years (23:24–25:14)

Festus—succeeded Felix as governor; reviewed Paul's case with Herod Agrippa II (24:27–26:32)

Herod Agrippa II—reviewed Paul's case with Festus; responded to the gospel with sarcasm (25:13—26:32)

Luke—medical physician who traveled with Paul; author of the Book of Acts (16:10–28:31)

BACKGROUND AND SETTING

Luke's purposes in writing the Gospel of Luke and the Acts of the Apostles form a powerful parallel. Luke sought to write "an orderly account" (Luke 1:3) of what Jesus had accomplished during His earthly ministry. Acts simply extended the effort, offering "an orderly account" of what Jesus had accomplished through the early church.

Beginning with Christ's ascension (His rise into heaven), through the birth of the church on the Day of Pentecost and to Paul's preaching in Rome, Acts chronicles the spread of the gospel and the growth of the church (see 1:15; 2:41,47; 4:4; 5:14; 6:7; 9:31; 12:24; 13:49; 16:5; 19:20). It also tells of the mounting opposition to the gospel (see 2:13; 4:1–22; 5:17–42; 6:9–8:4; 12:1–5; 13:6–12,45–50; 14:2–6,19–20; 16:19–20; 17:5–9; 19:23–41; 21:27–36; 23:12–21; 28:24).

Like the Gospel of Luke, Acts begins with a dedication to Theophilus, whose name means "lover of God." The name has no history apart from Luke's use in his two books. Whether this was a believer whom Luke was instructing or a pagan whom Luke was seeking to convert is unknown.

Luke's positive salutation, "most excellent Theophilus" (Luke 1:3), suggests that the recipient was a Roman official of some importance. Examples of this kind of greeting can be found in 24:3 and 26:25.

Acts begins in Jerusalem and ends in Rome. Luke's account captures the geographical spread of the gospel throughout the Roman Empire. He provides the story of how God "opened the door of faith to the Gentiles" (14:27).

KEY DOCTRINES IN ACTS

The establishment of the church—the history of how the faith spread (2:1; 4:23–24,32–37; 9:31; Matthew 16:18; Romans 12:5; 1 Corinthians 10:17; 12:12; Galatians 3:28; Ephesians 4:15–16; 1 Timothy 3:15; Revelation 19:8)

The work of the Holy Spirit—how the Spirit of God directed the church and individual believers (1:8; 2:2–4,16–18,38; 4:8; 8:29; 11:12; 13:2; 16:6; 21:11; Genesis 6:3; Numbers 11:25–27; Nehemiah 9:30; Isaiah 48:16; Zechariah 7:12; John 15:26; Romans 8:16,26; 1 Corinthians 2:4,9–10; Hebrews 2:4; 1 John 3:24; 4:13; Revelation 2:7,11,29)

GOD'S CHARACTER IN ACTS

God is accessible—14:27
God is glorious—7:2,55
God is good—14:17
God is just—17:31
God is Most High—7:48
God is a promise keeper—1:4; 2:33,39; 7:17; 13:22–23,32; 26:6–7
God is provident—1:26; 3:17–18; 12:5; 17:26; 27:22,31–32
God is righteous—17:31
God is wise—15:18

CHRIST IN ACTS

The Book of Acts gives the account of Jesus' ministry being passed on to His disciples. Their mission was to proclaim the resurrected Christ and fulfill the Great Commission given to them by Jesus (Matthew 28:19,20). The disciples acted as witnesses to the salvation brought about by Christ (4:12; 10:43).

KEY WORDS IN ACTS

Spirit: Greek *to pneuma*—2:4; 5:9; 8:39; 10:19; 11:12; 16:7; 19:21; 23:9—derived from the verb *pneō*, meaning "to breathe" or "to blow." It is sometimes used to refer to the wind and sometimes to life itself (see John 3:8; Revelation 13:15). It can refer to the life of angels (Hebrews 1:14), demons (Luke 4:33), and human beings (7:59). Yet this word is also used for the Spirit of God (see 1 Corinthians 2:11), that is, the Holy Spirit (Matthew 28:19), the third Person of the Trinity, the One who lives inside believers (see James 4:5; 1 John 4:13). This same Spirit is called "the Spirit of Jesus Christ" (Philippians 1:19); manuscripts have the title *the Spirit of Jesus* in 16:7. This title emphasizes the unity of action between Jesus and the Spirit that permeates this book and its companion volume, the Gospel of Luke. During the days of Jesus' earthly ministry, the disciples were directed by Jesus; now, after His resurrection and ascension, by the Spirit of Jesus.

Grace: Greek *charis*—4:33; 11:23; 13:43; 14:26; 15:11; 18:27; 20:32—probably equivalent to the Hebrew word *chesed* meaning "loving-kindness," a word frequently used by the psalmists to describe God's character. In the New Testament, the word *charis* usually signifies divine favor or goodwill, but it also means "that which gives joy" and "that which is a free gift." This is a noteworthy occurrence of the word *grace* because while it was one of Paul's favorite words for God's free gift of salvation, here we see Luke using it in the same way.

Together: Greek *epi to auto*—1:15; 2:1,44—idiom meaning "toward the same thing" or "in the same place"; it conveys the idea of united purpose or collective unity. In the early church it acquired a special meaning, indicating the union of the Christian body. All the members of the church not only gathered together regularly, they shared all things in common and were committed to each other and Christ with united fervor.

QUICK OVERVIEW

I. Prologue (1:1–8)
II. The Witness to Jerusalem (1:9–8:3)
    A. The Anticipation of the Church (1:9–26)
    B. The Founding of the Church (2:1–47)
    C. The Growth of the Church (3:1–8:3)
III. The Witness to Judea and Samaria (8:4–12:25)
    A. The Gospel to the Samaritans (8:4–25)
    B. The Conversion of a Gentile (8:26–40)
    C. The Conversion of Saul (9:1–31)
    D. The Gospel to Judea (9:32–43)
    E. The Gospel to the Gentiles (10:1–11:30)
    F. The Persecution by Herod (12:1–25)
IV. The Witness to the Ends of the Earth (13:1–28:31)
    A. Paul's First Missionary Journey (13:1–14:28)
    B. The Jerusalem Council (15:1–35)
    C. Paul's Second Missionary Journey (15:36–18:22)

D. Paul's Third Missionary Journey (18:23–21:16)
E. Paul's Jerusalem and Caesarean Trials (21:17–26:32)
F. Paul's Journey to Rome (27:1–28:31)

MEANWHILE, IN OTHER PARTS OF THE WORLD . . .
The Romans learn to use soap from the Gauls for cleaning purposes.

FREQUENTLY ASKED QUESTIONS

1. How can Luke's authorship of Acts of the Apostles be defended when his own name is not mentioned in the book?

Lack of the author's name is not an unusual challenge in establishing the authorship of a Bible book. Many books of the Bible come to us without obvious human authorship. In most cases, however, internal and external clues lead us to reasonable confidence in identifying the authors. One benefit created by initial anonymity involves recognizing that the Bible books originated by the inspiration of the Holy Spirit. It may take some effort to discover whom God used in writing one of those books, but the original Author is not in question.

The Gospel of Luke and Acts of the Apostles share numerous marks of common human authorship. They are addressed to the same person—Theophilus (Luke 1:3; Acts 1:1). They are parallel in style. The second book claims to be an extension of the first.

Luke was in a unique position to record Acts of the Apostles. He was Paul's close friend, traveling companion, and personal physician (Colossians 4:14). His work indicates that he was a careful researcher (Luke 1:1–4) and an accurate historian, displaying an intimate knowledge of Roman laws and customs. His records of the geography of Palestine, Asia Minor, and Italy offer flawless details.

In writing Acts, Luke drew on written sources (15:23–29; 23:26–30). He also, no doubt, interviewed key figures, such as Peter, John, and others in the Jerusalem church. Paul's two-year imprisonment at Caesarea (24:27) gave Luke ample opportunity to interview Philip and his daughters (important sources of information on the early days of the church). Finally, Luke's frequent use of the first person plural pronouns "we" and "us" (16:10–17; 20:5–21:18; 27:1–28:16) reveals that he was an eyewitness to many of the events recorded in Acts.

2. What can we learn about the Holy Spirit's special role from the Book of Acts?

One of the cautions we must exercise in studying and teaching from the Book of Acts has to do with the difference between description and prescription. The difference plays an important role in interpreting the historical biblical books. The Bible's description of an event does not imply that the event or action can, should, or will be repeated.

The role of the Holy Spirit in His arrival as the promised Helper (John 14:17), which Acts describes as a startling audiovisual event (2:1–13), had some partial and selected repetitions (8:14–19; 10:44–48; 19:1–7). These were special cases in which believers are reported to have received or been filled with the Holy Spirit. In each of these cases, the sound and the tongues as of fire that were present in the original event (2:1–13) were absent, but the people spoke in tongues they did not know (but others recognized). These events should not be taken as the basis for teaching that believers today should expect the same evidence—tongues—to accompany the filling of the Holy Spirit. Even in Acts itself, genuine conversions did not necessarily lead to extraordinary filling by the Holy Spirit. For example, a crowd of three thousand people believed and were baptized on that same Day of Pentecost (2:41) that started so dramatically with the gift of tongues, yet no mention of tongues is made with regard to the new converts. So, why in some cases did tongues accompany the confirmation of faith? This likely demonstrated that believers were being drawn from very different groups into the church. Each new group received a special welcome from the Holy Spirit. Thus, Samaritans (8:14–19), Gentiles (10:44–48), and believers from the Old Covenant (19:1–7) were added to the church, and the unity of the church was established. To demonstrate that unity, it was imperative to have some replication in each instance of what had occurred at Pentecost with the believing Jews, such as the presence of the apostles and the coming of the Spirit manifested through speaking in the languages of Pentecost.

3. How does the baptism with the Holy Spirit (1 Corinthians 12:13) relate to the Holy Spirit's activities in the Book of Acts?

Acts describes a number of occasions in which the Holy Spirit "fell on" or "filled" or "came upon" people (2:4; 10:44; 19:6). Peter identifies these actions by God as a fulfillment of Joel's prophecy (Joel 2:28–32). Viewed from the perspective of the entire New Testament, these experiences were neither the same nor replacements for what John the Baptist (Mark 1:8) and Paul described as the baptism with the Holy Spirit (1 Corinthians 12:13). The baptism with the Spirit is the one-time act by which God places believers into His body. The filling, on the other hand, is a repeated reality of Spirit-controlled behavior that God commands believers to maintain (Ephesians 5:18). Peter and others who experienced that special filling on Pentecost day (2:4) were filled with the Spirit again (4:8,31; 6:5; 7:55) and so boldly spoke the Word of God. That was just the beginning. The fullness of the Spirit affects all areas of life, not just speaking boldly (Ephesians 5:18–33).

QUICK STUDY ON ACTS

1. What event from the Book of Acts would you most like to have attended yourself? Why?
2. How did the church begin? How did it grow?
3. What different kinds of opposition did the early Christians face?
4. In what different ways did those Christians share their faith?
5. How was the Holy Spirit acknowledged and welcomed in the early church?
6. In what ways are you continuing to carry the gospel to your Jerusalem, Judea, Samaria, and the ends of the earth (Acts 1:8)?

ROMANS
Summary of Christian Doctrine

"For the wages of sin is death, but the gift of God is eternal life in Christ Jesus our Lord" (Romans 6:23).

Romans stands out among Paul's many books, not simply because it is first in line and length, but because it offers the most complete summary of Paul's thought. It was neither Paul's earliest nor latest writing. He composed Romans as a mature reflection, under the guidance of the Holy Spirit, on the central themes of the gospel. The study of the Epistle to the Romans remains a required course in the school of Christian discipleship.

AUTHOR AND DATE

Written by the Apostle Paul, approximately A.D. 56

No one disputes that the Apostle Paul wrote Romans. Raised as both a Roman citizen and a devout Jew, Paul benefited from the finest education available in his time. He grew up as a Pharisee (Acts 23:6), a member of the strictest Jewish sect (Philippians 3:5). In the months following the resurrection of Jesus, Paul gained a reputation as a ruthless enemy of the followers of Jesus Christ.

Yet, after his miraculous conversion, Paul helped spread Christianity throughout the Roman Empire. He made three missionary journeys through much of the Mediterranean world, tirelessly preaching the gospel he had once sought to destroy (Acts 26:9). He eventually suffered martyrdom at Rome in about A.D. 65 to 67 (2 Timothy 4:6). For more on Paul the apostle, see the **Frequently Asked Question,** "Who was Paul?"

KEY PEOPLE IN ROMANS

Paul—apostle and author of the Book of Romans (1:1–16:22)
Phoebe—deaconess of the church at Cenchrea; trusted by Paul to deliver his letter (the Book of Romans) to the Roman believers (16:1–2)

BACKGROUND AND SETTING

Rome was the capital and most important city of the Roman Empire. It was founded in 753 B.C. but is not mentioned in Scripture until New Testament times. In Paul's day, the city had a population of over one million people, many of whom were slaves. Rome boasted magnificent buildings, such as the emperor's palace, the Circus Maximus, and the Forum, but the slums that surrounded and infiltrated the city marred its beauty. According to tradition, Paul was martyred outside Rome on the Ostian Way during Nero's reign (A.D. 54 to 68).

Some of those converted on the Day of Pentecost in Jerusalem probably returned to Rome and founded the church (Acts 2:10). Paul had long wanted to visit the Roman church but had been prevented from doing so (1:13). As an example of God's providence, Paul's inability to visit Rome in person resulted in the gift of this inspired masterpiece of gospel doctrine.

Paul's primary purpose in writing Romans was to teach the great truths of the gospel of grace to believers who had never received apostolic instruction. The letter also introduced him to a church where he was personally unknown. Paul still hoped to visit for several important reasons: to edify the believers (1:11); to preach the gospel (1:15); and to get to know the Roman Christians. He also anticipated their ministry to him by encouragement (1:12; 15:32), by prayer (15:30), and by help with his planned ministry in Spain (15:28).

Unlike some of his other epistles, Paul's purpose for writing Romans was not to correct aberrant theology or rebuke ungodly living. The Roman church was doctrinally sound but, like all churches, needed the rich doctrinal and practical instruction that this letter provides.

KEY DOCTRINES IN ROMANS

Mankind's sinfulness—Sin separates every human from God; only Jesus Christ can reconcile God and man (3:9–20; Genesis 3:6–7; 18:20; Exodus 32:31; Deuteronomy 9:7; 1 Kings 8:46; 14:16; Psalm 38:18; Proverbs 20:9; Ecclesiastes 7:20; Jeremiah 2:22; Romans 5:12; 2 Corinthians 5:21; Hebrews 4:15; 7:26)

Justification by faith—Complete freedom from judgment and the bondage of sin comes by faith alone in Jesus Christ (1:16–17; 3:21–4:25; 5:1–2,18; Leviticus 18:5; Isaiah 45:25; 50:8; 53:11; Jeremiah 23:6; Habakkuk 2:4; John 5:24; Acts 13:39; 1 Corinthians 6:11; Galatians 2:14–21; 3:11; 5:4; Titus 3:7; James 2:10)

Sanctification—Through Christ's atonement, believers are glorified and set apart for the service of God (6:1–8:39; 15:16; Psalm 4:3; Ezekiel 37:28; Acts 20:32; 26:18; 2 Corinthians 6:17; Ephesians 5:26–27; 1 Thessalonians 4:3–4; 5:23; 2 Thessalonians 2:13; 2 Timothy 2:21; Hebrews 2:11; 13:12; 1 Peter 1:2; Jude 1:1)

Reconciliation—The sacrifice of Jesus Christ renews the relationship between God and man (5:1,10–11; Leviticus 8:15; 16:20; Daniel 9:24; Isaiah 53:5; Matthew 5:24–26; 2 Corinthians 5:18–20; Ephesians 2:14–16; Colossians 1:20–22; 2:14; Hebrews 2:17)

GOD'S CHARACTER IN ROMANS

God is accessible—5:2
God is eternal—1:20
God is forgiving—3:25
God is glorious—3:23; 6:4

God is good—2:4
God is incorruptible—1:23
God is just—2:11; 3:4,26
God is long-suffering—2:4–5; 3:25; 9:22
God is loving—5:5,8; 8:39; 9:11–13
God is merciful—9:15,18
God is powerful—1:16,20; 9:21–22
God is a promise keeper—1:1–2; 4:13,16,20; 9:4,8; 15:8
God is provident—8:28; 11:33
God is reconciling—5:1,10
God is righteous—2:5; 3:25–26
God is unsearchable—11:33
God is wise—11:33; 16:27
God is wrathful—1:18; 2:5–6,8; 3:5–6; 5:9; 9:18,20,22

CHRIST IN ROMANS

The Book of Romans, functioning primarily as a doctrinal work, presents Christ as the Redeemer of mankind. Paul declares that faith in Christ alone bridges the chasm between the almighty God and sinful humanity. Thus, man is justified through the work of Christ on the cross.

KEY WORDS IN ROMANS

Justification: Greek *dikaiōsis*—4:25; 5:18—derived from the Greek verb *dikaiō*, meaning "to acquit" or "to declare righteous," used by Paul in 4:2,5; 5:1. It is a legal term used of a favorable verdict in a trial. The word depicts a courtroom setting, with God presiding as the Judge, determining the faithfulness of each person to the law. In the first section of Romans, Paul makes it clear that no one can withstand God's judgment (3:9–20). The law was not given to justify sinners but to expose their sin. To remedy this deplorable situation, God sent His Son to die for our sins in our place. When we believe in Jesus, God imputes His righteousness to us, and we are declared righteous before God. In this way, God demonstrates that He is both a righteous Judge and the One who declares us righteous, our Justifier (3:26).

Reconciliation: Greek *katallagē*—5:11; 11:15—basically means "change" or "exchange." In the context of relationships between people, the term implies a change in attitude on the part of both individuals, a change from enmity to friendship. When used to describe the relationship existing between God and a person, the term implies the change of attitude on the part of both a person and God. The need for change in the sinful ways of a human being is obvious, but some argue that no change is needed on the part of God. Yet inherent in the doctrine of justification is the changed attitude of God toward the sinner. God declares a person who was formerly His enemy to be righteous before Him.

Hope: Greek *elpis*—4:18; 5:2; 8:20,24; 12:12; 15:4,13—denotes "confident expectation" or "anticipation," not "wishful thinking" as in common parlance. The use of the word *hope* in this context is unusual and ironic, for it suggests that the Gentiles, who know nothing or little about the Messiah, were anticipating His coming. However, we need only think of Cornelius (Acts 10) to realize that some Gentiles had anticipated the coming of the Jewish Messiah. Jesus was sent not only for the salvation of the Jews, but also for the Gentiles. Since God is the Author of our salvation, we can call Him the God of hope for He has given us hope (15:13).

Law: Greek *nomos*—2:12,27; 3:27; 4:15; 7:1,7,23; 9:31; 13:10—means an inward principle of action, either good or evil, operating with the regularity of a law. The term also designates a standard for a person's life. The Apostle Paul described three such laws. The first is called "the law of sin" which was operating through his flesh, causing him to sin. Paul, like all other believers, needed another law to overcome "the law of sin." This is "the law of the Spirit of life in Christ Jesus," which makes us "free from the law of sin and death" (8:2). By following this law, believers can actually fulfill the righteous requirements of God's law (8:4), which is the third law in this section. God's law is the standard for human action that corresponds to the righteous nature of God.

QUICK OVERVIEW

I. Greetings and Introduction (1:1–15)
II. Theme (1:16–17)
III. Condemnation: The Need of God's Righteousness (1:18–3:20)
  A. Unrighteous Gentiles (1:18–32)
  B. Unrighteous Jews (2:1–3:8)
  C. Unrighteous Humankind (3:9–20)
IV. Justification: The Provision of God's Righteousness (3:21–5:21)
  A. The Source of Righteousness (3:21–31)
  B. The Example of Righteousness (4:1–25)
  C. The Blessings of Righteousness (5:1–11)
  D. The Imputation of Righteousness (5:12–21)
V. Sanctification: The Demonstration of God's Righteousness (6:1–8:39)
VI. Restoration: Israel's Reception of God's Righteousness (9:1–11:36)
VII. Application: The Behavior of God's Righteousness (12:1–15:13)
VIII. Conclusion, Greetings, and Benediction (15:14–16:27)

MEANWHILE, IN OTHER PARTS OF THE WORLD . . .
Buddhism is introduced into China by the emperor Ming-Ti.

FREQUENTLY ASKED QUESTIONS

1. Who was Paul the apostle, and why does he seem to have two names?

Paul (Greek name) the apostle was also known as Saul, which was his Hebrew name. Along with his double name, Paul was also able to exercise dual citizenship as a Jewish descendant from the tribe of Benjamin (Philippians 3:5) and as a Roman (Acts 16:37; 22:25). Paul was born about the time of Christ's birth, in Tarsus, located in modern Turkey (Acts 9:11).

Young Saul spent much of his early life in Jerusalem as a student of the celebrated rabbi (teacher) Gamaliel (Acts 22:3). Like his father before him, Paul was a Pharisee (Acts 23:6), a member of the strictest Jewish sect (Philippians 3:5). He actively resisted those who followed Jesus. His first appearance in Scripture occurs in Acts 7:58 as he observed the martyrdom of Stephen.

Miraculously converted while on his way to Damascus (about A.D. 33 to 34) to persecute Christians, Paul immediately began proclaiming the gospel (Acts 9:20). After narrowly escaping Damascus (Acts 9:23–25; 2 Corinthians 11:32–33), Paul spent three years in the wilderness (Galatians 1:17–18). During those years, he received much of his doctrine as direct revelation from the Lord (Galatians 1:11–12).

More than any other individual, Paul was responsible for the spread of Christianity throughout the Roman Empire. He made three missionary journeys along the north side of the Mediterranean Sea, tirelessly preaching the gospel he had once tried to destroy (Acts 26:9). Eventually he was arrested in Jerusalem (Acts 21:27–31), appealed for a hearing before Caesar, and finally reached Rome (chapters 27–28). Later, he was released for a short time of ministry, then arrested again and martyred at Rome in about A.D. 65 to 67.

Though physically unimpressive (2 Corinthians 10:10; Galatians 4:14), Paul possessed an inner strength granted him through the Holy Spirit's power (Philippians 4:13). The grace of God proved sufficient to provide for his every need (2 Corinthians 12:9–10), enabling this noble servant of Christ to successfully finish his spiritual race (2 Timothy 4:7).

2. When Paul writes in Romans 5:12 that "through one man sin entered the world, and death through sin, and thus death spread to all men, because all sinned," what does he mean?

Paul's discussion of the perpetuation of Adam's sin (5:12–21) is one of the deepest, most significant theological passages in all of Scripture. It establishes the basis for Paul's teaching that one man's (Christ's) death can provide salvation for many. To prove his point, he uses Adam to develop the principle that it is possible for one man's actions to inexorably affect many other people.

In this passage, the word *sin* does not refer to a particular sin, but to the inherent propensity to sin that invaded the human realm through Adam. People became sinners by nature. Adam passed on to all his descendants that inherently sinful nature he possessed as a result of his first disobedience. He caught the infection; the rest of us inherit it. The sin nature is present from the moment of conception (Psalm 51:5), making it impossible for any person to live in a way that pleases God.

When Adam sinned, his sin transformed his inner nature and brought spiritual death and depravity that was then passed on seminally to his posterity. Because all humanity existed in the loins of Adam, and have through procreation inherited his fallenness and depravity, it can be said that all sinned in him. Therefore, humans are not sinners because they sin, but, rather, they sin because they are sinners.

3. In verses like Romans 5:12 and 6:23, to what kind of death is Paul referring?

The word *death* has three distinct manifestations in biblical terminology:

- Spiritual death or separation from God (Ephesians 1:1–2,4,18)
- Physical death (Hebrews 9:27)
- Eternal death (also called the second death), which includes not only eternal separation from God, but eternal torment in the lake of fire (Revelation 20:11–15)

When sin entered the human race through Adam, all these aspects of death came with it. Adam was not originally subject to death, but through his sin, death became a grim certainty for him and his posterity. The death referred to in Romans 6:23 includes the first and third descriptions above. That verse establishes two inexorable absolutes: 1) spiritual death and eternal separation from God make up the paycheck for every person's slavery to sin; and 2) eternal life is a free gift God gives undeserving sinners who believe in His Son (Ephesians 2:8,9).

4. In Romans 7:7–25, what is Paul's actual perspective? Is he describing his own experience as a believer or unbeliever, or is his style simply a literary device?

Paul uses the personal pronoun *I* throughout this passage, using his own experience as an example of what is true of unredeemed humanity (7:7–12) and of true Christians (7:13–25). Some interpret this chronicle of Paul's inner conflict as describing his life before Christ. They point out that

Paul describes the person as "sold under sin" (7:14), as having "nothing good" in him (7:18), and as a "wretched man" trapped in a "body of death" (7:24). Those descriptions seem to contradict Paul's earlier description of the believer (6:2,6–7,11,17–18,22).

It is correct, however, to understand Paul here to be speaking about a believer. This person desires to obey God's law and hates sin (7:15,19,21). He is humble, recognizing that nothing good dwells in his humanness (7:18). He sees sin in himself, but not as all that is there (7:17,20–22). And he serves Jesus Christ with his mind (7:25). Paul has already established that none of those attitudes ever describe the unsaved (1:18–21,32; 3:10–20). Paul's use of the present tense verbs in 7:14–25 strongly supports the idea that he was describing his current experience as a Christian.

Even those who agree that Paul was speaking as a genuine believer, however, still find room for disagreement. Some see a carnal, fleshly Christian under the influence of old habits. Others see a legalistic Christian, frustrated by his feeble attempts in his own power to please God by keeping the Mosaic Law. But the personal pronoun *I* refers to the apostle Paul, a standard of spiritual health and maturity. This leads to the conclusion that Paul, in 7:7–25, must be describing all Christians—even the most spiritual and mature—who, when they honestly evaluate themselves against the righteous standard of God's law, realize how far short they fall. Notice, particularly, Paul's honesty and transparency in the four laments (7:14–17,18–20,21–25).

5. Explain the process Paul refers to in Romans 8:28–30 and 9:6–29. What do words like *called, foreknew, predestined,* and *elect* tell us about our standing with God?

With these words, God reveals in human terms His divine role in the process of salvation. Paul's description offends the human spirit because it minimizes our role. Yet only those who see their own helplessness in the face of sin can come to see how gracious God has been in acting and choosing ahead of time. We never surprise God; He always anticipates us! "But God demonstrates His own love toward us, in that while we were still sinners, Christ died for us" (Romans 5:8).

The term *foreknew* (8:29) does not simply refer to God's omniscience—that in eternity past He knew who would come to Christ. Rather, it speaks of a predetermined choice by God to set His love on us and establish an intimate relationship. The term *election* (9:11) refers to the same action on God's part (1 Peter 1:1–2,20). Salvation is not initiated by human choice. Even faith is a gift of God (Romans 1:16; John 6:37; Ephesians 2:8–9).

The term *predestined* (8:29) literally means "to mark out, appoint, or determine beforehand." Those God chooses, He destines for His chosen end, that is, likeness to His Son (Ephesians 1:4–5,11). The goal of God's predestined purpose for His own is that they would be made like Jesus Christ.

The reality and security of our standing with God rests ultimately in His character and decision, not ours. Paul summarized his teaching about the believer's security in Christ with a thundering litany of questions and answers that haunt believers. They reach their peak with "Who shall separate us from the love of Christ" (8:35)? Paul's answer is an almost poetic expression of praise for God's grace in bringing salvation to completion for all who are chosen and believe. It is a hymn of security.

QUICK STUDY ON ROMANS

1. What major themes does Paul introduce in the first chapter of Romans?
2. How does Paul discuss the subject of sin both personally and in relation to the world at large?
3. In what ways do the following verses (3:23; 5:8; 6:23; 10:9–10) outline the gospel mentioned in Romans 1:16?
4. How do the last five chapters of Romans differ from the first eleven?
5. What key words have you had to take time to understand in your study of Romans?
6. Summarize what Paul writes about the character and work God in Romans.
7. In what ways has the message of Romans made a difference in your own life?

FIRST CORINTHIANS

Discipline for an Undisciplined Church

Source of the incomparable chapter on love, 1 Corinthians 13

Who will settle the argument? When people can't agree on an answer, sometimes they will agree to an arbitrator. One New Testament church became famous for its conflicts and questions—the church in Corinth. Fortunately, they had the Apostle Paul for an arbitrator. First Corinthians was one of several letters that Paul wrote to instruct this struggling church.

AUTHOR AND DATE

Written by the Apostle Paul, about A.D. 55

The first verse of this letter credits the Apostle Paul as the writer. His authorship cannot be seriously questioned, and the church has maintained that position since the first century. The letter repeatedly identifies its author (1:1,13; 3:4–6; 4:15; 16:21). External evidence for Pauline authorship includes the witness of Clement of Rome (A.D. 95), in a letter to the same Corinthian church. Other early Christian leaders also authenticated Paul as the author: Ignatius (about A.D. 110), Polycarp (about A.D. 135), and Tertullian (about A.D. 200).

KEY PEOPLE IN 1 CORINTHIANS

Paul—author of the letters to the Corinthian church (1:1–16:24)

Timothy—fellow missionary sent by Paul to assist the Corinthian church (4:17; 16:10–11)

Members of Chloe's household—informed Paul of the divisions among the Corinthian Christians (1:11)

BACKGROUND AND SETTING

Corinth was located in southern Greece, in what was the Roman province of Achaia, about forty-five miles west from Athens. Corinth sat on a narrow isthmus which not only funneled land traffic through its gates, but also controlled a portage for ships transported overland from the Gulf of Corinth on the west to the Saronic Gulf on the east. The city grew prosperous from all the trade traffic.

Although officially famous as the host city of the Isthmian games (rivaled in their time only by the Olympian games), Corinth was infamous for its depravity. Even by the pagan standards of the time, Corinth was so morally corrupt that its very name became synonymous with debauchery and moral depravity. In 6:9–10, Paul lists some of the specific sins for which the city was noted and which formerly had characterized many believers in the church there. Tragically, some of the worst sins were still found among church members. One of those sins, incest, was condemned even by most pagan Gentiles (5:1).

Like most ancient Greek cities, Corinth had an acropolis (high city) which rose some two thousand feet and was used both for defense and for pagan worship. Corinth boasted of a temple to Aphrodite, the Greek goddess of love. The temple and the city employed more than a thousand priestesses, who were "religious" prostitutes. Sexual immorality was rampant throughout Corinth.

Paul founded the church in Corinth on his second missionary journey (Acts 18). As usual, his ministry began among the Jews in the synagogue but then shifted to the Gentiles after his countrymen rejected the gospel. During the year and a half that Paul worked in Corinth he was assisted by Priscilla and Aquila, two Jewish believers, and by Paul's associates Silas and Timothy.

The most serious problem of the Corinthian church was worldliness, an unwillingness to divorce the culture around them. Most of the believers did not consistently separate themselves from their old, selfish, immoral, and pagan ways. Paul decided it was necessary for him to write to correct these patterns with disciplinary directions (5:9–13).

Before writing this inspired letter, Paul had exchanged other correspondence with the church (5:9), also corrective in nature. Because a copy of that correspondence has never been discovered, it has been referred to as the "lost epistle." Another noncanonical letter followed 1 Corinthians, usually called "the severe letter" (2 Corinthians 2:4).

KEY DOCTRINES IN 1 CORINTHIANS

Sexual sin—disobedience to God's plan for marriage and the family (6:13,18; 7:1–40; 2 Samuel 11:1–4; Proverbs 2:16–19; Matthew 5:32; 19:9; Mark 7:21; Acts 15:20; Romans 13:13; Galatians 5:19; Ephesians 5:5; Colossians 3:5; Hebrews 12:16; Jude 1:4,7)

Proper worship—God deserves our wholehearted worship and praise. Proper worship includes recognition of God's holy character (3:17); pure partaking of the Lord's Supper (11:17–34); and spiritual identification with the church (12:12–27; Matthew 2:1–2; 2:11; 28:16–17; John 4:20–24; 9:30–38; Romans 1:25; Hebrews 1:6; Revelation 4:10–11)

Spiritual gifts—divine enablements for ministry that the Holy Spirit gives in some measure to all believers (12:1–14:40; Isaiah 35:4–6; Joel 2:28–29; Matthew 7:22–23; 12:28; 24:24; Acts 2:1–4; 8:17–20; 10:44–46; 19:6; 1 Thessalonians 5:20; 2 Thessalonians 2:9; 1 Timothy 4:14; 2 Timothy 1:6; Revelation 13:13–14)

Resurrection of Jesus—central to the hope of Christians; without the Resurrection, faith in Christ would be useless (15:4,12–28; Psalms 2:7; 16:10; Isaiah 26:19; Matthew 20:19; Mark 9:9; 14:28; Luke 24:45–46; John 2:19–22; 10:18; Acts 1:3; 2:24; 3:15; 13:33–35; Romans 1:4; 4:25; 6:4; 8:11,34; Ephesians 1:20; Philippians 3:10; Colossians 2:12; 2 Timothy 2:8; 1 Peter 1:3,21; 3:18; Revelation 1:18)

GOD'S CHARACTER IN 1 CORINTHIANS

God is faithful—1:9; 10:13
God is glorious—11:7
God is holy—6:9–10
God is powerful—1:18,24; 2:5; 3:6–8; 6:14
God is unified—8:4,6
God is wise—1:24; 2:7
God is wrathful—10:22

CHRIST IN 1 CORINTHIANS

Paul's letter to the Corinthians helped the believers mature in their understanding of Christ and corrected some of the false teachings that had flourished. Paul stressed the reality of Christ's death and resurrection to people who had begun to deny the resurrection of the dead (15:12–28). Sanctification through Christ is also portrayed as an ongoing process by which believers strive for godliness in their daily lives (1:2,30).

KEY WORDS IN 1 CORINTHIANS

Resurrection: Greek *anastasis*—15:12,13,21,42—literally, "resurrection out from among the dead ones." This is the wording in the first half of 15:12 and in other verses (see Acts 17:31; 1 Peter 1:3). When Scripture speaks of the resurrection in general, commonly the phrase is "a resurrection of dead ones." This is the wording in the second half of 15:12 (see also 15:13,42). In Romans 1:4, Christ's resurrection is spoken of as "a resurrection of dead ones." The same terminology is used in 15:21, where the Greek text literally reads: "For since through a man death came, so also through a Man came a resurrection of dead persons." This shows that Christ's resurrection included the resurrection of believers to eternal life. When He arose, many arose with Him, for they were united with Him in His resurrection (see Romans 6:4–5; Ephesians 2:6; Colossians 3:1).

Spiritual Gifts: Greek *charisma*—12:4,9,28,30–31—closely akin to the word *charis*, which means "grace" or "favor"; *charisma* denotes "that which is graciously given." Paul used the term *charisma* synonymously with the Greek term *ta pneumatika*—literally, "the spiritual things"—because the things graciously given are spiritual gifts. These gifts were given by the Lord to various individuals in the church so as to enliven the meetings and to edify the believers in the church body. Each and every member has been gifted with at least one kind of *charisma*, whether it be the gift of teaching, prophesying, exercising faith, healing, performing miracles, discerning spirits, speaking in tongues, interpreting tongues, or other gifts.

QUICK OVERVIEW

I. Introduction: The Calling and Benefits of Sainthood (1:1–9)
II. Disunity in the Church (1:10–4:21)
  A. The Need for Unity (1:10–3:23)
  B. The Need for Servanthood (4:1–21)
III. Immorality in the Church (5:1–6:20)
IV. Marriage in the Church (7:1–40)
V. Liberty in the Church (8:1–11:1)
VI. Worship in the Church (11:2–14:40)
  A. Roles of Men and Women in the Church (11:2–16)
  B. The Lord's Supper (11:17–34)
  C. Spiritual Gifts (12:1–14:40)
VII. The Hope of the Church: Resurrection (15:1–58)
VIII. A Charge to the Church (16:1–24)
  A. Stewardship (16:1–4)
  B. Personal Plans and Greetings (16:5–24)

MEANWHILE, IN OTHER PARTS OF THE WORLD . . . Roman emperor Claudius I is poisoned by his fourth wife, Agrippina. Nero, the son of Agrippina by another marriage, succeeds Claudius as emperor.

FREQUENTLY ASKED QUESTIONS

1. What factors made it difficult for the gospel to take root in a healthy way in the city of Corinth?

The mind-set of the Corinthians made it almost impossible for the church to fully break with the surrounding culture. The congregation continually behaved in a factional way, showing its carnality and immaturity. After the gifted Apollos had ministered in the church for a while, some of his admirers established a clique that had little to do with the rest of the church. Another group, loyal to Paul, developed; another claimed special allegiance to Peter (Cephas); and still another to Christ alone (1:10–13; 3:1–9). Instead of the church having a significant impact on the city, the city had too much impact on the church.

Paul knew that this church would never become a faithful witness for Christ until they understood that those who claimed church participation but continued to be disobedient and unrepentant before God must be removed from the local body (5:9–13). The Corinthians seem to have been unwilling to pay the price of obedience.

2. How does Paul's teaching in 1 Corinthians help resolve the controversy over the gifts discussed in chapters 12–14?

Three chapters in this letter are devoted to the subject of spiritual gifts in the church. Paul knew that the subject was controversial but vital to a healthy church. The atmosphere of false religions that abounded in Corinth caused counterfeit spiritual manifestations that had to be confronted. Paul informed the church and challenged the believers in Corinth to regulate their behavior by the truth and the Spirit.

The categories of giftedness in these verses do not refer to natural talents, skills, or abilities. Believers and unbelievers alike possess such resources. These gifts are sovereignly and supernaturally bestowed by the Holy Spirit on all believers (12:7,11), enabling them to spiritually edify each other and thus honor the Lord.

The varieties of spiritual gifts fall roughly into two general types: 1) speaking gifts and 2) serving gifts (12:8–10; Romans 12:6–8; 1 Peter 4:10–11). The speaking or verbal gifts (prophecy, knowledge, wisdom, teaching, and exhortation) and the serving, nonverbal gifts (leadership, helps, giving, mercy, faith, and discernment) are all permanent and will operate throughout the church age. Their purpose is to build up the church and glorify God. The list here and in Romans 12:3–8 is best seen as representative of categories of giftedness from which the Holy Spirit draws to give each believer whatever kind or combination He chooses (12:11). Some believers may be gifted in similar ways to others, but each is personally unique because the Spirit suits each gift to the individual.

A special category made up of miracles, healing, languages, and the interpretation of languages served as a set of temporary sign gifts limited to the apostolic age and have, therefore, ceased. Their purpose was to authenticate the apostles and their message as the true Word of God. Once God's Word was complete and became self-authenticating, they were no longer required.

3. How does Paul address the issue of divorce for the Corinthian church?

Paul taught about divorce in the context of answering a number of questions that the church had sent to him. The first of those questions had to do with marriage, an area of trouble due to the moral corruption of the surrounding culture, which tolerated fornication, adultery, homosexuality, polygamy, and concubinage.

The apostle reminded the believers that his teaching was based on what Jesus had already made clear during His earthly ministry (Matthew 5:31–32; 19:5–8). Jesus Himself based His teaching on the previously revealed Word of God (Genesis 2:24; Malachi 2:16).

Paul's departure point for teaching affirmed God's prohibition of divorce. He wrote that in cases where a Christian has already divorced another Christian except for adultery (7:10–11), neither partner is free to marry another person. They should reconcile or at least remain unmarried.

Paul then added some helpful direction on the issue of marital conflicts created in cases where one spouse becomes a believer (7:12–16). First, the believing spouse lives under orders to make the best of the marriage, seeking to win his or her spouse to Christ. If the unbelieving spouse decides to end the marriage, Paul's response is "let him depart" (7:15). This term refers to divorce (7:10–11). When an unbelieving spouse cannot tolerate the partner's faith and wants a divorce, it is best to let that happen in order to preserve peace in the family (Romans 12:18). Therefore, the bond of marriage is broken only by death (Romans 7:2), adultery (Matthew 19:9), or an unbeliever's departure.

When the bond of marriage is broken in any of those ways, a Christian is free to marry another believer (7:15). Throughout Scripture, whenever legitimate divorce occurs, remarriage is an assumed option. When divorce is permitted, so is remarriage.

In general, conversion and obedience to Christ should lead us to greater faithfulness and commitment in every relationship. This extended passage (7:1–24) plainly repeats the basic principle that Christians should willingly accept the marital condition and social situations into which God has placed them and be content to serve Him there until He leads them elsewhere.

4. What difference would it make if the resurrection of Jesus never really happened?

Jesus' resurrection is the least optional part of the Christian faith. It is the first essential among the essential beliefs Christians hold. The Apostle Paul identified at least six disastrous consequences that would be unavoidable if the resurrection of Jesus proved to be a hoax:

- The preaching of Christ would be senseless and meaningless (15:14).
- Faith in Christ would be useless since He would still be dead (15:14).
- All the witnesses and preachers of the Resurrection would be liars (15:15).
- No one would be redeemed (saved) from sin (15:17).
- All former believers would have died as fools (15:18).
- Christians would be the most pitiable people in the world (15:19).

At the center of Christianity stands the risen Christ, victorious, and coming again.

5. Does 1 Corinthians 15:22 actually teach Universalism—the idea that all people will eventually be saved?

Some people, under a misguided notion of fairness and a woefully inadequate view of God, attempt to see in this verse a basis for their belief in *Universalism* (salvation of everyone without regard to faith). The two *alls* in 15:22 are alike only in the sense that they both apply to descendants. The second *all* applies only to believers. The immediate context (verse 23) limits the second *all* to "those who are Christ's." Many other passages clearly teach against Universalism by affirming the eternal punishment of unbelievers (Matthew 5:29; 10:28; 25:41,46; Luke 16:23; 2 Thessalonians 1:9; Revelation 20:15).

QUICK STUDY ON 1 CORINTHIANS

1. People were choosing sides and allegiances in the Corinthian church. How did Paul respond?
2. In handling questions about convictions regarding "meat offered to idols," what principles of Christian behavior does Paul explain and apply?
3. What kinds of immorality did Paul have to confront in the Corinthian church, and how did he do that?
4. Chapters 11–14 deal with many matters that affect corporate worship. What are the central teachings from these chapters, and how have you seen them applied or ignored in your church?
5. In what ways is Paul's description of the resurrection of Jesus and his explanation of its significance different from that of the Gospels?
6. How has the Resurrection of Jesus Christ affected your life?

SECOND CORINTHIANS

Words from a Caring Shepherd

Amazing insights about ministry and revealing glimpses of a minister's heart

In ancient times, letters were significant. They offered just about the only form of long-distance communication. In a world without electronics or even printing, a handwritten letter was a powerful tool, and only the person or their personal representative carried greater authority. When God revealed Himself in written form, He chose letters as one of His tools.

The letters written by the Apostle Paul were the result of the inspiration of the Holy Spirit. Thus, they are God's Word. They also reveal to us a great deal about their human author. Paul's concern and his compassion became part of the permanent record. The last letter he wrote to the Corinthians conveys to us Paul's heart and God's Word to a struggling church.

AUTHOR AND DATE

Written by Paul, approximately A.D. 55 to 56

That the Apostle Paul wrote 2 Corinthians is uncontested. The lack of any motive for a forger to write this highly personal and biographical epistle has led even the most critical scholars to affirm Paul as its author.

KEY PEOPLE IN 2 CORINTHIANS

Paul—author of the letters to the Corinthian church (1:1–13:14)
Timothy—fellow missionary sent by Paul to assist the Corinthian church (1:1–19)
Titus—Gentile man who helped collect money for the church in Jerusalem; trusted by Paul to deliver his letters to Corinth (2:13; 7:6–8:24; 12:18)
False apostles—false teachers in the Corinthian church who had disguised themselves as believers (11:13–15)

BACKGROUND AND SETTING

Paul's association with the important city of Corinth (see **Background and Setting** of 1 Corinthians) began during his second missionary journey (Acts 18:1–18). He spent eighteen months in Corinth planting and tending a new church. In the years that followed, Paul wrote at least four letters and visited the church twice. Second Corinthians was Paul's fourth letter to the Corinthian Christians.

The church in Corinth experienced almost continuous spiritual struggles from internal and external problems. Paul had to deal with rampant immorality and divisiveness within the church itself. He also had to confront outside influences in the form of self-styled false apostles (11:5–15).

In order to create a platform to teach their false gospel, the false prophets began assaulting Paul's character. They wanted to take advantage of the tension between the apostle and the church. If they could convince the people to turn from Paul, the congregation would then be completely vulnerable to their own demonic doctrines. The situation became so critical that Paul intervened personally. He referred to that episode as the "painful visit" (2:1). The tension in the church had broken out into public and personal attacks (2:5–8,10; 7:12). Paul, realizing he had done what he could, left the city but followed up his visit with what he called the "severe letter" (2:4) that Titus carried to Corinth on Paul's behalf (7:5–16).

Sometime later, eager for news about Corinth, Paul traveled to meet Titus (2:13). His younger associate gave Paul the news that the majority of the Corinthians had repented of their rebellion against him (7:7). When Paul wrote this letter (2 Corinthians), he was intent on rejoicing for the church (7:8–16), warning them about dangers ahead by confronting the false apostles (chapters 10–13), and, particularly, reestablishing his reputation and authority among them by defending his apostleship (chapters 1–7). Paul also encouraged the Corinthians to resume preparations for the collection for the poor at Jerusalem (chapters 8–9), which he planned to pick up on his next visit (12:14; 13:1–2). The Corinthians' participation in the Jerusalem offering (Romans 15:26) implies that Paul's third visit to that church was successful.

KEY DOCTRINES IN 2 CORINTHIANS

Reconciliation with God—the sacrifice of Jesus Christ renews the relationship between God and man (5:17–21; Romans 5:1,10–11; Leviticus 8:15; 16:20; Daniel 9:24; Isaiah 53:5; Matthew 5:24–26; Ephesians 2:14–16; Colossians 1:20–22; 2:14; Hebrews 2:17)

Christ's substitutionary atonement for sin—Christ's work upon the cross paid the penalty for sin (5:21; Isaiah 53; Daniel 9:24–27; Zechariah 13:1,7; John 1:29,36; 11:50–51; Acts 4:10; Romans 3:25; 5:8–11; Galatians 1:4; 1 Thessalonians 1:10; 1 Timothy 2:5–6; 1 Peter 1:11,20; 1 John 2:2; 4:10; Revelation 13:8)

Guarantee of believers' salvation—God adopts faithful believers as His own children (1:22; 5:5; Psalms 3:8; 37:39; Isaiah 45:21–22; 59:16; 63:9; Jeremiah 3:23; Mark 16:16; Acts 4:12; 16:31; Romans 10:9; Ephesians 2:8; 1 Thessalonians 5:9; 1 Timothy 2:4; Hebrews 5:9; 1 Peter 1:5)

The nature of Satan—the original rebel among God's creatures (4:4; 11:14–15; Genesis 3:1,14; Job 1:6; Zechariah 3:1; Matthew 4:3–10;

13:19; Luke 10:18; Ephesians 2:2; 6:11–12; 1 Thessalonians 2:18; 2 Thessalonians 2:9; 1 Timothy 3:6; 1 Peter 5:8; 2 Peter 2:4; 1 John 3:8; 5:19)

Judgment—God's righteous response to sin (5:9–11; Genesis 19:29; Deuteronomy 32:39; Isaiah 1:9; Matthew 12:36–37; Romans 1:18–2:16; 2 Peter 2:5–6)

GOD'S CHARACTER IN 2 CORINTHIANS

God is comforting—1:3; 7:6
God is glorious—4:6
God is loving—9:7; 13:11
God is merciful—1:3
God is powerful—6:7; 9:8; 13:4
God is a promise keeper—1:20; 6:18; 7:1
God is reconciling—5:18–19
God is spirit—3:17
God is true—1:20

CHRIST IN 2 CORINTHIANS

Paul's second letter to the Corinthians reveals Jesus Christ as the One who comforts the persecuted (1:5; 12:9), fulfills the promises of God (1:20), remains Lord over humanity (4:5), and perfectly reconciles believers to God (5:19). Paul declares believers to be new creations reconciled by Christ's atonement for sin "that we might become the righteousness of God in Him" (5:21).

KEY WORDS IN 2 CORINTHIANS

Service: Greek *leitourgia*—8:14; 12:8; 29:35; 31:16; 34:14; 35:10, 16—indicates "public ministry" or "official duty." The related word *leitourgos* is used frequently in Greek literature to designate a man who performed some public service (see Romans 13:6). In general, it means a public servant or administrator. Paul used *leitourgia* in connection with the service of those who labored to benefit the church.

Apostle: Greek *apostolos*—1:1; 11:5,13; 12:11–12—simply means "sent ones." Out of Jesus' many disciples, He selected twelve to be His apostles. These were the men who were sent by Jesus to take His message to the world and then raise up churches. Paul also became an apostle by the appointment of the risen Christ, who encountered Paul on the road to Damascus (see Acts 9). Paul's apostleship was accompanied by a great deal of suffering; and then, to add to it, some false teachers in the Corinthian church doubted his authority. Thus in 2 Corinthians, Paul repeatedly defended the genuineness of His apostleship.

QUICK OVERVIEW

I. Paul's Greeting (1:1–11)
II. Paul's Ministry (1:12–7:16)
  A. Paul's Plans (1:12–2:4)
  B. The Offender's Punishment (2:5–11)
  C. Titus's Absence (2:12–13)
  D. The Ministry's Nature (2:14–6:10)
  E. The Corinthians Exhorted (6:11–7:16)
III. Paul's Collection (8:1–9:15)
  A. The Patterns of Giving (8:1–9)
  B. The Purpose of Giving (8:10–15)
  C. The Procedures of Giving (8:16–9:5)
  D. The Promise of Giving (9:6–15)
IV. Paul's Apostleship (10:1–12:13)
  A. Apostolic Authority (10:1–18)
  B. Apostolic Conduct (11:1–15)
  C. Apostolic Suffering (11:16–33)
  D. Apostolic Credentials (12:1–13)
V. Paul's Visit (12:14–13:10)
  A. Paul's Unselfishness (12:14–18)
  B. Paul's Warnings (12:19–13:10)
VI. Paul's Benediction (13:11–14)

MEANWHILE, IN OTHER PARTS OF THE WORLD . . .
Nero is declared Roman emperor at age seventeen. During Nero's reign, two-thirds of Rome burns to the ground.

FREQUENTLY ASKED QUESTIONS

1. What does Paul mean when he writes about being "in Christ" and someone being "a new creation" (5:17)?

Paul uses the phrase *in Christ* when he writes about various aspects of our relationship with Jesus Christ as Lord and Savior. These two words comprise a brief but profound statement of the inexhaustible significance of the believer's redemption (salvation), which includes the following:

- The believer's security in Christ, who bore in His body God's judgment against sin
- The believer's acceptance in (through) Christ with whom God alone is well pleased
- The believer's future assurance in Him who is the resurrection to eternal life and the sole guarantor of the believer's inheritance in heaven

- The believer's participation in the divine nature of Christ, the everlasting Word (2 Peter 1:4)

All of the changes that Christ brings to the believer's life result in a state that can be rightly called "a new creation." The terms describe something created at a qualitatively new level of excellence. They parallel other biblical concepts like regeneration and new birth (John 3:3; Ephesians 2:1–3; Titus 3:5; 1 Peter 1:23; 1 John 2:29; 3:9; 5:4). The expression includes the Christian's forgiveness of sins paid for in Christ's substitutionary death (Galatians 6:15; Ephesians 4:24).

2. Why does the tone of 2 Corinthians change so abruptly between 9:15 and 10:1?

Even a casual reader usually notices the sudden change in tone that occurs between the ninth and tenth chapters of 2 Corinthians. This apparent difference has prompted various explanations of the relationship between chapters 1–9 and 10–13.

Some have argued that chapters 10–13 were actually part of the "severe letter" that Paul mentions in 2:4. Based on this theory, these four chapters belong chronologically before chapters 1–9. Chapters 10–13 cannot, however, have been written before chapters 1–9 because they refer to Titus's visit as a past event (see 8:6; 12:18). Further, the offender whose defiance prompted Paul's "severe letter" (2:5–8) is nowhere mentioned in chapters 10–13.

Others agree that chapters 10–13 belong after chapters 1–9 but suggest that they form a separate letter. They assume that Paul, after sending chapters 1–9 to the Corinthians, received reports of new trouble at Corinth and wrote chapters 10–13 in response. A variation of this view proposes that Paul paused after writing chapters 1–9, then heard bad news from Corinth before he resumed writing chapters 10–13. Although this view preserves the unity of 2 Corinthians, Paul gives no indication in the last four chapters that he received fresh news from Corinth.

The best interpretation sees 2 Corinthians as a unified letter with two distinct sections. Chapters 1–9 are addressed to the repentant majority (see 2:6) and chapters 10–13 to the minority still influenced by the false teachers. The following facts support this view: 1) no ancient authorities (Greek manuscripts, early church fathers, or early translations) indicate that chapters 10–13 ever circulated as a separate letter; 2) the overall differences in tone between the two sections have been exaggerated (compare 6:11; 7:2 with 11:11; 12:14); and 3) chapters 10–13 do form a logical conclusion to chapters 1–9, as Paul prepared the Corinthians for his promised visit (1:15–16; 2:1–3).

3. To what was Paul referring by the phrase *thorn in the flesh* (12:7)?

Paul began his account about the thorn in the flesh by indicating the reason it was given to him—"lest I should be exalted"—in other words, to keep him humble. As with Job, Satan was the immediate cause, but God was the ultimate cause behind Paul's thorn. This is why the thorn was not removed in spite of Paul's pleas (12:8). God had a purpose in allowing Paul to suffer in this way—to show him that "My grace is sufficient for you" (12:9).

Paul's use of the word *messenger* (Greek, *angellos,* or angel) from Satan suggests the thorn in the flesh (literally, "a stake for the flesh") was a demon, not a physical illness. Of the 188 uses of the Greek word *angellos* in the New Testament, at least 180 refer to angels. This particular angel was from Satan, a demon afflicting Paul.

Perhaps the best explanation for this demon is that he was indwelling the ringleader of the Corinthian conspiracy, the leader of the false apostles. Through them he was tearing apart Paul's beloved church and thus driving a painful stake through Paul. Added support for this view comes from the context of chapters 10–13, in which Paul engages his enemies (the false prophets). The verb translated "buffet" always refers to ill-treatment from other people (Matthew 26:67; Mark 14:65; 1 Corinthians 4:11; 1 Peter 2:20). Finally, the Old Testament frequently describes Israel's enemies as thorns (Numbers 33:55; Joshua 23:13; Judges 2:3; Ezekiel 28:24).

QUICK STUDY ON 2 CORINTHIANS

1. Based on his comments throughout this letter, what was Paul's relationship with the church in Corinth?
2. What principles of church discipline did Paul explain and apply in this letter?
3. What aspects of his own spiritual struggle and growth did Paul write about in this letter?
4. In 2 Corinthians 4, how does Paul explain the limits of ministry and the reasons behind the effectiveness of the gospel?
5. How do Paul's comments about the collection from the Asian churches for the church in Jerusalem help you understand some of the principles of giving among Christians?
6. In his response to those who are challenging his apostolic authority, what are Paul's central concerns?
7. In what ways can you identify with Paul's lessons about the *thorn in the flesh* (chapter 12)?

GALATIANS
Freed and Justified by Faith

Paul's first effort at writing under the inspiration of the Holy Spirit.

Paul's Epistle to the Galatians bears two significant distinctions. First, it represents the earliest of his many letters written under the inspiration of the Holy Spirit. Second, Galatians is the only one of Paul's messages targeted for a region, a group of churches, rather than a specific local church. First and always, Paul preached the gospel as the ultimate freedom found in Christ through justification by faith.

AUTHOR AND DATE

Written by Paul, about A.D. 50

There is no compelling reason to question the internal claims that the Apostle Paul wrote Galatians (1:1; 5:2). Further, Paul was familiar with this region, having been born in Tarsus, a city in the neighboring province of Cilicia. He also visited the southern area of Galatia and planted churches there during his first missionary journey. He would have had good reasons to follow up those visits with a letter, particularly in the light of news that struggling young churches needed to hear about the Jerusalem Council (Acts 15). For more on Paul, see the chapter on Romans and the **Frequently Asked Question** "Who was Paul?"

KEY PEOPLE IN GALATIANS

Paul—urged the Galatians to remember their freedom from the law through Christ Jesus (1:1–6:18)

Peter—leader of the church in Jerusalem; confronted by Paul for looking to the law for salvation (1:18–2:21)

Barnabas—traveled with Paul as a missionary; allowed Paul to correct several of his misguided beliefs (2:1–13)

Titus—Gentile believer and close friend to Paul; later served on the island of Crete (2:1–3)

Abraham—Paul used Abraham's life to exemplify God's salvation through faith alone (3:6–4:22)

False teachers—persuasive teachers who attempted to lure the people away from Paul's teaching (4:17–20)

BACKGROUND AND SETTING

In Paul's day, the word *Galatia* had two distinct meanings, one ethnic and the other political. In a strict ethnic sense, Galatia was the region of central Asia Minor (modern day Turkey) inhabited by a transplanted group called Galatians. They were a Celtic people who migrated to that region from Gaul (modern day France) in the third century B.C. The Romans conquered the Galatians in 189 B.C. but allowed them a measure of independence until 25 B.C., when Galatia became a Roman province.

When establishing the boundaries of the province of Galatia, Rome included some regions not populated by ethnic Galatians. This broader term was the primary meaning by the time of the New Testament.

Paul founded churches in the southern Galatian cities of Antioch, Iconium, Lystra, and Derbe (Acts 13:14–14:23). These were cities in the Roman province, but they were not inhabited by ethnic Galatians. Although Acts notes two brief visits by Paul into ethnic Galatia (Acts 16:6; 18:23), it makes no mention of any churches founded in that region.

Despite suggestions that Paul might have written his letter to the northern regions he had not visited, his concerns and the needs of the southern Galatian churches make them the more likely recipients of the letter. The apostle received word that the churches he had recently founded were under assault by Judaizing false teachers who were undermining the central New Testament doctrine of justification by faith. Ignoring the express decree of the Jerusalem Council (Acts 15:23–29), these teachers were insisting that Gentiles must first become Jewish proselytes and submit to all the Mosaic Law before they could become Christians (1:7; 4:17,21; 5:2–12; 6:12–13). Shocked by the Galatians' openness to that damning heresy (1:6), Paul wrote this letter to defend justification by faith and to warn these churches of the dire consequences of abandoning that essential doctrine. Galatians is the only Pauline letter without an opening commendation for its readers. That obvious omission reflects the urgency he felt about confronting the possible defection and defending the essential doctrine of justification.

KEY DOCTRINES IN GALATIANS

Justification by faith—complete freedom from judgment and from the bondage of sin comes by faith alone in Jesus Christ (2:14–21; 3:11; 5:4; Leviticus 18:5; Isaiah 45:25; 50:8; 53:11; Jeremiah 23:6; Habakkuk 2:4; John 5:24; Acts 13:39; Romans 1:16–17; 3:21–4:25; 5:1–2,18; 1 Corinthians 6:11; Titus 3:7; James 2:10)

The law—believers are freed from the bondage of the law (2:20–21; 5:1; Jeremiah 31:33; Romans 2:12; 6:14; 7:4–6; Galatians 3:10–13; Hebrews 8:10)

The role of the Holy Spirit—the Spirit remains in constant battle against the desires of the flesh (5:16–17; John 14:16; Romans 5:3–5; 7:23,25; 8:4–6; Philippians 3:3; 1 Peter 3:18)

GOD'S CHARACTER IN GALATIANS

God is merciful—6:16
God is powerful—2:8
God is a promise keeper—3:16–19,21–22,29; 4:4

CHRIST IN GALATIANS

The Book of Galatians deals with the freedom that Christ gives to believers. The Galatians were tempted by Jewish legalists to trade away that freedom and return to slavery under the law (2:4). Paul's letter urges believers to "not be entangled again with a yoke of bondage" but to hold to their position of liberty in Jesus Christ (5:1).

KEY WORDS IN GALATIANS

Elements: Greek *stoicheia*—4:3,9—can mean 1) "elementary or rudimentary principles" or 2) "elemental spirits." The word literally means things placed in line or in a row, like an alphabet. It was used to speak of rudimentary principles (Hebrews 5:12) or basic elements of the universe, whether physical (2 Peter 3:10) or spiritual. If Paul was thinking of elementary principles, he meant that people are in bondage to the basic elements of religion (see Colossians 2:20); if he meant spirits, he was saying that people are in bondage to the "elemental spirits," meaning certain gods or demons. *Principles* suits the overall context of Galatians, whereas *spirits* accords with 4:8–10. In either case, Paul was saying that people were in bondage until Christ came.

Flesh: Greek *sarx* —1:16; 2:20; 4:13–14; 5:17; 6:12–13—in Greek literature, the word *sarx* usually meant nothing more than the human body. It was also used this way in the New Testament (see John 1:14; Revelation 17:16; 19:18,21). However, Paul often used the word to denote the entire fallen human being—not just the sinful body but the entire being, including the soul and mind, as affected by sin. Thus Paul often pitted the *flesh* against the *Spirit* as being two diametrically opposed forces. The unbeliever can live only in the flesh, but the believer can live in the flesh or in the Spirit. Paul repeatedly encourages believers to overcome the deeds of the flesh by living in the Spirit.

QUICK OVERVIEW

I. Personal: The Preacher of Justifications (1:1–2:21)
   A. Apostolic Chastening (1:1–9)
   B. Apostolic Credentials (1:10–2:10)
   C. Apostolic Confidence (2:11–21)
II. Doctrinal: The Principles of Justification (3:1–4:31)

A. The Experience of the Galatians (3:1–5)
B. The Blessing of Abraham (3:6–9)
C. The Curse of the Law (3:10–14)
D. The Promise of the Covenant (3:15–18)
E. The Purpose of the Law (3:19–29)
F. The Sonship of Believers (4:1–7)
G. The Futility of Ritualism (4:8–20)
H. The Illustration from Scripture (4:21–31)

III. Practical: The Privileges of Justification (5:1–6:18)
A. Freedom from Ritual (5:1–6)
B. Freedom from Legalists (5:7–12)
C. Freedom in the Spirit (5:13–26)
D. Freedom from Spiritual Bondage (6:1–10)
E. Conclusion (6:11–18)

MEANWHILE, IN OTHER PARTS OF THE WORLD . . .
The Goths, traveling from present-day Sweden, establish a kingdom along the basin of the Vistula, the longest river in Poland.

FREQUENTLY ASKED QUESTIONS

1. How do the events mentioned in Galatians match the chronology of Acts?

A comparison of the references in Acts (11:27–30; 15:2,12,22,35) and Galatians (1:18; 2:1–10) seems to indicate at least three visits by Paul to Jerusalem, including his trip to participate in the Jerusalem Council. Other visits occurred after the Council (Acts 18:18–22; 21:15–17). The visit mentioned in Galatians 1:18 records Paul's first direct contact with the apostles in Jerusalem after his own conversion. Chapter 2:1 mentions a fourteen-year gap, after which Paul returned again to Jerusalem, most likely as a participant in the Jerusalem Council (Acts 15), called to resolve the issue of Gentile salvation.

Linguistically, the word *again* (2:1) need not refer to the next visit; it can just as easily mean "once again" or "another time" without respect to how many visits took place in between. And in fact, Paul did visit Jerusalem at least once during that fourteen-year period to deliver famine relief to the church there (Acts 11:27–30; 12:24–25). He simply did not mention that intervening visit in Galatians probably because it was not significant in his defense of his apostolic authority.

2. Galatians 3:27 seems to read as if baptism is necessary for salvation. What did Paul mean in that verse?

Paul's use of the term *baptized* in this verse does not refer to water baptism, which cannot save. Paul used the word here in a metaphorical manner to speak of being "immersed," or "placed into" Christ. The larger context here refers to faith and to the spiritual miracle of union with Him in His death and resurrection, not to an outward ceremony. The phrase that immediately follows, "put on Christ," pictures the result of the believer's spiritual union with Christ. Paul was emphasizing the fact that we have been united with Christ through salvation. Positionally before God, we have put on Christ, His death, resurrection, and righteousness. Practically we need to "put on Christ" before our family, friends, neighbors, and coworkers in our conduct (Romans 13:14).

3. How does Paul's statement about gender, race, and status equality in 3:28 affect other biblical teachings about roles?

This passage is sometimes quoted by those who wish to challenge the traditional concepts of authority and submission, particularly as they affect marriage. This verse does not deny that God's plan has included certain racial, social, and sexual distinctions among Christians, but it affirms that those do not imply spiritual inequality before God. In other words, the great doctrine of spiritual equality is not incompatible with the God-ordained roles of headship and submission in the church, society, and home. Even Jesus Christ, though fully equal with the Father, assumed a submissive role during His incarnation (Philippians 2:5–8).

4. What does the phrase *you have fallen from grace* (5:4) mean in relation to the doctrine of eternal security?

Paul uses two terms in this verse that imply separation, loss, and breakdown: "estranged from Christ" and "fallen from grace." The Greek word for *estranged* means "to be separated" or "to be severed." The word for *fallen* means "to lose one's grasp of something." The context clarifies Paul's meaning. Any attempt to be justified by the law equates to a rejection of salvation by grace alone through faith alone. Those who were once exposed to the gracious truth of the gospel and then turn their backs on Christ (Hebrews 6:4–6) and seek to be justified by the law are separated from Christ and lose all prospects of God's gracious salvation. Their desertion of Christ and the gospel only proves that their faith was never genuine (Luke 8:13–14; 1 John 2:19).

QUICK STUDY ON GALATIANS

1. How does Paul explain the relationship of the law to works of righteousness in Galatians?
2. Why does Paul call the Galatians "foolish"?
3. What does Paul tell the Galatians about faith? How does that description fit your own understanding of faith in your relationship with God?
4. When Paul discusses the concept of "freedom" with the Galatians, to what is he referring?
5. Paul discusses at length the effects of the Holy Spirit's presence in a Christian's life (5:16–26). What are those effects, and to what degree have you experienced them?

EPHESIANS
The Body of Christ Is Blessed

Ephesians offers a narrative blueprint for the church of Jesus Christ.

The church in the city of Ephesus received two letters recorded in Scripture. One came from the Apostle Paul, the other from Jesus (Revelation 2:1–6). When Jesus appeared to John and had him write letters to seven churches, He began with Ephesus. Both Jesus and Paul used the church in Ephesus as an example of the challenges and benefits of growing into an authentic living and loving Body of Christ in this world.

AUTHOR AND DATE

Written by Paul, between A.D. 60 and 62

No compelling evidence indicates that the authorship of Paul should be in question. His name appears in the opening salutation (1:1; 3:1). Parallel themes, context, and tone have made Ephesians one of the "Prison Epistles" (along with Philippians, Colossians, and Philemon). This group of letters were written while Paul awaited his trial in Rome (Acts 28:16–31).

KEY PEOPLE IN EPHESIANS

Paul—instructed the church at Ephesus about their position as the Body of Christ and their relationship with God (1:1–6:24)

Tychicus—sent by Paul to encourage the believers of Ephesus (6:21–22)

BACKGROUND AND SETTING

The church in Ephesus probably began under the ministry of Priscilla and Aquila (Acts 18:26), an exceptionally gifted couple who were left there by Paul during his second missionary journey (Acts 18:18–19). Later, Paul visited Ephesus during his third missionary journey (Acts 19) and spent three years establishing the fledgling church. After Paul's departure, Timothy pastored the congregation for perhaps a year and a half, providing corrective instruction against the false teaching of a few influential men who were probably elders in the congregation (1 Timothy 1:3,20).

Located at the mouth of the Cayster River, on the east shore of the Aegean Sea, Ephesus was perhaps best known for its Temple of Artemis, or Diana. That magnificent structure was one of the seven wonders of the ancient world. Ephesus also served as an important political, educational, and commercial center—a great city in its time.

KEY DOCTRINES IN EPHESIANS

The mystery of the church, the Body of Christ—all believers in Jesus Christ are equal before the Lord as His children and citizens of His eternal kingdom (1:22–23; 3:6; 5:32; Colossians 1:24; Revelation 21:9)

The blessings of Jesus Christ—all believers receive the unsearchable riches in Christ through His grace and inheritance (1:2,5–9; 2:7; 3:8,16,19; 4:13; 5:18; 6:10–13; Genesis 24:31; 26:29; Psalms 36:8; 63:5; 91:5–10; Isaiah 12:2; 40:11; Matthew 25:34; John 17:21; Ephesians 3:12; 2 Peter 1:4; Revelation 13:8)

GOD'S CHARACTER IN EPHESIANS

God is accessible—2:13,18; 3:12
God is glorious—1:12; 3:16
God is kind—2:7
God is loving—2:4–5
God is merciful—2:4
God is powerful—1:19; 3:7,20; 6:10
God is a promise keeper—1:13; 2:12; 3:6
God is reconciling—2:14,17
God is unified—4:6
God is wise—1:8; 3:10
God is wrathful—5:6

CHRIST IN EPHESIANS

In the Book of Ephesians, Paul explains the unique relationship between Jesus and the church as His Body. Christ is the Head of the church uniting believers together and strengthening the Body (4:15–16). Paul also focuses on the believer's position as being "in Christ" (1:1,3–7,11–13; 2:5–6,10,13,21; 3:6,12).

KEY WORDS IN EPHESIANS

Purpose; Counsel; Will: Greek *prothesis*—1:9,11; 3:11; Greek *boulē*—1:11; Greek *thelēma*—1:1,5,9,11; 5:17; 6:6—three key words, all related conceptually, appear in 1:11. One of these words (*thelēma*) has been used by Paul twice before (1:1,9). The word conveys the idea of desire, even a heart's desire, for the word primarily expresses emotion instead of volition. Thus God's will is not so much God's intention, as it is His heart's desire. The word *prothesis* denotes an intention or a plan; it literally means "a laying out beforehand" like a blueprint. This plan was created in God's counsel, a translation of the Greek word *boulē*, which means the result of deliberate determination. But behind the plan and the counsel was not just a mastermind but a heart of love.

New Man: Greek *kainos anthrōpos*—2:15; 4:24—word for *new* does not mean something more recent in time, but something having a different quality or nature. Thus the *new man* is the new humanity created in Christ, of which all believers partake, both individually and corporately. Since Paul has already spoken of the new man created in Christ in terms of a new, unified, corporate humanity (2:14–15), the new man in this verse must also be thought of corporately (see Colossians 3:9–11). In the immediate context, Paul is exhorting each believer to put on his or her new human nature.

QUICK OVERVIEW

I. Salutation (1:1–2)
II. God's Purpose for the Church (1:3–3:13)
  A. Predestination in Christ (1:3–6a)
  B. Redemption in Christ (1:6b–10)
  C. Inheritance in Christ (1:11–14)
  D. Resources in Christ (1:15–23)
  E. New Life in Christ (2:1–10)
  F. Unity in Christ (2:11–3:13)
III. God's Fullness for the Church (3:14–21)
IV. God's Plan for Faithful Living in the Church (4:1–6)
V. God's Son Endows and Builds the Church (4:7–16)
VI. God's Pattern and Principles for Members of the Church (4:17–32)
VII. God's Standards for Faithfulness in the Church (5:1–21)
  A. Walking in Love (5:1–7)
  B. Living in Light (5:8–14)
  C. Walking in Wisdom and Sobriety (5:15–18a)
  D. Filled with God's Spirit (5:18b–21)
VIII. God's Standards for Authority and Submission in the Church (5:22–6:9)
  A. Husbands and Wives (5:22–33)
  B. Parents and Children (6:1–4)
  C. Employers and Employees (6:5–9)
IX. God's Provision for His Children's Spiritual Battles (6:10–17)
  A. The Believer's Warfare (6:10–13)
  B. The Believer's Armor (6:14–17)
X. God's Appeal for Prayer in the Church (6:18–20)
XI. Benediction (6:21–24)

MEANWHILE, IN OTHER PARTS OF THE WORLD . . .
Jewish historian Josephus is training to become an invaluable resource on the historical background of much of the Bible.

FREQUENTLY ASKED QUESTIONS

1. Why does Paul use the word *mystery* so often in his letter to the Ephesians?

Paul actually uses the word *mystery* six times in this letter (1:9; 3:3–4, 9; 5:32; 6:19). By comparison, the word appears twice in Romans, once in 1 Corinthians, four times in Colossians, once in 1 Timothy, and nowhere else. Contrary to our use of mystery as a series of clues to be figured out, Paul's use of the word points to mystery as a heretofore unrevealed truth that has been made clear. The word *mystery* preserves the sense that the revealed truth has such awesome implications that it continues to amaze and humble those who accept it.

Ephesians introduces various aspects of the "mystery." Paul explained his use of the word in 3:4–6 by saying that "the Gentiles should be fellow heirs, of the same body, and partakers of His promise in Christ through the gospel." When the unsearchable riches of Christ are preached among the Gentiles, one result is an understanding of the "fellowship of the mystery" (3:9). And when God's plan for human marriage is used to explain the unique relationship between Christ and His bride, the church, Paul reminded his readers that the real subject is a great mystery (5:32). And finally, Paul asked the Ephesians to pray for him that he would be able "boldly to make known the mystery of the gospel" (6:19). The gospel is not mysterious because it is hard to understand. It is mysterious because it is unexpected, unmerited, and free. Though Paul didn't use the word in this passage, his summary of the mystery for the Ephesians can be found in 2:8–9: "For by grace you have been saved through faith, and that not of yourselves; it is the gift of God, not of works, lest anyone should boast."

2. How do grace, faith, and works make up the process of salvation that Paul describes in 2:8–10?

Paul describes the effective process of salvation as something God graciously accomplishes through faith. The word *that* in verse 8—"and that not of yourselves"—refers to the entire previous statement of salvation, not only the grace but also the faith. Although individuals are required to believe for salvation, even that faith is part of the gift of God that saves and cannot be exercised by one's own power. God's grace accomplishes the crucial action in every aspect of salvation.

Even *works,* which cannot produce salvation, are also part of God's gift. As with salvation, a believer's sanctification and good works are ordained before time. Opportunities, strength, and will to do good works are subsequent and resultant. They are God-empowered fruits and evidences that grace has accomplished salvation through faith (see John 15:8; Philippians 2:12–13; 2 Timothy 3:17; Titus 2:14; James 2:16–26).

3. Paul describes a number of leadership roles in 4:11. How do we understand these roles in the church today?

Christ possesses the authority and sovereignty to assign the spiritual gifts (4:7–8) to those He has called into service in His church. He gives not only gifts but also gifted people. This passage uses five terms to describe these roles: apostles, prophets, evangelists, pastors, and teachers.

Apostles is a New Testament term used particularly of the twelve disciples who had seen the risen Christ (Acts 1:22), including Matthias, who replaced Judas. Later, Paul was uniquely set apart as the Apostle to the Gentiles (Galatians 1:15–17). Those apostles were chosen directly by Christ, so as to be called "apostles of Christ" (Galatians 1:1; 1 Peter 1:1). They were given three basic responsibilities:

- To lay the foundation of the church (2:20)
- To receive, declare, and write God's Word (3:5; Acts 11:28; 21:10–11)
- To confirm that Word through signs, wonders, and miracles (2 Corinthians 12:12; Acts 8:6–7; Hebrews 2:3–4)

The term *apostle* is used in more general ways of others in the early church, including Barnabas (Acts 14:4), Silas, and Timothy (1 Thessalonians 2:6), and others (Romans 16:7; Philippians 2:25).

Prophets were not ordinary believers who had the gift of prophecy but those who had been especially commissioned by the early church. The office of prophet seems to have been exclusively for work within local congregations. They sometimes spoke practical direct revelation for a church about God (Acts 11:21–28), or they expounded revelation already given (implied in Acts 13:1). Since the offices of apostle and prophet ceased with the completion of the New Testament, the ongoing leadership needs of the church have been met by other offices.

Evangelists proclaimed the good news of salvation in Jesus Christ to unbelievers (Acts 21:8; 2 Timothy 4:5). The related verb translated "to preach the gospel" is used fifty-four times and the related noun translated "gospel" is used seventy-six times in the New Testament.

The phrase *pastors and teachers* is best understood in context as a single office of leadership in the church. The Greek word translated "and" can mean "in particular" (1 Timothy 5:17). Pastor is the equivalent of "shepherd," so the words pastor and teacher, and the two functions together define the teaching shepherd. This person is identified as one who is under the "great Pastor" Jesus (Hebrews 13:20–21; 1 Peter 2:25). One who holds this office is also called an "elder" and "bishop" (Acts 20:28; 1 Timothy 3:1–7; Titus 1:5–9; 1 Peter 5:1–2).

4. How do the principles of submission and love establish God's expectation of Christian marriage as described in 5:21–33?

The section that begins with a call to wise living (5:15) leads up to Paul's general counsel about submission (5:21). This last verse serves to introduce the next section (5:22–6:9), which spells out the godly expectations for various relationships. Here Paul stated unequivocally that every spirit-filled Christian is to be a humble, submissive Christian. This is foundational to all the relationships in this section. No believer is inherently superior to any other believer. In their standing before God, all believers are equal in every way (3:28).

Having established the foundational principle of submission (5:21), Paul applied it first to the wife. The command is unqualified and applicable to every Christian wife, no matter what her own abilities, education, knowledge of Scripture, spiritual maturity, or any other qualities might be in relation to those of her husband. The submission is not the husband's to command but for the wife to willingly and lovingly offer. The phrase *your own husband* limits the wife's submission to the one man that God has placed over her.

The Spirit-filled wife recognizes that her husband's role in giving leadership is not only God-ordained but also a reflection of Christ's own loving, authoritative headship of the church. As the Lord delivered His church from the dangers of sin, death, and hell, so the husband provides for, protects, preserves, and loves his wife, leading her to blessing as she submits (Titus 1:4; 2:13; 3:6).

Paul has much more to say to the man who has been placed in the role of authority within marriage. That authority comes with supreme responsibilities for husbands in regard to their wives. Husbands are to love their wives with the same sacrificial love that Christ has for His church. Christ gave everything He had, including His own life, for the sake of His church, and that is the standard of sacrifice for a husband's love of his wife.

The clarity of God's guidelines makes it certain that problems in marriage must always be traced in both directions so that each partner clearly understands his or her roles and responsibilities. Failure to love is just as often the source of marital trouble as failure to submit.

5. Why does Paul insist in 6:10–17 that Christians must be prepared for spiritual battle?

The true believer described in chapters 1 to 3, who lives the Spirit-controlled life described in 4:1–6:9, can be sure to encounter spiritual warfare. So, Paul closed his letter with warnings about upcoming battles and instructions about victorious living. The Lord provides His saints with sufficient armor to combat and defeat the adversary. Ephesians

6:10–13 briefly sets forth the basic truths regarding the believer's necessary spiritual preparation as well as truths about the enemy, the battle, and the victory. Verses 14–17 specify the six most necessary pieces of spiritual armor with which God equips His children to resist and overcome Satan's assaults. The spiritual equipment parallels the standard military equipment worn by soldiers in Paul's day:

- Belt of truth—The soldier wore a tunic of loose-fitting clothing. Since ancient combat was largely hand-to-hand, the tunic was a potential hindrance and danger. The belt cinched up the loose material. The belt that pulls together all the spiritual loose ends is "truth" or, better, "truthfulness."
- Breastplate of righteousness—A tough, sleeveless piece of leather or heavy material covered the soldier's full torso, protecting his heart and other vital organs. Because righteousness, or holiness, is such a distinctive characteristic of God Himself, it is easy to understand why it is the Christian's chief protection against Satan and his schemes.
- Boots of the gospel—Roman soldiers wore boots with nails in them to grip the ground in combat. The gospel of peace pertains to the good news that through Christ believers are at peace with God, and He is on their side (Romans 5:6–10).
- Shield of faith—This Greek word usually refers to the large shield that protected the soldier's entire body. The believer's continual trust in God's Word and promise is "above all" absolutely necessary to protect him or her from temptations to every sort of sin.
- Helmet of salvation—The helmet protected the head, always a major target in battle. This passage is speaking to those who are already saved; therefore, it does not refer to attaining salvation. Rather, since Satan seeks to destroy a believer's assurance of salvation with his weapons of doubt and discouragement, the believer must be as conscious of his or her confident status in Christ as he or she would be aware of a helmet on the head.
- Sword of the Spirit—A sword was the soldier's only weapon. In the same way, God's Word is the only weapon that a believer needs, infinitely more powerful than any of Satan's devices.

QUICK STUDY ON EPHESIANS

1. In what ways does Paul explain his description of the church as a mystery in Ephesians?
2. When Paul describes the church as the Body of Christ in chapter 4, what processes and relationships does he highlight?
3. In chapter 5, how does Paul use marriage as a pattern for understanding the relationship between Christ and the church?

4. What are the components of the armor of God that Paul describes in chapter 6? In what ways do you use those components in your spiritual life?
5. In what ways do Paul's guidelines for family living and work relationships affect your way of life?
6. To what degree does Ephesians 2:8–10 represent your own relationship with Christ?

PHILIPPIANS
Christ the Source of Joy and Strength

The church in Philippi was the first church in a European city.

If people were to search for joy, they probably would not think to look in prison. But that is where Paul wrote this marvelous letter about joy. Through Paul, the Holy Spirit taught that circumstances don't dictate the quality of joy believers have in Christ. How did Paul find joy in prison? He didn't. He took joy in Christ into jail with him; therefore, joy was his continual companion.

AUTHOR AND DATE

Written by Paul, approximately A.D. 61

The unanimous testimony of the early church was that the Apostle Paul wrote Philippians. The question of when this letter was written cannot be separated from where. The traditional view is that Philippians, along with the other Prison Epistles (Ephesians, Colossians, Philemon), was written during Paul's first imprisonment at Rome, about A.D. 60–62. The most natural understanding of the references to the "palace guard" (1:13) and the "saints . . . of Caesar's household" (4:22) is that Paul was in Rome, where the emperor lived. Paul's stated belief that his case would soon be decided (2:23–24) points to a writing date toward the close of the apostle's two-year Roman imprisonment (about A.D. 61).

KEY PEOPLE IN PHILIPPIANS

Paul—wrote to the Philippians about the joy and strength found in Christ (1:1–4:23)

Timothy—missionary of both Jewish and Gentile descent; prepared by Paul to carry on his ministry in Philippi (1:1–2:23)

Epaphroditus—faithful worker from Philippi; sent to Paul with supportive money (2:25–30; 4:18)

Euodia—faithful worker rebuked by Paul for her unreconciled relationship with Syntyche, another sister in the church (4:2–3)

Syntyche—faithful worker rebuked by Paul for her unreconciled relationship with Euodia (4:2–3)

BACKGROUND AND SETTING

In New Testament times, Philippi was known primarily as the site of one of the most famous events in Roman history. In 42 B.C., the forces of Antony and Cleopatra defeated those of Brutus and Cassius at the Battle of Philippi, thus ending the Roman Republic and ushering in the Empire.

After that battle, Philippi became a Roman colony (Acts 16:12), and many veterans of the Roman army settled there.

As a colony, Philippi had autonomy from the provincial government and the same rights granted to cities in Italy, including the use of Roman law, exemption from certain taxes, and Roman citizenship for its residents (Acts 16:21). Recognition as a colony provided a source for much civic pride for the Philippians, who used Latin as their official language, adopted Roman customs, and modeled their city government after that of Italian cities.

The church at Philippi, the first one founded by Paul in Europe, dates from the apostle's second missionary journey (Acts 16:12–40). Among the early converts were Lydia, a wealthy merchant dealing in expensive purple dyed goods (Acts 16:14), and the jailer whose prison housed Paul and Silas until an earthquake set them free and opened the jailer's heart to the gospel.

Both Acts and the letter to the Philippians reflect Philippi's status as a Roman colony. Paul's description of Christians as citizens of heaven (3:20) would have been particularly meaningful to the Philippians' pride over being citizens of Rome (Acts 16:21). Some of the retired veterans in Philippi may well have been former members of the elite palace guard (1:13) and part of Caesar's household (4:22).

KEY DOCTRINES IN PHILIPPIANS

Humility of Christ—Christ came into the world to serve and sacrifice Himself for humankind (2:5–8; Psalms 22:6; 69:9; Isaiah 50:6; 53:3,7; Zechariah 9:9; Matthew 11:29; 13:55; Luke 2:4–7,51; 9:58; John 5:41; 13:14–15; Romans 15:3; 2 Corinthians 8:9; Hebrews 2:16; 4:15; 5:7)

Submission to Christ—believers should pursue Christlikeness (1:21; 3:7–14; Genesis 43:14; Judges 10:15; 1 Samuel 3:18; 2 Samuel 15:26; Job 2:10; Psalms 37:7; 46:10; Matthew 6:10; Acts 7:59; Hebrews 12:6; 2 Peter 1:14)

Christ's provision for believers—God supplies the needs of His children (4:13,19; Nehemiah 9:19; Psalm 146:7–9; Matthew 9:36; John 7:37; 2 Corinthians 9:12; 12:9–10; Hebrews 4:16)

GOD'S CHARACTER IN PHILIPPIANS

God is glorious—2:11
God is merciful—2:27
God is provident—1:12

CHRIST IN PHILIPPIANS

Philippians presents one of the most poignant testimonies of the life lived in Christ. Paul intimately describes his relationship with his Lord with the words "to live *is* Christ and to die *is* gain" (1:21). Paul's selflessness leads not to feelings of loss but only to joy and peace in Jesus Christ (4:4–7). Therefore, he encourages believers to seek Christlikeness (2:5).

KEY WORDS IN PHILIPPIANS

Supply: Greek *epichorēgia*—1:19—used to describe what a choir manager would provide to all the members of a Greek choir who performed in Greek drama. In short, he took care of all their living expenses. The word came to mean a full supply of any kind. The Philippians' prayer would generate the Spirit's *supply.* Paul was looking forward to getting a full supply of Jesus Christ's Spirit as a result of the Philippians' prayers.

Form of God: Greek *morphē theou—*2:6*—morphē,* the word for *form,* was generally used to express the way in which a thing exists and appears according to what it is in itself. Thus, the expression *form of God* may be correctly understood as the essential nature and character of God. To say, therefore, that Christ existed in *the form of God* is to say that apart from His human nature, Christ possessed all the characteristics and qualities belonging to God because He is, in fact, God.

Virtue: Greek *aretē*—4:8—a rare word in the New Testament but generously used in Greek writings to denote moral excellence. Peter in his first letter used the word to describe the excellent nature or "excellencies" of God (see 1 Peter 2:9, where the word is translated *praises*). Such excellence is said to have been possessed by various people, but it is a quality that comes from God. Only those who are given divine power can be morally excellent on this earth (2 Peter 1:3).

QUICK OVERVIEW

I. Paul's Greeting (1:1–11)
II. Paul's Circumstances (1:12–26)
III. Paul's Exhortations (1:27–2:18)
  A. To Stand Firm amid Persecution (1:27–30)
  B. To Be United by Humility (2:1–4)
  C. To Remember the Example of Christ (2:5–11)
  D. To Be Light in a Dark World (2:12–18)
IV. Paul's Companions (2:19–30)
  A. Timothy (2:19–24)
  B. Epaphroditus (2:25–30)
V. Paul's Warnings (3:1–4:1)
  A. Against Legalism (3:1–16)
  B. Against Lawlessness (3:17–4:1)

VI. Paul's Admonition (4:2–9)
VII. Paul's Thankfulness (4:10–20)
VIII. Paul's Farewell (4:21–23)

MEANWHILE, IN OTHER PARTS OF THE WORLD . . .
Buddhist monks move from India into China bringing with them chants. Later, these chants were incorporated into Chinese music.

FREQUENTLY ASKED QUESTIONS

1. What can we learn about Jesus from the great eulogy in 2:6–11?

This is the classic Christological passage in the New Testament, summarizing the divinity, character, and incarnation of Jesus Christ. It stands so clearly as a unit that it was probably sung as a hymn in the early church.

This meditation begins by focusing on the eternal nature of Christ (2:6). The common Greek term for *being* is not used here. Instead, Paul chose another term that stresses the essence of a person's nature—his or her continuous state or condition. Also, of the two Greek words for *form,* Paul chose the one that specifically denotes the essential, unchanging character of something—what it is in and of itself. The fundamental doctrine of the deity of Christ has always included these crucial characteristics (see also John 1:1,3–4,14; 8:58; Colossians 1:15–17; Hebrews 1:3). Although Christ had all the rights, privileges, and honors of deity—for which He was eternally and continually worthy—His attitude was not to cling to His position but to willingly give it up for a time.

Next, the passage describes the process that Christ underwent in order to carry out the Incarnation. First, He "made Himself of no reputation" or better, "emptied Himself" (2:7). The Greek root word used here, *kenosis,* is now used as the theological term for the doctrine of Christ's self-emptying in His incarnation. This step did not mean that Jesus emptied Himself of deity. Jesus did, however, renounce or set aside His privileges in several areas:

- Heavenly glory (John 17:5)
- Independent authority—during His incarnation Christ completely submitted Himself to the will of His Father (Matthew 26:39; John 5:30; Hebrews 5:8)
- Divine prerogatives—Christ set aside the voluntary display of His divine attributes and submitted Himself to the Spirit's direction (Matthew 24:36; John 1:45–49)
- Eternal riches (2 Corinthians 8:9)
- A favorable relationship with God—Christ felt the Father's wrath for human sin while on the cross (Matthew 27:46).

Next, Christ took on the "form of a bondservant" and the "likeness of men" (2:7). The same Greek word for *form* occurs here as in verse 6. Christ became more than just God in a human body; He took on all the essential attributes of humanity (Luke 2:52; Galatians 4:4; Colossians 1:22), even to the extent that He identified with basic human needs and weaknesses (Hebrews 2:14,17; 4:15). He became the God-man: fully divine and fully human.

Next, Christ carried out the full purposes and implications of His divine action. He experienced every aspect of life as a human being. This included the ultimate obedience of dying as a criminal, following God's plan for Him (Matthew 26:39; Acts 2:23).

Christ's utter humiliation (2:5–8) is causally and inseparably linked to His exaltation by God (2:9–11). Jesus was honored in at least six distinct ways: 1) His resurrection; 2) His coronation (His position at the right hand of God); 3) His role as intercessor for believers (Acts 2:32–33; 5:30–31; Ephesians 1:20–21; Hebrews 4:15; 7:25–26); 4) His ascension (Hebrews 4:14); 5) His acknowledged role as the ultimate and perfect substitute for sin; and 6) His given title and name as Lord, which identifies Him fully as the divine and sovereign ruler (Isaiah 45:21–23; Mark 15:2; Luke 2:11; John 13:13; 18:37; 20:28; Acts 2:36; 10:36; Romans 14:9–11; 1 Corinthians 8:6; 15:57; Revelation 17:14; 19:16). Scripture repeatedly affirms Jesus' rightful title as the God-man.

2. To whom is Paul referring by the term "enemies of the cross" in 3:18?

As he had done in many of his contacts with churches he had founded (Acts 20:28–31), Paul warned the Philippians about the dangers of false teachers. Paul's language implies that these teachers did not openly claim to oppose Christ, His work on the cross, or salvation by grace alone through faith alone, but they did not pursue Christlikeness through godly living. Their faith was a fraud. Apparently, they had been posing as friends of Christ and possibly had even reached positions of leadership in the church. Their lives displayed their true allegiance.

3. How do the words *joy* and *rejoice* capture Paul's central message to this group of believers?

Paul uses the word *joy* four times in this letter (1:4,25; 2:2; 4:1). The word *rejoice* appears in the text nine times (1:18 twice, 26; 2:17–18; 3:1; 4:4 twice, 10). In the early chapters, these terms are used primarily to describe Paul's own experience of life in Christ. The beginning of chapter 3, however, is a transition point, shifting to a section of spiritual direction. Paul's expression "rejoice in the Lord" (3:1) is the first time in this letter for the phrase "in the Lord," signifying the reason and the sphere in which the believers' joy exists. Unrelated to the circumstances of life, the believers' joy flows from an unassailable, unchanging relationship with the sovereign Lord.

The theme of joy reaches a peak in 4:4 with the double command, "Rejoice in the Lord always. Again I will say, rejoice!" The verses that follow spell out the external behavior and the internal attitudes that characterize a person whose joy is genuine. Paul also included God's promise to supply both His presence and His peace to those who live rejoicing in the Lord.

QUICK STUDY ON PHILIPPIANS

1. Read Philippians 2:5–11 and then put it into your own words, describing how Christ's actions affect your life.
2. In Philippians 3, to what does Paul compare all his achievements when measured against what it means to know Christ?
3. In how many different ways can you identify Paul's emphasis on joy in this letter?
4. What guidelines does Paul offer in chapter 4 that relate to your prayer life and your thought life? How many of them do you practice?
5. What does Paul mean by Philippians 4:13, and to what degree have you experienced the truth of his discovery?

COLOSSIANS
Man Is Completed through God the Son

Colossians presents a powerful case for the divinity of Jesus Christ.

How does Christianity spread and grow? The church of Jesus in the city of Colosse began as a second-generation church. Paul and his team planted a church in Ephesus. Epaphras, who probably became a Christian in Ephesus, carried the gospel to Colosse and planted a new church. Later, when Paul heard that the Colossian believers were experiencing troubles, he wrote them this letter, a condensed handbook of the Christian faith.

AUTHOR AND DATE

Written by Paul, approximately A.D. 60 to 62

The opening verse identifies Paul as the author of this letter (1:1,23; 4:18). The early church, represented by Irenaeus, Clement of Alexandria, Tertullian, Origen, and Eusebius, confirms the genuineness of Paul's authorship. Additional evidence comes from the book's close parallels with Philemon, which is universally accepted as having been written by Paul.

Like Philemon and the other Prison Epistles (Ephesians and Philippians), Colossians was written during A.D. 60 to 62 while Paul was a prisoner in Rome (see **Frequently Asked Questions** on the Prison Epistles).

KEY PEOPLE IN COLOSSIANS

Paul—urged the church at Colosse to flee from false doctrines which deny Christ's deity (1:1–4:18)

Timothy—fellow missionary who traveled with Paul (1:1)

Tychicus—sent to the church at Colosse to bring letters and news from Paul (4:7–9)

Onesimus—faithfully served with Paul before returning to Colosse to reconcile with Philemon, his former master (see the Book of Philemon) (4:9)

Aristarchus—Thessalonian who traveled with Paul on his third missionary journey (4:10)

Mark—cousin of Barnabas who accompanied Paul and Barnabas on the first missionary journey (4:10)

Epaphras—founder of the Colossian church (1:7–8; 4:12–13)

BACKGROUND AND SETTING

Colosse was a city in Phrygia, in the Roman province of Asia (part of modern Turkey), about a hundred miles east of Ephesus. An ancient city, Colosse prospered through the marketing of black wool and dyes. Until

New Testament times, the city had served as an important regional crossroads. By Paul's day, however, the main road had been rerouted through nearby Laodicea, causing Colosse to gradually decline in importance. Although the population of Colosse consisted mainly of Gentiles, a sizable Jewish settlement had existed for several hundred years.

The church at Colosse began during Paul's three-year ministry at Ephesus (Acts 19). Epaphras, who probably had been saved during a visit to Ephesus, had returned home with such good news that the new church had sprung from his testimony. Several years after the founding of the Colossian church, a dangerous heresy arose to attack it. The threat to the church was real because the false teaching had elements that appealed to both the pagan and Jewish backgrounds of the church members. Epaphras was so concerned about this heresy that he made the long journey from Colosse to Rome (4:12–13) to consult with Paul who was a prisoner there. As a result, Paul composed this letter to warn the Colossians against the heresy. Epaphras stayed in Rome with Paul, but the letter was delivered by Tychicus, who was accompanied by Onesimus, the runaway slave returning to his master, Philemon, a member of the Colossian church (4:7–9; Philemon 23).

KEY DOCTRINES IN COLOSSIANS

The deity of Christ—Jesus did not only come from God; He is the one, true God and Messiah (1:15–20; 2:2–10; Psalms 24:7,10; 45:6–7; Isaiah 7:14; 8:13–14; 9:6; 40:3,11; Jeremiah 23:5–6; Zechariah 13:7; Matthew 1:23; 3:3; 12:8; 26:63–67; Mark 2:7,10; John 1:1,14,18; 3:16; Acts 10:36; Romans 9:5; Titus 2:13; Hebrews 13:20; 1 Peter 2:8)

Reconciliation—the sacrifice of Jesus Christ renews the relationship between God and man (1:20–22; 2:14; Leviticus 8:15; 16:20; Daniel 9:24; Isaiah 53:5; Matthew 5:24–26; Romans 5:1,10–11; 2 Corinthians 5:18–20; Ephesians 2:14–16; Hebrews 2:17)

Redemption—Jesus Christ bought our salvation for a price, His own death on the cross (1:13–14; 2:13–14; 3:9–11; Isaiah 43:1; 44:21–23; Matthew 20:28; Luke 1:68; Acts 20:28; 1 Corinthians 1:30; 6:20; 7:23; Galatians 3:13; 4:4–5; Hebrews 9:12; 1 Peter 1:19; Revelation 5:9)

Election—the life and future of each believer was intimately known by God before time began (3:12; Matthew 20:16; John 6:44; 13:18; 15:16; Acts 22:14; Romans 8:29; 9:11,15–16; 1 Corinthians 1:27; Ephesians 1:4–5,11; 1 Thessalonians 1:4; 2 Thessalonians 2:13; Titus 1:1; 1 Peter 1:2)

Forgiveness—we are to forgive others in the same merciful manner God forgives us (3:13; Psalm 7:4; Proverbs 19:11; Matthew 18:22; Mark 11:25; Luke 6:36; 17:4; 23:34; Romans 12:19; Ephesians 4:32; 1 Peter 4:8)

The nature of the church as the Body of Christ—all believers in Jesus Christ are equal before the Lord as His children and citizens of His eternal kingdom (1:18,24–25; 2:19; 3:11,15; Ephesians 1:22–23; 3:6; 5:32; Revelation 21:9)

GOD'S CHARACTER IN COLOSSIANS

God is accessible—1:21–22
God is invisible—1:15
God is just—3:25
God is powerful—1:11; 2:12
God is reconciling—1:20
God is wrathful—3:6

CHRIST IN COLOSSIANS

The message of Colossians affirms the believer's perfect completion in Christ (1:28). Paul stressed the deity of Jesus against those who attacked the Person of Christ with "philosophy and empty deceit" (2:8–9). Accepting the fullness of Christ as God allows believers to come to fullness of life in Him (2:10).

KEY WORDS IN COLOSSIANS

Jesus Christ: Greek *Iēsous Christos*—1:1–4,28; 2:6; 3:17. Many people believe *Jesus Christ* refers to the first and last names of Jesus. However, *Jesus* is a human name which means "the Lord saves" (see Matthew 1:21). The title *Christ* describes a unique position: Jesus is "the Anointed One." He serves as the perfect King, Prophet, and High Priest of humanity. The name *Jesus Christ* was used prolifically after Jesus revealed Himself as the promised Messiah. Paul indicated the supremacy of Jesus Christ by using this combined name to begin his letter to the Colossians.

First Born: Greek *prōtotokos*—1:15,18—literally, "first in time" or "first in place." In this context, *prōtotokos* should be translated as preeminent or "first in place." Therefore, Jesus Christ is the "chief born" who reigns over all creation (see Exodus 4:22; Deuteronomy 21:16–17; Psalm 89:23). This title reveals the humanity of the Son as the foremost creature of all creation. However, this designation in no way suggests that Christ Himself was created by God. The next verse clearly declares Christ as the Creator of all things. Thus, Christ cannot be a created being. Instead He is the eternal Son of God and the second Person of the Godhead.

Perfect: Greek *teleios*—1:28; 4:12—literally, "end," "limit," or "fulfillment." Paul uses *teleios* to describe the completion or perfection of believers in Christ (Colossians 1:28; 4:12). Christians move towards "perfection" and godliness when their faith matures through trials (James 1:4).

Christians are made more complete by expressing God's love to others (3:14; 1 John 4:12). Just as Paul pressed on towards the goal of perfection in his Christian walk (Philippians 3:12–14), so we too should make perfection in Christ our goal. For humanity, the goal of perfection will be completed when "that which is perfect" comes (1 Corinthians 13:10).

QUICK OVERVIEW

- I. Personal Matters (1:1–14)
  - A. Paul's Greeting (1:1–2)
  - B. Paul's Thankfulness (1:3–8)
  - C. Paul's Prayer (1:9–14)
- II. Doctrinal Instruction (1:15–2:23)
  - A. About Christ's Deity (1:15–23)
  - B. About Paul's Ministry (1:24–2:7)
  - C. About False Philosophy (2:8–23)
- III. Practical Exhortations (3:1–4:18)
  - A. Christian Conduct (3:1–17)
  - B. Christian Households (3:18–4:1)
  - C. Christian Speech (4:2–6)
  - D. Christian Friends (4:7–18)

MEANWHILE, IN OTHER PARTS OF THE WORLD . . .
An ambassador from the king of Nu, a country formerly located on the island of modern-day Japan, arrives in China to give homage to the Han emperor Guang Wudi.

FREQUENTLY ASKED QUESTIONS

1. How does a passage like 1:15–20, which describes Christ as the "firstborn over all creation," fit with the biblical doctrine of Christ's deity?

This passage, 1:15–20, includes a powerful defense of Christ's deity. Apparently, a central component of the heresy that threatened the Colossian church was the denial of the deity of Christ. Ironically, throughout the centuries some cults have used the phrase "firstborn over all creation" (1:15) to undermine Christ's deity. The assumption is that if Jesus was born at creation, then He is more like us than He is God.

The Greek word for firstborn, however, can refer to one who was born first chronologically, but it most often refers to preeminence in position or rank (Hebrews 1:6; Romans 8:9). *Firstborn* in this context clearly means highest in rank, not first created (Psalm 89:27; Revelation 1:5) for several reasons:

- Christ cannot be both "first begotten" and "only begotten" (see John 1:14,18; 3:16,18; 1 John 4:9); and, when the firstborn is one of a class, the class is in the plural form (1:18; Romans 8:29), but "creation," the class here, is in a singular form.
- If Paul were teaching that Christ was a created being, he would be agreeing with the heresy that he was writing to refute.
- It is impossible for Christ to be both created and the Creator of everything (1:16). Thus, Jesus is the firstborn in the sense that He has the preeminence (1:18) and that he possesses the right of inheritance "over all creation" (Hebrews 1:2; Revelation 5:1–7,13).

2. What does the conditional statement "if indeed you continue in the faith" (1:22,23) have to do with whether or not believers can lose their salvation?

The Christian doctrine that deals with this question is often called "the perseverance of the saints." Scripture, as here, sometimes calls us to hold fast to our faith (Hebrews 10:23; Revelation 3:11) or warns us against falling away (Hebrews 10:26–29). Such admonitions do not negate the many promises that true believers will persevere (John 10:28–29; Romans 8:38–39; 1 Corinthians 1:8–9; Philippians 1:6). Rather, the warnings and pleas are among the means God uses to secure our perseverance in the faith. Conditional statements like the one in 1:22 and 23 simply underscore the point that those who do fall away from Christ give conclusive proof that they were never truly believers to begin with (1 John 2:19). To say that God secures our perseverance is not to say that we are passive in the process, however. God keeps us "through faith" (1 Peter 1:5)—our faith.

3. What were the Prison Epistles, and what prison was Paul in when he wrote them?

Four of Paul's letters are grouped as the Prison Epistles: Ephesians, Philippians, Colossians, and Philemon. Each of them includes clear internal references to the writer's prison surroundings (Ephesians 3:1; 4:1; 6:20; Philippians 1:7,13–14,17; Colossians 4:3,10,18; Philemon 1,9–10,13,23). The similarities between the details of Paul's imprisonment given in Acts and in the Prison Epistles support the traditional position that the letters were written from Rome. Among these details are these:

- Paul was guarded by soldiers (Acts 28:16; Philippians 1:13–14).
- Paul was permitted to receive visitors (Acts 28:30; Philippians 4:18).
- Paul had the opportunity to preach the gospel (Acts 28:31; Ephesians 6:18–20; Philippians 1:12–14; Colossians 4:2–4).

Caesarea and Ephesus have also been suggested as Paul's possible location when he wrote at least some of these letters. Paul was imprisoned in Caesarea for two years (Acts 24:27), but his opportunities to receive visitors and proclaim the gospel were severely limited during that time (Acts 23:35). The Prison Epistles express Paul's hope for a favorable verdict (Philippians 1:25; 2:24; Philemon 23). In Caesarea, however, Paul's only hope for release was to either bribe Felix (Acts 24:26) or agree to stand trial at Jerusalem under Festus (Acts 25:9). In the Prison Epistles, Paul expected the decision in his case to be final (Philippians 1:20–23; 2:17,23). That could not have been true at Caesarea, since Paul could and did appeal his case to the emperor.

Ephesus has been the other suggested location. Most of the same difficulties faced by the Caesarea suggestion face those who support Ephesus. The most telling argument against Ephesus as the point of origin for the Prison Epistles, however, is that there is no evidence that Paul was ever imprisoned at Ephesus.

In light of the serious difficulties faced by both the Caesarean and Ephesian views, no reason remains for rejecting the traditional view that Paul wrote the Prison Epistles from Rome while awaiting a hearing before the emperor on his appeal for justice as a Roman citizen.

QUICK STUDY ON COLOSSIANS

1. Based on his counterarguments, what false teaching was Paul refuting in Colossians?
2. What particular themes about the character of Jesus Christ did Paul emphasize in Colossians?
3. How does Paul spell out the requirements of a genuine disciple of Christ in Colossians?
4. In the last chapter of Colossians, what kind of help does Paul ask of the Colossian Christians?
5. In what different ways do you rely on other Christians to encourage your efforts to follow Christ?

FIRST THESSALONIANS

Christ Will Come Again

First Thessalonians mentions the return of Jesus in each of its five chapters.

Christians were dying, and Christ hadn't returned. When the gospel was first preached to the Thessalonians, a strong part of the message focused on the expectation of Christ's return. Several years later, the death of some of the believers raised questions in the church. How long would Christ delay? What about those who died in the meantime? How should Christians live? In response to these questions and other concerns, Paul sent the Thessalonians a letter.

AUTHOR AND DATE

Written by Paul, about A.D. 51

As was his custom, Paul identified himself as the author of this letter (1:1; 2:18). This has not been questioned until recently by radical critics. Their attempts to undermine Pauline authorship have failed in light of the combined weight of evidence favoring the traditional view, such as 1) direct assertions of Paul's authorship; 2) the letter's perfect correlation with Paul's travels in Acts 16–18; 3) the multitude of intimate details concerning Paul; 4) the confirmation by multiple, early historical witnesses starting with Marcion's canon in A.D. 140.

Based in part on the archeological evidence verifying the dates of Gallio's service as proconsul in Achaia as A.D. 51 to 52 (Acts 18:12–17), the first letter to the Thessalonians is dated about A.D. 51. This makes 1 Thessalonians second only to Galatians in the chronological order of Paul's letters.

KEY PEOPLE IN 1 THESSALONIANS

Paul—wrote to the church at Thessalonica to confirm the second coming of Christ and commend them for their faithfulness (1:1–5:28)
Timothy—attested to the faithfulness of the church at Thessalonica (1:1–3:10)
Silas—traveled with Paul as a missionary (1:1)

BACKGROUND AND SETTING

Thessalonica (modern Salonica) stood at the northern end of the Thermaic Gulf in the Aegean Sea. The city became the capital of Macedonia (about 168 B.C.) and enjoyed the status of a "free city" (one ruled by its own citizenry) under the Roman Empire (Acts 17:6). Thessalonica served as a key commercial and political hub on the Via Egnatia, the primary east-west Roman highway in the region. The population in Paul's day reached two hundred thousand people.

Paul's original visit to Thessalonica during his second missionary journey (A.D. 50—Acts 16:1–18:22) was brief but effective. A church was planted there before the apostle and his companions were evicted (Acts 17:1–9). Within a year, Paul sent Timothy back into the region to obtain a report on the new churches at Berea and Thessalonica. Timothy's good news prompted Paul to write his first letter. At that point the apostle was in Corinth, where he remained long enough to write his second letter to the church.

Timothy's report about Thessalonica must have included some details that delighted and some that concerned Paul. Some of these became the purposes behind his letter:

- To encourage the church (1:2–10)
- To answer false allegations (2:1–12)
- To comfort a persecuted flock (2:13–16)
- To express his joy in their faith (2:17–3:13)
- To remind them of the importance of moral purity (4:1–8)
- To condemn the sluggard lifestyle (4:9–12)
- To correct a wrong understanding of prophetic events (4:13–5:11)
- To defuse tensions within the church (5:12–15)
- To exhort the church in the basics of Christian living (5:16–22)

KEY DOCTRINES IN 1 THESSALONIANS

Sanctification—through Christ's atonement, believers are glorified and set apart for the service of God (3:12–13; 4:3–4,16–18; 5:23; Psalm 4:3; Ezekiel 37:28; Acts 20:32; 26:18; Romans 6:1–8:39; 15:16; 2 Corinthians 6:17; Ephesians 5:26–27; 2 Thessalonians 2:13; 2 Timothy 2:21; Hebrews 2:11; 13:12; 1 Peter 1:2; Jude 1:1)

Christ's second coming—Christ's return will mark the judgment of all mankind (1:10; 2:19; 3:13; 4:16; 5:23; Psalm 50:3–4; Daniel 7:13; Matthew 24:36; 25:31; Mark 13:32; John 14:3; 1 Corinthians 1:8; Titus 2:13; 2 Peter 3:12; Jude 1:14; Revelation 1:7)

GOD'S CHARACTER IN 1 THESSALONIANS

God is faithful—5:24
God is wrathful—1:10; 2:16

CHRIST IN 1 THESSALONIANS

First Thessalonians discusses the believer's hope in Christ, particularly in His second coming (1:10; 2:19; 3:13; 4:16; 5:23). Paul instructs believers to prepare for the Day of the Lord, for it shall come "as a thief in the night" (5:2). However, this Day is not to be feared by believers, for Christ obtains our salvation and guards against the wrath of God.

KEY WORDS IN 1 THESSALONIANS

Sanctification: Greek *hagiasmos*—4:3–4—literally, "set apart"—refers to a process whereby God sets aside that which is holy. However, sanctification is perfect only in principle; it is not yet attained by humanity. But though we still remain in a fallen world, we stand in relation to God as though we were already made perfect (Hebrews 10:10). Christ's one and only sacrifice sanctified us, and that sanctification has the lasting result that it continues to work in us, making us holy (Hebrews 10:14).

Spirit; Soul; Body: Greek *pneuma*—4:8; 5:19,23—literally, "spirit"; Greek *psuchē*—5:23—literally, "life"; Greek *sōma*—5:23—literally, "body." First Thessalonians 5:23 is the only place in the New Testament where the being of a person is delineated into three portions. Yet in this passage, all three make up a whole person. The *spirit* enables a person to contact and be regenerated by the divine Spirit (John 3:6; Romans 8:16). The *psuchē*, which is translated *soul*, speaks of a person's personality or essence. Finally the New Testament writers identify the *body* as a physical entity separate from one's soul or spirit. As this verse indicates, God works from the inside out, sanctifying our entire being for eternal life.

Coming: Greek *parousia*—2:19; 3:13; 4:15; 5:23—literally, "presence," commonly used in the New Testament to describe the visitation of important people such as royalty. Thus the word points to a unique and distinct "coming." This term is used in the New Testament to designate the second coming of Christ. This glorious coming will reveal Christ as King over all.

QUICK OVERVIEW

I. Paul's Greeting (1:1)
II. Paul's Personal Thoughts (1:2–3:13)
  A. Thanksgiving for the Church (1:2–10)
  B. Reminders for the Church (2:1–16)
  C. Concerns for the Church (2:17–3:13)
III. Paul's Practical Instructions (4:1–5:22)
  A. On Moral Purity (4:1–8)
  B. On Disciplined Living (4:9–12)
  C. On Death and the Rapture (4:13–18)
  D. On Holy Living and the Day of the Lord (5:1–11)

E. On Church Relationships (5:12–15)
F. On the Basics of Christian Living (5:16–22)
IV. Paul's Benediction (5:23–24)
V. Paul's Final Remarks (5:25–28)

MEANWHILE, IN OTHER PARTS OF THE WORLD . . .
Caractacus, a Welsh chieftain, is taken captive by Roman invaders after being betrayed by Cartimandua, the queen of the Yorkshire Brigantes.

FREQUENTLY ASKED QUESTIONS

1. How did Paul answer the Thessalonians' concerns about the fate of those Christians who had already died?

The statement in 4:13–18 provides an enduring and powerful answer to some of the recurring questions that trouble Christians when they face the death of loved ones in Christ. The Thessalonians had the same practical concerns. Even though Paul's ministry in Thessalonica was brief, it is clear that the people came to believe in and hope for the reality of their Savior's return (1:3,9–10; 2:19; 5:1–2; 2 Thessalonians 2:1,5). They were living in expectation of that coming, eagerly awaiting Christ. They knew that His return was the climactic event in redemptive history and anticipated their participation in it. Verse 13 (see also 2 Thessalonians 2:1–3) indicates that the believers were agitated about those who might miss Christ's return. Based on Paul's answers, their major questions seem to have been: "What happens to the Christians who die before He comes? Do they miss His return?"

Clearly, the Thessalonians had an imminent view of Christ's return. Evidently they had interpreted Paul's teaching to mean that Christ would definitely come back very soon, during their lifetime. Quite naturally, they became confused as they were being persecuted, an experience from which they assumed they would be delivered by the Lord's return.

Paul's answer begins with a note about grief. It does not say that Christians shouldn't "sorrow" over the death of another Christian. Instead, Paul's point is that sorrow for the Christian is hopeful, not hopeless. Then the letter offers a series of promises that affect those who "fall asleep in Christ"—believers who die: As Jesus died and rose again, so too will those who have died in Christ (4:14 and John 14:1–3; 1 Corinthians 15:51–58). These texts describe the rapture of the church (including dead Christians) which will occur when Jesus comes to collect His redeemed and take them back to heaven.

Those who are alive and those who have died will experience the Lord's return at the same time (4:15). Apparently, the Thessalonians were informed fully about the Day of the Lord judgment (5:1–2) but not the preceding event—the rapture of the church. Until Paul revealed it as the revelation from God to him, it had been a secret, with the only prior mention being Jesus' teaching in John 14:1–3. Because Paul didn't know God's timing, he lived and spoke as if this event could happen in his lifetime. As with all early Christians, he believed it was near (Romans 13:11; 1 Corinthians 6:14; 10:11; 16:22; Philippians 3:20–21; 1 Timothy 6:14; Titus 2:13).

"The Lord Himself will descend" (4:16). This fulfills the pledge by Jesus in John 14:1–3. Until then, He remains in heaven (1:10; Hebrews 1:1–3). Believers who have died will rise first, in time to participate in Christ's return (4:16; 1 Corinthians 15:52). Those alive at the Rapture will accompany those dead who rise first (4:17) and "meet the Lord in the air."

Paul assured the Thessalonians, and all believers, that Jesus will not have any of His own miss out on His return. The final verse of the chapter reveals Paul's central intent in the passage—to encourage those Christians whose loved ones have died. The comfort here is based on the following:

- The dead will be resurrected and will participate in the Lord's coming for His own.
- When Christ comes the living will be reunited forever with their loved ones.
- All believers, both the living and the dead, will be with the Lord eternally (4:17–18).

2. What did Paul mean by the "times and seasons" (5:1), and why did he find no need to write the church about them?

Chapter 5 begins with Paul's shifting the specific subject from his discussion of the blessings of the rapture of believers (4:13–18) to the judgment of unbelievers (5:1–11). The two terms *times* and *seasons* refer to the measurement of time and the character of the times respectively (Daniel 2:21; Acts 1:7). Instead of writing to them about this subject, Paul needed only to remind them of what they had already been taught.

Apparently, the Thessalonians knew all God intended believers to know about coming judgment, and once Paul had taught them what they needed to know about the Rapture (4:13–18), his remaining duty was to encourage. Paul exhorted them to live godly lives in the light of coming judgment on the world, rather than to be distracted by probing into issues of prophetic timing. They could not know the timing of God's final judgment, but they knew well that it would come unexpectedly (5:2).

3. How does Paul add his voice to the rest of Scripture in using the expression *Day of the Lord* (5:2)?

Nineteen indisputable uses of *the Day of the Lord* occur in the Old Testament and four in the New Testament (Acts 2:20; 1 Thessalonians

5:2; 2 Thessalonians 2:2; 2 Peter 3:10). The Old Testament prophets used *Day of the Lord* to describe:

- Near historical judgments (Isaiah 13:6–12; Ezekiel 30:2–19; Joel 1:15; 3:14; Amos 5:18–20; Zephaniah 1:14–18)
- Far eschatological divine judgments (Joel 2:30–32; Zechariah 14:1; Malachi 4:1,5). Six times it is referred to as the "day of doom" and four times "day of vengeance."

The New Testament calls it a day of "wrath," day of "visitation," and the "Great Day of God Almighty" (Revelation 16:4).

These are terrifying judgments from God (Joel 2:30–31; 2 Thessalonians 1:7) for the overwhelming sinfulness of the world. The future Day of the Lord, which unleashes God's wrath, falls into two parts: the end of the seven-year tribulation period (Revelation 19:11–21) and the end of the Millennium. These two are actually one thousand years apart. Peter refers to the end of the one-thousand-year period in connection with the final Day of the Lord (2 Peter 3:10; Revelation 20:7–15).

Here the reference to the Day of the Lord refers to the conclusion of the tribulation period. The descriptive phrase "a thief in the night" is never used in Scripture to refer to the rapture of the church. It is used of Christ's coming in judgment on the Day of the Lord at the end of the seven-year tribulation that is distinct from the rapture of the church (4:15) which occurs immediately prior to this seven-year period. It is also used of the judgment that concludes the Millennium (2 Peter 3:10). As a thief comes unexpectedly and without warning, so will the Day of the Lord come in both its final phases.

QUICK STUDY ON 1 THESSALONIANS

1. What does Paul teach about the second coming of Christ in 1 Thessalonians?
2. How does Paul use his own experiences to encourage the Thessalonians?
3. What comments and counsel did Paul record about the persecution of Thessalonian believers?
4. What encouraging statements does Paul have to make about the faith of the Thessalonians?
5. What evidence from your life demonstrates that you are prepared for Christ's second coming?

SECOND THESSALONIANS

Comfort, Correction, and Confrontation

In 2 Thessalonians, Christians learn that Christ's coming is no excuse for complacency.

No one can accuse the Apostle Paul of lacking in persistence. If one of his letters didn't accomplish its goal, he simply would write another one. Within a short time of writing his first letter to the church in Thessalonica, Paul wrote a second time. As before, his primary purpose was to encourage those believers. He saw in them a persistent need for encouragement that matched his own persistent need to minister.

AUTHOR AND DATE

Written by Paul, about late A.D. 51 or early A.D. 52

As with 1 Thessalonians and most of his letters, Paul identified himself twice as the author of this letter (1:1; 3:17). Evidence, both within this letter and with regard to vocabulary, style, and doctrinal content, strongly supports Pauline authorship.

The time of this writing was apparently a few months after the first epistle, while Paul was still in Corinth with Silas and Timothy (1:1; Acts 18:5) in late A.D. 51 or early A.D. 52.

KEY PEOPLE IN 2 THESSALONIANS

Paul—wrote to give guidance on how to maintain a healthy church with an effective testimony (1:1–3:18)

Silas—traveled with Paul as a missionary (1:1)

Timothy—traveled with Paul as a missionary (1:1)

BACKGROUND AND SETTING

For background information on Thessalonica, see Thessalonians **Background and Setting.** Some have suggested that Paul penned this letter from Ephesus (Acts 18:18–21), but his eighteen-month stay in Corinth provided ample time for him to write both the Thessalonian letters.

Paul apparently managed to stay apprised of the happenings in Thessalonica. Perhaps the bearer of the first letter had returned with an update on the condition of the church. Paul was aware of the maturity and expansion of that church (1:3), but he also knew of their suffering under pressure and persecution. There were signs of danger in the seeds being sown of false teaching about the Lord, as well as in the disorderly behavior of some people.

As Paul took up his pen, he had the following picture of the church in his mind: 1) discouraged by persecution and needing incentive to persevere; 2) deceived by false teachers who confused them about the Lord's return; 3) disobedient to divine commands, particularly by refusing to work. For each of these, Paul had something to offer: 1) comfort for the persecuted believers (1:3–12); 2) correction for falsely taught and frightened believers (2:1–15); 3) confrontation for the disobedient and undisciplined believers (3:6–15).

KEY DOCTRINES IN 2 THESSALONIANS

Church discipline—clear guidelines about godly conduct are necessary for a healthy church (3:6–15; Matthew 18:15–20; 1 Corinthians 5:1–13; Galatians 6:1–5; 1 Timothy 5:19–20)

Eternal reward and retribution—each human after death will either be with God forever (eternal reward) or absent from God's presence and glory forever (eternal punishment) (1:5–12; Matthew 8:12; 22:13; 25:30; Luke 16:24–26; Romans 2:7; 2 Corinthians 5:10; Colossians 3:24; Hebrews 11:6; Revelation 20:14–15; 22:5)

GOD'S CHARACTER IN 2 THESSALONIANS

God is good—1:11
God is loving—2:16
God is righteous—1:6
God is wrathful—1:8

CHRIST IN 2 THESSALONIANS

Paul's second letter to the Thessalonians describes the effects of Christ's second coming. While 1 Thessalonians reveals the expectation of Christ's return, 2 Thessalonians describes the glorification of believers on that day and God's judgement of unbelievers (1:10,12; 2:8–12).

KEY WORDS IN 2 THESSALONIANS

Destruction: Greek *olethros*—1:9—does not mean annihilation or extinction, in which one would cease to exist, but rather the loss of everything good and worthwhile. In 1 Corinthians, Paul uses the word to speak of the immediate consequences of sin (1 Corinthians 5:5). Yet, in 1 Thessalonians 1:91, he uses the same word to describe the eternal consequences of sin (see also 1 Timothy 6:9). The punishment for sin is not annihilation, but eternal separation from the love of Christ. Just as eternal life belongs to believers, endless suffering awaits those who rebel against Christ.

The Lawless One: Greek *ho anomos*—2:8—literally, "without law," points to a man consumed with rebellion. This evil figure is also called "the

Antichrist" (1 John 4:2–3) and "the beast" (Revelation 13:1). He stands in direct defiance to Jesus Christ, the embodiment of righteousness. Yet, in the end, this man will be conquered by the sovereign Ruler of the universe.

QUICK OVERVIEW

I. Paul's Greeting (1:1–2)
II. Paul's Comfort for Affliction (1:3–12)
  A. By Way of Encouragement (1:3–4)
  B. By Way of Exhortation (1:5–12)
III. Paul's Correction for Prophetic Error (2:1–17)
  A. Prophetic Crisis (2:1–2)
  B. Apostolic Correction (2:3–12)
  C. Pastoral Comfort (2:13–17)
IV. Paul's Concern for the Church (3:1–15)
  A. Regarding Prayer (3:1–5)
  B. Regarding Undisciplined Living (3:6–15)
V. Paul's Benediction (3:16–18)

MEANWHILE, IN OTHER PARTS OF THE WORLD . . .
Lake Fucino, located in central Italy, is drained for cultivation under the direction of Claudius.

FREQUENTLY ASKED QUESTIONS

1. How does Paul expand on some of his teaching about the Day of the Lord in 2:1–5?

The Christians in Thessalonica had a persistent problem with the tension between an attitude of expectation for the Lord's soon return and the realities of daily living that required hard work and commitment. False teachers were fanning the flames of confusion. The idea that the Day of the Lord had already arrived conflicted with what Paul had previously taught them about the Rapture. Whoever was telling them they were already in the Day of the Lord claimed that the message had come from Paul. Thus the lie was given supposed apostolic authority. The results were shock, fear, and alarm. This error, which so upset the Thessalonians, Paul corrected in 2:1–12. He showed that the Day of the Lord hadn't come and couldn't come until certain realities were in place, most especially, "the man of sin" (verse 3).

The same verse refers to "the falling away." The language indicates a specific event, not general apostasy that exists now and always will. Rather, Paul had in mind the apostasy. This is a clearly and specifically identifiable unique event, the consummate act of rebellion, an event of final magnitude. The key to identifying the event depends on the identity of the main person involved. Paul calls him the "man of sin." This figure is also called "the prince who is to come" (Daniel 9:26) and "the little horn" (Daniel 7:8). John calls him "the beast" (Revelation 13:2–10,18), but most know him as the Antichrist.

This statement is referring to the very act of ultimate apostasy that reveals the final Antichrist and sets the course for the events that usher in the Day of the Lord. Apparently, he will be seen as supportive of religion so that God and Christ will not appear as his enemies until the apostasy. He exalts himself and opposes God by moving into the temple, the place for worship of God, declaring himself to be God and demanding the world's worship (verse 4). In this act of Satanic self-deification, he commits the great apostasy in defiance of God. The seven-year tribulation that follows under the reign of Antichrist (Daniel 7:25; 11:36–39; Matthew 24:15–21; Revelation 13:1–8) culminates with the Day of the Lord.

This section of Paul's letter continues to emphasize that the Thessalonians did not need to be agitated or troubled, thinking that they had missed the Rapture and thus were in the Day of Judgment. They were destined for glory, not judgment, and would not be included with those deceived and judged in that Day.

2. How does Paul's teaching on church discipline in 3:6–15 fit with other major passages of Scripture on this subject?

Paul addressed a particular issue of church discipline with the Thessalonians in 3:6–15. Helpful parallel passages that should be consulted in studying this one include Matthew 18:15–20; 1 Corinthians 5:1–13; Galatians 6:1–5; and 1 Timothy 5:19–20.

This passage (3:6–15) gives specific direction on the nature of the church's response to someone who deliberately refuses to follow God's Word, expecting to benefit from fellowship with God's people while being unwilling to participate in a meaningful way. In Paul's words, "If anyone will not work, neither shall he eat" (3:10). These were fellow-believers acting in a parasitic way, sapping the generosity of other believers. Paul had already addressed this pattern in his first letter (1 Thessalonians 4:11).

This passage offers an emphatic command, a personal confrontation, and a compassionate caution. First, verses 6 and 14 instruct the rest of the church to "withdraw" and "not keep company" with such a person. In other words, Paul was commanding the church to disfellowship blatantly disobedient Christians in order to produce shame (verse 14) and, hopefully, repentance. Second, Paul was giving the sluggards a direct command to "work in quietness and eat their own bread" (verse 12), removing any excuse that they had not been warned about discipline. Third, Paul added two crucial words of caution. He reminded the believers that genuinely needy people deserved help. He urged them, "Do not grow weary in doing good" (verse 13). He also cautioned them to limit their disciplinary withdrawal. "Yet do not count him as an enemy, but admonish him as a brother" (verse 15). While an unrepentant pattern of sin should be handled decisively, they should continually remember that the person being disciplined is a brother or sister in the Lord. All further warnings to this person about his or her sin should be done with love and concern, praying for this fellow believer's restoration.

QUICK STUDY ON 2 THESSALONIANS

1. In what ways does the message of 2 Thessalonians compare and contrast with Paul's message in 1 Thessalonians?
2. Outline Paul's description of final events.
3. What kind of outlook and attitude does Paul expect Christians to have in the light of Christ's coming?
4. How would you describe your attitude to the possibility of being persecuted for being a Christian?

FIRST TIMOTHY
The Youthful Minister

First Timothy provides the basis for church organization.

The Apostle Paul surrounded himself with some amazing friends. Paul, Timothy, Luke, Mark, Titus, and Philemon together wrote or received sixteen out of twenty-seven books in the New Testament. Three of his friends Paul called "sons in the faith"—Timothy, Titus, and Onesimus. Paul honored his friends by writing them powerful letters. This one to young Timothy reflects the unique accountability and friendship that grew between Paul and his protégé.

AUTHOR AND DATE

Written by Paul, about A.D. 62 to 64

Many modernist critics deny that Paul wrote the Pastoral Epistles (1 Timothy, 2 Timothy, and Titus). To do so, they must dismiss the testimony of the letters themselves (1:1; 2 Timothy 1:1; Titus 1:1). They must also ignore the testimony of the early church, which is as strong in favor of Pauline authorship of the Pastoral Epistles as for any of the letters, except for Romans and 1 Corinthians (which enjoys impregnable support). These critics maintain that a devout follower of Paul wrote the Pastoral Epistles in the second century. They offer extensive, but refutable, support for their argument. And, since the "latest evidence" often turns out to be flawed, and Scripture repeatedly turns out to be right, it is best in this case to maintain the straightforward scriptural claim of Pauline authorship for the Pastoral Epistles.

KEY PEOPLE IN 1 TIMOTHY

Paul—encouraged Timothy in his ministry in Ephesus (1:1–6:21)

Timothy—name means "one who honors God"; served as the pastor of the church at Ephesus (1:2–6:21)

BACKGROUND AND SETTING

Timothy was from Lystra (Acts 16:1–3), a city in the Roman province of Galatia. Paul had led Timothy to Christ (1:2,18; 1 Corinthians 4:17; 2 Timothy 1:2), undoubtedly during his ministry in Lystra on his first missionary journey (Acts 14:6–23). Timothy would be Paul's disciple, friend, and colaborer for the rest of the apostle's life, ministering with him in Berea (Acts 17:4), Athens (Acts 17:15), and Corinth (Acts 18:5; 2 Corinthians 1:19), and accompanying him on his trip to Jerusalem (Acts 20:4). He was with Paul in his first Roman imprisonment, and he went to Philippi (Philippians 2:19–23) after Paul's release. In addition, Paul's epistles frequently mention

Timothy (Romans 16:21; 2 Corinthians 1:1; Philippians 1:1; Colossians 1:1; 1 Thessalonians 1:1; 2 Thessalonians 1:1; Philemon 1). Paul often would send Timothy to churches as his representative (1 Corinthians 4:17; 16:10; Philippians 2:19; 1 Thessalonians 3:2); thus this letter finds him on another assignment, serving as pastor of the church at Ephesus (1:3).

After being released from his first Roman imprisonment (Acts 28:30), Paul revisited several of the cities in which he had previously ministered, including Ephesus. He left Timothy in Ephesus to deal with problems that had arisen in the church there, such as false doctrine (1:3–7; 4:1–3; 6:3–5), disorder in worship (2:1–15), the lack of qualified leaders (3:1–14), and materialism (6:6–19). Paul continued on to Macedonia, from where he wrote Timothy this letter to help him carry out his task in the church (3:14–15).

KEY DOCTRINES IN 1 TIMOTHY

Salvation—comes through Jesus Christ alone (1:14–16; 2:4–6; Genesis 3:15; Psalms 3:8; 37:39; Isaiah 45:21–22; 49:6; 59:16; 63:9; Luke 1:69; John 1:1–18; 6:35,48; 8:12; 10:7,9; 10:11–14; 11:25; 14:6; 17:3; Acts 4:12; 16:31; Romans 5:8; 10:9; Ephesians 2:8; 5:23; 2 Timothy 1:10; Hebrews 2:10; 5:9; 1 Peter 1:5; 1 John 1:1–4)

The Fall—sin entered all mankind through the disobedience of the first two humans (2:13–14; Genesis 3:6,11–12; 6:5; Job 15:14; 25:4; Psalm 51:5; Isaiah 48:8; Jeremiah 16:12; Matthew 15:19; Romans 5:12,15,19; 2 Corinthians 11:3)

The person of Christ—Christ is fully God and fully man (3:16; 6:15–16; Isaiah 7:14; Matthew 4:11; John 1:14; Romans 1:3–4; Acts 1:9; 1 John 4:2–3; 5:6)

Election—before time began, God intimately knew the life and future of His children (6:12; Deuteronomy 7:6; Matthew 20:16; John 6:44; 13:18; 15:16; Acts 22:14; Ephesians 1:4; 1 Thessalonians 1:4; Titus 1:1)

The second coming of Christ—Christ's return will mark the judgment of all mankind (6:14–15; Psalm 50:3–4; Daniel 7:13; Matthew 24:36; 25:31; Mark 13:32; John 14:3; 1 Corinthians 1:8; 1 Thessalonians 1:10; 2:19; 3:13; 4:16; 5:23; Titus 2:13; 2 Peter 3:12; Jude 1:14; Revelation 1:7)

GOD'S CHARACTER IN 1 TIMOTHY

God is eternal—1:17
God is immortal—1:17; 6:16
God is invisible—1:17
God is long-suffering—1:16
God is merciful—1:2,13
God is a promise keeper—4:8

God is unified—2:5
God is wise—1:17

CHRIST IN 1 TIMOTHY

Paul's letter to Timothy describes the person of Christ as "manifested in the flesh, justified in the Spirit, seen by angels, preached among the Gentiles, believed on in the world, received up in glory" (3:16). Paul also speaks of the actions of Christ as the ransom and Savior of humanity (2:6; 4:10). Paul reminds Timothy to keep faith in Christ (1:14) and to "fight the good fight of faith" (6:12).

KEY WORDS IN 1 TIMOTHY

Ransom: Greek *antilutron*—2:6—literally, "ransom"—actually composed of two words: *anti* meaning substitution, and *lutron* ransom of a slave or prisoner. The *antilutron* is a payment given in substitution for a slave. The slave's owner accepts the payment for the release of their slave. Galatians 3:13 shows how Christ paid the ransom for sinners under the curse of the law. Christ's sacrifice on the cross redeemed us from the bondage of sin.

Bishop: Greek *episkopos*—3:1–2—literally, "one who oversees." In the New Testament, elders functioned as overseers of their congregations (Acts 20:17,28). Elders were responsible to maintain the internal affairs of the church. To accomplish this task, several elders held positions of responsibility in any given congregation (see Acts 14:23; Titus 1:5–7). After New Testament times, the term *elder* was replaced with *bishop,* and it became customary for only one bishop to oversee each congregation.

Idle Babblings: Greek *kenophōnia*—6:20—literally, "empty words." Paul uses this term to express a total void of spiritual meaning. In other words, human achievement amounts to nothing if it does not come from the will of God. In Paul's time, Judaizers were trying to entice believers by using clever-sounding philosophies. Paul described their hollow talk as *idle babblings* (see 6:20; Ephesians 5:6; Colossians 2:8; 2 Timothy 2:16). On the other hand, the teaching of Paul and the apostles was not futile; it would last throughout eternity because it originated in God's unchanging will (Matthew 5:18; 1 Corithians 15:12–15).

QUICK OVERVIEW

I. Greeting (1:1–2)
II. Instructions concerning False Doctrine (1:3–20)
  A. The False Doctrine at Ephesus (1:3–11)
  B. The True Doctrine of Paul (1:12–17)
  C. The Exhortation to Timothy (1:18–20)

III. Instructions concerning the Church (2:1–3:16)
  A. The Importance of Prayer (2:1–8)
  B. The Role of Women (2:9–15)
  C. The Qualifications for Leaders (3:1–13)
  D. The Reason for Paul's Letter (3:14–16)
IV. Instructions concerning False Teachers (4:1–16)
  A. The Description of False Teachers (4:1–5)
  B. The Description of True Teachers (4:6–16)
V. Instructions concerning Pastoral Responsibilities (5:1–6:2)
  A. The Responsibility to Sinning Members (5:1–2)
  B. The Responsibility to Widows (5:3–16)
  C. The Responsibility to Elders (5:17–25)
  D. The Responsibility to Slaves (6:1–2)
VI. Instructions concerning the Man of God (6:3–21)
  A. The Peril of False Teaching (6:3–5)
  B. The Peril of Loving Money (6:6–10)
  C. The Proper Character and Motivation of a Man of God (6:11–16)
  D. The Proper Handling of Treasure (6:17–19)
  E. The Proper Handling of Truth (6:20–21)

MEANWHILE, IN OTHER PARTS OF THE WORLD . . .
Pit houses, circular dwellings composed of mud, were constructed by the Mogollon tribe in the Southeast region of present-day United States.

FREQUENTLY ASKED QUESTIONS

1. When Paul writes, "This is a faithful saying," is he quoting other Scripture?

Paul used this phrase a number of times in the Pastoral Epistles (1:15; 3:1; 4:9; 2 Timothy 2:11; Titus 3:8). The statement that follows in each case summarizes a key doctrine. The added phrase *worthy of all acceptance* gives the statement added emphasis. Apparently, these sayings were well known in the churches as concise expressions of cardinal gospel truth. In their travels together, Timothy and Titus would have heard Paul expand on these statements many times.

These sayings do not quote other Scripture directly but summarize biblical teaching. For example, the saying in 1:15 that "Christ Jesus came into the world to save sinners" is based on Jesus' statements recorded in Matthew 9:13 and Luke 19:10. Naturally, their usage by Paul under the inspiration of the Holy Spirit confirmed that these sayings were God's Word.

2. If 2:4–6 states that God "desires all men to be saved," why isn't everyone saved? How far does salvation extend?

The Greek word for *desires* is not the one usually used to express God's will of decree (His sovereign eternal purpose). Rather, it expresses God's will of desire. There is a distinction between God's desire and His eternal saving purpose, which must transcend His desires. God does not want people to sin. He hates sin with all His being (see Psalms 5:4; 45:7). Thus, He hates its consequences—eternal wickedness in hell. God does not want people to remain wicked forever in eternal remorse and hatred of Him. Yet God, for His own glory, and to manifest that glory in wrath, chose to endure "vessels . . . prepared for destruction" for the supreme fulfillment of His will (see Romans 9:22). In His eternal purpose, He chose only the elect out of the world (see John 17:6) and passed over the rest, leaving them to the consequences of their sin, unbelief, and rejection of Christ (see Romans 1:18–32). Ultimately, God's choices and action are determined by His sovereign, eternal purpose, not His desires.

Paul describes Christ's role in salvation with the phrase *a ransom for all* (verse 6). Jesus Himself used similar wording when He described His purpose to be "a ransom for many" (Matthew 20:28). The *all* is qualified by the *many.* Not all will be ransomed (though His death would be sufficient), but only the many who believe by the work of the Holy Spirit and for whom the actual atonement was made. The *for all* should be taken in two senses:

- Temporal benefits of the atonement that accrue to people universally (for example, daily experiences of God's compassion and grace)
- Christ's death was sufficient to cover the sins of all people. Yet the substitutionary aspect of His death is applied to the elect alone. Christ's death is therefore unlimited in its sufficiency but limited in its application. The fact that not all are saved has no bearing on Christ's ability to save but rather rests in humanity's profound sinfulness and God's sovereign plan.

3. What specific instructions did Paul give Timothy that would apply to a young person?

A young person seeking to live as a disciple of Jesus Christ can find essential guidelines in 4:12–16, where Paul listed five areas (verse 12) in which Timothy was to be an example to the church:

- In "word" or speech—see also Matthew 12:34–37; Ephesians 4:25,29,31
- In "conduct" or righteous living—see also Titus 2:10; 1 Peter 1:15; 2:12; 3:16
- In "love" or self-sacrificial service for others—see also John 15:13

- In "faith" or faithfulness or commitment, not belief—see also 1 Corinthians 4:2
- In "purity" and particularly sexual purity—see also 4:2

The verses that follow hold several other building blocks to a life of discipleship:

- Timothy was to be involved in the public reading, study, and application of Scripture (verse 13).
- Timothy was to diligently use his spiritual gift that others had confirmed and affirmed in a public way (verse 14).
- Timothy was to be committed to a process of progress in his walk with Christ (verse 15).
- Timothy was to "take heed" to pay careful attention to "yourself and to the doctrine" (verse 16).

The priorities of a godly leader should be summed up in Timothy's personal holiness and public teaching. All of Paul's exhortations in verses 6–16 fit into one or the other of those two categories. By careful attention to his own godly life and faithful preaching of the Word, Timothy would continue to be the human instrument God would use to bring the gospel and to save some who heard him. Though salvation is God's work, it is His pleasure to do it through human instruments.

4. What are the characteristics of a false teacher?

Paul provided for Timothy a helpful profile of false teachers by identifying three primary characteristics in 6:3. False teachers reveal themselves in these ways: 1) they "teach otherwise"—a different doctrine, or any teaching that contradicts God's revelation in Scripture (see Galatians 1:6–9); 2) they do "not consent to wholesome words"—they do not agree with sound, healthy teaching, specifically the teaching contained in Scripture (see 2 Peter 3:16); 3) they reject "doctrine which accords with godliness"—teaching not based on Scripture will always result in an unholy life. Instead of godliness, the lives of false teachers will be marked by sin (see 2 Peter 2:10–22; Jude 4,8–16).

5. What directions did Paul give Timothy about dealing with people who are wealthy?

Paul counseled Timothy (6:17–19) concerning what to teach those who are rich in material possessions—that is, those who have more than the mere essentials of food, clothing, and shelter. Paul had already made the case (6:6–8) that Christians should be satisfied and sufficient, and not to seek for more than what God has already given them, for He is the source of true contentment. Instead of condemning wealthy people or commanding them to get rid of their wealth, Paul called them to be good stewards of their God-given resources (see also Deuteronomy 8:18; 1 Samuel 2:7; 1 Chronicles 29:12; 2 Corinthians 3:5; 9:8; Philippians 4:11–13,19).

Those who have an abundance face a constant temptation to look down on others and act superior—haughty (6:17). Paul reminded Timothy that riches and pride often go together; thus, the wealthier a person becomes, the more he or she is tempted to be proud (see Proverbs 18:23; 28:11; James 2:1–4). In fact, those who have much tend to trust in their wealth (see Proverbs 23:4–5). But God provides far more security than any earthly investment can ever give (see Ecclesiastes 5:18–20; Matthew 6:19–21).

QUICK STUDY ON 1 TIMOTHY

1. What clues about Timothy's youthfulness and relationship with Paul are found in this letter?
2. What duties did Paul give to Timothy?
3. How does Paul describe the kind of leaders Timothy should seek to appoint in the church?
4. In chapter 4, Paul gives Timothy several guidelines for personal discipline. What are these?
5. What relationships did Paul highlight in describing how the church should function within a community?
6. In what ways do you identify with Timothy?

SECOND TIMOTHY

Final Words

Second Timothy represents the last will and testament of a great apostle of the gospel.

Last words often carry special significance. The Apostle Paul saw that the end of life was near, so he wrote to share some final thoughts with his "son in the faith," Timothy. Paul's words take the form of a powerful, Spirit-inspired last will and testament. The letter also expresses a tribute to the Lord Jesus Christ, of whom Paul could say, "I know whom I have believed and am persuaded that He is able to keep what I have committed to Him until that Day" (2 Timothy 1:12).

AUTHOR AND DATE

Written by Paul, about A.D. 66 to 67

Paul's authorship is claimed by the first word in the first verse of this letter. Suggestions to the contrary are discussed in the **Frequently Asked Question** "Did Paul write the Pastoral Epistles?" Scripture and tradition attest that Paul wrote 2 Timothy, the last of his inspired letters, shortly before his martyrdom in about A.D. 66–67. For more biographical information on Timothy, see 1 Timothy **Background and Setting.**

KEY PEOPLE IN 2 TIMOTHY

Paul—wrote to encourage and instruct Timothy in his pastoral ministry at Ephesus (1:1–4:22)

Timothy—name means "one who honors God"; served as the pastor of the church at Ephesus (1:2–4:22)

Luke—Paul's traveling companion; only person to stay with Paul through his imprisonment (4:11)

Mark—traveled with Paul and Barnabas on their first missionary journey (4:11)

BACKGROUND AND SETTING

Paul was released from his first Roman imprisonment for a short period of ministry. During that time, he wrote the epistles 1 Timothy and Titus. By the time he wrote this letter, however, he was imprisoned again (1:16; 2:9). His rearrest probably occurred during Nero's persecution of Christians. Unlike Paul's confident hope of release during his earlier imprisonment (Philippians 1:19,25–26; 2:24; Philemon 22), this time he had no such hopes (4:6–8). In his first imprisonment in Rome (about A.D. 60–62), before Nero began aggressively persecuting believers (A.D. 64), Paul was only under house arrest and enjoyed much interaction and ministry with people (Acts 28:16–31). Five or six years later when he wrote 2 Timothy (about A.D. 66–67), however, the apostle was in a cold cell (4:13), in chains (2:9), and with no hope of deliverance (4:6). Fearful of their own persecution, nearly all those close to Paul had abandoned him (1:15; 4:9–12,16). So facing imminent execution, Paul wrote to Timothy, urging him to hurry to Rome for one last visit (4:9,21). History does not report whether Timothy made it there before Paul's death. According to tradition, Paul remained in Roman custody until he suffered the martyrdom that he had foreseen (4:6).

In this letter, Paul, aware that the end was near, passed the mantle of ministry to Timothy (2:2). The older disciple challenged the younger one in the following areas: He exhorted Timothy 1) to continue to be faithful in his duties (1:6); 2) to hold on to sound doctrine (1:13–14); 3) to avoid error (2:15–18); 4) to accept persecution for the gospel (2:3–4; 3:10–12); and 5) to put his confidence in the Scripture and to preach it relentlessly (3:15–4:5).

KEY DOCTRINES IN 2 TIMOTHY

Salvation by God's sovereign grace—comes through Jesus Christ alone (1:9–10; 2:10; Genesis 3:15; Psalms 3:8; 37:39; Isaiah 45:21–22; 49:6; 59:16; 63:9; Luke 1:69; John 1:1–18; 6:35,48; 8:12; 10:7,9; 10:11–14; 11:25; 14:6; 17:3; Acts 4:12; 16:31; Romans 5:8; 10:9; Ephesians 2:8; 5:23; 1 Timothy 1:14–16; 2:4–6; Hebrews 2:10; 5:9; 1 Peter 1:5; 1 John 1:1–4)

The person of Christ—both divine Judge over the world and the Messiah descending from the seed of David (2:8; 4:1,8; Isaiah 7:14; Matthew 4:11; John 1:14; Romans 1:3–4; Acts 1:9; 1 Timothy 3:16; 6:15–16; 1 John 4:2–3; 5:6)

Perseverance—believers who persevere give evidence of the genuineness of their faith (2:11–13; Job 17:9; Psalm 37:24; Proverbs 4:18; John 8:31; 1 Corinthians 15:58; Galatians 6:9; Philippians 1:6; Colossians 1:21–23; Hebrews 3:6,14)

Inspiration of Scripture—God used the minds, vocabularies, and experiences of the biblical writers to produce His own infallible and inerrant Word (3:16–17; Acts 1:16; Romans 3:2; 9:17; Galatians 3:8; Hebrews 3:7; 1 Peter 4:11; 2 Peter 1:21)

GOD'S CHARACTER IN 2 TIMOTHY

God is powerful—1:8
God is a promise keeper—1:1
God is wise—2:19

CHRIST IN 2 TIMOTHY

Paul's second letter encourages Timothy to keep close to the "sound words which you have heard from me, in the faith and love which are in Christ Jesus" (1:13). Left to carry on Paul's ministry, Timothy was reminded of the person of Christ (2:8; 4:1,8), and his call to "Preach the word" (4:2). Timothy was promised persecution by following Christ (3:12), yet he was urged to keep strong in the faith "which is in Christ Jesus" (3:15).

KEY WORDS IN 2 TIMOTHY

Appearing: Greek *epiphaneia*—1:10; 4:1,8—literally means "a shining forth" and was used in Greek literature to denote a divine appearance. The English word *epiphany* is a close equivalent. The New Testament writers use the word to refer to Jesus' first coming, the time when He entered this world as a man (see 1:10). They also use the word to speak of Jesus' second coming, specifically to His appearance to all the world (see Matthew 24:27).

Books, Parchments: Greek *biblion*—4:13; Greek *membrana*—4:13, the word *biblion* is common in the New Testament but not the word *membrana*, which occurs only here. It is a word derived from Latin that means an animal skin used for writing. The two words in this passage have been interpreted in three different ways: 1) *the scrolls* were copies of Old Testament books, and *the parchments* were copies of various New Testament books; 2) *the books* were copies of both Old Testament and New Testament books, and *the parchments* were blank writing material or notebooks containing rough drafts; or 3) the two words signified the same thing: *the books*—that is, the *parchment notebooks.* If the third interpretation is correct, it suggests that Paul was anxious to recover some rough drafts he had left behind when he was arrested.

Inspiration of God: Greek *theopneustos*—3:16—means "God-breathed," from *theos* (God) and *pneō* (to breathe). Although it is difficult to fully recreate the thought of this Greek expression in English, we are sure that Paul meant to say that all Scripture was breathed out from God. This definition affirms the Bible's divine origin; thus God not only inspired the authors who wrote the words of the Bible but He also inspires those who read it with a heart of faith.

QUICK OVERVIEW

I. Greeting and Thanksgiving (1:1–5)
II. The Perseverance of a Man of God (1:6–18)
  A. The Exhortation (1:6–11)
  B. The Examples (1:12–18)

III. The Patterns of a Man of God (2:1–26)
   A. Paul (2:1–2)
   B. A Soldier (2:3–4)
   C. An Athlete (2:5)
   D. A Farmer (2:6–7)
   E. Jesus (2:8–13)
   F. A Worker (2:14–19)
   G. A Vessel (2:20–23)
   H. A Servant (2:24–26)
IV. The Perils of a Man of God (3:1–17)
   A. Facing Apostasy (3:1–9)
   B. Defeating Apostasy (3:10–17)
V. The Preaching of the Man of God (4:1–5)
   A. The Charge to Preach (4:1–2)
   B. The Need for Preaching (4:3–5)
VI. Concluding Remarks (4:6–18)
   A. Paul's Triumph (4:6–8)
   B. Paul's Needs (4:9–18)
VII. Paul's Farewells (4:19–22)

MEANWHILE, IN OTHER PARTS OF THE WORLD . . .
Events in Israel that will lead to the destruction of Jerusalem in A.D. 70 have begun.

FREQUENTLY ASKED QUESTIONS

1. In 1:7, to what or whom does the term *spirit* refer?

This statement is contrasting two attitudes rather than describing the Holy Spirit, whose presence (1:14) produces the second of the two "spirits" mentioned here. The spirit of fear that could be translated "timidity" denotes a cowardly, shameful fear caused by a weak, selfish character. Since this is not a by-product of God's presence, it must be coming from somewhere else.

The threat of Roman persecution, which was escalating under Nero, the hostility of those in the Ephesians church who resented Timothy's leadership, and the assaults of false teachers with their sophisticated systems of deception may have been overwhelming Timothy. But if he was fearful, his fear didn't come from God.

As an antidote to fear, Paul reminded Timothy of the resources God does supply. God has already given believers all the spiritual resources they need for every trial and threat (see Matthew 10:19,20). First, divine "power"—effective, productive spiritual energy—belongs to believers (see Zechariah 4:6; Ephesians 1:18–20; 3:20). Second, God provides "love." This love centers on pleasing God and seeking other's welfare before one's own (see Romans 14:8; Galatians 5:22,25; Ephesians 3:19; 1 Peter 1:22; 1 John 4:18). Third, God promotes a "sound mind." This refers to a disciplined, self-controlled, and properly prioritized mind. This is the opposite of the fear and cowardice that causes disorder and confusion. Focusing on the sovereign nature and perfect purposes of our eternal God allows believers to control their lives with godly wisdom and confidence in every situation (see Romans 12:3; 1 Timothy 3:2; Titus 1:8; 2:2).

2. How many generations of discipleship does 2:2 include?

As Paul directed Timothy in the process of transmitting the gospel message, he mentioned four generations of lives transformed by the grace of Christ. The first mentioned was his own generation. He reminded Timothy that the source of his message for others was the countless hours of preaching and teaching he had heard the apostle deliver "among many witnesses." The next generation was Timothy's. What he had heard, he was charged to deliver to others. These others would be the next generation. They were not to be a random audience, but "faithful" believers with teaching abilities. These in turn would teach the next generation about the "grace that is in Christ Jesus." The process of spiritual reproduction, which began in the early church, is to continue until the Lord returns.

3. Did Paul write the Pastoral Epistles (1 Timothy, 2 Timothy, and Titus)?

The question implies that Pauline authorship has been debated. It has. Many modernist critics, who seem to delight in attacking the plain statement of Scripture, deny that Paul wrote these three letters called the Pastoral Epistles. Despite the internal evidence (1:1; 2 Timothy 1:1; Titus 1:1) and the ancient testimony of the early church, these critics maintain that a devout follower of Paul wrote these letters in the second century.

As proof of their assertions, these critics offer five lines of supposed evidence against Pauline authorship:

1. The historical references in the Pastoral Epistles cannot be harmonized with the chronology of Paul's life recorded in Acts.
2. The false teaching described in the Pastoral Epistles is the fully developed Gnosticism of the second century.
3. The church organizational structure in the Pastoral Epistles is that of the second century and is too well developed for Paul's day.
4. The Pastoral Epistles do not contain the great themes of Paul's theology.
5. The Greek vocabulary of the Pastoral Epistles contains many words not found in Paul's other letters, nor in the rest of the New Testament.

In reply to the critic's arguments, the following facts refute each of their points of evidence:

1. The suggestion of historical incompatibility proves valid only if Paul never left his Roman imprisonment recorded in Acts. But he was released. Acts does not record Paul's execution, and Paul himself expected to be released (see Philippians 1:19,25–26; 2:24; Philemon 22). The historical events mentioned in these letters fall after the close of the Book of Acts.
2. While similarities exist between the heresy of the Pastoral Epistles and second-century Gnosticism, so do important differences. Unlike second-century Gnosticism, the false teachers faced by Timothy were still within the church (1:3–7), and their teaching was based on Judaistic legalism (1:7; Titus 1:10,14; 3:9). The church organizational structure mentioned in the Pastoral Epistles is, in fact, consistent with that established elsewhere by Paul (see Acts 14:23; Philippians 1:1).
3. The Pastoral Epistles do mention the central themes of Paul's theology, including the inspiration of Scripture (3:15–17), election (1:9; Titus 1:1–2), salvation (Titus 3:5–7), the deity of Christ (Titus 2:13), Christ's mediatorial work (1 Timothy 2:5), and substitutionary atonement (2:6).
4. The different subject matter in the Pastoral Epistles required a different vocabulary from that in Paul's other epistles.

The idea that a "pious forger" wrote the Pastoral Epistles faces several further difficulties:

- The early church did not approve of such practices.
- Why forge three letters that include similar material and deviant doctrine?
- If a counterfeit, why not invent an itinerary for Paul that would have harmonized with Acts?
- Would a later, devoted follower of Paul have put the words of 1:13,15 into his master's mouth?
- Why would he include warning against deceivers (3:13; Titus 1:10) if he himself were one?

Pauline authorship of the Pastoral Epistles continues to be the most reasonable, defendable, and, certainly, biblical position.

4. What is a *valedictory,* and why did Paul include one in his second letter to Timothy?

A valedictory is a speech or action done in parting. It is a farewell message. While hints of Paul's mood appear throughout the letter, 4:6–8 centers on Paul's self-evaluation. Nearing the end of his life, Paul was able to look back without regret or remorse. In these verses, he examined his life from three perspectives: 1) the present reality of the approaching end of his life, for which he was ready (verse 6); 2) the past, when he had been faithful (verse 7); 3) the future, as he anticipated his heavenly reward (verse 8).

QUICK STUDY ON 2 TIMOTHY

1. What specific directions did Paul give Timothy about the attitude of a minister of the gospel?
2. What does Paul repeat in 2 Timothy that he emphasized in his first letter?
3. How does chapter 2 describe the process by which the gospel spreads?
4. How does Paul's statement in 2 Timothy 3:16 fit in with the rest of the letter?
5. What dangers does Paul point out to his young disciple about ministry in troubled times?
6. Who gives you the most encouragement in your Christian life, and what kind of response have you given them?

TITUS
Valued Messenger

In a rapidly darkening world, Paul encouraged Titus to teach Christians to live faithfully for Christ.

The Apostle Paul often extended his ministry by sending letters. He also sent people. Titus served as one of Paul's trusted messengers. He went where Paul could not go. When Paul was imprisoned, men like Titus and Timothy carried on his ministry. Even when he was free, Paul found that the work far exceeded his personal reach. By using Titus, Paul expanded his impact. Paul then used this letter to instruct and encourage Titus on his mission for the gospel.

AUTHOR AND DATE

Written by Paul, around A.D. 62 to 64

The letter to Titus (along with 1 and 2 Timothy) is the third of the Pastoral Epistles. Authorship by the Apostle Paul (1:1) is essentially uncontested. Paul wrote Titus sometime between A.D. 62–64 while he ministered in Macedonia between his first and second Roman imprisonments.

KEY PEOPLE IN TITUS

Paul—wrote to give Titus encouragement and counsel regarding his leadership position in the church (1:1–3:15)

Titus—Greek believer sent by Paul to pastor the church on the island of Crete (1:4–3:15)

BACKGROUND AND SETTING

Although Titus is not mentioned by name in the Book of Acts, it seems probable that he, a Gentile (Galatians 2:3), was led to faith in Christ by Paul (1:4) either before or during the apostle's first missionary journey. Titus then accompanied Paul and Barnabas to the Council of Jerusalem (Acts 15; Galatians 2:1–5), where he witnessed the debate over the way in which new Gentile believers would be treated and welcomed into the church. As a Gentile, Titus would have been particularly sensitive to the impact of the Judaizers, false teachers in the church, who among other things insisted that all Christians, Gentiles as well as Jews, were bound by the Mosaic Law.

Titus traveled with Paul during the third missionary journey, making his presence felt, especially in Corinth. Paul later mentioned him nine times in 2 Corinthians (2:13; 7:6,13–14; 8:6,16,23; 12:18). Paul considered Titus to be a "brother" (2 Corinthians 2:13), "my partner and fellow worker" (2 Corinthians 8:23), and "a true son" (Titus 1:4).

Later, Titus ministered for a while with Paul on the island of Crete and was left behind to continue and strengthen the work (1:5), in much the same way as when Paul left Timothy in Ephesus (1 Timothy 1:3). Paul indicated that he intended to send Artemas or Tychicus (3:12) to relieve Titus in the ministry on Crete. The apostle wanted Titus to join him in Nicopolis, in the Grecian province of Achaia, for the winter months (3:12). Paul's letter informed Titus of the upcoming plans and offered him direction for his ongoing ministry in Crete.

KEY DOCTRINES IN TITUS

God's sovereign election of believers—before time began, God intimately knew the life and future of His children (1:1–2; Deuteronomy 7:6; Matthew 20:16; John 6:44; 13:18; 15:16; Acts 22:14; Ephesians 1:4; 1 Thessalonians 1:4; 1 Timothy 6:12)

God's saving grace—God's gracious gift to fallen humanity is Jesus Christ (2:11; 3:5; Psalm 84:11; John 1:14; 3:16–18; Romans 5:15,17; Ephesians 1:6; 1 Timothy 2:5–6; 4:10; Hebrews 4:16; James 1:17; 1 Peter 5:10; 1 John 2:2)

Christ's deity and second coming—the second coming of Jesus Christ will reveal His full glory as God (2:13; Romans 8:22–23; 1 Corinthians 15:51–58; Philippians 3:20–21; 1 Thessalonians 4:13–18; 2 Peter 1:1; 1 John 3:2–3)

Christ's substitutionary atonement—Christ gave Himself as a sacrifice so that believers in Him might be pardoned from sin (2:14; Isaiah 53:4–12; John 15:13; Acts 4:12; Romans 5:8–11; 8:32; 2 Corinthians 5:18–19; Galatians 1:4; Hebrews 10:14; 1 Peter 3:18; 1 John 2:2; 4:10)

The Holy Spirit's regeneration and renewing of believers—salvation brings the gift of a new, Spirit-generated, Spirit-empowered, Spirit-protected life as God's own children and heirs (3:5; Ezekiel 36:25–29; Joel 2:28; John 3:3–6; Romans 5:5; 8:2; Ephesians 5:26; James 1:18; 1 Peter 1:23; 1 John 2:29; 3:9; 4:7; 5:1)

GOD'S CHARACTER IN TITUS

God is kind—3:4–6
God is loving—3:4–7
God is merciful—1:18; 3:5
God is a promise keeper—1:2
God is true—1:2

CHRIST IN TITUS

The deity of Christ is strongly maintained in the Book of Titus: "Looking for the blessed hope and glorious appearing of our great God and Savior Jesus Christ" (2:13). Paul refers to God and Christ as the Savior throughout the book, emphasizing both the person of Christ as God and the plan of salvation (1:3–4; 2:10,13; 3:4,6).

KEY WORDS IN TITUS

God Our Savior: Greek *tou sōtēros hēmōn theou*—1:3; 2:10; 3:4—in the Pastoral Epistles, this expression or similar ones appear often. In each of these verses, the appellation describes God the Father. The Old Testament writers speak of God as Savior (see Psalm 24:5; Isaiah 12:2; 45:15,21) and so do a few other New Testament writers (Luke 1:47; Jude 25). The Son is called Savior in the Pastoral Epistles (1:4; 2:13; 3:6; 2 Timothy 1:10), and in 2:13 the Son is called "our God and Savior," thus clearly identifying Jesus as God.

Washing of Regeneration: Greek *loutron palingenesias*—3:5—this word for *washing* can signify the receptacle of washing itself. In Ephesians 5:26, the only other New Testament occurrence of this word, the natural meaning is washing. Here the action of washing is also presented. Quite simply, the text says that regeneration is characterized by or accompanied by the action of washing. The regenerative activity of the Holy Spirit is characterized elsewhere in Scripture as cleansing and purifying (see Ezekiel 36:25–27; John 3:5). The Greek term for *regeneration* literally means "being born again"—indicating the new birth effected by the Holy Spirit (see John 3:6; Romans 8:16; Galatians 4:6). Thus God saved us through one process with two aspects: the washing of regeneration and the renewing of the Holy Spirit.

QUICK OVERVIEW

I. Salutation (1:1–4)
II. Essentials for Effective Evangelism (1:5–3:11)
  A. Among Leaders (1:5–16)
  B. In the Church (2:1–15)
  C. In the World (3:1–11)
III. Conclusion (3:12–14)
IV. Benediction (3:15)

MEANWHILE, IN OTHER PARTS OF THE WORLD . . .
Rome burns and Christians are blamed, even though Nero is widely acknowledged as the arsonist.

FREQUENTLY ASKED QUESTIONS

1. In what ways does Paul's letter to his disciple Titus indicate that the message was intended for more than just Titus and the Christians on Crete?

Titus 2:11–13 presents the heart of Paul's letter to Titus. The apostle had already emphasized God's sovereign purpose in calling out elders as leaders (1:5) and in commanding His people to live righteously (2:1–10). That purpose is to provide the witness that brings God's plan and purpose of salvation to fulfillment. As always, the apostle had a larger audience in mind. The gospel has a universal scope. Here Paul condensed God's saving plan into three realities: 1) salvation from the penalty of sin (verse 11); 2) salvation from the power of sin (verse 12); and 3) salvation from the presence of sin (verse 13).

As he described the "grace of God that brings salvation" (verse 11), Paul was not simply referring to the divine attribute of grace but to Jesus Christ Himself, grace incarnate, God's supremely gracious gift to fallen humankind (see John 1:14). The term "all men" (verse 11), in spite of efforts to make it a proof text for Universalism, does not provide support for that error. "Mankind" is translated as "man" in 3:4, to refer to humanity in general, as a category, not to every individual. Jesus Christ made a sufficient offering to cover the sins of everyone who believes (see John 3:16–18; 1 Timothy 2:5–6; 4:10; 1 John 2:2). The opening words of this letter to Titus make it clear that salvation becomes effective only through "the faith of God's elect" (1:1). Paul was well aware that the gospel had universal implications. Out of all humanity, only those who believe will be saved (see John 1:12; 3:16; 5:24,38,40; 6:40; 10:9; Romans 10:9–17).

2. How does 3:1–11 make a case for the value of evangelism?

Throughout this letter, Paul made it clear that Titus had a larger role than simply to maintain the existing church in Crete. Paul's purpose was evangelistic. He wanted Titus's work to bring more people to faith in Christ. In order for this to occur, Paul's directions focused on equipping the churches of Crete for effective evangelism. Even Paul's standards for leadership required godly leaders who would not only shepherd believers under their care (1:5–9) but also equip those Christians for evangelizing their pagan neighbors. Paul's consistent pattern is best described in 2 Timothy 2:2.

Paul's closing remarks admonish Titus to remind believers under his care of 1) the importance of having a good attitude toward the unsaved rulers (3:1) and people in general (3:2); 2) their previous state as unbelievers lost in sin (3:3); 3) of their gracious salvation through Jesus Christ (3:4–7); 4) of their righteous testimony to the unsaved world (3:8); and 5) their responsibility to oppose false teachers and factious members within the church (3:9–11). All these matters prove essential to effective evangelism. A humble and compassionate witness by a well-ordered body of believers offers the most compelling message of the gospel.

QUICK STUDY ON TITUS

1. As you study Titus, review the location of the island of Crete.
2. Compare Titus with 1 Timothy. What points of similarity do you note between the two letters?
3. How does Paul summarize the gospel for Titus?
4. What are the key church leadership roles according to Paul's guidelines for Titus?
5. To what degree does the character of church leaders matter to Paul?
6. What group of Christians do you represent, and how seriously do you take that responsibility?

PHILEMON
Spiritual Equality and True Forgiveness

Paul wrote a reference letter for a runaway slave.

Philemon owned a slave who ran away. His slave, Onesimus, eventually met the Apostle Paul and became a Christian. Paul sent Onesimus back to Philemon with this letter of explanation. The letter provides an insightful look into the realities of slavery in the ancient world and shows how Christ elevated the value of a slave from being property to being "a beloved brother" (verse 16).

AUTHOR AND DATE

Written by Paul while in prison, about A.D. 60 to 62

This letter to Philemon, along with the epistles to the Ephesians, Philippians, and Colossians, completes the group called the Prison Epistles. (For more on this, see the **Frequently Asked Question** "What were the Prison Epistles?" on page 267) Paul's authorship is based on internal evidence (verses 1,9,19) as well as the testimony of early church fathers (Jerome, Chrysostom, and Theodore of Mopsuestia) and the Muratorian canon (about A.D. 170). For biographical information on Paul, see the **Frequently Asked Question** "Who was Paul?" (in the chapter on Romans).

KEY PEOPLE IN PHILEMON

Paul—wrote to urge Philemon to forgive and accept Onesimus as his brother (verses 1–25)

Philemon—prominent member of the church at Colosse; former master of Onesimus (verses 1–25)

Onesimus—runaway slave of Philemon; became a Christian after meeting Paul in Rome (verses 10–22)

BACKGROUND AND SETTING

Philemon was a prominent member of the Colossian church. He had been saved under Paul's ministry, probably in Ephesus (verse 19). Wealthy enough to have a large house (verse 2), Philemon also owned at least one slave, a man named Onesimus.

Onesimus was not a believer when he stole money (verse 18) from Philemon and ran away. Like thousands of other runaway slaves, Onesimus fled to Rome, seeking to lose himself in the imperial city's teeming population. Through circumstances not recorded in Scripture, Onesimus met Paul in Rome and became a Christian.

The apostle grew to love the runaway slave (verses 12,16) and considered keeping Onesimus with him in Rome (verses 11,13). But by stealing and running away from Philemon, Onesimus had broken Roman law and defrauded his master. Paul knew those issues had to be resolved, and he decided to send Onesimus back to Colosse. It was too hazardous for him to make the trip alone (because of the danger of slave-catchers), so Paul sent him back with Tychicus. The two of them carried Paul's letters to Philemon and the church at Colosse (Colossians 4:7–9). Paul's beautiful epistle to Philemon urged the master to forgive the slave and welcome him back into service as a brother in Christ (verses 15–17).

KEY DOCTRINES IN PHILEMON

Forgiveness—Christ offers the perfect example of forgiveness (verses 16–17; Matthew 6:12–15; 18:21–35; Ephesians 4:32; Colossians 3:13)

Equality—Christianity undermined the evils of slavery by changing the hearts of slaves and masters and stressing the spiritual equality of master and slave (verse 16; Matthew 20:1–16; Mark 10:31; Galatians 3:28; Ephesians 6:9; Colossians 4:1; 1 Timothy 6:1–2)

GOD'S CHARACTER IN PHILEMON

God is forgiving—verses 16–17
God is impartial—verse 16

CHRIST IN PHILEMON

The relationship between Paul, Onesimus, and Philemon presents a beautiful illustration of Christ's mediation between the Father and humanity. Paul freely accepted Onesimus's penalty in order to renew the relationship between Onesimus and Philemon, his former master. Paul's work of forgiveness also portrays the strength given to Christians by God to show compassion and mercy.

QUICK OVERVIEW

I. Greeting (1–3)
II. The Character of One Who Forgives (4–7)
III. The Actions of One Who Forgives (8–18)
IV. The Motives of One Who Forgives (19–25)

MEANWHILE, IN OTHER PARTS OF THE WORLD . . .
The Romans begin to manufacture brass and develop a system to extract gold from its ores.

FREQUENTLY ASKED QUESTIONS

1. Who was Onesimus, and why did Paul write a letter to Philemon about him?

Onesimus was a slave owned by Philemon, a prominent member of the church at Colosse. Through happy and divine coincidence, Onesimus met Paul after he ran away from Philemon. At the time, Onesimus was a double lawbreaker, on the run as a thief and an escaped slave. Shortly after meeting Paul, Onesimus became a Christian.

Although Onesimus was providing useful service to Paul, the apostle decided to send him back to Philemon. With him, he sent both Tychicus as an escort and a personal cover letter as an explanation to Philemon. The wealthy Colossian owed Paul much, for Paul was the messenger who had brought him the gospel. Paul didn't hesitate to mention that debt to awaken Philemon's awareness of the importance of welcoming and forgiving his vagabond slave.

Paul's letter to Philemon provides an insightful glimpse into the New Testament's handling of slavery. Rather than a direct attack on this terrible practice, Christianity disarmed the institution from within by radically changing the relationship between slaves and masters. See the introduction to this letter for more on this subject.

2. How did Paul intervene with Philemon on Onesimus's behalf?

Paul reintroduced the slave Onesimus to the master Philemon as his own son in the faith (verse 10). Paul had led the slave to Christ while in prison at Rome. Since Onesimus was a common slave name that meant "useful," Paul offered a play on words as a tribute to Onesimus's new life in Christ. Paul's description (verse 11) basically means, "Useful—formerly was useless, but now really is useful." Onesimus had been radically transformed by God's grace.

Although Paul did not challenge Onesimus's existing legal standing with Philemon as a slave (verse 16), he did challenge Philemon to a new relationship with Onesimus. Paul did not call for the slave's freedom (1 Corinthians 7:20–22) but called for the master to receive his slave as a fellow-believer in Christ (see Ephesians 6:9; Colossians 4:1; 1 Timothy 6:2). Paul was not trying to abolish slavery but rather to make the relationship within this institution just and kind. The master and the slave were to enjoy spiritual oneness and fellowship as they worshiped and ministered together.

Paul also recognized that Philemon's forgiveness would involve a cost. The original theft as well as the loss due to Onesimus's absence were justifiable concerns that Paul was willing to address. If Philemon felt the need for restitution, Paul declared that he would pay Onesimus's debt. He also gently hinted, however, that Philemon might consider what he owed Paul as he was reckoning his losses.

QUICK STUDY ON PHILEMON

1. How does Paul handle the issue of slavery in writing to Philemon?
2. On what principles does Paul base his encouragement to Philemon to forgive Onesimus?
3. What is the tone of Paul's letter?
4. How would you resolve the tension between Onesimus, Philemon, and Paul in such a way that each one would be satisfied?

HEBREWS
Christ Is Our High Priest

Hebrews brings the richness of the Old Testament background into the world of the New Testament church.

All thirty-nine books of the Old Testament were originally given to the Jews. Only one New Testament book was aimed specifically at their needs. That single epistle was Hebrews. This certainly does not mean that God had forgotten the Jews. Other books, like Matthew, Romans, and Galatians have Jewish believers much in mind. All the New Testament books with the exception of Luke and Acts were given by the Holy Spirit's inspiration through Jews.

AUTHOR AND DATE

Written by an unknown author, around A.D. 67 to 69

The author of Hebrews is unknown. Paul, Barnabas, Silas, Apollos, Luke, Philip, Priscilla, Aquila, and Clement of Rome have been suggested by different scholars. The epistle's history, vocabulary, style, and various literary characteristics, however, do not clearly support any particular authorship claim. It is significant that the writer includes himself among those people who had received confirmation of Christ's message from others (2:3). That would seem to rule out someone like Paul who claimed that he had received such confirmation directly from God and not from any human being (Galatians 1:12). Regardless of his identity, the author preferred citing Old Testament references from the Greek Old Testament (LXX) rather than the Hebrew text.

Even the early church expressed various opinions on authorship. Current scholarship admits the puzzle still has no solution. Therefore, it seems best to accept the epistle's anonymity. The ultimate author, of course, was the Holy Spirit.

KEY PEOPLE IN HEBREWS

Abel—son of Adam and Eve; offered a more acceptable sacrifice to God than his brother did (11:4; 12:24)

Enoch—lived in close fellowship with God; taken up to heaven without dying (11:5)

Noah—obeyed God and built the ark (11:7)

Abraham—followed God to become the father of the Jewish nation (2:16; 6:13–11:19)

Sarah—trusted God to give her a child in her old age (11:11)

Isaac—son of Abraham and Sarah; blessed his sons, Jacob and Esau, according to the will of God (11:9–20)

Jacob—son of Isaac; blessed and adopted Joseph's sons before his death (11:9,20–21)

Joseph— believed God would deliver the nation of Israel out from Egypt (11:22)

Moses—courageously served God and led Israel out of Egypt (3:2–16; 7:14–12:25)

Rahab—obeyed God by sheltering Israelite spies in her home (11:31)

Old Testament people of faith—accomplished great deeds for God and also suffered great persecution (11:32–40)

BACKGROUND AND SETTING

Extensive use of the Old Testament, an emphasis on the Levitical priesthood and on sacrifices, as well as the absence of any reference to the Gentiles, support the conclusion that a community of Hebrews was the original recipient of the epistle. Although these Jews were primarily converts to Christ, probably a number of unbelievers were in their midst who were attracted by various degrees to the message of salvation but who had not yet made a full commitment of faith in Christ.

The contents of the epistle make it clear that this community of Hebrews was facing the possibility of intensified persecution (10:32–39; 12:4). Under this pressure, the Hebrews were tempted to cast aside any identification with Christ. They may have considered demoting Christ from God's Son to a mere angel. Others had certainly done so. These kinds of doctrinal aberrations would explain the emphasis in Hebrews on the superiority of Christ over angels.

KEY DOCTRINES IN HEBREWS

The New Covenant—all believers now have direct access to God and may approach God's throne without fear (4:16; 6:19–20; 9:8; 10:19–22; Deuteronomy 4:7; Psalm 65:4; John 10:7,9; 14:6; Romans 5:2; Ephesians 2:18; 3:12; Colossians 1:21–22; 1 Peter 3:18)

Christ as High Priest—(3:1–2; 4:14; 5:5–11; 6:20; 7:15–17,26; 9:11; Zechariah 6:13; Psalm 110:4)

GOD'S CHARACTER IN HEBREWS

God is accessible—4:16; 7:25; 9:6–15; 10:19–22; 11:16

God is a consuming fire—12:29

God is glorious—1:3

God is loving—12:6

God is a promise keeper—4:1; 6:12,15,17; 8:6,10,12; 10:23,36; 11:9,11,33

God is wrathful—3:17–19; 10:26–27

CHRIST IN HEBREWS

Directed towards Jewish readers, this is a work of contrasts. The Jewish believers were in danger of falling back into the rituals of the law. Yet Hebrews exhorts its readers to remember God's provision for a perfect priest and sacrifice in Christ to free those under the law. Hebrews presents Christ as the perfect sacrifice over the inadequate sacrifices of the Jews (9:9,12–15). Christ is also superior as the High Priest, Prophet, and King to all those who came before Him (4:14–16; 12:1–2).

KEY WORDS IN HEBREWS

Covenant: Greek *diathēkē*—8:6,8–10; 9:4; 10:16,29; 12:24—literally, "agreement," "will," or "testament." In 9:15–20, the author of Hebrews explains why the New Covenant (8:7) has completed the first covenant made at Mount Sinai. The author uses the word *diathēkē* throughout the section as an analogy to a "will." Just as the contents of a will go into effect when a person dies, so Christ's death initiated the New Covenant that frees us from bondage to the first covenant.

Mediator: Greek *mesitēs*—8:6; 9:15; 12:24—literally, "a go-between" or "intermediary." Paul characterizes Moses as a mediator of the covenant at Mount Sinai. Moses acted as a communication link between God and the Israelites. He informed the Israelites of their covenant obligations and also appealed to God on Israel's behalf (see Galatians 3:19–20). Acting in the same position, Jesus is the Mediator of the New Covenant. He activated this covenant through His own sacrifice on the cross. He now sits at the right hand of the Father interceding for us (7:25).

Redemption: Greek *apolutrōsis*—9:15—literally, "redemption." When used by the New Testament writers, this word, and its related term, *lutrōsis*, signify redemption. *Redemption* reflects the act of freeing, releasing, or buying back by paying a ransom price. The ransom price for humanity's sin is death. Yet, Christ paid this ransom price through His own sacrifice (1 Peter 1:18–19) and thus freed us from the bondage of sin, to be brought back into the family of God (Galatians 3:13; 4:5).

QUICK OVERVIEW

- I. The Superiority of Jesus Christ's Position (1:1–4:13)
  - A. A Better Name (1:1–3)
  - B. Better than the Angels (1:4–2:18)
  - C. Better than Moses (3:1–19)
  - D. A Better Rest (4:1–13)
- II. The Superiority of Jesus Christ's Priesthood (4:14–7:28)
  - A. Christ as High Priest (4:14–5:10)

B. Exhortation to Full Commitment to Christ (5:11–6:20)
C. Christ's Priesthood like Melchizedek's (7:1–28)

III. The Superiority of Jesus Christ's Priestly Ministry (8:1–10:18)
A. Through a Better Covenant (8:1–13)
B. In a Better Sanctuary (9:1–12)
C. By a Better Sacrifice (9:13–10:18)

IV. The Superiority of the Believer's Privileges (10:19–12:29)
A. Saving Faith (10:19–25)
B. False Faith (10:26–39)
C. Genuine Faith (11:1–3)
D. Heroes of the Faith (11:4–40)
E. Persevering Faith (12:1–29)

V. The Superiority of Christian Behavior (13:1–21)
A. In Relation to Others (13:1–3)
B. In Relation to Ourselves (13:4–9)
C. In Relation to God (13:10–21)

VI. Postscript (13:22–25)

MEANWHILE, IN OTHER PARTS OF THE WORLD . . .
In east Africa, the art of pottery developed in Tanzania and Kenya migrates to Mozambique.

FREQUENTLY ASKED QUESTIONS

1. To which Hebrews was this book written?

Although the author and the original recipients of this letter are unknown, the title, dating as early as the second century A.D., has been "To the Hebrews." The title certainly fits the content. The epistle exudes a Jewish mind-set. References to Hebrew history and religion abound. And since no particular Gentile or pagan practice gains any attention in the book, the church has kept the traditional title.

A proper interpretation of Hebrews, however, requires the recognition that it addresses three distinct groups of Jews:

- Hebrew Christians formed the primary addressees. These had already suffered rejection and persecution by fellow Jews (10:23–34), although none had yet been martyred (12:4). They were an immature group of believers who were tempted to hold on to the symbolic and spiritually powerless rituals and traditions of Judaism. This letter was written to give them encouragement and confidence in Christ, their Messiah and High Priest.
- Jewish unbelievers who were intellectually convinced of the gospel were also addressed. They gave mental assent to the truth of the gospel but had not placed their faith in Jesus Christ as their Savior

and Lord. They were intellectually persuaded but spiritually un-committed. These unbelievers are addressed in such passages as 2:1–3; 6:4–6; 10:26–29; 12:15–17.

- Jewish unbelievers who were attracted by the gospel and the person of Christ but who had reached no final conviction about Him. Chapter 9 of Hebrews speaks specifically to this group (particularly verses 11,14–15,27–28).

Failure to acknowledge these groups will lead to interpretations that are inconsistent with the rest of Scripture.

2. What does 4:14–16 teach about prayer?

This passage offers two very personal benefits that come to those who have trusted in Jesus the Son of God as the great High Priest. First, we have Someone who can "sympathize with our weaknesses" because He "was in all points tempted as we are, yet without sin" (verse 15). Second, we can be confident of access to the "throne of grace" (verse 16) because Someone knows our need. Christian prayer accepts God's invitation to enjoy the access provided through Christ.

The Christian's unique access to God was a radical idea in the ancient world. Most ancient rulers were unapproachable by anyone but their highest advisers. In contrast, the Holy Spirit calls for all to come confidently before God's throne to receive mercy and grace through Jesus Christ (see 7:25; 10:22; Matthew 27:51). It was at the throne of God that Christ made atonement for sins, and it is there that grace is dispensed to believers for all the issues of life (see 2 Corinthians 4:15; 9:8; 12:9; Ephesians 1:7; 2:7).

3. To whom is 6:4–6, and particularly the phrase *once enlightened,* directed?

The phrase *once enlightened* is often taken to refer to Christians. The accompanying warning, then, is taken to indicate the danger of losing their salvation if they "fall away" and "crucify again for themselves the Son of God." But the immediate context has no mention of their being saved. They are not described with any terms that apply only to believers (such as *holy, born again, righteous,* or *saints*).

The interpretive problem arises from inaccurately identifying the spiritual condition of the ones being addressed. In this case, they were unbelievers who had been exposed to God's redemptive truth and, perhaps, had made a profession of faith but had not exercised genuine saving faith. Another passage (10:26) addresses the same issue. The subject here is people who came in contact with the gospel but were spiritually unchanged by it. These apostates were Christians in name only and were never genuine believers, who are often incorrectly thought to lose their salvation because of their sins.

There is no possibility of these verses referring to someone losing salvation. Many Scripture passages make unmistakably clear that salvation is eternal (see, for example, John 10:27–29; Romans 8:35,38–39; Philippians 1:6; 1 Peter 1:4–5). Those who want to make this passage mean that believers can lose salvation will have to admit that it would then also make the point that one could never get it back again.

4. Who was Melchizedek and why was he so important?

Melchizedek shows up abruptly and briefly in the Old Testament, but his special role in Abraham's life makes him a significant figure. He is mentioned again in Psalm 110:4, the passage under consideration in 4:14–7:28. As the king of Salem and priest of the Most High God in the time of Abraham, Melchizedek offered a historical precedent for the role of king-priest (Genesis 14:18–20) that was later filled perfectly by Jesus Christ.

By using the two Old Testament references to Melchizedek, the writer (7:1–28) explains the superiority of Christ's priesthood by reviewing Melchizedek's unique role as a type of Christ and his superiority to the Levitical high priesthood. The Levitical priesthood was hereditary, but Melchizedek's was not. Through Abraham's honor, Melchizedek's rightful role was established. The major ways in which the Melchizedekan priesthood was superior to the Levitical priesthood are these:

- The receiving of tithes (7:2–10), as when Abraham the ancestor of the Levites gave Melchizedek a tithe of the spoils
- The giving of the blessing (7:1,6–7), as when Abraham accepted Melchizedek's blessing
- The continual replacement of the Levitical priesthood (7:11–19), which passed down from father to son the perpetuity of the Melchizedekan priesthood (7:3,8,16–17,20–28), since the record about his priesthood does not record his death

5. What significance can be found in the statement, "And as it is appointed for men to die once, but after this the judgment" (9:27)?

First, this passage offers a direct answer to those tempted to flirt with any form of reincarnation. Second, it states the general rule for all humankind, with very rare and only partial exceptions. Lazarus and the multitudes who were resuscitated at Christ's resurrection had to die again (see Matthew 27:51–53; John 14:43–44). Those, like Lazarus, who were raised from the dead by a miraculous act of our Lord were not resurrected to a glorified body and unending life. They only experienced resuscitation. Another exception will be those who don't die even once, but who will be "caught up . . . to meet the Lord in the air" (1 Thessalonians 4:17). Enoch (Genesis 5:24) and Elijah (2 Kings 2:11) are also part of this last group.

The general rule for all human beings includes another shared event—judgment. The judgment noted here refers to the judgment of all people, believers (2 Corinthians 5:10) and unbelievers (Revelation 20:11–15).

QUICK STUDY ON HEBREWS

1. In explaining Christ's uniqueness and excellence, what does the writer of Hebrews use for comparison?
2. What specific examples of practical teaching can you find in Hebrews?
3. Did the writer of Hebrews actually think Christians might entertain angels (13:2)?
4. What is the role of the Old Testament saints, particularly in chapter 11?
5. How does Hebrews explain Christ's dual role of priest and sacrifice?
6. What insights from Hebrews have you gained about your own prayer life?

JAMES
Faith in Action

James provided a hands-on, practical manual of the Christian faith.

Jesus had four half brothers—James, Joses, Judas, and Simon. The Bible makes it clear that after Jesus' miraculous birth, Mary and Joseph had other children (Mark 6:3). Eventually, Judas (whom we know as Jude) and James became believers in their brother Jesus as Lord. But neither James (Mark 6:3) nor Jude (Matthew 13:55) was an early follower. At first, James rejected Jesus as Messiah (John 7:5), but he later believed (1 Corinthians 15:7). He became one of the leaders in the Jerusalem church and authored a very practical handbook of Christian living that bears his name.

AUTHOR AND DATE

Written by James, the half brother of Jesus, between A.D. 44 to 49

James was a common name in New Testament times. At least four men with that name actively participated in Jesus' ministry and the early years of the church. Although some have suggested James the son of Zebedee and brother of John for a likely candidate for the author of this book, he was martyred too early to have written it (Acts 12:2). Only James, the oldest half brother of Jesus, fits the profile of the author of the book that bears his name. After James believed in Christ (1 Corinthians 15:7), he became the key leader in the Jerusalem church (Acts 12:17; 15:13; 21:18; Galatians 3:12). He was called one of the "pillars" of the church (Galatians 2:9).

Textual evidence from a comparison between James's vocabulary in the letter that he authored after the Jerusalem Council (Acts 15) and this letter further corroborates his authorship. James wrote with the authority of one who had personally seen the resurrected Christ (1 Corinthians 15:7), who was a recognized associate of the apostles (Galatians 1:9), and who was the leader of the Jerusalem church.

KEY PEOPLE IN JAMES

The believers—persecuted Jewish believers dispersed throughout the Roman Empire (1:1–5:20)

BACKGROUND AND SETTING

The recipients of this letter were Jewish believers who were scattered (1:1), possibly as a result of Stephen's martyrdom (Acts 7; A.D. 31–34), but more likely due to the persecution under Herod Agrippa I (Acts 12; about A.D. 44). Fifteen times the author refers to his audience as "brethren"

(1:2,16,19; 2:1,5,14; 3:1,10,12; 4:11; 5:7,9–10,12,19), which was a common epithet among the first-century Jews. Not surprisingly, then, James displays a distinct Jewish flavor in style and content. His letter contains more than forty allusions to the Old Testament and more than twenty to the Sermon on the Mount (Matthew 5–7).

KEY DOCTRINES IN JAMES

Works—salvation is determined by faith alone and is demonstrated by faithfulness to obey God's will (2:14–26; Matthew 7:16–17,21–23,26; 21:28–32; Romans 3:28; 11:6; Galatians 5:6; Ephesians 2:8–10; 2 Timothy 1:9; Titus 3:5; 2 Peter 1:3–11)

Godly behavior—wise living through uncompromising obedience to the Word of God (1:22; 3:13,17; 4:7–11; 5:7–12; Job 9:4,28; Psalms 104:24; 111:10; Proverbs 1:7; 2:1–7; 3:19–20; 9:10; Jeremiah 10:7,12; Daniel 1:17; 2:20–23; Matthew 7:21,26; Luke 6:46–49; Romans 2:13)

GOD'S CHARACTER IN JAMES

God is accessible—4:8
God is immutable—1:17
God is Light—1:17
God is a promise keeper—1:12; 2:5
God is unified—2:19–20

CHRIST IN JAMES

James openly refers to Christ only twice (1:1; 2:1), yet his epistle abounds with references to Christ's teachings, particularly to the Sermon on the Mount (1:2; see Matthew 5:10–12; 1:4; see Matthew 5:48; 2:13; see Matthew 6:14–15; 4:11; see Matthew 7:1–2; 5:2; see Matthew 6:19). James's application of truth to his reader's lives gives believers a clearer understanding of Christ's wisdom.

KEY WORDS IN JAMES

Anointing: Greek *aleiphō*—5:14—literally, "to daub" or "to smear." Greek *chriō*—5:14—literally, "to anoint." The term *aleiphō* was commonly used to describe a medicinal anointing. A similar Greek word *chriō* was used to express a sacramental anointing. In biblical times, oil was commonly used as a medicine (Luke 10:30–37). Yet, oil also symbolized the Spirit of God (1 Samuel 16:1–13).

Good Gift; Perfect Gift: Greek *dosis agathē*—1:17—literally, "the act of giving" and "good." Greek *dōrēma teleion*—1:17—literally, "actual gifts" and "perfect." The Greek text uses two separate words to describe gifts from God. The first expression, *good gift,* reveals the value of receiving something from God, while *perfect gift* represents the flawless quality of God's gifts. God's giving is continuously good, and His gifts are always perfectly suited for His children.

QUICK OVERVIEW

I. Introduction (1:1)
II. The Test of Perseverance in Suffering (1:2–12)
III. The Test of Blame in Temptation (1:13–18)
IV. The Test of Response to the Word (1:19–27)
V. The Test of Impartial Love (2:1–13)
VI. The Test of Righteous Works (2:14–26)
VII. The Test of the Tongue (3:1–12)
VIII. The Test of Humble Wisdom (3:13–18)
IX. The Test of Worldly Indulgence (4:1–12)
X. The Test of Dependence (4:13–17)
XI. The Test of Patient Endurance (5:1–11)
XII. The Test of Truthfulness (5:12)
XIII. The Test of Prayerfulness (5:13–18)
XIV. The Test of True Faith (5:19–20)

MEANWHILE, IN OTHER PARTS OF THE WORLD . . .
The sea route used for trade between India and Egypt becomes increasingly more important than the main land routes through Persia.

FREQUENTLY ASKED QUESTIONS

1. How can James expect Christians to somehow "count it all joy" when they face difficulties and trials (1:2)?

The Greek word for *count* may also be translated "consider" or "evaluate." The natural human response to hardships and difficulties is rarely rejoicing. Therefore, the believer must make a conscious commitment to face trials with joy. Trials, then, are reminders to rejoice (Philippians 3:1).

Trials translates a Greek word that connotes trouble, or something that breaks the pattern of peace, comfort, joy, and happiness in someone's life. The verb form of this word means "to put someone or something to the test," with the purpose of discovering that person's nature or that thing's quality. God brings such tests to prove—and increase—the strength and quality of one's faith and to demonstrate its validity (verses 2–12). Every trial becomes a test of faith designed to strengthen: If the believer fails the test by responding wrongly, that test then becomes a temptation, or a solicitation to evil. The choice to rejoice avoids greater trouble later.

2. When James writes about the "perfect law of liberty" how does he use those terms—*law* and *liberty*—that appear to be contradictory (1:25)?

In both the Old Testament and the New Testament, God's revealed, inerrant, sufficient, and comprehensive Word is called "law" (Psalm 19:7). The presence of God's grace does not mean the absence of a moral law or code of conduct for believers to obey. Believers are enabled by the Spirit to keep God's standards.

True liberty is not the license to do what we want but rather the assistance to do what we ought. The law of liberty frees us from sin (2:12–13). It liberates us when we have sinned by showing us a gracious God, and it directs us away from sin as we obey Him. As the Holy Spirit applies the principles of Scripture to believers' hearts, they are freed from sin's bondage and enabled to live in true freedom (John 8:34–36).

3. What is the *royal law* (2:8)?

The phrase *royal law* translates better as "sovereign law." The idea is that this law is supreme or binding. James quotes the second half of what Jesus taught was the whole of the sovereign law. "Love your neighbor as yourself," which James quotes from Leviticus 19:18 as well as from Mark 12:31, when combined with the command to love God (Deuteronomy 6:4–5), summarizes all the Law and the Prophets (Matthew 22:36–40; Romans 13:8–10).

James has already alluded to the first part of the great commandment (2:5). Here he focuses on the theme of this section, which is human relationships. James is not advocating some kind of emotional affection for oneself—self-love is clearly a sin (2 Timothy 3:2). Rather, the command is to pursue meeting the physical and spiritual needs of one's neighbors with the same intensity and concern as one does naturally for one's self (Philippians 2:3–4), while never forgetting we are under royal law to do so.

4. If salvation is by faith in Christ, how can James write, "Faith without works is dead" (James 2:14–26)?

This passage comes within a longer section, in which James provides his readers with a series of tests they can use to evaluate whether their faith is living or dead. Here is the central test—the one that pulls the others together: the test of works or righteous behavior. James defines this behavior as actions that obey God's Word and manifest a godly nature (1:22–25).

James's point is not that a person is saved by works. He has already strongly and clearly asserted that salvation is a gracious gift from God (1:17–18). Rather, his concern is to show that there is a kind of apparent faith that is dead and does not save (2:14,17,20,24,26). His teaching parallels the rest of Scripture (Matthew 3:7–8; 5:16; 7:21; 13:18–23; John

8:30–31; 15:6). It is possible that James was writing to Jews who had turned away from the works righteousness of Judaism and had instead embraced the mistaken notion that since righteous works and obedience to God's will were not efficacious for salvation, they were not necessary at all. Thus, they reduced faith to a mere mental assent to the facts about Christ, to which James rightly declares that such faith is, in fact, dead.

5. What does James mean by the closing words of his letter, "he who turns a sinner from the error of his way will save a soul from death and cover a multitude of sins" (5:20)?

The language used by James makes it clear that the "sinner" he has in mind here is someone whose faith is dead (2:14–26), not a believer who sins. The term is used throughout Scripture to describe those who are outside of Christ and unregenerate (Proverbs 11:31; 13:6,22; Matthew 9:13; Luke 7:37,39; 15:7,10; 18:13; Romans 5:8; 1 Timothy 1:9,15; 1 Peter 4:18).

A person who wanders from the truth and never allows it to transform him puts his soul in jeopardy. This "death" is not physical death, but eternal death—eternal separation from God and eternal punishment in hell (Isaiah 66:24; Daniel 12:2; Matthew 13:40,42,50; 25:41,46; Mark 9:43–49; 2 Thessalonians 1:8–9; Romans 6:23; Revelation 20:11–15; 21:8). Knowing how high the stakes are should motivate Christians to aggressively pursue such people.

Since even one sin is enough to condemn a person to hell, James's use of the word *multitude* emphasizes the hopeless condition of lost, unregenerate sinners. The good news of the gospel is that God's forgiving grace (which is greater than any sin, Romans 5:20) is available to those who turn from their sins and exercise faith in the Lord Jesus Christ (Ephesians 2:8–9).

QUICK STUDY ON JAMES

1. Explain James's view of the benefits of difficulties and suffering.
2. How does James view harmful discrimination between Christians?
3. How does James discuss the tension between faith and works?
4. How do the ten commands that fill James 4:7–10 relate to grace?
5. How does James explain the difference between the two kinds of wisdom in the world (3:13–18)?
6. What command in James do you find most challenging to carry out?

FIRST PETER
Persecution of the Church

The New Testament letter with the widest specific geographic address (1 Peter 1:1).

Among the disciples of Jesus, Peter remains the most recognizable name. He was probably the first of those Jesus specifically called to follow Him (Mark 1:16–17). Jesus' last recorded words to Peter had the same theme, "You follow Me" (John 21:22). Along the way, Christ replaced his name, Simon, with Peter (Greek) or Cephas (Aramaic), both meaning "stone" or "rock."

The Lord clearly singled out Peter for special lessons throughout the Gospels (Matthew 10; 16:13–21; 17:1–9; 24:1–7; 26:31–33; John 6:6; 21:3–7; 15–17). He was the spokesman for the twelve, articulating their thoughts and questions as well as his own. He was probably the primary source for Mark's gospel. Eventually, he wrote two canonical (inspired) letters himself, of which this is the first.

AUTHOR AND DATE

Written by Peter about A.D. 64 to 65

The opening verse of the epistle claims Peter as the author. He was clearly the leader among the apostles. The gospel writers emphasize this by placing his name at the head of each list of the apostles (Matthew 10; Mark 3; Luke 6; Acts 1), and including more information about him in the four gospels than any person other than Christ.

Because of his unique prominence, there was no shortage in the early church of documents falsely claiming to be written by Peter. That the Apostle Peter is the author of 1 Peter, however, is certain. The material in this letter bears definite resemblance to Peter's messages in the Book of Acts. Compare 2:7–8 with Acts 4:10–11, both of which have Peter teaching that Christ is the Stone rejected by the builders. Similarly, 1:17 and Acts 10:34 point out that Christ is no respecter of persons. In addition to these and other internal evidences, it is noteworthy that the early Christians universally recognized the letter as the work of Peter.

KEY PEOPLE IN 1 PETER

Peter—one of Jesus' twelve disciples; wrote to encourage persecuted believers (1:1–5:14)

Silas—missionary who traveled with Paul; assisted Peter in writing his letters (5:12)

Mark—leader in the church; used Peter's testimony to write the Gospel of Mark (5:13)

BACKGROUND AND SETTING

Peter's audience of believers was facing increasing signs of persecution throughout the Roman Empire. Conditions were ripe for the tactics used by Nero to deflect blame for the burning of Rome from himself to the Christians. Once Nero spread the word that Christians had set the fires, the accusation stuck because the Christians were already hated as those who associated with Jews and were hostile to Roman culture. The vicious persecution that ensued touched the far corners of the empire, reaching the very places mentioned by Peter's salutation (1:1).

The general addressees of the letter and the ambiguous location of the writer (Babylon—5:13) underscore the tension of the times. Believers established underground networks that would have directed Peter's letter and his envoy to the necessary places. It is likely that Babylon was an alias for Rome. By the way he identified his location, Peter was protecting his own companions. Nevertheless, the apostle realized the scattered and battered Christians needed spiritual strengthening because of the sufferings. Under the inspiration of the Holy Spirit, Peter wrote this epistle to encourage them.

KEY DOCTRINES IN 1 PETER

Persecution—Christians are able to identify with Christ's sufferings when they are persecuted for their faith (1:6; 2:12,19–21; 3:9,13–18; 4:1, 12–16,19; Psalm 69:26; Isaiah 50:6; 53:7; Jeremiah 15:15; Daniel 3:28; Zechariah 2:8; Mark 10:30; Luke 21:12; John 5:16; 15:20; Romans 8:35; 2 Corinthians 1:10; 4:9; 2 Timothy 3:12)

GOD'S CHARACTER IN 1 PETER

God is accessible—1:17; 3:18
God is faithful—4:19
God is holy—1:15–16
God is just—1:17
God is long-suffering—3:20
God is merciful—1:3
God is righteous—2:23

CHRIST IN 1 PETER

Since the Christians addressed in 1 Peter lived in the midst of great persecution, Peter directs them to identify with the sufferings of Christ (1:10–12; 2:24; 4:12–13). First Peter balances this message with reminders of the numerous blessings bestowed on Christians for their perseverance (1:13–16). Christ remains the believer's "living hope" in a hostile world (1:3–4).

KEY WORDS IN 1 PETER

Word: Greek *logos*—1:23; 2:8; 3:1—literally, "word" or "idea," also Greek *rhēma*—1:25. "The word of God" (1:23) is the gospel message about the Lord Jesus Christ. The Spirit uses the Word to produce life. It is the truth of the gospel that saves and regenerates men and women. Peter used Isaiah 40:6–8 which says "the word of our God" in a New Testament context.

Example: Greek *hupogrammos*—2:21—literally, "tracing tablet." In biblical times, this term denoted tablets that contained the entire Greek alphabet. Students would practice tracing each letter of the alphabet on these tablets. When believers use the life of Jesus as their example, His life of suffering becomes their tracing tablet. Christians who trace the life of Jesus learn godliness and wisdom in the face of persecution.

Love: Greek *agapē*—4:8—literally, "love." Most of the ancient occurrences of this Greek word appear in the New Testament. *Agapē* describes the love of one who shows kindness to strangers, gives hospitality, and acts charitably. In the New Testament, the word *agapē* took on a special meaning: It denoted a love in action as opposed to the purely emotional kind. *Agapē* love is the self-sacrificial love naturally demonstrated by God.

QUICK OVERVIEW

I. Salutation (1:1–2)
II. Remember Our Great Salvation (1:3–2:10)
  A. The Certainty of Our Future Inheritance (1:3–12)
  B. The Consequences of Our Future Inheritance (1:13–2:10)
III. Remember Our Example before Men (2:11–4:6)
  A. Honorable Living before Unbelievers (2:11–3:7)
  B. Honorable Living before Believers (3:8–12)
  C. Honorable Living in the Midst of Suffering (3:13–4:6)
IV. Remember Our Lord Will Return (4:7–5:11)
  A. The Responsibilities of Christian Living (4:7–11)
  B. The Rewards of Christian Suffering (4:12–19)
  C. The Requirements for Christian Leadership (5:1–4)
  D. The Realization of Christian Victory (5:5–11)
V. Conclusion (5:12–14)

MEANWHILE, IN OTHER PARTS OF THE WORLD . . .
Fire destroys much of the city of Rome. Nero blames Christians for setting the fire, which begins an Empire-wide persecution of all believers.

FREQUENTLY ASKED QUESTIONS

1. How did a fisherman like Peter write a masterpiece like 1 Peter?

Some have argued that Peter, being an "unlearned" fisherman (Acts 4:13), could not have written in the kind of sophisticated Greek style employed in the writing of 1 Peter. The less formal Greek of 2 Peter is then placed into evidence as proof that one person could not have written both letters.

Though superficially persuasive, these arguments do not stand up to careful scrutiny. In the first place, the fact that Peter was "unlearned" (a conclusion drawn by those who had ulterior motives in minimizing the apostle's authority), does not mean he was illiterate, but only that he was without formal, rabbinical training in the Scriptures. Moreover, though Aramaic may have been Peter's primary language, there is no particular reason to believe he could not speak Greek, which was a widely spoken second language in Palestine. It is also apparent that at least some of the authors of the New Testament, though not highly educated, could read the Greek of the Old Testament Septuagint (Acts 15:14–18 records James quoting it).

Beyond these evidences of Peter's own ability in Greek, another linguistic factor underscores Peter's authorship. He notes in 5:13 that he wrote this letter "by Silvanus," also known as Silas. The implication of this statement is that Silvanus served as his secretary, or *amanuensis*. Dictation was common in the ancient Roman world, and secretaries often aided with syntax and grammar. There is evidence that Paul used a similar method (Romans 16:22). Christians have long held, therefore, that Peter, under the superintendence of the Spirit of God, dictated this letter to Silvanus. Silvanus, in turn, who also was a prophet (Acts 15:32), may have aided in some of the composition of the more classical Greek.

2. Why does Peter call his readers "elect" (1:2)?

Peter uses a term here that in Greek also connotes "called out ones." The word means "to pick out" or "to select." In the Old Testament, the word was used of Israel (Deuteronomy 7:6), indicating that God sovereignly chose Israel from among all the nations of the world to believe in and belong to Him (Deuteronomy 14:12; Psalms 105:43; 135:4). In 1 Peter, the word is used for Christians, those chosen by God for salvation (Romans 8:33; Colossians 3:12; 2 Timothy 2:10). The word is also used for those who receive Christ during the tribulation time (Matthew 24:22,24) and for holy, unfallen angels (1 Timothy 5:21). To be reminded that they were elected by God was a great comfort to those persecuted Christians.

By using this and other terms of ownership, Peter was establishing the basis from which he would encourage them not to see their suffering as evidence of a different standing with God. Their ultimate security, even in the face of persecution and suffering, was in God's hands.

3. What is the "pure milk of the word" (2:2)?

The Scriptures frequently use startling but clear figurative language to teach spiritual truth. Daily life often mirrors heavenly realities. God's Word offers pure spiritual nourishment. Spiritual growth is always marked by a craving for and delight in God's Word with the same intensity with which a baby craves milk (Job 23:12; Psalms 1:1–2; 19:7–11; 119:16,24,35,47–48,72,92,97,103,111,113,127,159,167,174; Jeremiah 15:16). That initial by-product of spiritual rebirth ought to be a consistent part of the Christian's life.

Christians develop and maintain a desire for the truth of God's Word by remembering their life's source (1:25; Isaiah 55:10–11; John 15:3; Hebrews 4:12), eliminating sin from their lives (2:1), admitting their need for God's truth (2:2, "as newborn babes"; Matthew 4:4), pursuing spiritual growth (2:2, "that you may grow thereby"), and surveying their blessings (2:3, "the Lord is gracious").

4. Do Christians need a priesthood to intercede for them with God (2:9)?

Along with "royal priesthood" Peter uses several Old Testament concepts to emphasize the privileges of New Testament Christians (Deuteronomy 7:6–8). This phrase gave rise to the theological expression "the priesthood of believers." For believers, the need for a representative priest has been met by Jesus Christ, the ultimate royal priest (Hebrews 4:14–9:15). The role of priest is not eliminated but altered. This verse indicates that a central role of the priesthood of all believers is to "proclaim the praises of Him who called you out of darkness into His marvelous light."

The concept of a kingly priesthood is drawn from Exodus 19:6. Israel temporarily forfeited this privilege because of its apostasy and because its wicked leaders executed the Messiah. At the present time, the church is a royal priesthood united with the royal priest, Jesus Christ. A royal priesthood is not only a priesthood that belongs to and serves the king, but is also a priesthood that exercises rule. This will ultimately be fulfilled in Christ's future kingdom (1 Corinthians 6:1–4; Revelation 5:10; 20:6).

5. How does Peter use familiar terms like *spirit, abyss, flood,* and *baptism* in 1 Peter 3:18–22?

This passage proves to be one of the most difficult texts in the New Testament to translate and interpret. The line between Old Testament allusions and New Testament applications gets blurred. Peter's overall purpose in this passage, which was to encourage his readers in their suffering, must be kept in mind during interpretation. The apostle repeatedly reminds them and demonstrates that even Christ suffered unjustly because it was God's will (verse 11) and was accomplishing God's purposes.

Therefore, although Jesus experienced a violent physical execution that terminated His earthly life when He was "put to death in the flesh" (verse 18; Hebrews 5:7), nevertheless He was "made alive by the Spirit" (verse 18). This is not a reference to the Holy Spirit but to Jesus' true inner life, His own spirit. Contrasted with His flesh (humanness), which was dead for three days, His spirit (deity) remained alive, literally, "in spirit" (Luke 23:46).

Part of God's purpose in Christ's death involved His activities between His death and resurrection. His living spirit went to the demon spirits bound in the abyss and proclaimed victory in spite of death. Peter further explains that the abyss is inhabited by bound demons that have been there since the time of Noah. They were sent there because they overstepped the limits of God's tolerance with their wickedness. Not even 120 years of Noah's example and preaching had stemmed the tide of wickedness in his time (Genesis 6:1–8). Thus God bound these demons permanently in the abyss until their final sentencing.

Peter's analogy spotlights the ministry of Jesus Christ in saving us as surely as the ark saved Noah's family. He is not referring to water baptism here but to a figurative immersion in Christ that keeps us safe from the flood of God's sure judgment. The resurrection of Christ demonstrates God's acceptance of Christ's substitutionary death for the sins of those who believe (Acts 2:30–31; Romans 1:4). God's judgment fell on Christ just as the judgment of the floodwaters fell on the ark. The believer who is in Christ is thus in the ark of safety that will sail over the waters of judgment into eternal glory (Romans 6:1–4).

QUICK STUDY ON 1 PETER

1. Peter clearly wants his readers to be secure in their relationship with Christ. What points does he make about salvation?
2. What special titles, names, and roles does Peter assign to Christ in this letter?
3. In 1 Peter 2:21–25, how does Jesus serve as a model for those facing suffering for their faith?
4. Compare the first seven verses of chapter 3 with Ephesians 5:21–33. How does the teaching of these two apostles regarding marriage overlap and where does it differ in emphasis?
5. What does Peter have to say about the conduct of relationships among Christians in general?
6. In 1 Peter 1:14–25, the apostle includes a major section emphasizing the important of holy living. To what extent does your life match the pattern given by Peter?

SECOND PETER

False Teachers among God's People

Second Peter was the last letter from the leader of the apostles.

Peter's final written message has much of the warmth, concern, and passion that fills the pages of Paul's final letter (2 Timothy). These great men of the faith knew their days were numbered. Peter was keenly aware of the warfare between good and evil that would outlast his life (1:12–15). He wanted to leave a strong dose of encouragement for those believers who would remain. The hope of Christ's coming consistently shines through in the background of his letter. Among his closing thoughts were these words: "Therefore, beloved, looking forward to these things, be diligent to be found by Him in peace, without spot and blameless" (3:14).

AUTHOR AND DATE

Written by Peter, about A.D. 67 to 68

A number of internal references point to authorship of this letter by the Apostle Peter. The first verse of the epistle states the claim. In 1:14, he refers to the Lord's unique prediction of his own death (John 21:18–19). In 1:16–18, the author claims to have been present at the transfiguration of Christ (Matthew 17:1–4). Later, in 3:1, Peter refers to his earlier letter (1 Peter).

It must be noted, however, that critics have generated more controversy over 2 Peter's authorship and rightful place in the canon of Scripture than over any other New Testament book. True, the church fathers were slow in giving the letter their acceptance. No church father refers to 2 Peter by name until Origen near the beginning of the third century. The ancient church historian Eusebius grouped 2 Peter with several other disputed books: James, Jude, 2 John, and 3 John. To this it must be responded that 2 Peter has not been questioned about the orthodoxy of its contents. But there was no shortage in the early church of documents falsely claiming to be written by Peter. Therefore, it is not surprising that even a genuine epistle from the apostle received added scrutiny.

Nero died in A.D. 68, and tradition says Peter died during Nero's persecution. The epistle may have been written shortly before his death (1:14; around A.D. 67–68).

KEY PEOPLE IN 2 PETER

Peter—one of Jesus' twelve disciples; wrote his second letter to warn against false teachers in the church (1:1–3:18)

Paul—great missionary and apostle whose writings were twisted by false teachers in the church (3:15–16)

BACKGROUND AND SETTING

Since writing and sending his first letter, Peter had become increasingly concerned about false teachers who were infiltrating the churches in Asia Minor. Though these false teachers had already caused trouble, Peter expected that their heretical doctrines and immoral lifestyles would result in more damage in the future. Thus Peter, in an almost last will and testament (1:13–15), wrote to warn the beloved believers in Christ about the doctrinal dangers they would face. Although Peter mentioned no specific recipients in the salutation of the letter, later reference to his earlier letter (3:2) indicates he was writing to the same people who had received his earlier letter.

Peter does not explicitly say where he was when he wrote this letter, as he does in 1 Peter (1 Peter 5:13). But the consensus seems to be that he wrote this letter from prison in Rome, where he was facing imminent death. Shortly after writing this letter, Peter was martyred, according to reliable tradition, by being crucified upside down.

KEY DOCTRINES IN 2 PETER

False teachers—their teachings deny Christ and twist the Scriptures (chapter 2; Deuteronomy 13:1–18; 18:20; Jeremiah 23; Ezekiel 13; Matthew 7:15; 23:1–36; 24:4–5; Romans 16:17; 2 Corinthians 11:13–14; Galatians 3:1–2; 2 Timothy 4:3–4)

Scripture—the Holy Spirit, as divine author and originator of all Scripture, worked through humans to convey the Word of God (1:20–21; Jeremiah 1:4; 3:2; John 10:34–35; 17:17; Romans 3:2; 1 Corinthians 2:10; 1 Thessalonians 2:13; 2 Timothy 3:16; Titus 1:2; 1 Peter 1:10–11)

Christian character—God gives all believers the power to grow in faith, virtue, knowledge, self-control, perseverance, godliness, brotherly kindness, and love (1:5–11; Psalm 4:3; Proverbs 28:1; 1 Corinthians 9:27; Galatians 5:23; Colossians 1:4; 1 Thessalonians 4:9; 1 Peter 4:8; 1 John 4:20; Revelation 17:14)

Christ's second coming—God has continual patience to allow people to repent before Christ returns (3:1–13; Daniel 7:13; Matthew 24:30; 25:31; John 14:3; 1 Thessalonians 4:16; 2 Thessalonians 1:10; 1 Timothy 6:14; Hebrews 9:28; Jude 14; Revelation 1:7)

GOD'S CHARACTER IN 2 PETER

God is long-suffering—3:9,15
God is a promise keeper—1:4; 3:3–4,13

CHRIST IN 2 PETER

In his second letter, Peter anticipates the second coming of the Lord Jesus Christ "as a thief in the night" (3:10). He also speaks repeatedly of the knowledge of Christ that produces peace, grace, and power for the believer (1:2–3,8; 3:18).

KEY WORDS IN 2 PETER

Knowledge: Greek *gnōsis*—1:5–6; 3:18—literally, "knowledge." This Greek word expresses a knowledge that grows and progresses. As Christians, we need to grow in our personal knowledge of Jesus Christ. The greatest protection against false teachings comes from a solid foundation in the Word of God. Peter's epistle encourages believers to attain a fuller, more thorough knowledge of their Lord Jesus Christ (1:8; 2:20; 3:18).

Morning Star: Greek *phōsphoros*—1:19—literally, "light-bearer" or "light-bringer." In 1 Peter, Christ is called the Morning Star. He is also called the Bright and Morning Star in Revelation 22:16, and the Dayspring in Luke 1:78. Christians today have the light of Christ within their hearts. When Jesus returns to earth, He will bring all believers into a perfect day. His outward coming will bring light to all people. On this day, the spirits of the godly will take on "an illuminating transformation" as the light of Christ fills them.

QUICK OVERVIEW

I. Salutation (1:1–2)
II. Know Your Salvation (1:3–11)
  A. Sustained by God's Power (1:3–4)
  B. Confirmed by Christian Graces (1:5–7)
  C. Honored by Abundant Reward (1:8–11)
III. Know Your Scriptures (1:12–21)
  A. Certified by Apostolic Witness (1:12–18)
  B. Inspired by the Holy Spirit (1:19–21)
IV. Know Your Adversaries (2:1–22)
  A. Deceptive in Their Infiltration (2:1–3)
  B. Doomed by Their Iniquity (2:4–10a)
  C. Disdainful in Their Impurity (2:10b–17)
  D. Devastating in Their Impact (2:18–22)
V. Know Your Prophecy (3:1–18)
  A. The Sureness of the Day of the Lord (3:1–10)
  B. The Sanctification of God's People (3:11–18)

MEANWHILE, IN OTHER PARTS OF THE WORLD . . .

Nero commits suicide in A.D. 68 and is succeeded by Galba.

FREQUENTLY ASKED QUESTIONS

1. How can two letters (1 and 2 Peter) from the same author be so different in style?

The differences between 1 Peter and 2 Peter lie in three areas: style, vocabulary, and theme. These differences must be resolved in the context of the clear claim by the author of 2 Peter to be the author of 1 Peter (2 Peter 3:2).

Questions about the difference in Greek style between the two letters can be satisfactorily answered. Peter reported that he used a secretary (amanuensis), Silvanus, in writing 1 Peter (5:12). When he wrote 2 Peter, the apostle either used a different secretary or took up a pen himself. These methods of composition were not unusual in ancient times. Paul occasionally used an *amanuensis* (Romans 16:22). The role of a secretary or scribe did not cast doubt on the origin of the contents of writing.

2. Who were the false teachers in the early church that Peter addressed in 2 Peter?

Second Peter offers the most graphic and penetrating exposé of false teachers in Scripture, comparable only to Jude. Peter does not identify a specific false religion, cult, or system of teaching. He is more concerned with general principles of recognizing and resisting false instruction in the church.

In his broadest characterization of false teachers, Peter points out that they teach destructive heresies. They deny Christ and twist the Scriptures. They bring true faith into disrepute. They mock the Second Coming of Christ. It is not too much to claim that Peter's primary response to false teaching is knowledge of true doctrine. Falsehood may come in a variety of shades, but they stand revealed as wrong when compared with the truth.

Peter was just as concerned to show the immoral character of false teachers as he was to expose their teaching. He describes them in more detail than he does their doctrine. He knows that the quality of fruit reveals the soundness of the tree. Wickedness is not the product of sound doctrine but of "destructive heresies" (2:1). Peter urges Christians to pursue a deliberate plan of spiritual growth (1:5–9), allowing a life of integrity to expose what is false.

3. What does Peter mean by the counsel to "make your call and election sure" (1:10)?

This phrase hits the theological bull's-eye Peter was aiming at in 1:5–9. Though God is "sure" who His elect are and has given them an eternally secure salvation (1 Peter 1:1–5; Romans 8:31–39), the Christian might not always have inward assurance of salvation. Security is the fact revealed by the Holy Spirit that salvation is forever. Assurance is one's confidence that he or she possesses that eternal salvation. In other words, the believers who pursue the spiritual qualities mentioned in the context of this phrase will guarantee to themselves by spiritual fruit that they were called (Romans 8:30; 1 Peter 2:21) and chosen (1 Peter 1:2) by God to salvation.

4. How does Peter explain the doctrine of the inspiration of Scripture (1:19–21)?

This particular section of 2 Peter provides crucial insights regarding the nature and authenticity of Scripture. Even the apostle expected his readers to provide a reasonable defense for their confidence in the Scriptures. He realized that false teachers would attempt to discredit his letter as well as his past ministry, so he countered their arguments. He knew they would accuse him of concocting fables and myths as a way to manipulate his audience. (This charge by the false teachers actually revealed their own approach and purpose.) So, Peter gave evidence in this passage to prove that he wrote the truth of God as a genuinely inspired writer.

Peter details the process of inspiration. Scripture, claims Peter, is not of human origin. Neither is Scripture the result of human will (1:21). The emphasis in this phrase is that no part of Scripture was produced solely because men wanted it so. The Bible is not the product of sheer human effort. The prophets, in fact, often wrote what they could not understand (1 Peter 1:10–11), but they were nevertheless faithful to write what God revealed to them.

Instead of relying on their own purposes, men were "moved by the Holy Spirit" (1:21) to write. Grammatically, this means that they were continually carried or borne along by the Spirit of God (Luke 1:70; Acts 27:15,17). The Holy Spirit thus is the divine author and originator, the producer of the Scriptures. In the Old Testament alone, the human writers refer to their writings as the words of God over 3,800 times (Jeremiah 1:4; 3:2; Romans 3:2; 1 Corinthians 2:10). Though the human writers were active rather than passive in the process of writing Scripture, God the Holy Spirit superintended them so that, using their own individual personalities, thought processes, and vocabulary, they composed and recorded without error the exact words God wanted written. The original documents of Scripture are therefore inspired (God-breathed, 2 Timothy 3:16), and inerrant (without error, John 10:34–35; 17:17; Titus 1:2). Peter here has described the process of inspiration that created an inerrant original text (Proverbs 30:5; 1 Corinthians 14:36; 1 Thessalonians 2:13).

5. How does "with the Lord one day is as a thousand years, and a thousand years as one day" (3:8) affect our understanding of God's plan?

God understands time very differently from us. From a human point of view, Christ's coming seems like a long time away (Psalm 90:4). From God's viewpoint, it will not be long. Peter reminds his readers of this fact before pointing out that any delay in Christ's return from the human perspective should never be taken as an indication that God is loitering or late. The passage of time actually is a clearer signal of God's immense capacity for patience before He breaks forth in judgment (Joel 2:13; Luke 15:20; Romans 9:22; 1 Peter 3:15).

Beyond that general frame of reference, this text may be a specific indication of the fact that there are actually a thousand years between the first phase of the Day of the Lord at the end of the tribulation (Revelation 6:17) and the second phase at the end of the millennial kingdom when the Lord creates the new heaven and new earth.

6. If the Lord is "not willing that any should perish" (3:9), why does it appear that many will have that very end?

The *any* in this passage must refer to those whom the Lord has chosen and will call to complete the redeemed, the *us* mentioned earlier in the same verse. Since the whole passage is about God's destroying the wicked, His patience is not so He can save all of them, but so that He can receive all His own. He can't be waiting for everyone to be saved, since the emphasis is that He will destroy the world and the ungodly. Those who do perish and go to hell, go because they are depraved and worthy only of hell—they have rejected the only remedy, Jesus Christ—not because they were created for hell and predetermined to go there. The path to damnation is the path of an unrepentant heart; it is the path of one who rejects the person and provision of Jesus Christ and holds on to sin (Isaiah 55:1; Jeremiah 13:17; Ezekiel 18:32; Matthew 11:28; 13:37; Luke 13:3; John 3:16; 8:21,24; 1 Timothy 2:3–4; Revelation 22:17).

The *all* which begins the next phrase "but that all should come to repentance," must refer to all who are God's people who will come to Christ to make up the full number of the people of God. The reason for the delay in Christ's coming and the attendant judgments is not because He is slow to keep His promise, or because He wants to judge more of the wicked, or because He is impotent in the face of wickedness. He delays His coming because He is patient and desires the time for His people to repent.

QUICK STUDY ON 2 PETER

1. What does Peter's comment about Paul's letters mean (3:15)?
2. What indications can you discover in the letter that indicate it might have been Peter's last?
3. How does Peter explain the apparent delay in the return of Christ?
4. In what ways does Peter attack and undermine the false authority of the false teachers?
5. What practical steps for spiritual growth does Peter include in this letter?

FIRST JOHN
The Fundamentals of Faith

First John serves like a cover letter for the Gospel of John, filled with practical ways to live out the Christian life that begins by believing in Jesus.

The Apostle John made a significant contribution to the New Testament with five books (Gospel of John, 1, 2, and 3 John, and Revelation). His writing represents a wider variety than that of any of the other authors. He composed a gospel, three letters, and a lengthy prophetic work.

AUTHOR AND DATE

Written by John in about A.D. 90 to 95

The epistle does not identify the author, but the strong, consistent, and earliest testimony of the church ascribes it to John the disciple and apostle (Luke 6:13–14). This anonymity strongly affirms the early church's identification of the epistle as John's, for only someone with his well-known and preeminent status as an apostle would be able to write with such unmistakable authority. The author expected complete obedience from his readers even without clearly identifying himself (4:6). He and his message were so well known to the readers that he didn't need to mention his own name.

John and James, his older brother (Acts 12:2), were known as "the sons of Zebedee" (Matthew 10:2–4). Jesus also called them "Sons of Thunder" (Mark 3:17). John was one of the three most intimate associates of Jesus (along with Peter and James—Matthew 17:1; 26:37). He was an eyewitness and participant in Jesus' earthly ministry from the start, which explains the intimate tone of the opening of this letter (1:1–4). In addition to the three epistles, John also authored the Fourth Gospel, in which he identified himself as the disciple "whom Jesus loved" and as the one who reclined on Jesus' breast during the Last Supper (John 13:23; 19:26; 20:2; 21:7,20). He also wrote the Book of Revelation (Revelation 1:1).

KEY PEOPLE IN 1 JOHN

John—wrote to reassure believers about the fundamental truth of the Christian faith (1:1–5:21)

Jesus—Christ is the Word of Life who sacrificed Himself and rose from the grave to give eternal life to all who believe (1:1–5:20)

BACKGROUND AND SETTING

Although he was advanced in age when he penned this epistle, John was still actively ministering to churches in and around Ephesus in Asia

Minor. By then, he was the sole remaining apostolic survivor who had had an intimate, eyewitness association with Jesus throughout His earthly ministry, death, resurrection, and ascension. The church fathers indicate that John eventually settled in Ephesus. There he gave oversight to many churches, conducted an extensive evangelistic program, and wrote much of his contribution to the New Testament. One church father (Papias), who had direct contact with John, described him as a "living and abiding voice." As the last remaining apostle, John's testimony was highly authoritative among Christians at the end of the first century.

Ephesus (Acts 19:10) lay within the intellectual center of Asia Minor. As predicted years before by the Apostle Paul (Acts 20:28–31), false teachers had arisen from within the church's own ranks. These leaders, saturated with the prevailing climate of philosophical trends, began infecting the church with false doctrine, perverting fundamental apostolic teaching. These false teachers advocated new ideas that eventually became known as "Gnosticism" (from the Greek word for "knowledge"). Second only to the battle over the influence of legalistic Judaism in the early church, Gnosticism was the most dangerous heresy that threatened the church during the first three centuries. Most likely, John was combating the early strains of that virulent heresy. Since even the primitive forms of this false teaching were spiritually lethal, John took action. With gentleness and love, but with unquestionable apostolic authority, he sent this letter to churches in his sphere of influence to stem this spreading plague of false doctrine.

KEY DOCTRINES IN 1 JOHN

Fundamentals of the faith—sound faith, obedience, and love work together to produce happiness, holiness, and assurance in the lives of believers (1:4,9; 2:1,3,15; 4:4–6; 5:13; Psalm 32:3–5; Proverbs 28:13; John 14:30; 16:11; Romans 6:12–14; 8:12–13; 1 Corinthians 15:34; Ephesians 4:32; Colossians 2:13)

Demonic teachings—false teachers denied the humanity of Jesus Christ (2:18, 26; 3:7; 4:1–7; Isaiah 53:3–4; Matthew 1:18; Luke 1:31; 1 Corinthians 15:21; Galatians 4:4; Hebrews 2:14–17; 2 John 1:7)

GOD'S CHARACTER IN 1 JOHN

God is faithful—1:9
God is just—1:9
God is light—1:5
God is loving—2:5; 3:1; 4:8–10,12,16,19
God is a promise keeper—2:25
God is true—1:10; 5:10
God is unified—5:7

CHRIST IN 1 JOHN

In this epistle, John combats Gnostic doctrine that denied the humanity of Jesus Christ. John proclaims the identity of Jesus Christ as the incarnation of God the Son into human flesh: "This is He who came by water and blood" (5:6). This verse describes the genuine life and death of Christ as the Son of Man.

KEY WORDS IN 1 JOHN

Sin: Greek *hamartia*—1:7–8; 3:4–5,8–9; 5:16–17—literally, "to miss the mark." John speaks of a kind of sin one can recover from and another kind of sin from which one can not recover. John's readers, unlike readers today, apparently understood the difference between these two kinds of sin. The overall teaching of this epistle suggests that those who denied the Christian community (2:18–19) to follow heretical, "antichrist" teachings were irrecoverable. Their rebellion and denial of Jesus' true identity (4:1–3) leads to unrepentant sin. In the end, their sin produces spiritual death.

Advocate: Greek *paraklētos*—2:1—literally, "one who is called to our side." This Greek term refers to the position of a comforter, consoler, or defense attorney. In John 14:26 and 15:26, the Holy Spirit is called the Advocate for believers. The Holy Spirit works within us to comfort and help us and also pleads our case before the Father in heaven (Romans 8:26–27,34).

QUICK OVERVIEW

I. The Fundamental Test of Genuine Fellowship—Spiral I (1:1–2:17)
   A. The Fundamental Test of Doctrine (1:1–2:2)
   B. The Fundamental Tests of Morals (2:3–17)
II. The Fundamental Tests of Genuine Fellowship—Spiral II (2:18–3:24)
   A. Part 2 of the Doctrinal Test (2:18–27)
   B. Part 2 of the Moral Test (2:28–3:24)
III. The Fundamental Test of Genuine Fellowship—Spiral III (4:1–21)
   A. Part 3 of the Doctrinal Test (4:1–6)
   B. Part 3 of the Moral Test (4:7–21)
IV. The Fundamental Tests of Genuine Fellowship—Spiral IV (5:1–21)
   A. The Victorious Life in Christ (5:1–5)
   B. The Witness of God for Christ (5:6–12)
   C. Christian Certainties Because of Christ (5:13–21)

MEANWHILE, IN OTHER PARTS OF THE WORLD . . .
The empires of Rome and China expand towards each other, separated only by the Armenian mountains and the Caspian Sea.

FREQUENTLY ASKED QUESTIONS

1. How does 1 John help us understand some of the destructive teaching that attacked Christianity in the first century?

Paul, Peter, and John all faced early forms of a system of false teaching that later became known as Gnosticism. That term (derived from the Greek word for "knowledge") refers to the Gnostics' claiming of an elevated knowledge, a higher truth known only to those in on the deep things. Those initiated into this mystical knowledge of truth had a higher internal authority than Scripture. This resulted in a chaotic situation in which instead of divine revelation standing as judge over man's ideas, man's ideas judged God's revelation (1 John 2:15–17).

Philosophically, the heresy relied on a distortion of Platonism. It advocated a dualism in which matter was inherently evil and spirit was good. One of the direct errors of this heresy involved attributing some form of deity to Christ but denying His true humanity, supposedly to preserve Him from evil (which they concluded He would be if He actually came in the flesh). Such a view destroys not only the true humanity of Jesus but also the atonement work of Christ. Jesus must not only have been truly God, but also the truly human (physically real) man who actually suffered and died upon the cross in order to be the acceptable substitutionary sacrifice for sin (Hebrews 2:14–17). The biblical view of Jesus affirms His complete humanity as well as His full deity.

The Gnostic heresy, even in John's day, featured two basic forms: Docetism and the error of Cerinthus. Docetism (from a Greek word that means "to appear") asserted that Jesus' physical body was not real but only "seemed" to be physical. John forcefully and repeatedly affirmed the physical reality of Jesus. He reminded his readers that he was an eyewitness to Him ("heard," "seen," "handled," "Jesus Christ has come in the flesh"; 1 John 1:1–4; 4:2–3). The other form of early Gnosticism was traced back to Cerinthus by the early church apologist Irenaeus. Cerinthus taught that Christ's "spirit" descended on the human Jesus at His baptism but left Him shortly before His crucifixion. John asserted that the Jesus who was baptized at the beginning of His ministry was the same person who was crucified on the cross (1 John 5:6).

John does not directly specify the early Gnostic beliefs, but his arguments offer clear clues about his targets. Further, John's wisdom was to avoid direct attacks on rapidly shifting heresies, but to provide a timely positive restatement of the fundamentals of the faith that would provide timeless truth and answers for later generations of Christians.

2. What are the nonnegotiable basics of the faith that John spells out in 1 John?

John presents the basics or fundamentals of the Christian life in absolute, nonrelative terms. Unlike Paul, who often included exceptions when discussing spiritual principles, John does not deal with the "what if I fail" issues. John does recognize the importance of forgiveness and Christ's role as Advocate when we fail (1:8–9; 2:1), but most of his letter presents truths in black and white rather than shades of gray. His stark contrasts allow little room for compromise: "light" versus "darkness" (1:5,7; 2:8–11); truth versus lies (2:21–22; 4:1); children of God versus children of the devil (3:10).

Those who claim to be Christians must absolutely display the characteristics of genuine Christians: sound doctrine, obedience, and love. Those who are truly born again have been given a new nature, which gives evidence of itself. Those who do not display characteristics of the new nature don't have it, so were never truly born again. The issues do not center (as much of Paul's writing does) on maintaining temporal or daily fellowship with God but on the application of basic tests in one's life to confirm that salvation has truly occurred. Such absolute distinctions were also characteristic of John's gospel.

3. Why are there so many seemingly repeated thoughts in 1 John?

In a unique fashion, John challenges his readers and interpreters by his repetition of similar themes over and over to emphasize the basic truths about genuine Christianity. Some have likened John's repetitive style to a spiral that moves outward, becoming larger and larger, each cycle spreading the same truth over a wider territory and encompassing a larger area of life. Others have seen the spirals moving inward, penetrating deeper and deeper into the same themes while expanding on his thoughts. However one views the spiraling pattern, John clearly uses repetition of basic truths as a means to accentuate their importance and to help his readers understand and remember them.

4. What does confession have to do with gaining forgiveness in 1 John 1:9?

The false teachers that John was resisting shared a characteristic with many modern people. They walked in spiritual darkness (sin) but went so far as to deny the existence of a sin nature in their lives. If someone never admits to being a sinner, salvation cannot result (see Matthew 19:16–22 for the account of the young man who refused to recognize his sin). Confession (admission of sin) is like opening a hand to release an object. Once the hand is open, it can receive forgiveness.

Continual confession of sin is an indication of genuine salvation. While the false teachers would not admit their sin, the genuine Christians admitted and forsook it (Psalm 32:3–5; Proverbs 28:13). The term *confess* means to say the same thing about sin that God says, to acknowledge His perspective about sin. Confession of sin characterizes genuine Christians, and God continually cleanses those who are confessing. Rather than focusing on confession for every single sin as necessary, John has especially in mind here a settled recognition and acknowledgment that one is a sinner in need of cleansing and forgiveness (Ephesians 4:32; Colossians 2:13).

5. Why are we not to love the world (2:15)?

Although John often repeats the importance of love and that God is love (4:7–8), he also reveals that God hates a certain type of love: love of the world (John 15:18–20). An absence of love for the world must habitually characterize the love life of those to be considered born again. Conversely, Christians love God and their fellow Christians.

Love here signifies affection and devotion. God, not the world, must have the first place in the Christian's life (Matthew 10:37–39; Philippians 3:20). The term *world* is not a reference to the physical, material world but to the invisible spiritual system of evil, dominated by Satan, and all that it offers in opposition to God, His Word, and His people (5:19; John 12:31; 1 Corinthians 1:21; 2 Corinthians 4:4; James 4:4; 2 Peter 1:4).

QUICK STUDY ON 1 JOHN

1. What does John teach about confession and forgiveness in the first chapter?
2. What four reasons does John give for why true Christians cannot habitually practice sin (3:4–10)?
3. John's letter includes five specific reasons why Christians love (4:7–21). What are they?
4. How does John use Cain as an example in his letter?
5. According to John, why is it impossible to love God and hate our neighbor?
6. How do you apply the statement "We love because He first loved us" in your life?

SECOND JOHN
A Lesson in Hospitality

Second John is the only New Testament letter specifically addressed to a woman.

Even a memo from one of the original disciples has great value—particularly if it was inspired by the Holy Spirit. This shortest of the New Testament books fits on a single sheet of papyrus. In it, John includes only crucial encouragement and warnings. There was much more to say, but he hoped to visit soon (verse 12).

AUTHOR AND DATE

Written by the Apostle John in about A.D. 90 to 95

The author describes himself in 2 John 1 as "the Elder." It fits the apostle's pattern of not using his own name in his writings. In the Gospel of John he called himself the disciple "whom Jesus loved" (John 13:23; 19:26; 20:2; 21:7,20). "The Elder" conveys the advanced age of the apostle, his authority, and his status during the foundational period of Christianity.

KEY PEOPLE IN 2 JOHN

John—apostle of Jesus writing to emphasize Christian fellowship and hospitality (verses 1–13)

The elect lady—personal acquaintance of John and a believer (verse 1)

The lady's children—reference to the sons and daughters of the chosen lady (verse 1)

BACKGROUND AND SETTING

The primary difference between 1 John and 2 John has to do with the audience. First John is addressed in a general way to Christians. 2 John is written to a particular person and a particular church (verse 1). Both letters warn of the dangers of those false teachers who, influenced by early Gnostic thought, were threatening the church.

Based on the internal evidence, John was concerned that the individual addressed in the greeting (verse 1) inadvertently or unwisely may have shown these false prophets hospitality (verses 10–11). Apparently, false teachers were conducting an itinerant ministry among John's congregations, seeking to make converts and taking advantage of Christian hospitality to advance their cause. The apostle urgently warned his readers against showing hospitality to such deceivers (verses 10–11). Although his exhortation may appear on the surface to be harsh or unloving, the acutely dangerous nature of the false teaching justified such actions, especially since it threatened to destroy the very foundations of the faith (verse 9).

KEY DOCTRINES IN 2 JOHN

Christian fellowship—sound doctrine must serve as the test of fellowship and the basis of separation between those who profess to be Christians and those who actually are (verses 9–11; Romans 16:17; Galatians 1:8–9; 2 Thessalonians 3:6,14; Titus 3:10).

Fundamentals of the faith—the basics of Christianity are summarized by adherence to the truth, love, and obedience (verses 4–6; John 13:34–35; 14:15,21; 15:10,12,17; 1 Thessalonians 2:19–20; 1 John 2:7–11; 3:11; 4:7–12).

GOD'S CHARACTER IN 2 JOHN

God is loving—1:6
God is truth—1:1–2

CHRIST IN 2 JOHN

Similar to John's first letter, the apostle stresses the basic truth of Christ's identity (verses 7–11). To deny Christ's humanity is to deny the bodily suffering and sacrifice Christ endured to redeem the world of sin: "Many deceivers have gone out into the world who do not confess Jesus Christ as coming in the flesh. This is a deceiver and an antichrist" (verses 7–8).

QUICK OVERVIEW

I. The Basis of Christian Hospitality (1–3)
II. The Behavior of Christian Hospitality (4–6)
III. The Bounds of Christian Hospitality (7–11)
IV. The Blessings of Christian Hospitality (12–13)

MEANWHILE, IN OTHER PARTS OF THE WORLD . . .
Most of northern Germany is still occupied by barbarians. However, Rome invades and conquers parts of the Black Forest, located between the Rhine and the Danube.

FREQUENTLY ASKED QUESTIONS

1. Why was it so important to John to "confess Jesus Christ as coming in the flesh" (verse 7)?

John's purpose was to strengthen Christians to resist the tide of heresy that was rising against the church. Much of this false teaching was an early form of Gnosticism. For more on the heresy itself, see the **Frequently Asked Question** "How does 1 John help us understand some of the destructive teaching that attacked Christianity in the first century?"

The Gnostic idea that matter was evil and only spirit was good led to the idea that either the body should be treated harshly, a form of asceticism

(Colossians 2:21–23), or that sin committed in the body had no connection or effect on one's spirit. In other words, the false teaching sought to drive a wedge between body and soul. This is why it often maintained that Jesus could not have been God and man at the same time.

The result of this error in teaching was compounded when some, including John's opponents, concluded that sins committed in the physical body did not matter. Absolute indulgence in immorality was permissible. One could deny sin even existed (1 John 1:8–10) and disregard God's law (1 John 3:4).

As a bulwark against this heresy, John lifted the confession that Jesus Christ came "in the flesh" (verse 7). What Christians do in their physical life is directly connected with what they do in their spiritual life. John emphasized the need for obedience to God's laws, for he defined the true love for God as obedience to His commandments (1 John 5:3). Jesus, in His human living, offered the perfect example of that kind of love.

2. How does John's teaching about truth and love affect discussions about Christian unity today (verses 4–6)?

John's teaching stands in direct antithesis to the frequent cry for ecumenism and Christian unity among believers. Love and truth are inseparable in Christianity. Truth must always guide the exercise of love (Ephesians 4:5). Love must stand the test of truth. The main lesson of John's second letter is that truth determines the bounds of love and, as a consequence, the bounds of unity. Therefore, truth must exist before love can unite, for truth generates love (1 Peter 1:22). When someone compromises the truth, true Christian love and unity are destroyed. Only shallow sentimentalism exists where truth is not the foundation of unity.

QUICK STUDY ON 2 JOHN

1. How does John highlight his consistent theme of love in his short letter?
2. How does John emphasize the importance of truth?
3. What is the cause of John's warnings in this brief letter?
4. What positive counsel about Christian relationships does John offer?

THIRD JOHN
Serving the Servants of the Lord

Third John records John's tribute to the practice of hospitality.

Like 2 John, 3 John is marked by brevity. It fit on a single sheet of papyrus. In it, the apostle announces his intention to visit soon. John's note to a leader named Gaius challenges and encourages him by using the behavior of two other leaders as negative and positive examples of effective spiritual leadership. John hoped to add much more teaching when he arrived.

AUTHOR AND DATE

Written by the Apostle John about A.D. 90 to 95

John used the same identifying term that he used in 2 John. In both letters, he referred to himself as "the Elder." The term conveys the advanced age of the apostle, as well as his authority, and his privileged role as one of the remaining eyewitnesses of Jesus' ministry.

The precise date of the epistle cannot be determined. Since the structure, style, and vocabulary closely approximate 2 John, most likely John composed the letters at the same time, about A.D. 90 to 95. Compare the following passages for those similarities: compare verse 1 to 2 John 2; verse 4 to 2 John 4; verse 13 to 2 John 12; verse 14 to 2 John 12. As with 1 and 2 John, the apostle probably wrote this letter during his ministry at Ephesus near the end of his life.

KEY PEOPLE IN 3 JOHN

John—wrote to commend Gaius for his generous hospitality (verses 1–14)

Gaius—sole recipient of John's letter; member of one of the churches under John's spiritual oversight (verse 1)

Diotrephes—self-centered and domineering member of the church (verses 9–10)

Demetrius—faithful servant and excellent role model in the church (verse 12)

BACKGROUND AND SETTING

Third John is perhaps the most personal of John's three epistles. While 1 John appears to be a general letter addressed to congregations scattered throughout Asia Minor, and 2 John was sent to a lady and her family (2 John 1), in 3 John the apostle clearly names the sole recipient as "the beloved Gaius" (verse 1). The name Gaius was common in the first century, and men bearing it appear in a number of New Testament passages (Acts 19:29; 20:4; Romans 16:23; 1 Corinthians 1:14). Beyond this letter, however, no other specific identity for Gaius has been found.

The composition of this letter was motivated by those who returned from Gaius with a report of the hospitality and support they had received from that brother. Meanwhile, others, like Diotrephes (verse 9), had refused to extend a welcome to visiting teachers from John. The apostle followed up those reports with this note of gratitude and encouragement for Gaius.

KEY DOCTRINES IN 3 JOHN

Hospitality—should be shown to faithful ministers of the Word (verses 9–10; Genesis 14:18; 18:3–8; Exodus 2:20; 1 Samuel 9:22; 2 Kings 6:22–23; Job 31:32; Isaiah 58:7; Luke 14:13–14; Romans 12:13,20; 1 Timothy 3:2; 5:10; Titus 1:8; Hebrews 13:2; 1 Peter 4:9)

GOD'S CHARACTER IN 3 JOHN

God is good—verse 11

CHRIST IN 3 JOHN

Unlike 1 and 2 John, 3 John does not directly mention the name of Jesus Christ. However, in verse 7, John describes the missionaries as going "forth for His name's sake" (see Romans 1:5). The truth of Christ's sacrifice on the cross remains the basis of spreading the Good News to all people.

KEY WORD IN 3 JOHN

Church: Greek *ekklēsia*—verses 6,9–10—literally, "an assembly." In secular Greek literature, this term described any gathering of people to an important event or assembly. The writers of the New Testament used this term to mean a local assembly of believers, or the worldwide body of believers. John uses *ekklēsia* in two ways: "the church" in verse 6 refers to the general group of believers, whereas "the church" in verses 9 and 10 has to be a specific local church. In biblical times, Christians of each city were organized under one group of elders (see Acts 14:23; 15:2,4; 20:17–18; Titus 1:5). Several "assemblies" of believers, held in various homes, comprised the local church in each city.

QUICK OVERVIEW

I. The Commendation regarding Christian Hospitality (1–8)
II. The Condemnation regarding Violating Christian Hospitality (9–11)
III. The Conclusion regarding Christian Hospitality (12–14)

MEANWHILE, IN OTHER PARTS OF THE WORLD . . .
John's disciple Polycarp may already be ministering in Smyrna.

FREQUENTLY ASKED QUESTIONS

1. What guidelines about Christian hospitality are found in 3 John?

John offers both encouragement and counsel regarding hospitality. He certainly believed that Christians should practice the kind of hospitality that could be judged in a "manner worthy of God" (verse 6). First, Christians must show hospitality to those who have pure motives. He described these as itinerant missionaries who went out "for the sake of the name" (verse 7; Romans 1:5). They must be doing ministry for God's glory, not their own. Second, Christians must show hospitality to those who are not in ministry for money. Since these missionaries were "taking nothing from the Gentiles" (verse 7), the church was their only means of support. Third, when Christians practice hospitality, they become participants in the ministry of those to whom they extend a welcome (verse 8).

2. Why was John so upset about this person called Diotrephes in his third letter?

John mentioned Diotrephes to Gaius as an example of the kind of negative effect caused by a leader who contradicts Jesus' teaching on servant-leadership in the church (Matthew 20:20–28; Philippians 2:5–11; 1 Timothy 3:3; 1 Peter 5:3) and who violates the standards of hospitality required of Christians. John noted at least six errors in Diotrephes's behavior that form helpful warnings to others:

- He loved to have preeminence (the desire to be first, verse 9).
- He rejected John's authority and therefore the authority of God's Word by refusing to receive John's letter (verse 9).
- John charged Diotrephes with "prating against us" (a term that conveys the idea of someone talking nonsense, verse 10).
- Diotrephes acted "with malicious words" (his false accusations against John were also evil, verse 10).
- He "does not receive the brethren" (his hostility extended to other Christians, verse 10).
- He was even "putting them out of the church" (he was excommunicating those who resisted his authority, verse 10).

QUICK STUDY ON 3 JOHN

1. What are the high points and low points of John's third letter?
2. In what ways is Christian hospitality important?
3. What character traits are creating problems in the church John is writing?
4. For what actions and traits are Gaius and Demetrius complimented?
5. What has been your most memorable experience of giving or receiving Christian hospitality?

JUDE
Profile of an Apostate

Jude presents a great warning shout from the Lord's brother to stand firm!

Jude was the second half brother of Jesus to write a New Testament letter (Matthew 13:55; Mark 6:3). Although Jude had earlier rejected Jesus as Messiah (John 7:1–9), he, along with other half brothers of our Lord, was converted after Christ's resurrection (Acts 1:14). Like his brother James, Jude became a significant leader in the church in Jerusalem following Jesus' death, resurrection, and ascension into heaven. He was also active on missionary journeys with other brothers (1 Corinthians 9:5).

AUTHOR AND DATE

Written by Jude about A.D. 68 to 70

Although Jude (Judas) was a common name in Palestine (at least eight men by that name are in the New Testament), the author of Jude generally has been accepted as Jude, Christ's half brother. Three internal clues reinforce this conclusion:

- Jude's appeal to being the "brother of James," the leader of the Jerusalem Council (Acts 15) and another half brother of Jesus (verse 1; Galatians 1:19)
- The similarities between Jude's and James's salutations (verse 1; James 1:1)
- Jude's not identifying himself as an apostle (verse 1), but rather distinguishing himself from them (verse 17). These clues negate the other main candidate for authorship, the Apostle Judas (not Judas Iscariot), the son of James (Luke 6:16; Acts 1:13), also known as Thaddaeus.

Early questions about the canonicity of Jude revolve around its relationship with 2 Peter. Jude quotes directly from 2 Peter 3:3 and acknowledges that it is from an apostle (verses 17–18). If Peter had quoted Jude, there would have been no question about canonicity, since Peter would thereby have given Jude apostolic affirmation. The authenticity of Jude, however, was attested by Clement of Rome (about A.D. 96) and Clement of Alexandria (about A.D. 200).

Since no mention of Jerusalem's destruction in A.D. 70 was included by Jude, and though Jude most likely came after 2 Peter (A.D. 67–68), the former fits into the same narrow time frame as the latter. Jude was probably written about A.D. 68 to 70.

KEY PEOPLE IN JUDE

Jude—Christ's half brother who earlier rejected Jesus as Messiah and then converted after the resurrection (1:1–25)

James—brother of Jude; well-known leader of the Jerusalem church and author of the book of James (1:1)

BACKGROUND AND SETTING

Jude lived at a time when Christianity was under severe political pressure from Rome and aggressive spiritual infiltration from Gnostic-like apostates who sowed abundant seed for a gigantic harvest of doctrinal error. The exact audience of believers with whom Jude corresponded is unknown but seems to be Jewish in light of Jude's illustrations. He undoubtedly wrote to a region recently plagued by false teachers.

Except for John, who lived until the close of the first century, all the other apostles had likely been martyred by the time Jude wrote. Christianity was thought to be extremely vulnerable. Thus, Jude called the church to fight, in the midst of intense spiritual warfare, for the truth.

KEY DOCTRINES IN JUDE

Apostasy—defection from the true, biblical faith (verses 3–4,8,10,16–19; 2 Thessalonians 2:10; Hebrews 10:29; 2 Peter 2:1–22; 1 John 2:18–23)

GOD'S CHARACTER IN JUDE

God is glorious—verses 24–25
God is gracious—verse 4
God is judging—verses 5–6,14–15
God is Lord—verse 4
God is loving—verses 1–3,21
God is wise—verse 25

CHRIST IN JUDE

Jude opens his attack on apostasy by first addressing believers: "To those who are called, sanctified by God the Father, and preserved in Jesus Christ" (verse 1). Unlike the condemned apostate, Christ keeps believers secure for eternal life. Jude concludes his epistle by bolstering the courage of believers in Christ's power. Jude proclaims Jesus as "Him who is able to keep you from stumbling, and to present you faultless" (verse 24).

QUICK OVERVIEW

I. Desires of Jude (1–2)
II. Declaration of War against Apostates (3–4)

III. Damnable Outcome of Apostates (5–7)
IV. Denunciation of Apostates (8–16)
V. Defenses against Apostates (17–23)
VI. Doxology of Jude (24–25)

MEANWHILE, IN OTHER PARTS OF THE WORLD . . .
Vespasian enters Rome triumphantly and is adopted as the new emperor by the senate.

FREQUENTLY ASKED QUESTIONS

1. Since Jude quotes from books that are not in the Bible, does this give those other books a special value?

Jude quoted specifically from two extra-biblical books: 1 Enoch (verse 14) and Assumption of Moses (verse 9). The authors of these books are unknown. Jude referred to them to support and illustrate his points.

Christians have held that Jude was writing under the inspiration of the Holy Spirit (2 Timothy 3:16; 2 Peter 1:20–21) and included material that was accurate and true in its affirmations. His use of extra-biblical material was selective and not meant to extend any special authority to those texts. Paul followed the same pattern in quoting or referring to nonbiblical authors (Acts 17:28; 1 Corinthians 15:33; Titus 1:12).

2. What does Jude mean by *the faith which was once delivered to the saints* (verse 3)?

Jude is referring to the whole body of revealed salvation truth contained in the Scriptures (Galatians 1:23; Ephesians 4:5,13; Philippians 1:27; 1 Timothy 4:1). Here, and later in verse 20, Jude is describing a fixed body of spiritual revelation that can be known as sound doctrine (Ephesians 4:14; Colossians 3:16; 1 Peter 2:2; 1 John 2:12–14), used in discerning and sorting out truth from error (1 Thessalonians 5:20–22), and effective in confronting and attacking error (2 Corinthians 10:3–5; Philippians 1:17,27; 1 Timothy 1:18; 6:12; 2 Timothy 1:13; 4:7–8; Titus 1:13).

God's revelation was delivered once as a unit, at the completion of the Scripture, and is not to be edited by either deletion or addition (Deuteronomy 4:2; 12:32; Proverbs 30:6; Revelation 22:18–19). Scripture is complete, sufficient, and finished; therefore it is fixed for all time. Nothing is to be added to the body of the inspired Word (2 Timothy 3:16–17; 2 Peter 1:19–21) because nothing else is needed.

3. Why are the last verses in Jude called a "doxology"?

The word itself is not found in the Bible but is an ancient term referring to special passages that express high praise to God. The first part of the word comes from the Greek word *doxa,* which means "glory." The second part of the word comes from the Greek word *logos,* which means "word." These words in Jude express in the most exalted terms the glory of God. They stand alongside other splendid examples in the New Testament (Romans 11:33–36; 16:25–27; 2 Corinthians 13:14; Hebrews 13:20–21).

Jude's doxology includes Christians in a powerful way, highlighting what God can do for them that no one else can do. Jude reemphasized his theme of salvation and bolstered the courage of the believers to know that Christ would protect them from the present apostasy.

QUICK STUDY ON JUDE

1. How does Jude describe himself in relation to his brother James and his half brother, Jesus? Why is that significant?
2. What figures and events from biblical history did Jude use to base his warnings?
3. In what way does he describe the false teachers?
4. What does the word *apostasy* mean and how does Jude characterize an apostate?
5. What specific aspects of our relationship with God through Christ are lifted up in the doxology of verses 24–25?

REVELATION
The Final Judgment

Unlike most books of the Bible, Revelation contains its own title: "The Revelation of Jesus Christ" (1:1).

God made sure His Word had a grand finale. What opened with the overture of Genesis comes to a dramatic conclusion in Revelation. In all its uses, *revelation* refers to something or someone, once hidden, becoming visible. What this book reveals or unveils is Jesus Christ in glory. Truths about Him and His final victory that the rest of Scripture merely alludes to John describes in this expanded revelation about Jesus Christ.

AUTHOR AND DATE

Written by the Apostle John in about A.D. 94 to 96

Four times the author identifies himself as John (1:1,4,9; 22:8). Early tradition unanimously identifies him as John the apostle, author of the Fourth Gospel and three epistles. Important second-century witnesses to the Apostle John's authorship include Justin Martyr, Irenaeus, Clement of Alexandria, and Tertullian. Many of the book's original readers were still alive during the lifetimes of Justin Martyr and Irenaeus—both of whom held to apostolic authorship.

There are differences in style between Revelation and John's other writings, but these are insignificant considering the radical difference in subject matter and setting. There are, however, some striking parallels between Revelation and John's other works. In the New Testament, only John's gospel and Revelation refer to Jesus Christ as the Word (19:13; John 1:1). Revelation (1:7) and John's gospel (19:37) translate Zechariah 12:10 differently from the Septuagint (the Greek Old Testament), but in agreement with each other. Further, only Revelation and the Gospel of John describe Jesus as the "Lamb" (5:6,8; John 1:29) and as a "witness" (1:5; John 5:31–32).

Revelation was written in the last decade of the first century (about A.D. 94–96), near the end of Emperor Domitian's reign (A.D. 81–96). Although some date it during Nero's reign (A.D. 54–68), their arguments are unconvincing and conflict with the view of the early church. Writing in the second century, Irenaeus declared that Revelation had been written toward the end of Domitian's reign. Other early writers, Clement of Alexandria, Origen, Victorinus (who wrote one of the earliest commentaries on Revelation), Eusebius, and Jerome affirm the Domitian date.

The spiritual decline of the seven churches (chapters 2–3) also argues for the later date. Those churches were strong and spiritually healthy in the mid–A.D. 60s, when Paul last ministered in Asia Minor. The brief time between Paul's ministry there and the end of Nero's reign was too short for such a decline to have occurred. The longer time gap also explains the rise of the heretical sect known as the Nicolaitans (2:6,15), who are not mentioned in Paul's letters. Finally, dating Revelation during Nero's reign does not allow time for John's ministry in Asia Minor to reach the point at which the authorities would have felt the need to exile him.

KEY PEOPLE IN REVELATION

John—apostle of Jesus Christ who received the revelation of Jesus Christ from an angel (1:1,4,9; 22:8)

Jesus—the revealed Son of God who will come again to claim His people (1:1–22:21)

BACKGROUND AND SETTING

Revelation begins with John, the last surviving apostle and an old man, in exile on the small, barren island of Patmos, located in the Aegean Sea southwest of Ephesus. The Roman authorities had banished him there because of his faithful preaching of the gospel (1:9). While on Patmos, John received a series of visions that laid out the future history of the world.

When he was arrested, John was in Ephesus, ministering to the church there and in surrounding cities. Although he could no longer minister to those congregations in person, John received a divine command to address Revelation to them (1:4,11). Those churches had begun to feel the effects of violent persecution. At least one man—probably a pastor—had already been martyred (2:13). John himself had been exiled. But the storm of persecution was about to break in full fury upon the seven churches so dear to the apostle's heart (2:10). To those churches, Revelation provided a message of hope: God is in control of all the events of human history, and though evil often seems pervasive and wicked men all powerful, their ultimate doom is certain. Christ will come in glory to judge and rule.

KEY DOCTRINES IN REVELATION

Revelation—Jesus Christ's true identity and saving work is unveiled (1:1–22:21; Isaiah 11:5; 53:1–11; Zechariah 9:9; Luke 1:35; John 1:1–14; 7:18; Acts 4:27; 2 Corinthians 8:9; Philippians 2:8; 1 Thessalonians 5:24; Hebrews 1:9; 1 John 5:20)

Holiness—the church is warned about sin and exhorted to holiness (22:11; Leviticus 11:45; 19:2; 20:7; Psalm 24:3–4; Romans 8:29; 12:1; Ephesians 5:1,8; Colossians 3:12; Hebrews 12:14; 1 Peter 1:15–16; 1 John 2:6)

Worship—God is worthy of man's worship and praise (4:10–11; 5:12; 2 Samuel 22:44; Psalms 22:23; 50:23; 96:2; 145:3; Ezekiel 3:12; Daniel

2:20; Matthew 2:1–2,11; 28:16–17; John 4:20–24; 9:30–38; Luke 1:68–69; Hebrews 1:6; Jude 1:25)

Eschatology—the doctrine of the last things (4:1–22:21)

GOD'S CHARACTER IN REVELATION

God is eternal—4:8–10; 16:5
God is glorious—21:11,23
God is holy—4:8; 15:4; 21:27
God is just—19:2
God is powerful—4:11; 5:13; 11:17
God is righteous—16:5,7; 19:2
God is true—15:3; 16:7
God is wrathful—6:17; 11:18; 16:6–7; 19:15

CHRIST IN REVELATION

In the last book of the Bible, Jesus triumphantly reveals Himself as the Almighty One (1:8); the Alpha and Omega (1:8; 21:6); the Beginning and the End (1:8; 21:6). Other voices in the Book of Revelation proclaim Jesus Christ as the Lion of the tribe of Judah (5:5); Heir to David's throne (5:5); the Lamb of God (5:6–22:3); the Word of God (19:13); King of kings and Lord of lords (19:16).

KEY WORDS IN REVELATION

Hades: Greek *hadēs*—1:18; 6:8; 20:13–14—literally, "the place of the unseen." This Greek word, translated from the Hebrew word *sheol*, describes the invisible world of the dead. All people who die go to Hades in the sense that death leads from the visible world to the invisible. Therefore, death and Hades can be used interchangeably. Unfortunately, many people mistakenly associate Hades with hell, a place of eternal punishment. But the Greek word for hell is *gehenna* (see Mark 9:43–45). While we will all one day go to Hades, we can avoid hell by believing in Jesus Christ's work of salvation.

Almighty: Greek *pantokratōr*—1:8; 4:8; 11:17; 15:3; 16:7,14; 19:15; 21:22—literally, "one who has power over everything," in other words, the One in total control. God commands all the hosts of powers in heaven and earth, and He is able to overcome all His foes. The title *Almighty* occurs often in Revelation as this book unveils God's awesome control over all the universe and throughout all history.

Devil; Satan: Greek *diabolos*—2:10; 12:9,12; 20:2,10—literally, "slanderer," and Greek *Satanas*—20:2,7—literally, "Adversary." The word *diabolos* signifies one who accuses another. Hence that other name given him: "the accuser of our brethren" (see 12:10). The name Satan signifies one who lies in wait for or sets himself in opposition to another. These and other names of the same fallen spirit point to different features of his evil character and deceitful operations.

New Jerusalem: Greek *Ierousalēm kainē*—3:12; 21:2,10. The New Jerusalem that comes out of heaven is plainly distinct from the earthly Jerusalem, the former capital of Israel. This is the city Abraham looked for, the city whose builder and maker is God (Hebrews 11:10). This is the city that exists even now in heaven, for Paul calls it the Jerusalem that is above (Galatians 4:26).

The Alpha and the Omega: Greek *to Alpha kai to O*—1:8,11; 21:6; 22:13. Alpha and omega are the first and last letters of the Greek alphabet. This phrase is used of both God the Father and God the Son. God in Christ comprises everything, all that goes between the Alpha and the Omega, as well as being the First and the Last. This expresses God's fullness, comprehensiveness, and all-inclusiveness. He is the Source of all things and will bring all things to their appointed end.

QUICK OVERVIEW

I. The Things Which You Have Seen (1:1–20)
   A. The Prologue (1:1–8)
   B. The Vision of the Glorified Christ (1:9–18)
   C. The Apostle's Commission to Write (1:19–20)
II. The Things Which Are (2:1–3:22)
   A. The Letter to the Church at Ephesus (2:1–7)
   B. The Letter to the Church at Smyrna (2:8–11)
   C. The Letter to the Church at Pergamos (2:12–17)
   D. The Letter to the Church at Thyatira (2:18–29)
   E. The Letter to the Church at Sardis (3:1–6)
   F. The Letter to the Church at Philadelphia (3:7–13)
   G. The Letter to the Church at Laodicea (3:14–22)
III. The Things Which Will Take Place after This (4:1–22:21)
   A. Worship in Heaven (4:1–5:14)
   B. The Great Tribulation (6:1–18:24)
   C. The Return of the King (19:1–21)
   D. The Millennium (20:1–10)
   E. The Great White Throne Judgment (20:11–15)
   F. The Eternal State (21:1–22:21)

MEANWHILE, IN OTHER PARTS OF THE WORLD . . .
Clement I becomes bishop of Rome (A.D. 88–97). Emperor Trajan expands the Roman Empire to its largest state (A.D. 98–117).

FREQUENTLY ASKED QUESTIONS

1. What are the different ways in which the Book of Revelation can be interpreted?

No other New Testament book poses more interpretive challenges than Revelation. The book's vivid imagery and striking symbolism have produced four main interpretive approaches:

- The *preterist* approach interprets Revelation as a description of first-century events in the Roman Empire. This view conflicts with the book's own repeated claim to be prophecy (1:3; 22:7,10,18–19). It is impossible to see all the events in Revelation as already fulfilled. The Second Coming of Christ, for example, obviously did not take place in the first century.
- The *historicist* approach views Revelation as a panoramic description of church history from apostolic times to the present, seeing in the symbolism such events as the barbarian invasions of Rome, the rise of the Roman Catholic Church, the emergence of Islam, and the French Revolution. This interpretive method, however, robs Revelation of any meaning for those to whom it was originally written. It also ignores the time limitations the book itself places on the unfolding events (11:2; 12:6,14; 13:5). Historicism has produced many different, often conflicting, interpretations of the actual historical events contained in Revelation.
- The *idealist* approach interprets Revelation as a timeless depiction of the cosmic struggle between the forces of good and evil. In this view, the book contains neither historical allusions nor predictive prophecy. Since this view ignores Revelation's stated prophetic character, however, it tends to sever the book from any connection with actual historical events. Revelation then becomes merely a collection of stories designed to teach spiritual truth.
- The *futurist* approach insists that the events recorded in chapters 6–22 are yet future, and that those chapters literally and symbolically depict actual people and events yet to appear on the world scene. The chapters describe the events surrounding the Second Coming of Jesus Christ (chapters 6–19), the Millenium and final judgment (chapter 20), and the eternal state (chapters 21–22). Only this view does justice to Revelation's claim to be prophecy and interprets the entire book by the consistent grammatical-historical method used for the rest of Scripture.

2. What do we know about these seven churches to which John wrote his letters?

Revelation 2:1–3:22 includes seven letters dictated to John by the Lord Jesus. Each of these churches displays a significant character trait about which the Lord was pleased or displeased. The churches were named for the cities in which they were located:

- Ephesus, the loveless church
- Smyrna, the persecuted church
- Pergamos, the compromising church
- Thyatira, the corrupt church
- Sardis, the dead church
- Philadelphia, the faithful church
- Laodicea, the lukewarm church

Although these seven churches were actual, historical churches in Asia Minor, they also represent the types of churches that perennially exist throughout the church age. What Christ says to each of these churches is relevant in all times.

3. Does Revelation 3:20 mean that Christ is standing at each person's life, knocking to come in?

Rather than allowing for the common interpretation of Christ's knocking on a person's heart, the context demands that we say that Christ was seeking to enter this church that bore His name but lacked a single true believer. The poignant letter to the church in Laodicea was Christ's knocking. If one member would recognize his spiritual bankruptcy and respond in saving faith, Christ would enter the church.

4. What is the "tribulation" and where does it fit in the Book of Revelation?

The tribulation refers to that seven-year time period immediately following the removal of the church from the earth (John 14:1–3; 1 Thessalonians 4:13–18), when the righteous judgments of God will be poured out upon an unbelieving world (Jeremiah 30:7; Daniel 9:27; 12:1; 2 Thessalonians 2:7–12; Revelation 16). These judgments will be climaxed by the return of Christ in glory to the earth (Matthew 24:27–31; 25:31–46; 2 Thessalonians 2:7–12).

In the Book of Revelation, the lengthy section from 6:1 to 19:21 details the judgments and events of the time of tribulation from its beginning with the opening of the first seal through the seven seal, trumpet, and bowl judgments of God, to the return of Christ to destroy the ungodly (19:11–21). The passage of time during this period is tracked in Revelation (11:2–3; 12:6,14; 13:5). The second half of the seven-year period is specifically called in Revelation 7:14 "the great tribulation."

5. Why does the number *666* get so much attention?

Numbers are important in Scripture in two ways: 1) they speak to God's exactness; and 2) they represent certain recurring ideas. The number *666* is mentioned in Revelation 13:18. The significance of the number itself is not emphasized, so speculation about the meaning must be cautious and limited.

The number represents the essential number of a man. The number 6 falls one short of God's perfect number, 7, and thus points to human imperfection. Antichrist, the most powerful human the world will ever know, will still be a man—a 6. The ultimate in human and demonic power is a 6, not perfect, as God is. The threefold repetition of the number is intended to emphasize man's identity. He is emphatically imperfect, not almost perfect. When Antichrist is finally revealed, there will be some way to identify him with this basic number, or his name may have the numerical equivalent of 666. In many languages, including Hebrew, Greek, and Latin, letters from the alphabet were used to represent numbers.

Beyond these basic observations, the text reveals very little about the meaning of 666. It is unwise, therefore, to speculate beyond what God's Word gives us.

6. Why does the great multitude in Revelation 19:1–6 keep saying "Alleluia"?

The term is a transliterated Hebrew that appears only four times in the New Testament, all in this chapter (verses 1,3–4,6). This exclamation, meaning "Praise the Lord," occurs frequently in the Old Testament (Psalms 104:35; 105:45; 106:1; 111:1; 112:1; 113:1; 117:1; 135:1; 146:1).

In the case of this great multitude gathered in heaven, they have five reasons for repeatedly shouting "Alleluia—Praise the Lord!"

- They praise God for delivering His people from their enemies (verses 1–2).
- They praise God for meting out justice (verse 2).
- They praise God for permanently crushing man's rebellion (verse 3).
- They praise God for His sovereignty (verse 6).
- They praise God for communing (being) with His people (verse 7).

7. What is the Millennium and where does it fit in Revelation?
Revelation 20 includes six mentions of a kingdom that will last a thousand years (verses 2–7). There are three main views regarding the nature and duration of this period:

- *Premillennialism* sees this as a literal thousand-year period during which Jesus Christ, in fulfillment of numerous Old Testament prophecies (2 Samuel 7:12–16; Psalm 2; Isaiah 11:6–12; 24:23; Hosea 3:4–5; Joel 3:9–21; Amos 9:8–15; Micah 4:1–8; Zephaniah

3:14–20; Zechariah 14:1–11) and Jesus' own teaching (Matthew 24:29–31,36–44) will reign on the earth. Using the same general principles of interpretation for both prophetic and nonprophetic passages leads most naturally to premillennialism. This view is also strongly supported by the fact that so many biblical prophecies have already been literally fulfilled and therefore suggests that future prophecies will likewise be fulfilled literally.

- *Postmillennialism* understands the reference to a thousand-year period as only symbolic of a golden age of righteousness and spiritual prosperity. It will be ushered in by the spread of the gospel during the present church age and brought to completion when Christ returns. According to this view, references to Christ's reign on earth primarily describe His spiritual reign in the hearts of believers in the church.
- *Amillennialism* understands the thousand years to be merely symbolic of a long period of time. This view interprets Old Testament prophecies of a Millennium as being fulfilled spiritually now in the church (either on earth or in heaven) or as references to the eternal state.

In summary, nothing in the text leads directly to the conclusion that "a thousand years" is symbolic. Never in Scripture when the term *year* is used with a number is its meaning not literal. The weight of biblical evidence points to the premillennialist position.

QUICK STUDY ON REVELATION

1. What statements about its purpose does the Book of Revelation declare?
2. What are the seven churches to which John writes and what comments does Jesus make about each one?
3. How does Revelation illustrate the sovereignty of God?
4. Throughout the Book of Revelation, what happens to people who continue to trust Christ?
5. What, according to chapter 20, will happen at the last judgment?
6. Whose names are recorded in the Book of Life, and why?

APPENDICES

- *Quick Notes on Theology*
- *Chronology of Old Testament Patriarchs and Judges*
- *Chronology of Old Testament Kings and Prophets*
- *The Ministries of Jesus Christ*
- *Index of Key Words*

QUICK NOTES ON THEOLOGY

THE CONDUCT OF THE GOSPEL

God's instructions to those who have believed in Jesus on how to spread the good news, the gospel.

Proclaim it
"And Jesus went about all Galilee, teaching in their synagogues, preaching the gospel of the kingdom" (Matthew 4:23).

Defend it
"I found it necessary to write to you exhorting you to contend earnestly for the faith which was once for all delivered to the saints" (Jude 3b).

Demonstrate it
"Only let your conduct be worthy of the gospel of Christ, so that whether I come and see you or am absent, I may hear of your affairs, that you stand fast in one spirit, with one mind striving together for the faith of the gospel" (Philippians 1:27).

Share it
"I thank my God . . . for your fellowship in the gospel from the first day until now" (Philippians 1:3a,5).

Suffer for it
"Therefore do not be ashamed of the testimony of our Lord, nor of me His prisoner, but share with me in the sufferings for the gospel according to the power of God" (2 Timothy 1:8).

Do not hinder it
"Nevertheless we have not used this right, but endure all things lest we hinder the gospel of Christ" (1 Corinthians 9:12b).

Do not be ashamed of it
"For I am not ashamed of the gospel of Christ, for it is the power of God to salvation for everyone who believes" (Romans 1:16a).

Preach it
"For if I preach the gospel, I have nothing to boast of, for necessity is laid upon me; yes, woe is me if I do not preach the gospel" (1 Corinthians 9:16).

Be empowered by it
"For our gospel did not come to you in word only, but also in power, and in the Holy Spirit and in much assurance, as you know what kind of men we were among you for your sake" (1 Thessalonians 1:5).

Guard it
"I marvel that you are turning away so soon from Him who called you in the grace of Christ, to a different gospel, which is not another; but there are some who trouble you and want to pervert the gospel of Christ. But even if we, or an angel from heaven, preach any other gospel to you than what we have preached to you, let him be accursed" (Galatians 1:6–8).

THE HOLY SCRIPTURES

"All Scripture is given by inspiration of God, and is profitable for doctrine, for reproof, for correction, for instruction in righteousness, that the man of God may be complete, thoroughly equipped for every good work" (2 Timothy 3:16–17).

The Bible is God's written revelation to humankind. The sixty-six books of the Bible given to us by the Holy Spirit constitute the plenary (inspired equally in all parts) Word of God (1 Corinthians 2:7–14; 2 Peter 1:20–21).

The Word of God is an objective, propositional revelation (1 Corinthians 2:13; 1 Thessalonians 2:13), verbally inspired in every word (2 Timothy 3:16), absolutely inerrant in the original documents, infallible, and God-breathed. The literal, grammatical-historical interpretation of Scripture supports this view of the Bible. For example, this position affirms the belief that the opening chapters of Genesis present creation in six literal days (Genesis 1:31; Exodus 31:17).

The Bible constitutes the only infallible rule of faith and practice (Matthew 5:18; 24:35; John 10:35; 16:12–13; 17:17; 1 Corinthians 2:13; 2 Timothy 3:15–17; Hebrews 4:12; 2 Peter 1:20–21).

God spoke in His written Word by a process of dual authorship. The Holy Spirit so superintended the human authors that, through their individual personalities and different styles of writing, they composed and recorded God's Word to humankind (2 Peter 1:20–21) without error in the whole or in the part (Matthew 5:18; 2 Timothy 3:16).

Whereas there may be several applications of any given passage of Scripture, there is but one true interpretation. The meaning of Scripture is to be found as one diligently applies the literal, grammatical-historical method of interpretation under the enlightenment of the Holy Spirit (John 7:17; 16:12–15; 1 Corinthians 2:7–15; 1 John 2:20). It is the responsibility of believers to ascertain carefully the true intent and meaning of Scripture, recognizing that proper application is binding on all generations. Yet the truth of Scripture stands in judgment of people; never do people stand in judgment of Scripture.

THE TRIUNE GOD

"Hear, O Israel: The Lord our God, the Lord is one! You shall love the Lord your God with all your heart, with all your soul, and with all your strength" (Deuteronomy 6:4–5). There is but one living and true God (Deuteronomy 6:4; Isaiah 45:5–7; 1 Corinthians 8:4). God is an infinite, all-knowing Spirit (John 4:24), perfect in all His attributes, one in essence, eternally existing in three Persons—Father, Son, and Holy Spirit (Matthew 28:19; 2 Corinthians 13:14).

Christianity teaches that man doesn't find God, because God has already found us. He has disclosed Himself through His Word. He spoke to Adam, to Abraham, to Moses, and to the prophets (Genesis 1:28; 12:1–3; Exodus 3:4–22; Jeremiah 1:4–10; Ezekiel 2:1; 3:3–4,10; Zechariah 1:3).

God has revealed Himself to us in two ways: through *natural revelation* (Romans 1:20) and through *special revelation* (Jeremiah 9:23–24). Through natural revelation (the created order) God discloses three things about Himself: His power, His sovereignty, His wrath (Romans 1:20–23). Another aspect of natural revelation is found in the human conscience, which also points to God (Romans 1:19). Because of the Fall and the entry of sin into the world, people often deny and resist the evidence of natural revelation (Psalm 14:1).

Special revelation picks up where creation and conscience leave off. This revelation involved God's communication of His Word to the writers of Scripture, the various miracles recorded in the Old and New Testaments, and the ultimate revelation of His own incarnation (Hebrews 1:1–4).

GOD THE FATHER

"For as many as are led by the Spirit of God, these are sons of God. For you did not receive the spirit of bondage again to fear, but you received the Spirit of adoption by whom we cry out, 'Abba, Father'" (Romans 8:14,15). God the Father, the first person of the Trinity, orders and disposes all things according to His own purpose and grace (Psalm 145:8–9; 1 Corinthians 8:6).

God the Father is the Creator of all things (Genesis 1:1–31; Ephesians 3:9). As the only absolute and omnipotent ruler in the universe, He is sovereign in creation, providence, and redemption (Psalm 103:19; Romans 11:36).

God's fatherhood involves both His designation within the Trinity and His relationship with humanity. As Creator, He is Father to all people (Ephesians 4:6), but He is the spiritual Father only to believers (Romans 8:14; 2 Corinthians 6:18).

God the Father has decreed for His own glory all things that come to pass (Ephesians 1:11). He continually upholds, directs, and governs all creatures and events (1 Chronicles 29:11). In His sovereignty, He is neither author nor approver of sin (Habakkuk 1:13), nor does He abridge the accountability of moral, intelligent creatures (1 Peter 1:17). He has graciously chosen from eternity past those whom He would have as His own (Ephesians 1:4–6). He saves from sin all those who come to Him, and He becomes, upon adoption, Father to His own (John 1:12; Romans 8:15; Galatians 4:5; Hebrews 12:5–9).

ANGELS

But when He again brings the firstborn into the world, He says, "Let all the angels of God worship Him." And of the angels He says, "Who makes His angels spirits And His ministers a flame of fire" (Hebrews 1:6–7).

Angels are created beings and are therefore not to be worshiped (Revelation 19:10; 22:8). Although they are a higher order of creation than humans (Psalm 8:5), they are created to serve God and to worship Him (Luke 2:9–14; Hebrews 1:6–7,14; 2:6–7; Revelation 5:11–14).

FALLEN ANGELS

Satan is a created angel and the author of sin. He incurred the judgment of God by rebelling against his Creator (Isaiah 14:12–17; Ezekiel 28:11–19), by taking numerous angels with him in his fall (Matthew 25:41; Revelation 12:1–14), and by introducing sin into the human race by his temptation of Eve (Genesis 3:1–15).

Satan is the open and declared enemy of God and humanity (Isaiah 14:13–14; Matthew 4:1–11; Revelation 12:9–10), and he is the prince of this world who has been defeated through the death and resurrection of Jesus Christ (Romans 16:20). He shall be eternally punished in the lake of fire (Isaiah 14:12–17; Ezekiel 28:11–19; Matthew 25:41; Revelation 20:10).

GOD THE SON

"And a cloud came and overshadowed them; and a voice came out of the cloud, saying, 'This is My beloved Son. Hear Him'" (Mark 9:7)!

Jesus Christ, the second person of the Trinity, possesses all the divine excellencies, and in these He is co-equal, co-substantial, and co-eternal with the Father (John 10:10; 14:9). God the Father created "the heavens and the earth and all that is in them" according to His own will, through

His Son, Jesus Christ, by whom all things continue in existence and in operation (John 1:3; Colossians 1:15–17; Hebrews 1:2).

In His Incarnation (God becoming man), Christ surrendered only the prerogatives of deity but nothing of the divine essence, either in degree or kind. In His Incarnation, the eternally existing Second Person of the Trinity accepted all the essential characteristics of humanity and so became the God-man, deity and humanity in indivisible oneness (Micah 5:2; John 5:23; 14:9–10; Philippians 2:5–8; Colossians 2:9).

Our Lord Jesus Christ was virgin born (Isaiah 7:14; Matthew 1:23,25; Luke 1:26–35). He was God incarnate (John 1:1,14), and the purpose of the Incarnation was to reveal God, to redeem people, and to rule over God's kingdom (Psalm 2:7–9; Isaiah 9:6; John 1:29; Philippians 2:9–11; Hebrews 7:25–26; 1 Peter 1:18–19).

Our Lord Jesus Christ accomplished our redemption through the shedding of His blood and sacrificial death on the cross, and His death was voluntary, vicarious, substitutionary, propitiatory, and redemptive (John 10:15; Romans 3:24–25; 5:8; 1 Peter 2:24).

Our justification is made sure by His literal, physical resurrection from the dead. He is now ascended to the right hand of the Father, where He mediates as our Advocate and High Priest (Matthew 28:6; Luke 24:38–39; Acts 2:30–31; Romans 4:25; 8:34; Hebrews 7:25; 9:24; 1 John 2:1).

In the Resurrection of Jesus Christ from the grave, God confirmed the deity of His Son and gave proof that God has accepted the atoning work of Christ on the cross. Jesus' bodily Resurrection is also the guarantee of a future resurrection life for all believers (John 5:26–29; 14:19; Romans 4:25; 6:5–10; 1 Corinthians 15:20,23).

Jesus Christ will return to receive the church, which is His body, unto Himself at the Rapture. Returning with His church in glory, He will establish His millennial kingdom on earth (Acts 1:9–11; 1 Thessalonians 4:13–18; Revelation 20).

The Lord Jesus Christ is the One through whom God will judge all people (John 5:22–23): 1) believers (1 Corinthians 3:10–15; 2 Corinthians 5:10); 2) living inhabitants of the earth at His glorious return (Matthew 25:31–46); and 3) unbelieving dead at the Great White Throne (Revelation 20:11–15). As the mediator between God and people (1 Timothy 2:5), the head of His body the church (Ephesians 1:22; 5:23; Colossians 1:18), and the coming universal King who will reign on the throne of David (Isaiah 9:6–7; Ezekiel 37:24–28; Luke 1:31–33), He is the final Judge of all who fail to place their trust in Him as Lord and Savior (Matthew 25:14–46; Acts 17:30–31).

GOD THE HOLY SPIRIT

"But the Helper, the Holy Spirit, whom the Father will send in My name, He will teach you all things, and bring to your remembrance all things that I said to you" (John 14:26). The Holy Spirit is a divine person, eternal, underived, possessing all the attributes of personality and deity, including intellect (1 Corinthians 2:10–13), emotions (Ephesians 4:30), will (1 Corinthians 12:11), eternality (Hebrews 9:14), omnipresence (Psalm 139:7–10), omniscience (Isaiah 40:13–14), omnipotence (Romans 15:13), and truthfulness (John 16:13). In all the divine attributes He is co-equal and co-substantial with the Father and the Son (Matthew 28:19; Acts 5:3–4; 28:25–26; 1 Corinthians 12:4–6; 2 Corinthians 13:14; and Jeremiah 31:31–34 with Hebrews 10:15–17).

It is the work of the Holy Spirit to execute the divine will with relation to all people. We recognize His sovereign activity in the creation (Genesis 1:2), the Incarnation (Matthew 1:18), the written revelation (2 Peter 1:20–21), and the work of salvation (John 3:5–7).

A unique work of the Holy Spirit in this age began at Pentecost when He came from the Father as promised by Christ (John 14:16–17; 15:26) to initiate and complete the building of the Body of Christ. His activity includes convicting the world of sin, of righteousness, and of judgment; glorifying the Lord Jesus Christ; and transforming believers into the image of Christ (John 16:7–9; Acts 1:5; 2:4; Romans 8:29; 2 Corinthians 3:18; Ephesians 2:22).

The Holy Spirit is the supernatural and sovereign agent in regeneration, baptizing all believers into the Body of Christ (1 Corinthians 12:13). The Holy Spirit also indwells believers from the moment of salvation. He sanctifies, instructs, and empowers them for service and seals them unto the day of redemption (2 Corinthians 3:6; Ephesians 1:13). It is the duty of those born and indwelt by the Spirit to be filled with (controlled by) the Spirit (Romans 8:9–11; Ephesians 5:18; 1 John 2:20,27).

The Holy Spirit is the divine teacher who guided the apostles and prophets into all truth as they committed to writing God's revelation, the Bible (2 Peter 1:19–21).

The Holy Spirit administers spiritual gifts to the church. The Holy Spirit glorifies neither Himself nor His gifts by ostentatious displays, but He does glorify Christ by implementing His work of redeeming the lost and building up believers in the most holy faith (John 16:13–14; Acts 1:8; 1 Corinthians 12:4–11; 2 Corinthians 3:18).

God the Holy Spirit is sovereign in the bestowing of all His gifts for the perfecting of the saints today. Speaking in tongues and the working of sign miracles in the beginning days of the church were for the purpose of pointing to and authenticating the apostles as revealers of divine truth, and were never intended to be characteristic of the lives of believers (1 Corinthians 12:4–11; 13:8–10; 2 Corinthians 12:12; Ephesians 4:7–12; Hebrews 2:1–4).

HUMANITY

> "When I consider Your heavens, the work of Your fingers,
> The moon and the stars, which You have ordained,
> What is man that You are mindful of him,
> And the son of man that You visit him?
> But You made him a little lower than the angels,
> And crowned him with glory and honor"(Psalm 8:3–5).

Humans were directly and immediately created by God in His image and likeness. They were created free of sin with a rational nature, intelligence, volition, self-determination, and moral responsibility to God (Genesis 2:7,15–25; James 3:9).

God's intention in the creation of people was that they should glorify God, enjoy His fellowship, live their lives in the will of God, and by this accomplish God's purpose for them in the world (Isaiah 43:7; Colossians 1:16; Revelation 4:11).

Through Adam's sin of disobedience to the revealed will and Word of God, people lost their innocence, incurred the penalty of spiritual and physical death; became subject to the wrath of God; and became inherently corrupt and utterly incapable of choosing or doing that which is acceptable to God apart from divine grace. With no recuperative powers to enable them to recover themselves, humans are hopelessly lost. Humanity's salvation is thereby wholly of God's grace through the redemptive work of our Lord Jesus Christ (Genesis 2:16–17; 3:1–19; John 3:36; Romans 3:23; 6:23; 1 Corinthians 2:14; Ephesians 2:1–3; 1 Timothy 2:13–14; 1 John 1:8).

Because all people were in Adam, a nature corrupted by Adam's sin has been transmitted to all people of all ages, Jesus Christ being the only exception. All people are thus sinners by nature, by choice, and by divine declaration (Psalm 14:1–3; Jeremiah 17:9; Romans 3:9–18,23; 5:10–12).

On the basis of the efficacy of the death of our Lord Jesus Christ, the believing sinner is freed from the punishment, the penalty, the power, and one day the very presence of sin. He or she is declared righteous, given eternal life, and adopted into the family of God (Romans 3:25; 5:8–9; 2 Corinthians 5:14–15; 1 Peter 2:24; 3:18).

Every saved person is involved in a daily conflict—the new creation in Christ doing battle against the flesh—but adequate provision is made for victory through the power of the indwelling Holy Spirit. The struggle nevertheless plagues the believer all through this earthly life and is never completely ended. All claims to complete eradication of sin in this life are unscriptural. The complete absence of sin is not possible, but the

Holy Spirit does provide for victory over sin (Galatians 5:16–25; Ephesians 4:22–24; Philippians 3:12; Colossians 3:9–10; 1 Peter 1:14–16; 1 John 3:5–9).

THE PROCESS OF SALVATION

"For by grace you have been saved through faith, and that not of yourselves; it is the gift of God, not of works, lest anyone should boast" (Ephesians 2:8–9). Salvation is wholly of God by grace on the basis of the redemption of Jesus Christ, the merit of His shed blood, and not on the basis of human merit or works (John 1:12; Ephesians 1:4–7; 2:8–10; 1 Peter 1:18–19). The following terms describe the process of salvation.

Election

Election is the act of God by which, before the foundation of the world, He chose in Christ those whom He graciously regenerates, saves, and sanctifies (Romans 8:28–30; Ephesians 1:4–11; 2 Thessalonians 2:13; 2 Timothy 2:10; Titus 3:4–7; 1 Peter 1:1–2).

Sovereign election does not contradict or negate the responsibility of humanity to repent and trust Christ as Savior and Lord (Ezekiel 18:23,32; 33:11; John 3:18–19,36; 5:40; 2 Thessalonians 2:10–12; Revelation 22:17). Nevertheless, since sovereign grace includes the means of receiving the gift of salvation, as well as the gift itself, sovereign election will result in what God determines. All whom the Father calls to Himself will come in faith, and all who come in faith the Father will receive (John 6:37–40,44; Acts 13:48; James 4:8).

The unmerited favor that God grants to totally depraved sinners is not related to any initiative of their own part nor to God's anticipation of what they might do by their own will, but is solely of His sovereign grace and mercy (Ephesians 1:4–7; Titus 3:4–7; 1 Peter 1:2).

God is truly sovereign, but He exercises His sovereignty in harmony with his other attributes, especially His omniscience, justice, holiness, wisdom, grace, and love (Romans 9:11–16). This sovereignty will always exalt the will of God in a manner totally consistent with His character as revealed in the life of our Lord Jesus Christ (Matthew 11:25–28; 2 Timothy 1:9).

Regeneration

Regeneration is the supernatural work of the Holy Spirit by which the divine nature and divine life are given (John 3:3–8; Titus 3:5). It is instantaneous and is accomplished solely by the power of the Holy Spirit through the instrumentality of the Word of God (John 5:24), when the repentant sinner, as enabled by the Holy Spirit, responds in faith to the divine provision of salvation. Genuine regeneration is manifested by fruits worthy of repentance, as demonstrated in righteous attitudes and conduct. Good works will be the proper evidence and fruit (1 Corinthians 6:19–20; Ephesians 5:17–21; Philippians 2:12b; Colossians 3:12–17; 2 Peter 1:4–11). This obedience causes the believer to be increasingly conformed to the image of our Lord Jesus Christ (2 Corinthians 3:18). Such a conformity climaxes in the believer's glorification at Christ's coming (Romans 8:16–17; 2 Peter 1:4; 1 John 3:2–3).

Justification

Justification before God is an act of God (Romans 8:30,33) by which He declares righteous those who, through faith in Christ, repent of their sins (Luke 13:3; Acts 2:38; 3:19; 11:18; Romans 2:4; 2 Corinthians 7:10; Isaiah 55:6–7) and confess Him as sovereign Lord (Romans 10:9–10; 1 Corinthians 12:3; 2 Corinthians 4:5; Philippians 2:11). By this means, God is enabled to "be just, and the justifier of the one who has faith in Jesus" (Romans 3:26).

Sanctification

Every believer is sanctified (set apart) unto God by justification and is therefore declared to be holy and rightly identified as a saint. This sanctification is positional and instantaneous and should not be confused with progressive sanctification. This sanctification has to do with the believer's standing, not his present walk or condition (Acts 20:32; 1 Corinthians 1:2,30; 6:11; 2 Thessalonians 2:13; Hebrews 2:11; 3:1; 10:10,14; 13:12; 1 Peter 1:2).

THE RESULTS OF SALVATION

"For this is the will of God, your sanctification" (1 Thessalonians 4:3). Salvation is wholly of God by grace on the basis of the redemption of Jesus Christ, the merit of His shed blood, and not on the basis of human merit or works (John 1:12; Ephesians 1:4–7; 2:8–10; 1 Peter 1:18–19). The following three terms describe the results of salvation.

Sanctification

There is a progressive sanctification by which the state of the believer is brought closer to the likeness of Christ through obedience to the Word of God and the empowering of the Holy Spirit. The believer is able to live a life of increasing holiness in conformity to the will of God, becoming more and more like our Lord Jesus Christ (John 17:17,19; Romans 6:1–22; 2 Corinthians 3:18; 1 Thessalonians 4:3–4; 5:23).

Security

All the redeemed, once saved, are kept by God's power and are thus secure in Christ forever (John 5:24; 6:37–40; 10:27–30; Romans 5:9–10; 8:1,31–39; 1 Corinthians 1:4–9; Ephesians 4:30; Hebrews 7:25; 13:5; 1 Peter 1:4–5; Jude 24).

It is the privilege of believers to rejoice in the assurance of their salvation through the testimony of God's Word, which, however, clearly forbids the use of Christian liberty as an excuse for sinful living and carnality (Romans 6:15–22; 13:13–14; Galatians 5:13,16–17,25–26; Titus 2:11–14).

Separation

Separation from sin is clearly called for throughout the Old and New Testaments, and the Scriptures clearly indicate that in the last days, apostasy and worldliness shall increase (2 Corinthians 6:14–7:1; 2 Timothy 3:1–5).

Out of deep gratitude for the undeserved grace of God granted to us and because our glorious God is so worthy of our total consecration, all the saved should live in such a manner as to demonstrate our adoring love to God and so as not to bring reproach upon our Lord and Savior. Separation from any association with religious apostasy and worldly, sinful practices is commanded of us by God (Romans 12:1–2; 1 Corinthians 5:9–13; 2 Corinthians 6:14–7:1; 1 John 2:15–17; 2 John 9–11).

Believers should be separated unto our Lord Jesus Christ (2 Thessalonians 1:11–12; Hebrews 12:1–2) and affirm that the Christian life is a life of obedient righteousness demonstrated by a beatitude attitude (Matthew 5:2–12) and a continual pursuit of holiness (Romans 12:1–2; 2 Corinthians 7:1; Hebrews 12:14; Titus 2:11–14; 1 John 3:1–10).

THE IDENTITY OF THE CHURCH

"For as the body is one and has many members, but all the members of that one body, being many, are one body, so also is Christ" (1 Corinthians 12:12). All who place their faith in Jesus Christ are immediately placed by the Holy Spirit into one united spiritual body, the church (1 Corinthians 12:12–13), the bride of Christ (2 Corinthians 11:2; Ephesians 5:23–32; Revelation 19:7–8), of which Christ is the head (Ephesians 1:22; 4:15; Colossians 1:18).

The formation of the church, the Body of Christ, began on the day of Pentecost (Acts 2:1–21,38–47) and will be completed at the coming of Christ for His own at the Rapture (1 Corinthians 15:51–52; 1 Thessalonians 4:13–18).

The church is thus a unique spiritual organism designed by Christ, made up of all born-again believers in this present age (Ephesians

2:11–3:6). The church is distinct from Israel (1 Corinthians 10:32), a mystery not revealed until this age (Ephesians 3:1–6; 5:32).

The establishment and continuity of local churches is clearly taught and defined in the New Testament (Acts 14:23,27; 20:17,28; Galatians 1:2; Philippians 1:1; 1 Thessalonians 1:1; 2 Thessalonians 1:1). The members of the one scriptural body are directed to associate themselves together in local assemblies (1 Corinthians 11:18–20; Hebrews 10:25).

The one supreme authority for the church is Christ (Ephesians 1:22; Colossians 1:18). Church leadership, gifts, order, discipline, and worship are all appointed through His sovereignty as found in the Scriptures. The biblically designated officers serving under Christ and over the assembly are elders (males, who are also called bishops, pastors, and pastor-teachers; Acts 20:28; Ephesians 4:11) and deacons, both of whom must meet biblical qualifications (1 Timothy 3:1–13; Titus 1:5–9; 1 Peter 5:1–5).

These leaders lead or rule as servants of Christ (1 Timothy 5:17–22) and have His authority in directing the church. The congregation is to submit to their leadership (Hebrews 13:7,17).

Vitally important to the church are the practices of discipleship (Matthew 28:19–20; 2 Timothy 2:2), the mutual accountability of all believers to each other (Matthew 18:15–17), and the need for discipline of sinning members of the congregation in accord with the standards of Scripture (Matthew 18:15–22; Acts 5:1–11; 1 Corinthians 5:1–13; 2 Thessalonians 3:6–15; 1 Timothy 1:19,20; Titus 1:10–16).

The local church should be autonomous, free from any external authority or control, with the right of self-government and freedom from the interference of any hierarchy of individuals or organizations (Titus 1:5). It is scriptural for true churches to cooperate with each other for the presentation and propagation of the faith. Local churches, however, through their pastor and their interpretation and application of Scripture, should be the sole judges of the measure and method of their cooperation (Acts 15:19–31; 20:28; 1 Corinthians 5:4–7,13; 1 Peter 5:1–4).

THE PURPOSE OF THE CHURCH

"To Him be glory in the church by Christ Jesus to all generations forever and ever. Amen" (Ephesians 3:21). The purpose of the church is to glorify God (Ephesians 3:21) by building itself up in the faith (Ephesians 4:13–16) by instruction of the Word (2 Timothy 2:2,15; 3:16–17), by fellowship (Acts 2:47; 1 John 1:3), by keeping the ordinances (Luke 22:19; Acts 2:38–42), and by advancing and communicating the gospel in the entire world (Matthew 28:19; Acts 1:8).

All saints are called to the work of service (1 Corinthians 15:58; Ephesians 4:12; Revelation 22:12).

The church must cooperate with God as he accomplishes His purpose in the world. To that end, He gives the church spiritual gifts. First, He chooses people to equip the saints for the work of the ministry (Ephesians 4:7–12), and He also gives unique and special spiritual abilities to each member of the Body of Christ (Romans 12:5–8; 1 Corinthians 12:4–31; 1 Peter 4:10–11).

There are two kinds of gifts given the early church: miraculous gifts of divine revelation and healing, given temporarily in the apostolic era for the purpose of confirming the authenticity of the apostles' message (Hebrews 2:3–4; 2 Corinthians 12:12); and ministering gifts, given to equip believers for edifying one another. With the New Testament revelation complete, Scripture becomes the sole test of the authenticity of a person's message, and confirming gifts of a miraculous nature are no longer necessary (1 Corinthians 13:8–12). Miraculous gifts can even be counterfeited by Satan so as to deceive believers (Matthew 24:24). The only gifts in operation today are those nonrevelatory equipping gifts for edification (Romans 12:6–8).

No one possesses the gift of healing today, but God does hear and answer the prayer of faith and will answer in accordance with His own perfect will for the sick, suffering, and afflicted (Luke 18:1–8; John 5:7–9; 2 Corinthians 12:6–10; James 5:13–16; 1 John 5:14–15).

Two ordinances have been committed to the local church: baptism and the Lord's Supper (Acts 2:38–42). Christian baptism by immersion (Acts 8:36–39) is the solemn and beautiful testimony of believers showing forth their faith in the crucified, buried, and risen Savior, and their union with Him in death to sin and resurrection to a new life (Romans 6:1–11). It is also a sign of fellowship and identification with the visible Body of Christ (Acts 2:41–42).

The Lord's Supper is the commemoration and proclamation of His death until He comes and should be always preceded by solemn self-examination (1 Corinthians 11:23–32). Whereas the elements of communion are only representative of the flesh and blood of Christ, the Lord's Supper is nevertheless an actual communion with the risen Christ, who is present in a unique way to fellowship with His people (1 Corinthians 10:16).

THE LAST THINGS (ESCHATOLOGY): A PERSONAL VIEW

"So also is the resurrection of the dead. The body is sown in corruption, it is raised in incorruption. It is sown in dishonor, it is raised in glory. It is sown in weakness, it is raised in power. It is sown a natural body, it is raised a spiritual body" (1 Corinthians 15:42–44a).

DEATH

Physical death involves no loss of our immaterial consciousness (Revelation 6:9–11). There is a separation of soul and body (James 2:26), and the soul of the redeemed passes immediately into the presence of Christ (Luke 23:43; 2 Corinthians 5:8; Philippians 1:23). For the redeemed, such separation will continue until the Rapture (1 Thessalonians 4:13–17), which initiates the first resurrection (Revelation 20:4–6), when our soul and body will be reunited to be glorified forever with our Lord (1 Corinthians 15:35–44; 50–54; Philippians 3:21). Until that time, the souls of the redeemed in Christ remain in joyful fellowship with our Lord Jesus Christ (2 Corinthians 5:8).

RESURRECTION

All people will experience bodily resurrection—the saved to eternal life (John 6:39; Romans 8:10–11,19–23; 2 Corinthians 4:14), and the unsaved to judgment and everlasting punishment (Daniel 12:2; John 5:29; Revelation 20:13–15).

The souls of the unsaved at death are kept under punishment until the second resurrection (Luke 16:19–26; Revelation 20:13–15), when the soul and the resurrection body will be united (John 5:28–29). This resurrection of the unsaved dead to judgment will be a physical resurrection. They shall then appear at the Great White Throne judgment (Revelation 20:11–15) and shall be cast into hell, the lake of fire (Matthew 25:41–46), cut off from the life of God forever (Daniel 12:2; Matthew 25:41–46; 2 Thessalonians 1:7–9), which involves an eternal conscious punishment.

ETERNITY

After the closing of the Millennium, the temporary release of Satan, and the judgment of unbelievers (2 Thessalonians 1:9; Revelation 20:7–15), the saved will enter the eternal state of glory with God, after which the elements of this earth are to be dissolved (2 Peter 3:10) and replaced with a new earth, wherein only righteousness dwells (Ephesians 5:5; Revelation 20:15,21–22). Following this, the heavenly city will come down out of heaven (Revelation 21:2) and will be the dwelling place of the saints, where they will forever enjoy fellowship with God and one another (John 17:3; Revelation 21–22). Our Lord Jesus Christ, having fulfilled His redemptive mission, will then deliver up the kingdom to God the Father (1 Corinthians 15:23–28) so that in all spheres the triune God may reign forever and ever (1 Corinthians 15:28).

THE LAST THINGS (ESCHATOLOGY): A PROPHETIC VIEW

"For as in Adam all die, even so in Christ all shall be made alive. But each one in his own order: Christ the firstfruits, afterward those who are Christ's at His coming. Then comes the end, when He delivers the kingdom to God the Father, when He puts an end to all rule and all authority and power" (1 Corinthians 15:22–24).

THE RAPTURE OF THE CHURCH

Our Lord Jesus Christ will personally return in bodily form before the seven-year tribulation (1 Thessalonians 4:16; Titus 2:13) to translate His church from this earth (John 14:1–3; 1 Corinthians 15:51–53; 1 Thessalonians 4:15–5:11), and between this event and His glorious return with His saints, to reward believers according to their works (1 Corinthians 3:11–15; 2 Corinthians 5:10).

THE TRIBULATION PERIOD

Immediately following the removal of the church from the earth (John 14:1–3; 1 Thessalonians 4:13–18), the righteous judgments of God will be poured out upon an unbelieving world (Jeremiah 30:7; Daniel 9:27; 12:1; 2 Thessalonians 2:7–12; Revelation 16). These judgments will be climaxed by the return of Christ in glory to the earth (Matthew 24:27–31; 25:31–46; 2 Thessalonians 2:7–12). At that time, the Old Testament and tribulation saints will be raised, and the living will be judged (Daniel 9:24–27; 12:2–3; Matthew 24:15–31; 25:31–46; Revelation 20:4–6).

THE SECOND COMING AND THE MILLENNIAL REIGN

After the tribulation period, Christ will come to earth to occupy the throne of David (Matthew 25:31; Luke 1:32–33; Acts 1:10–11; 2:29–30) and to establish His messianic kingdom for a thousand years on the earth (Revelation 20:1–7). During this time the resurrected saints will reign with Him over Israel and all the nations of the earth (Ezekiel 37:21–28; Daniel 7:17–22; Revelation 19:11–16). This reign will be preceded by the overthrow of the Antichrist and the False Prophet and by the removal of Satan from the world (Daniel 7:17–27; Revelation 20:1–6).

The kingdom itself will be the fulfillment of God's promise to Israel (Isaiah 65:17–25; Ezekiel 37:21–28; Zechariah 8:1–17) to restore them to the land that they forfeited through their disobedience (Deuteronomy 28:15–68). The result of their disobedience was that Israel was temporarily set aside (Matthew 21:43; Romans 11:1–26) but will again be awakened through repentance to enter into the land of blessing (Jeremiah 31:31–34; Ezekiel 36:22–32; Romans 11:25–29).

Our Lord's reign will be characterized by harmony, justice, peace, righteousness, and long life (Isaiah 11; 65:17–25; Ezekiel 36:33–38), and will be brought to an end with the release of Satan (Revelation 20:7).

THE JUDGMENT OF THE LOST

Following the release of Satan after the thousand-year reign of Christ (Revelation 20:7), Satan will deceive the nations of the earth and gather them to battle against the saints and the beloved city. Satan and his army will be devoured by fire from heaven (Revelation 20:9). Then Satan will be thrown into the lake of fire (Matthew 24:41; Revelation 20:10) whereupon Christ will resurrect and judge the great and small at the Great White Throne judgment (John 5:22; Revelation 20:11–15).

CHRONOLOGY OF OLD TESTAMENT PATRIARCHS AND JUDGES

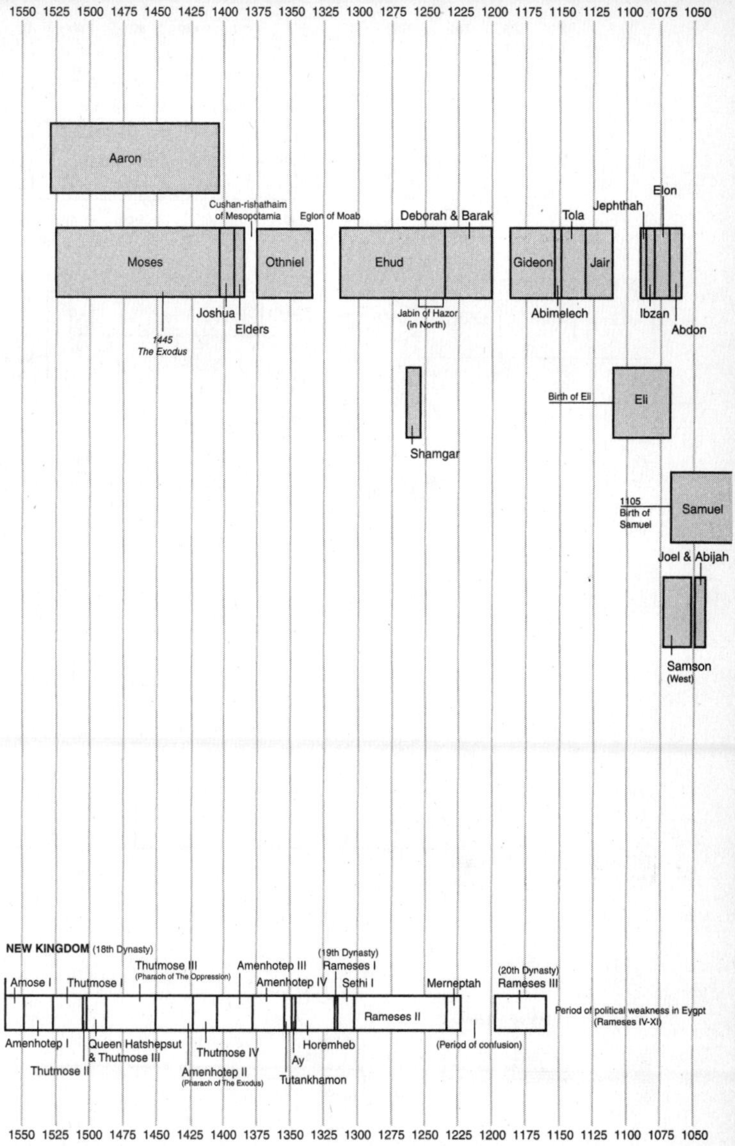

CHRONOLOGY OF OLDTESTAMENT KINGS AND PROPHETS

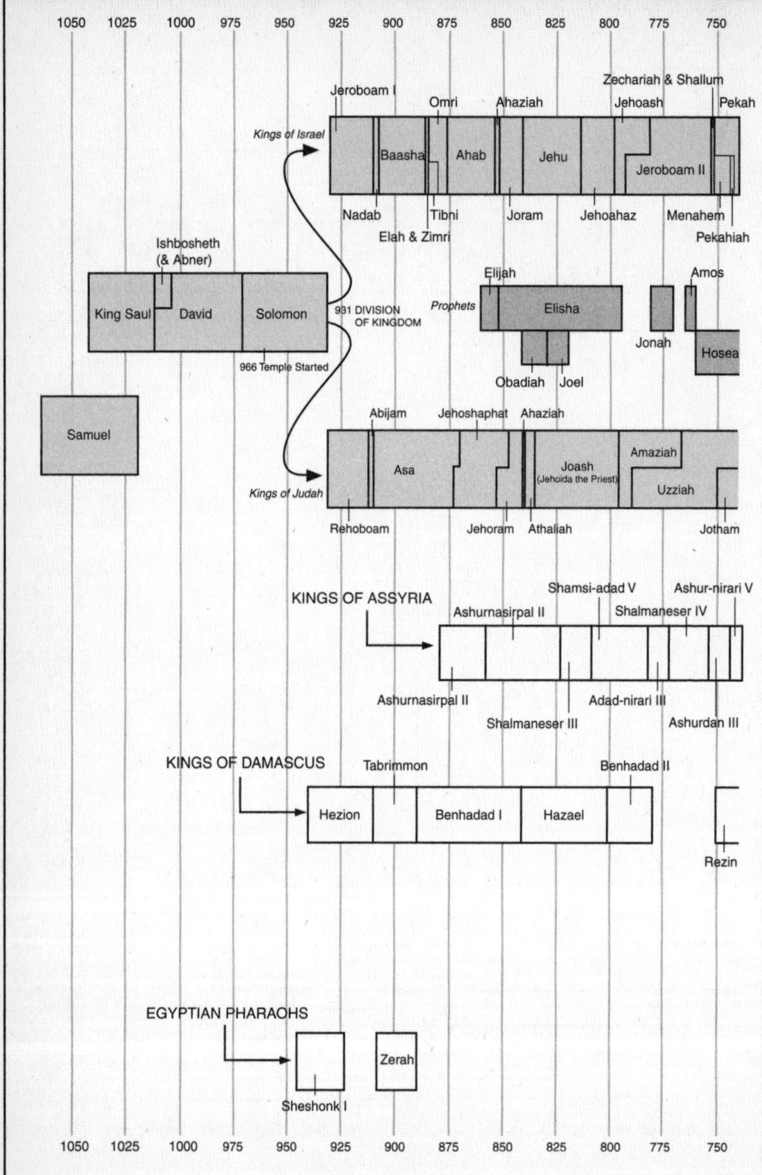

CHRONOLOGY OF OLD TESTAMENT KINGS AND PROPHETS

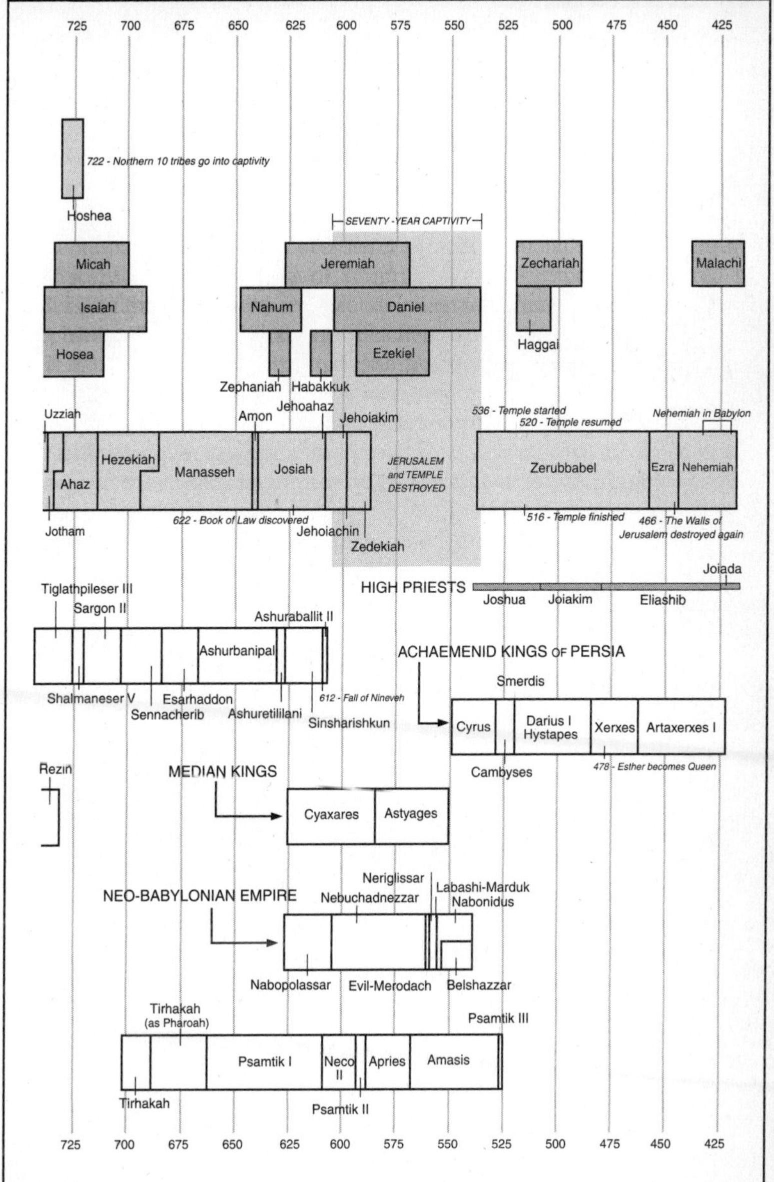

THE MINISTRIES OF JESUS CHRIST

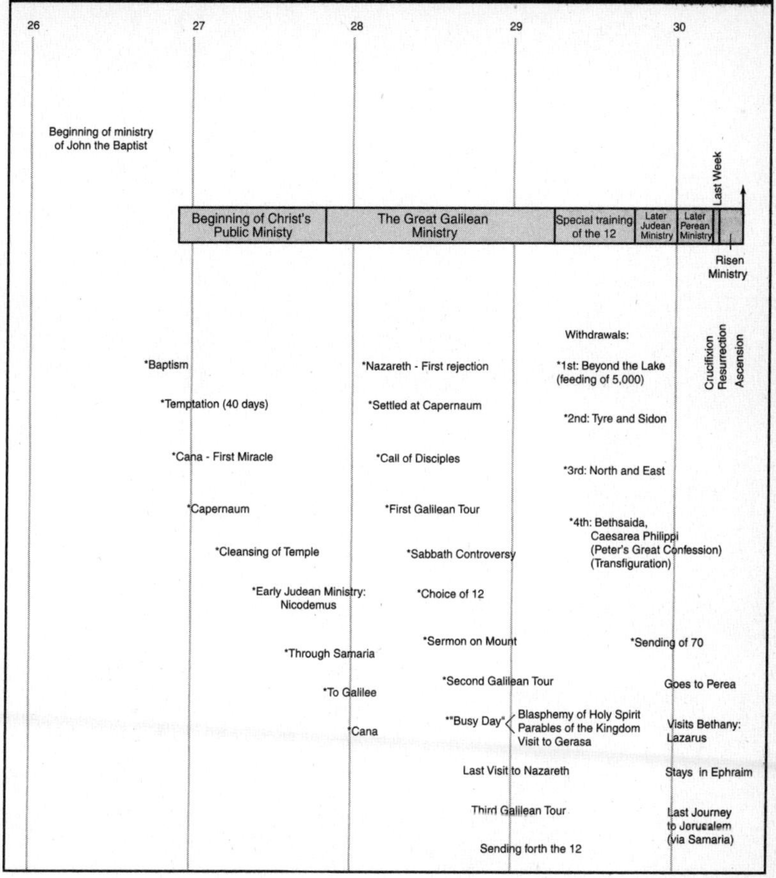

INDEX OF KEY WORDS

Prophet—Jeremiah
Purpose, counsel, will—Ephesians
Ransom—1 Timothy
Reconciliation—Romans
Redemption—Hebrews
Renew—Lamentations
Resurrection—1 Corinthians
Salvation—Isaiah
Sanctification—1 Thessalonians
Satan, Devil—Revelation
Scribes—Mark
Seek—Amos
Servant—Isaiah
Service—2 Corinthians
Setting Apart—1 Samuel
Shepherd—Jeremiah
Signet ring—Haggai
Sin—1 John
Slow to anger—Jonah
Son of Man—Ezekiel
Spirit, soul, body—1 Thessalonians
Spirit— Joel; Acts
Stumble—Hosea
Supply—Philippians
The Word—John
Together—Acts
Try—Malachi
Virtue—Philippians
Vision—Daniel
Washing of regeneration—Titus
Weeps—Lamentations
Word—Jeremiah; 1 Peter

NOTES

NOTES

NOTES

NOTES